Scott Lindsay

Scott
Best Wishes
Harold Kerzner

Scott Lindsay

PROJECT

MANAGEMENT

BEST PRACTICES

PROJECT

MANAGEMENT

BEST PRACTICES

Achieving Global Excellence

HAROLD KERZNER, Ph.D.

WILEY

John Wiley & Sons, Inc.

Published by John Wiley & Sons, Inc., Hoboken, New Jersey
Published simultaneously in Canada

For general information on our other products and services or for technical support, please contact our Customer Care Department within the United States at (800) 762-2974, outside the United States at (317) 572-3993 or fax (317) 572-4002.

Wiley also publishes its books in a variety of electronic formats. Some content that appears in print may not be available in electronic books. For more information about Wiley products, visit our web site at www.wiley.com.

Library of Congress Cataloging-in-Publication Data:

Kerzner, Harold.
    Project management best practices : achieving global excellence / Harold
Kerzner.
        p. cm.
    A new follow-up to Advanced project management (2nd ed. c2004), containing
contributions from over 50 Fortune 500 companies.
    ISBN-13 978-0-471-79346-5
    ISBN-10 0-471-79368-X (cloth)
    1. Project management.   2. Six Sigma (Quality control standard)   3. Project
management—Case studies.   I. Kerzner, Harold. Advanced project management.
II. Title.
    HD69.P75K4715 2006
    658.4'04—dc22
                                                                    2005036656
Printed in the United States of America.

10 9 8 7 6 5 4 3 2 1

*To
my wife, JO ELLYN,
who showed me that excellence
can be achieved in
marriage, family, and life,
as well as at work*

Contents

Preface _____

For almost 35 years, project management was viewed as a process that might be nice to have, but not one that was necessary for the survival of the firm. Companies reluctantly invested in some training courses simply to provide their personnel with basic knowledge on planning and scheduling. Project management was viewed as a threat to established lines of authority and, in many companies only partial project management was used. This half-hearted implementation occurred simply to placate lower- and middle-level personnel.

During this 35-year period, we did everything possible to prevent excellence in project management from occurring. We provided only lip service to empowerment, teamwork, and trust. We hoarded information because the control of information was viewed as power. We placed personal and functional interests ahead of the best interest of the company in the hierarchy of priorities. And we maintained the faulty belief that time was a luxury rather than a constraint.

By the mid-1990s, this mentality began to subside, largely due to two recessions. Companies were under severe competitive pressure to create quality products in a shorter period of time. The importance of developing a long-term trusting relationship with the customers had come to the forefront. Businesses were being forced by the stakeholders to change for the better. The survival of the firm was now at stake.

Today, businesses have changed for the better. Trust between the customer and contractor is at an all-time high. New products are being developed at a faster rate than ever before. Project management has become a competitive weapon during competitive bidding. Some companies are receiving sole-source contracts because of the faith that the customer has in the contractor's ability to deliver a continuous stream of successful projects using a project management methodology. All of these factors have allowed a multitude of companies to achieve some degree of excellence in project management. Business decisions are now being emphasized ahead of personal decisions.

Words that were commonplace six years ago have taken on new meanings today. Change is no longer being viewed as being entirely bad. Today, change implies continuous improvement. Conflicts are no longer seen as detrimental. Conflicts managed well can be beneficial. Project management is no longer viewed as a system entirely internal to the organization. It is now a competitive weapon that brings higher levels of quality and increased value added opportunities to the customer.

Companies that were considered excellent in management in the past may no longer be regarded as excellent today, especially with regard to project management. Consider the book entitled *In Search of Excellence,* written by Tom Peters and Robert Waterman in 1982. How many of those companies identified in their book are still considered as excellent today? How many of those companies have won the prestigious Malcolm Baldrige Award? How many of those companies that have won the award are excellent in project management?

The differentiation between the first 30 years of project management and the last ten years is in the implementation of project management. For more than three decades, we emphasized the quantitative and behavioral tools of project management. Basic knowledge and primary skills were emphasized. However, within the past six years, emphasis has been on implementation. What was now strategically important was how to put 30 years of basic project management theory into practice. Today it is the implementation of project management that constitutes advanced project management. Subjects such as earned value analysis, situational leadership, and cost and change control are part of basic project management courses today whereas 15 years ago they were considered as advanced topics in project management. So, what constitutes applied project management today? Topics related to project management implementation are advanced project management concepts.

This book covers the advanced project management topics necessary for implementation of and excellence in project management. The book contains numerous quotes from people in the field who have benchmarked best practices in project management and are currently implementing these processes within their own firms. The quotes are invaluable because they show the thought process of these leaders and the direction in which their firms are heading. These companies have obtained some degree of excellence in project management, and what is truly remarkable is the fact that this happened in less than five or six years. Best practices in implementation will be the future of project management well into the twenty-first century. Companies have created best practices libraries for project management. Many of the libraries are used during competitive bidding for differentiation from other competitors. Best practices in project management are now viewed as intellectual property.

Seminars and correspondence courses on project management principles and best practices in project management are available using this text and my text, *Project Management: A Systems Approach to Planning, Scheduling, and Controlling.* Seminars on advanced project management are also available using this text. Information on these courses, E-learning courses, and on in-house and public seminars can be obtained by contacting the author at

Phone: 216-765-8090
Fax: 216-765-8090
E-mail: hkerzner@bw.edu

Harold Kerzner
Baldwin-Wallace College

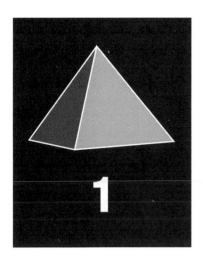

Understanding Best Practices

1.0 INTRODUCTION

Project management has evolved from a set of processes that were once considered "nice" to have to a structured methodology that is considered mandatory for the survival of the firm. Companies are now realizing that their entire business, including most of the routine activities, can be regarded as a series of projects. Simply stated, we are managing our business by projects.

As the relative importance of project management permeates each facet of the business, knowledge is captured on best practices in project management. Some companies view this knowledge as intellectual property to be closely guarded in the vaults of the company. Others share this knowledge in hope of discovering other best practices. Companies are now performing strategic planning for project management.

One of the benefits of performing strategic planning for project management is that it usually identifies the need for capturing and retaining best practices. Unfortunately this is easier said than done. One of the reasons for this difficulty, as will be seen later in the chapter, is that companies today are not in agreement on the definition of a best practice, nor do they understand that best practices lead to continuous improvement, which in turn leads to the capturing of more best practices.

1.1 PROJECT MANAGEMENT BEST PRACTICES: 1945–1960

During the 1940s, line managers functioned as project managers and used the concept of over-the-fence management to manage projects. Each line manager, wearing the hat of a project manager, would perform the work necessitated by his or her line organization and, when completed, would throw the "ball" over the fence in hopes that someone would catch it. Once the ball was thrown over the fence, the line managers would wash their hands of any responsibility for the project because the ball was no longer in their yard. If a project failed, blame was placed on whichever line manager had the ball at that time.

The problem with over-the-fence management was that the customer had no single contact point for questions. The filtering of information wasted precious time for both the customer and the contractor. Customers who wanted first-hand information had to seek out the manager in possession of the ball. For small projects, this was easy. But as projects grew in size and complexity, this became more difficult.

During this time period, very few best practices were identified. If there were best practices, then they would stay within a given functional area never to be shared with the remainder of the company. Suboptimal project management decision-making was the norm.

Following Word War II, the United States entered into the Cold War. To win a Cold War, one must compete in the arms race and rapidly build weapons of mass destruction. The victor in a Cold War is the one who can retaliate with such force as to obliterate the enemy. Development of weapons of mass destruction was comprised of very large projects involving potentially thousands of contractors.

The arms race made it clear that the traditional use of over-the-fence management would not be acceptable to the Department of Defense (DoD) for projects such as the B52 bomber, the Minuteman Intercontinental Ballistic Missile, and the Polaris submarine. The government wanted a single point of contact, namely, a project manager who had total accountability through all project phases. In addition, the government wanted the project manager to possess a command of technology rather than just an understanding of technology, which mandated that the project manager be an engineer preferably with an advanced degree in some branch of technology. The use of project management was then mandated for some of the smaller weapon systems such as jet fighters and tanks. The National Aeronautics and Space Administration (NASA) mandated the use of project management for all activities related to the space program.

Projects in the aerospace and defense industries were having cost overruns in excess of 200–300 percent. Blame was erroneously placed upon improper implementation of project management when, in fact, the real problem was the inability to forecast technology, resulting in numerous scope changes occurring. Forecasting technology is extremely difficult for projects that could last 10–20 years.

By the late 1950s and early 1960s, the aerospace and defense industries were using project management on virtually all projects, and they were pressuring their suppliers to use it as well. Project management was growing, but at a relatively slow rate except for aerospace and defense.

Because of the vast number of contractors and subcontractors, the government needed standardization, especially in the planning process and the reporting of information. The government established a life-cycle planning and control model and a cost-monitoring system and created a group of project management auditors to make sure that the government's money was being spent as planned. These practices were to be used on all government programs above a certain dollar value. Private industry viewed these practices as an overmanagement cost and saw no practical value in project management.

In the early years of project management, because many firms saw no practical value in project management, there were misconceptions concerning project management. Some of the misconceptions included:

- Project management is a scheduling tool such as PERT/CPM (program evaluation and review technique/critical path method) scheduling.
- Project management applies to large projects only.
- Project management is designed for government projects only.
- Project managers must be engineers and preferably with advanced degrees.
- Project managers need a "command of technology" to be successful.
- Project success is measured in technical terms only. (Did it work?)

1.2 PROJECT MANAGEMENT BEST PRACTICES: 1960–1985

During this time period, with a better understanding of project management, the growth of project management had come about more through necessity than through desire, but at a very slow rate. Its slow growth can be attributed mainly to lack of acceptance of the new management techniques necessary for its successful implantation. An inherent fear of the unknown acted as a deterrent for both managers and executives.

Other than aerospace, defense, and construction, the majority of companies in the 1960s maintained an informal method for managing projects. In informal project management, just as the words imply, the projects were handled on an informal basis whereby the authority of the project manager was minimized. Most projects were handled by functional managers and stayed in one or two functional lines, and formal communications were either unnecessary or handled informally because of the good working relationships between line managers. Those individuals that were assigned as project managers soon found that they were functioning more as project leaders or project monitors rather than as real project managers. Many organizations today, such as low-technology manufacturing, have line managers who have been working side by side for 10 or more years. In such situations, informal project management may be effective on capital equipment or facility development projects and project management is not regarded as a profession.

By 1970 and through the early 1980s, more companies departed from informal project management and restructured to formalize the project management process, mainly because the size and complexity of their activities had grown to a point where they were unmanageable within the current structure.

Not all industries need project management, and executives must determine whether there is an actual need before making a commitment. Several industries with simple tasks, whether in a static or a dynamic environment, do not need project management. Manufacturing industries with slowly changing technology do not need project management, unless of course they have a requirement for several special projects, such as capital equipment activities, that could interrupt the normal flow of work in the routine manufacturing operations. The slow growth rate and acceptance of project management were related to the fact that the limitations of project management were readily apparent yet the advantages were not completely recognizable. Project management requires organizational restructuring. The question, of course, is "How much restructuring?" Executives have avoided the subject of project management for fear that "revolutionary" changes must be made in the organization.

Project management restructuring has permitted companies to:

- Accomplish tasks that could not be effectively handled by the traditional structure
- Accomplish one-time activities with minimum disruption of routine business

The second item implies that project management is a "temporary" management structure and, therefore, causes minimum organizational disruption. The major problems identified by those managers who endeavored to adapt to the new system all revolved around conflicts in authority and resources.

Another major concern was that project management required upper-level managers to relinquish some of their authority through delegation to middle managers. In several situations, middle managers soon occupied the power positions, even more so than upper-level managers.

Project management became a necessity for many companies as they expanded into multiple product lines, many of which were dissimilar, and organizational complexities grew. This growth can be attributed to:

- Technology increasing at an astounding rate
- More money invested in research and development (R&D)
- More information available
- Shortening of project life cycles

To satisfy the requirements imposed by these four factors, management was "forced" into organizational restructuring; the traditional organizational form that had survived for decades was inadequate for integrating activities across functional "empires."

By 1970, the environment began to change rapidly. Companies in aerospace, defense, and construction pioneered in implementing project management, and other industries soon followed, some with great reluctance. NASA and the DoD "forced" subcontractors into accepting project management.

Because current organizational structures are unable to accommodate the wide variety of interrelated tasks necessary for successful project completion, the need for project management has become apparent. It is usually first identified by those lower-level and middle managers who find it impossible to control their resources effectively for the diverse activities within their line organization. Quite often middle managers feel the impact of changing environment more than upper-level executives.

Once the need for change is identified, middle management must convince upper-level management that such a change is actually warranted. If top-level executives cannot recognize the problems with resource control, then project management will not be adopted, at least formally. Informal acceptance, however, is another story.

As project management developed, some essential factors in its successful implementation were recognized. The major factor was the role of the project manager, which became the focal point of integrative responsibility. The need for integrative responsibility was first identified in complex R&D projects.

The R&D technology has broken down the boundaries that used to exist between industries. Once-stable markets and distribution channels are now in a state of flux. The industrial environment is turbulent and increasingly hard to predict. Many complex facts about markets, production methods, costs, and scientific potentials are related to investment decisions in R&D.

All of these factors have combined to produce a king-size managerial headache. There are just too many crucial decisions to have them all processed and resolved through regular line hierarchy at the top of the organization. They must be integrated in some other way.

Providing the project manager with integrative responsibility resulted in:

- Total project accountability assumed by a single person
- Project rather than functional dedication
- A requirement for coordination across functional interfaces
- Proper utilization of integrated planning and control

Without project management, these four elements have to be accomplished by executives, and it is questionable whether these activities should be part of an executive's job description. An executive in a Fortune 500 corporation stated that he was spending 70 hours each week working as both an executive and a project manager, and he did not feel that he was performing either job to the best of his abilities. During a presentation to the staff, the executive stated what he expected of the organization after project management implementation:

- Push decision-making down in the organization
- Eliminate the need for committee solutions
- Trust the decisions of peers

Those executives who chose to accept project management soon found the advantages of the new technique:

- Easy adaptation to an ever-changing environment
- Ability to handle a multidisciplinary activity within a specified period of time
- Horizontal as well as vertical work flow
- Better orientation toward customer problems
- Easier identification of activity responsibilities
- A multidisciplinary decision-making process
- Innovation in organizational design

As project management evolved, best practices became important. Best practices were learned from both successes and failures. In the early years of project management, private industry focused on learning best practices from successes. The government, however, focused on learning about best practices from failures. When the government finally focused on learning from successes, the knowledge of best practices came from their relationships with both their prime contractors and the subcontractors. Some of these best practices that came out of the government included:

- Use of life-cycle phases
- Standardization and consistency
- Use of templates [e.g., for statement of work (SOW), work breakdown structure (WBS), and risk management]
- Providing military personnel in project management positions with extended tours of duty at the same location
- Use of integrated project teams (IPTs)
- Control of contractor-generated scope changes
- Use of earned value measurement

1.3 PROJECT MANAGEMENT BEST PRACTICES: 1985–2006

By the 1990s, companies had begun to realize that implementing project management was a necessity, not a choice. By 2006, project management had spread to virtually every industry and best practices were being captured. In the author's opinion, the appearance of best practices from an industry perspective might be:

- 1960–1985: Aerospace, defense, and construction
- 1986–1993: Automotive suppliers
- 1994–1999: Telecommunications
- 2000–2003: Information technology
- 2004–present: Health care

The question now was not how to implement project management, but how fast could it be done? How quickly can we become mature in project management? Can we use the best practices to accelerate the implementation of project management?

Table 1–1 shows the typical life-cycle phases that an organization goes through to implement project management. In the first phase, the embryonic phase, the organization recognizes the apparent need for project management. This recognition normally takes place at the lower and middle levels of management where the project activities actually take place. The executives are then informed of the need and assess the situation.

There are six driving forces that lead executives to recognize the need for project management:

- Capital projects
- Customer expectations
- Competitiveness
- Executive understanding
- New project development
- Efficiency and effectiveness

TABLE 1–1.　THE FIVE PHASES OF THE PROJECT MANAGEMENT LIFE CYCLE

Embryonic	Executive Management Acceptance	Line Management Acceptance	Growth	Maturity
Recognize need	Get visible executive support	Get line management support	Recognize use of life cycle phases	Develop a management cost/schedule control system
Recognize benefits	Achieve executive understanding of project management	Achieve line management commitment	Develop a project management methodology	Integrate cost and schedule control
Recognize applications	Establish project sponsorship at executive levels	Provide line management education	Make the commitment to planning	Develop an educational program to enhance project management skills
Recognize what must be done	Become willing to change way of doing business	Become willing to release employees for project management training	Minimize creeping scope Select a project tracking system	

Manufacturing companies are driven to project management because of large capital projects or a multitude of simultaneous projects. Executives soon realize the impact on cash flow and that slippages in the schedule could end up idling workers.

Companies that sell products or services, including installation, to their clients must have good project management practices. These companies are usually non-project-driven but function as though they were project-driven. These companies now sell solutions to their customers rather than products. It is almost impossible to sell complete solutions to customers without having superior project management practices because what you are actually selling is your project management expertise.

There are two situations where competitiveness becomes the driving force: internal projects and external (outside customer) projects. Internally, companies get into trouble when they realize that much of the work can be outsourced for less than it would cost to perform the work themselves. Externally, companies get into trouble when they are no longer competitive on price or quality or simply cannot increase their market share.

Executive understanding is the driving force in those organizations that have a rigid traditional structure that performs routine, repetitive activities. These organizations are quite resistant to change unless driven by the executives. This driving force can exist in conjunction with any of the other driving forces.

New product development is the driving force for those organizations that are heavily invested in R&D activities. Given that only a small percentage of R&D projects ever make it into commercialization, where the R&D costs can be recovered, project management becomes a necessity. Project management can also be used as an early warning system that a project should be canceled.

Efficiency and effectiveness, as driving forces, can exist in conjunction with any other driving forces. Efficiency and effectiveness take on paramount importance for small companies experiencing growing pains. Project management can be used to help such companies remain competitive during periods of growth and to assist in determining capacity constraints.

Because of the interrelatedness of these driving forces, some people contend that the only true driving force is survival. This is illustrated in Figure 1–1. When the company recognizes that survival of the firm is at stake, the implementation of project management becomes easier.

The speed by which companies reach some degree of maturity in project management is most often based upon how important they perceive the driving forces to be. This is illustrated generically in Figure 1–2. Non-project-driven and hybrid organizations move quickly to maturity if increased internal efficiencies and effectiveness are needed. Competitiveness is the slowest path because these types of organizations do not recognize that project management affects their competitive position directly. For project-driven organizations, the path is reversed. Competitiveness is the name of the game and the vehicle used is project management.

Once the organization perceives the need for project management, it enters the second life-cycle phase of Table 1–1, executive acceptance. Project management cannot be implemented rapidly in the near term without executive support. Furthermore, the support must be visible to all.

The third life-cycle phase is line management acceptance. It is highly unlikely that any line manager would actively support the implementation of project management without

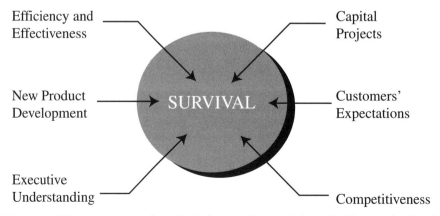

FIGURE 1–1. The components of survival. *Source:* Reprinted from H. Kerzner, *In Search of Excellence in Project Management.* New York: Wiley, 1998, p. 51.

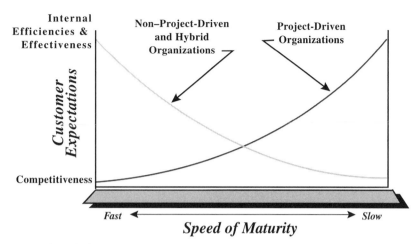

FIGURE 1–2.   Speed of maturity.

first recognizing the same support coming from above. Even minimal line management support will still cause project management to struggle.

The fourth life-cycle phase is the growth phase, where the organization becomes committed to the development of the corporate tools for project management. This includes the processes and project management methodology for planning, scheduling, and controlling as well as selection of the appropriate supporting software. Portions of this phase can begin during earlier phases.

The fifth life-cycle phase is maturity. In this phase, the organization begins using the tools developed in the previous phase. Here, the organization must be totally dedicated to project management. The organization must develop a reasonable project management curriculum to provide the appropriate training and education in support of the tools as well as the expected organizational behavior.

By the 1990s, companies finally began to recognize the benefits of project management. Table 1–2 shows the benefits or project management and how our view of project management has changed. Many of these benefits were identified through the discovery and implementation of best practices.

Recognizing that the organization can benefit from the implementation of project management is just the starting point. The question now becomes, "How long will it take us to achieve these benefits?" This can be partially answered from Figure 1–3. In the beginning of the implementation process, there will be added expenses to develop the project management methodology and establish the support systems for planning, scheduling, and control. Eventually, the cost will level off and become pegged. The question mark in Figure 1–3 is the point at which the benefits equal the cost of implementation. This point can be pushed to the left through training and education.

TABLE 1–2.   CRITICAL FACTORS IN PROJECT MANAGEMENT LIFE CYCLE

Critical Success Factors	Critical Failure Factors
Executive Management Acceptance Phase	
Consider employee recommendations	Refuse to consider ideas of associates
Recognize that change is necessary	Unwilling to admit that change may be necessary
Understand the executive role in project management	Believe that project management control belongs at executive levels
Line Management Acceptance Phase	
Willing to place company interest before personal interest	Reluctant to share information
Willing to accept accountability	Refuse to accept accountability
Willing to see associates advance	Not willing to see associates advance
Growth Phase	
Recognize the need for a corporate-wide methodology	View a standard methodology as a threat rather than as a benefit
Support uniform status monitoring/reporting	Fail to understand the benefits of project management
Recognize the importance of effective planning	Provide only lip service to planning
Maturity Phase	
Recognize that cost and schedule are inseparable	Believe that project status can be determined from schedule alone
Track actual costs	See no need to track actual costs
Develop project management training	Believe that growth and success in project management are the same

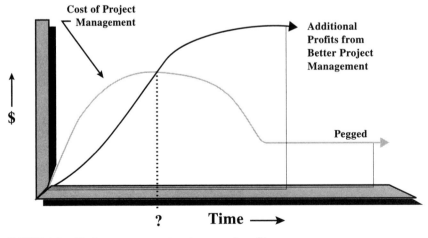

FIGURE 1–3.   Project management costs versus benefits.

1.4 BEST PRACTICES PROCESS

Understanding best practices is a four-step process. The first step is the answer to a critical question facing many companies: is "Why capture best practices?" The reasons or objectives for capturing best practices might include:

- Continuous improvements (efficiencies, accuracy of estimates, waste reduction, etc.)
- Enhanced reputation
- Winning new business
- Survival of the firm

The answer to this question also addresses how the company plans to use the best practice, such as for internal use or possibly for external use.

The next step is to decide where to look for best practices. Typical places to look include:

- Forms, guidelines, templates, and checklists that can impact the execution of the project.
- Forms, guidelines, templates, and checklists that can impact our definition of success on a project.
- Each of the PMBOK® Guide areas of knowledge or domain areas
- Companywide or isolated units

The third step is to decide on the amount of depth to go into the best practice. Should it be generic and at a high level or detailed and at a low level? High-level best practices may not achieve the efficiencies desired whereas highly detailed best practices may have limited applicability.

The fourth step is the identification of the drivers or metrics that affect each best practice. It is possible to have several drivers for each best practice. It is also possible to establish a universal set of drivers for each best practice, such as:

- Reduction in risk by a certain percentage, cost, or time
- Improve estimating accuracy by a certain percentage or dollar value
- Cost savings of a certain percentage or dollar value
- Efficiency increase by a certain percentage
- Reduction in waste, paperwork, or time by a certain percentage

There are several advantages of this approach. First, the drivers can change over time. Second, the best practices process is more of a science than an art. And third, we can establish levels of best practices such as shown in Figure 1–4. In this figure, a level 4 best practice, which is the best, would satisfy 60 percent or more of the list of drivers or characteristics of the ideal best practice.

The overall four-step process discussed here can easily lead to a clear definition of what is or is not a best practice.

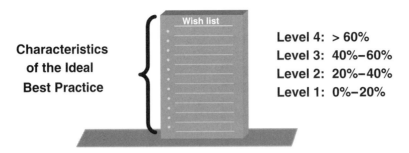

Level 4: > 60%
Level 3: 40%–60%
Level 2: 20%–40%
Level 1: 0%–20%

FIGURE 1–4. Best practices levels. Each level contains a percentage of the ideal characteristics.

1.5 DEFINITION OF A BEST PRACTICE

As project management evolved, so did the definitions of a best practice. Some definitions of a best practice are highly complex while others are relatively simplistic. Yet, they both achieve the same purpose of promoting excellence in project management throughout the company. Every company can have its own definition of a best practice and there might even be industry standards on the definition of a best practice. Typical definitions of a best practice might be:

- Something that works
- Something that works well
- Something that works well on a repetitive basis
- Something that leads to a competitive advantage
- Something that can be identified in a proposal to generate business
- Something that keeps the company out of trouble and, if trouble occurs, the best practice will assist in getting the company out of trouble

At Orange Switzerland, a best practice is defined as an experience based, proven, and published way of proceeding to achieve an objective. According to it's project management office (PMO) team[1]:

> The first good (best) practices at Orange Switzerland were created as an immediate response to some urgent needs. They were labeled "quick wins" at that time. Once disseminated, they allowed affirming openly the need for the existence of the PMO, which created them.

---

1. All information on Orange Switzerland's PMO and project management methodology is provided jointly by Martin Troxler, Director Corporate Quality; Daniel Heller, PMO Manager; and Alexander Matthey, Project Management Professional (PMP®), former PMO Manager, today Amontis Consulting Group, Associate Partner. Orange Communications AG, Lausanne, is 100% owned by Orange SA/France Telecom Group. On May 29, 1998, the Federal Communications Office (BAKOM) granted Orange a license to build and operate an 1800-MHz GSM (Global System for Mobile Communications) network. On June 29, 1999, Orange entered the Swiss market as a provider and its network now covers almost 99% of the Swiss population. In December 2000 Orange acquired one of the four UMTS licenses. At the end of 2004 Orange achieved a total revenue of 1288 million francs and earnings before interest, tax, depreciation, and amortization (EBITDA) of 395 million francs. By the end of March 2005 Orange had 1,126,000 customers, had invested over 3 billion francs, and employed 1400 people. For more information on Orange, go to www.orange.ch <http://www.orange.ch>.

As another example of the complexity in defining a best practice, consider the following comments made by Nani Sadowski, Manager of the Enterprise Project Management Office at Halifax Community Health Systems (HCHS):

> Best practices (according to HCHS) consist of a broad definition. We do have best practices that are detailed in our policies/procedures and workflows. These are guidelines and templates as well as processes that we all (members of the EPMO—enterprise project management office) have agreed to abide by as well as that they are effective and efficient methods for all parties involved. In addition, when we wrap up (conclude) a project, we conduct a formal lessons learned session (involving the project manager, sponsors, core team, and other parties impacted by the project) which is stored in a collective database and reviewed with the entire team. These lessons learned are in effect what create our best practices. We share these with other health care organizations for those vendors for which we are reference sites. All of our templates, policies/procedures, and workflows are accessible by request and, when necessary, we set meetings to review as well as explain them in detail.
>
> We have created standardized templates for all documentation that leaves our EPMO and have created a checkpoint process to ensure that all documents are up to "par." We have found that this instills consistency and professionalism as well as sets expectations for those who have been involved in projects run by the EPMO at HCHS.

According to Kelly Workman, PMP®, Senior Manager Field Service Engineering at etalk:

> Generally we view a best practice as any activity or process that improves a given situation, eliminates the need of other more cumbersome methods, or significantly enhances an existing process. Each best practice is a living entity and subject to review, amendments, or removal.
>
> From the senior management team (SLT) perspective, we (senior management, below director level) are given the freedom and responsibility of managing the departmental processes. We are expected to deliver the business with the most efficient use of resources. It is the project and line managers' decision to deem a practice as best; however the processes that surface in this category are in themselves generally self-evident as best—answering or classifying themselves as best practices by their effect on cost, quality, or schedule.

Companies often have well-defined approaches to defining best practices, as stated above by Kelly Workman at etalk. These approaches can be implemented on either a formal or an informal basis. For example, Doug Bolzman, Consultant Architect, PMP®, ITIL Service Manager at EDS, discusses the approach at EDS for defining a best practice and how the final decision is made[2]:

> Within EDS, specific work activities are identified, promoted and leveraged as best practices. With thousands of clients, many innovative methods are discovered and utilized to support specific client needs. These innovations that can be leveraged are identified and promoted as part of an existing best practice or as a new best practice. By leveraging these

---

2. Doug Bolzman has been with EDS 20 years and is currently a member of the EDS Project Management Delivery-IT Enterprise Management/ITIL capability. EDS has been awarded a patent on behalf of Doug's processes titled, "System and Method for Identifying and Monitoring Best Practices of an Enterprise."

efforts, all innovations can benefit all clients, thus improving the maturity of service provision by the organization.

A best practice is a work package comprised of a process, tool (or templates), and people that when used together can enable a project team to produce a consistent and stable deliverable for a client with increased accuracy and efficiency. Best practices are project management—based work types that at the start of a project can be identified during the planning stage and leveraged by the project team.

In order to manage each best practice consistently, each practice is documented following the best practice profile template. Some of the information contained within the profile includes the description of the practice, the type, the value to the company, and a list of practitioners to use the practice. Each practice documents all of the assets and asset status, and finally all of the practices document the business drivers that have been used to develop the practice.

EDS established a Client Facing Best Practice Design Board (comprised of best practice owners) to define and oversee the framework used to manage best practices. EDS has registered and has received a patent for the process and tools used to manage its best practices.

Once a practice has been nominated and approved to be a best practice, it is only sanctioned until the next yearly review cycle. Over time, best practices have the tendency to lose value and become ineffective if they are allowed to age. To allow for continuous improvement, a new level of maturity is assigned to all of the sanctioned best practices for a yearly resanctioning. By continually moving the bar higher, it is necessary to prove the value of each best practice and demonstrate improvements from the previous version of the process, tools, and people designs.

Being part of the integrated set of client facing best practices involves an assessment of a "candidate" best practice against a standard set of maturity criteria. Three levels of best practice maturity have been defined with minimum requirements for an "associate" best practice, "best practice," and "mastery" best practice. The requirements are centered on the following sections:

- Value
- Client
- User community
- Training
- Assets

- Governance
- Release management
- Integration with internal structures
- Integration with external structures, if applicable

Motorola also has a process by which best practices are identified and approved. According to Tama McBride, PMP®, Program Manager at Motorola:

> In essence we do (identify best practices), but not through a formalized process. When a new process or practice is felt to be of significance, it is documented in our PMO internal website and then, as appropriate, incorporated into our stage gate checklist.
>
> The decision as to what is termed a best practice is made within the community that performs the practice. Process capabilities are generally known and baselined. To claim best practice status, the practice or process must quantitatively demonstrate significant improvements in quality, efficiency, cost, and/or cycle time. The management of the organization affected as well as process management must approve the new practice prior to institutionalization.

Everyone seems to have his or her own definition of a best practice. In the author's opinion, for simplicity sake, *best practices are those actions or activities undertaken by the company or individuals that lead to a sustained competitive advantage in project management while providing value for both the company and the client.* What is important in this definition is the term "sustained competitive advantage." In other words, best practices are what differentiate you from your competitors.

This definition of a best practice focuses more on the private sector than on the public sector. A comparison of possible incentives for discovery and implementation of best practices in the public and private sectors is shown in Table 1–3.

Best practices may not be transferable from company to company, nor will they always be transferable from division to division within the same company. As an example, consider the following best practice discovered by a telecommunications company:

- A company institutionalized a set of values that professed that quality was everything. The result was that employees were focusing so much on quality that there was a degradation of customer satisfaction. The company then reprioritized its values with customer satisfaction being the most important, and quality actually improved.

In this company, customer satisfaction emphasis led to improved quality. However, in another company, emphasis on quality could just as easily have led to an improvement in customer satisfaction. Care must be taken during benchmarking activities to make sure that whatever best practices are discovered are in fact directly applicable to your company.

Best practices need not be overly complex. As an example, the following list of best practices is taken from companies discussed in this textbook, and as you can see, some of the best practices were learned from failures rather than successes:

- Changing project managers in midstream is bad even if the project is in trouble. Changing project managers inevitably elongates the project and can make it worse.
- Standardization yields excellent results. The more standardization placed in a project management methodology, usually the better are the results.
- Maximization of benefits occurs with a methodology based upon templates, forms, guidelines, and checklists rather than policies and procedures.
- Methodologies must be updated to include the results of discovering best practices. The more frequently the methodology is updated, the quicker the benefits are realized.

TABLE 1–3. BEST PRACTICES INCENTIVES

Private Sector:	Public Sector:
Profit	Minimization of cost
Competitiveness	On-time delivery
Efficiency	Efficiency
Effectiveness	Effectiveness
Customer satisfaction	Stakeholder satisfaction
Partnerships	Sole-source procurement

Best practices need not be complex. Even though some best practices seem simplistic and common sense, the constant reminder and use of these best practices lead to excellence and customer satisfaction. As an example, Antares Management Solutions developed a small handout listing eight best practices. This handout was given to all employees, inserted into proposals during competitive bidding, and also shown to customers. The eight best practices in its brochure are:

- Making use of project management concepts and terminology throughout the enterprise, not just in information systems
- Providing ongoing project management training throughout the enterprise
- Structuring every major project in a consistent manner, including scope, responsibilities, risks, high-level milestones, and project planning
- Communicating and updating project plans on an ongoing basis, using online tools when appropriate
- Maintaining an official project issue list, including who is responsible, what are the potential impacts, and how the issues are being resolved
- Using a formal change control process, including an executive steering committee to resolve major change issues
- Periodically auditing the project management process and selected projects to determine how well the methodology is working and to identify opportunities for improvement
- Concluding every major project with an open presentation of results to share knowledge gained, demonstrate new technology, and gain official closure

There is nothing proprietary or classified about these eight best practices. But at Antares Management Solutions, these best practices serve as constant reminders that project management is seen as a strategic competency and continuous improvement is expected.

Properly designed forms, checklists, and templates can become best practices if they are used correctly. As an example, Kelly Workman, PMP®, Senior Manager Field Service Engineering at etalk, believes:

> A recent example of a best practice is the use Outlook forms. These forms are readily available to all, revision control is extremely easy, and there is no need to save, attach and so on. We currently use these for a variety of events, including request for resources, material procurement, training, and implementation daily updates. Also they can be tailored to automatically address specific individuals. They have been a true improvement of past templates and have streamlined several operations.

Best practices can support other processes or other processes can support best practices. According to Tama McBride, PMP®, iDEN Subscriber Group, Program Manager:

> The single best practice which is remarkable is a combination of schedule templates, a stage-gate framework, biweekly program roll-ups, and a matrix organizational structure (cross-functional core teams) that has enabled us to have five plus years of consistent on-time, high-quality deliveries. In addition we have supporting processes as follows:

- We have a readily navigable central repository of all processes with supporting templates/tools that simplifies implementation.
- We have a schedule roll-up dashboard that provides rapid assessment of the health of every project currently under development.
- We have formalized design reviews with our customer on all projects to ensure understanding of the technology and the challenges and to prevent surprises later in the program.

1.6 STRATEGIC BEST PRACTICES

Previously, we stated that project management has evolved from a series of processes that were nice to have into a mandatory grouping of processes that are necessary for the survival of the firm. In such a situation, project management is viewed as a strategic competency providing the firm with a competitive advantage. This requires strong executive leadership for project management as well as an understanding at the executive levels of the importance of project management. At Nortel Networks, project management is a strategic competency. According to Sue Spradley, President, Global Operations at Nortel Networks:

> In this age of instant communications and rapidly evolving networks, Nortel continues to maximize use of its project management discipline to ensure the successful deployment of increasingly complex projects. We foster an environment that maintains a focus on sharing best practices and leveraging lessons learned across the organization, largely driven by our project managers. We are also striving to further integrate project management capabilities with supply chain management through the introduction of SAP business management software. Project management remains an integral part of Nortel's business and strategy as it moves forward in a more services- and solutions-oriented environment.

When project management is recognized as a strategic competency, best practices are discovered and developed such that the entire company benefits. As an example, consider the following four best practices provided by Nortel Networks:

- Nortel has commercialized project management (PM) as a service and included PM in Nortel's Global Services Portfolio. This enables Nortel to leverage extensive PM expertise as a competitive advantage in today's services environment. Formal service description documents have been established for the standard PM services, with customized PM services also available to meet specific customer requirements.

  Linda Talbot, Leader, North America Wireless PM Process & Quality, Nortel Networks

- Nortel has created customer-centric organizations that provide dedicated PM support for major accounts and that utilize PM talent pools for resource flexibility on other accounts. Use of dedicated project managers enables Nortel to consistently leverage PM expertise to meet customer expectations on projects while enhancing customer relationships. Utilizing PM talent pools in some markets enables Nortel to retain critical PM skills and experience while providing the flexibility required to support the fluctuating resource demands of the business.

  Jennifer Day, Area Operations Leader, Nortel Networks

- Nortel has established a standardized global PM process as well as a comprehensive suite of tools and templates.
  - The global PM process has been fully documented, approved, and implemented as a discipline across all products and regions.
  - Standard templates and tools have been established, based on best practices, for use by project managers across the organization, for example, risk mitigation template, SOW, communication plan, action register, project plans, quality plan, project financial tracking tool, responsibility assignment matrix, and change management tracking tool.

Bill Gasikowski, Senior Project Manager, Global Services, Nortel Networks

- Nortel strives to ensure timely and consistent communications to all project managers to help drive continued success in the application of the global PM process. Examples of the various communications methods include:
  - The *PM Newsflash* is published on a monthly basis to facilitate communications across the PM organization and related functions.
  - PM communications sessions are held regularly, with a strong focus on providing training, metrics reviews, process and template updates, and so on.
  - Broadcast bulletins are utilized to communicate time-sensitive information.
  - A centralized repository has been established for project managers to facilitate easy access to and sharing of PM-related information.

Linda Talbot, Leader, North America Wireless PM Process & Quality

The comments by these Nortel personnel make it clear that best practices in project management can now permeate all business units of a company, especially those companies that are multinational. One of the reasons for this is that we now view all activities in a company as a series of projects. Therefore, we are managing our business by projects. Given this fact, best practices in project management are now appearing throughout the company.

Another strategic importance of best practices in project management can be seen from the comments below by Suzanne Zale, Global Program Manager at EDS:

Driven by the world economy, there is a tendency toward an increasing number of large-scale global or international projects. Project managers who do not have global experience tend to treat these global projects as large national projects. However, they are completely different. A more robust project management framework will become more important for such projects. Planning up front with a global perspective becomes extremely important. As an example, establishing a team that has knowledge about geographic regions relevant to the project will be critical to the success of the projects. Project managers must also know how to operate in those geographic areas. It is also essential that all project team members are trained and understand the same overall project management methodology.

Globalization and technology will make sound project management practice even more important.

Suzanne Zale's comments illustrate the importance of extracting best practices from global projects. This could very well be the future of best practices by the end of this decade.

1.7 SOURCES OF BEST PRACTICES _____

Best practices can be captured either within your organization or external to your organization. Benchmarking is one way to capture external best practices possibly by using the project management office as the lead for external benchmarking activities. However, there are external sources other than benchmarking for identifying best practices:

- Project Management Institute (PMI®) publications
- Seminars and symposiums on general project management concepts
- Seminars and symposiums specializing on project management best practices
- Relationships with other professional societies
- Graduate-level theses

With more universities offering masters- and doctorate-level work in project management, graduate-level theses can provide up-to-date research on best practices.

The problem with external benchmarking is that best practices discovered in one company may not be transferable to another company. In the author's opinion, most of the best practices are discovered internally and are specifically related to the company's use of its project management methodology and processes. Good project management methodologies allow for the identification and extraction of best practices. As an example, consider Orange Switzerland, which created a unique approach to extracting best practices:

> The project management system is based on three pillars, like the pylons of an ancient Greek temple; there is no one pillar more important than the other two. Care has been taken at Orange that all three "pylons" be developed in parallel (as shown in Figure 1–5).[3]

Orange Switzerland maintains a best practices library that is presently considered to be in the initial stage of development. The best practices library is accessible directly from its PMO Intranet website, which is one click away from its main Intranet site. This is shown in Figure 1–6.

At present, the drop-down list under best practices on Orange's PMO Intranet page contains four best practices within the best practices library:

- Red–Yellow–Green (RYG) traffic light rules (see Figure 1–7)
- Project hierarchy (see Figure 1–8)
- Project management self-assessment
- Capital expenditure (Capex) and operating expenses (Opex) definitions

The project hierarchy is an excellent best practice because it reinforces the relationship and importance of projects to the enterprise and the objectives of the enterprise. This type of best practice usually accelerates the maturity toward long-term project management excellence.

---

3. An explanation of Orange Switzerland's project management system, along with the three pillars, will be discussed in detail in a later chapter that describes project management methodologies.

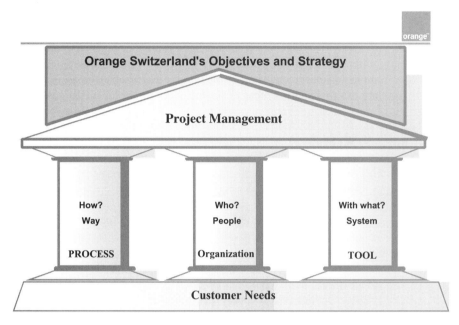

FIGURE 1–5. Orange Switzerland project management: based on three pillars process, organization, and tool.

There are several conclusions that can be drawn from the four best practices at Orange Switzerland. First, having the right few best practices can produce better results than having hundreds of so-called best practices that are meaningless. Second, involving the PMO in the identification of best practices is another best practice. Third, even with a few best practices, a Web-based best practices library can produce beneficial results. Fourth, every

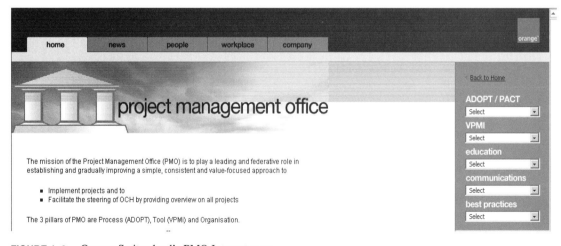

FIGURE 1–6. Orange Switzerland's PMO Intranet page.

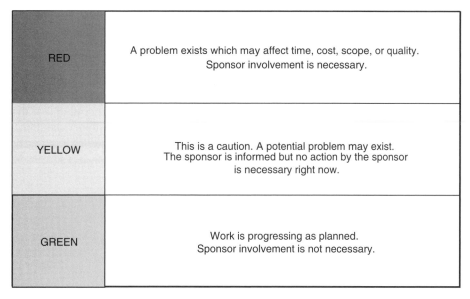

RED	A problem exists which may affect time, cost, scope, or quality. Sponsor involvement is necessary.
YELLOW	This is a caution. A potential problem may exist. The sponsor is informed but no action by the sponsor is necessary right now.
GREEN	Work is progressing as planned. Sponsor involvement is not necessary.

FIGURE 1–7. Orange Switzerland's traffic light rules.

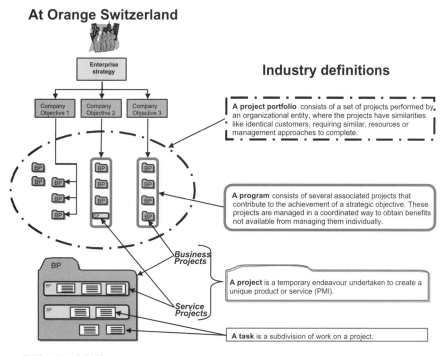

PMO, 6 March 2003

FIGURE 1–8. Project hierarchy.

company should strive to identify at least one best practice, no matter how simple, that relates the importance of project management to the successful completion of corporate objectives.

Another way to identify sources of best practices is from the definition of project success, critical success factors (CSFs), and key performance indicators (KPIs). Extracting best practices from the definition of success on a project may be difficult and misleading. The problem with defining success as on time, within cost, and at the desired quality is an internal definition of success only. The ultimate customer should have some say in the definition of success, and ultimately there may be numerous best practices discovered that relate to customer interfacing. Today, our definition of project success is measured in terms of both primary and secondary factors:

- Primary factors
  - Within time
  - Within cost
  - Within quality
  - Accepted by the customer
- Secondary factors
  - Customer reference
  - Follow-on work
  - Commercialization
  - Financial success
  - Technical superiority
  - Strategic alignment
  - Regulatory agency relationships
  - Health and safety
  - Environmental protection
  - Corporate reputation
  - Employee alignment
  - Ethical conduct

Today, we recognize that the customer rather than the contractor defines quality. The same holds true for project success. There must be customer acceptance included in any definition of project success. You can complete a project internally within your company within time, within cost, and within quality limits and yet the project is not fully accepted by the customer.

Perhaps one of the best definitions of project success was provided by Orange Switzerland. According to a spokesperson from Orange Switzerland, project success must be an evolving definition:

The definition of success has evolved from:

- Delivering a project (four years ago) to
- Delivering a project in time (two years ago) to
- Providing the project deliverables in a timely manner while respecting quality characteristics (today)

We are currently in the process of formalizing the project success definition covering:

- The delivery of the "product" within the scope of time, cost, and quality characteristics
- The successful management of changes during project life cycle
- The management of the project team
- The success of the product against defined criteria and targets during project initiation phase [e.g., adoption rates, return on investment (ROI)]

Although the definition of project success seems quite simple, many companies have elaborated on the primary definition of project success. Consider the comments below provided by Colin Spence, Project Manager/Partner at Convergent Computing (CCO):

General guidelines for a successful project are as follows:

- Meeting the technology and business goals of the client on time, on budget, and on scope
- Setting the resource or team up for success, so that all participants have the best chance to succeed and have positive experiences in the process
- Exceeding the client's expectations in terms of abilities, teamwork, and professionalism and generating the highest level of customer satisfaction
- Winning additional business from the client and being able to use the client as a reference account and/or agree to a case study
- Creating or fine-tuning processes, documentation, and deliverables that can be shared with the organization and leveraged in other engagements

Another critical question today is, "Who is defining success on a project?" Colin Spence responded to this question by stating:

Both the client stakeholders and CCO team members ultimately define whether a project is successful.

Success criteria for the project are defined during the initial steps in the engagement by the client and the project team in designing the proposal/scope-of-work (SOW) document. The creation of the scope of work typically involves stakeholders from the client side, a technical consultant from CCO, and an account manager from CCO. Depending on the size and complexity of the project, this process can be completed in one meeting with the client or may involve a more complete discovery and design process. CCO consultants are trained to focus on the business concerns of the client as well as their technology goals and to ensure that the solution recommended meets the full set of requirements.

Once the information has been gathered, the CCO team will create the SOW document that may involve assistance from additional resources (such as a technical writer or other expert on the technologies involved). The draft of the SOW is reviewed by the CCO team, delivered to the client, and then presented to the client. Often a project plan accompanies the SOW, but if not, one is created prior to the commencement of the work.

Once the project starts, regular checkpoint meetings are critical to ensure the project is successful on all fronts and for change management purposes. These meetings involve client stakeholders and members of the CCO team as appropriate. If a project manager is not assigned to the project full time, one will be allocated to attend in an advisory role. Team members are encouraged to raise flags at any time during the project.

Once the project is complete, a satisfaction review meeting is scheduled, where the results of the project are discussed and the client can freely report on what worked and what did not and make suggestions for perfecting the relationship. A project can be successful in that it met the goals set forth in the SOW but still be a failure if the client is not satisfied and chooses to not engage in other projects with CCO. Additionally the client may be satisfied with the results, but the CCO team may not be, so it is important to assess success from both the external point of view and the internal one.

Project success can be measured intermittently throughout the phase or gate review meetings that are part of the project management methodology. This allows a company to establish interim metrics for measuring success. An example of this will appear in a later chapter on project management methodologies.

Project success can also be measured by repeat business or sales volume. As an example, the definition of success in one of the units of Motorola, according to Thomas Dye, Director of Program Management at Motorola, is:

> Program success is measured by whether the product achieves its sales, volume, and margin goals. From a pure project management standpoint, a project is successful if it meets its objectives for scope, schedule, and cost.

Thomas Dye also believes that, in his group at Motorola, "The customer defines success by how many units are purchased."

Another element that is becoming important in the definition of success is the word *value*. Doug Bolzman, Consultant Architect, PMP®, ITIL Service Manager at EDS, believes:

> At one point, customers were measuring project success as being on time and under budget. But if the project provided no real business value, what good is it being on time or under budget? Value for projects are being transformed within the planning of the project to depict the value to the user or the client of the project.
>
> The users or the customers of the project define success. This can be difficult to identify at the start of the project (especially if not the norm). The executives can determine the overall value of how the projects map to the success of a program or initiative, but the users or customers will be the entity to receive the value of the project.

The comments by Doug Bolzman indicate that perhaps the single most important criterion for defining a potential best practice is that it must add value to the company and/or the client. Hewlett-Packard also sees the necessity for understanding the importance of value. According to Jack Calkins, Program Manager, Enterprise Infrastructure Practice Consulting and Integration at Hewlett-Packard, the following three best practices are added-value best practices:

- Project collaboration portals with standardized project management templates and integrated tool kits with ability to request additional features by a support staff: One such feature I have requested is the ability to implement Carl Pritchard's status reporting format virtually. (Each person walks virtually around a table and looks at other team

members' status reports and can ask questions directly in lieu of taking up the time of the group.) Actually, two best practices are combined here—project status and collaboration technology.
- Project retrospectives: Very helpful for group learning and eliciting/recognizing/documenting "best practices" but indeed communication beyond the immediate team is the challenge.
- Virtual projects: Given sufficient infrastructure I feel virtual projects are more productive and effective than burning up time and money on travel. I think HP utilizes these capabilities internally very well.

The ultimate definition of success might very well be when the customer is so pleased with the project that the customer allows you to use his or her name as a reference. This occurred in one company that bid on a project at 40 percent below its cost of doing the work. When asked why the bid was so low, company representatives responded that they knew they were losing money but what was really important was getting the customer's name on the corporate resume of clients. Therefore, the secondary factors may be more important than the primary factors.

The definition of success can also change based upon whether you are project- or non-project-driven. In a project-driven firm, the entire business of the company is projects. But in a non-project-driven firm, projects exist to support the ongoing business of production or services. In a non-project-driven firm, the definition of success also includes completion of the project *without* disturbing the ongoing business of this firm. It is possible to complete a project within time, within cost, and within quality and at the same time cause irrevocable damage to the organization. This occurs when the project manager does not realize that the project is *secondary* in importance to the ongoing business.

Some companies define success in terms of CSFs and KPIs. Critical success factors identify those factors necessary to meet the desired deliverables of the customer. Typical CSFs include:

- Adherence to schedules
- Adherence to budgets
- Adherence to quality
- Appropriateness and timing of signoffs
- Adherence to the change control process
- Add-ons to the contract

Critical success factors measure the end result usually as seen through the eyes of the customer. KPI's measure the quality of the process to achieve the end results. KPIs are internal measures and can be reviewed on a periodic basis throughout the life cycle of a project. Typical KPIs include:

- Use of the project management methodology
- Establish control processes
- Use of interim metrics
- Quality of resources assigned versus planned for
- Client involvement

Key performance indicators answer such questions as: Did we use the methodology correctly? Did we keep management informed and how frequently? Were the proper resources assigned and were they used effectively? Were there lessons learned which could necessitate updating the methodology or its use? Excellence companies measure success both internally and externally using KPIs and CSFs. As an example, consider the following remarks from Jennifer Day, Area Operations Leader at Nortel Networks:

> Nortel defines project success based on schedule, cost, and quality measurements, as mutually agreed-upon by the customer, the project team, and key stakeholders. Examples of key performance indicators may include completion of key project milestones, product installation/integration results, change management results, completion within budget, and so on. Project status and results are closely monitored and jointly reviewed with the customer and project team on a regular basis throughout a project to ensure consistent expectations and overall success. Project success is ultimately measured by customer satisfaction.

Examples of industrial definitions of CSFs and KPIs include:

- CSFs:
  - Typically projects either improve something or reduce something. These improvements come in the form of capability or functionality of the company (through the employees/users). These produce additional productivity, new products and services, or more efficiency for existing products. Critical success factors are mapped to the overall business objectives. (Provided by Doug Bolzman, Consultant Architect, PMP®, ITIL Service Manager at EDS)
  - Obviously, CSFs vary with projects and intent. Below are ones that apply over a large variety of projects:
    - Early customer involvement
    - High quality standards
    - Defined processes and formalized gate reviews
    - Cross-functional team organizational structure
    - Control of requirements, prevention of scope creep
    - Commitment to schedules—disciplined planning to appropriate level of detail and objective and frequent tracking
    - Commitment of resources—right skill level at necessary time
    - Communication among internal teams and with customer
    - Early risk identification, management, and mitigation—no surprises
    - Unequaled technical execution based on rigorous Engineering.
      (Provided by Thomas Dye, Director of Program Management, Motorola)
  - CCO has identified a number of CSFs involved in delivering outstanding technology services:
    - Have experienced and well-rounded technical resources. These resources need to not only have outstanding technical skills but also be good communicators, work well in challenging environments, and thrive in a team environment.

- Make sure we understand the full range of the clients' needs, including both technical and business needs, and document a plan of action (the scope of work) for meeting these needs.
- Have well-defined policies and processes for delivering technology services that leverage "best practice" project management concepts and practices.
- Have carefully crafted teams, with well-defined roles and responsibilities for the team members, designed to suit the specific needs of the client.
- Enhance collaborations and communications both internally (within the team and from the team to CCO) and externally with our clients.
- Leverage our experience and knowledge base as much as possible to enhance our efficiency and the quality of our deliverables.

(Provided by Colin Spence, Project Manager/Partner, Convergent Computing)

- KPIs:
  - Key performance indicators allow the customer to make a series of measurements to ensure the performance is within the stated thresholds (success factors). This is called "keeping the pulse of the company" by the executives. KPIs are determined, measured, and communicated through mechanisms such as dashboards or metrics.

(Provided by Doug Bolzman, Consultant Architect, PMP®, ITIL Service Manager at EDS)

  - Postship acceptance indicators:
    - Profit and loss
    - Warranty returns
    - Customer reported unique defects
    - Satisfaction metrics
  - In-process indicators:
    - Defect trends against plan
    - Stability for each build (part count changes) against plan
    - Feature completion against plan
    - Schedule plan versus actual performance
    - Effort plan versus actual performance
    - Manufacturing costs and quality metrics
    - Conformance to quality processes and results of quality audits
    - System test completion rate and pass/fail against plan
    - Defect/issue resolution closure rate
    - Accelerated life-testing failure rates against plan
    - Prototype defects per hundred units (DPHU) during development against plan

(Provided by Thomas Dye, Director of Program Management, Motorola)

- The statement of work (SOW) provides a checklist of basic indicators for the success of the project, but client satisfaction is also important. The SOW will indicate what the deliverables are and provide information on costs and timelines that are easily tracked.

  However, it is also critical that the SOW identify not only the goals of the project but also which are the most important to the client. For example, one client may not be overly concerned about the budget but must have the project meet certain deadlines. Part of the project manager's job is to understand which are the key criteria to meet and manage the project accordingly. If no project manager is assigned, this task is assigned to one of the other team members, typically the consultant.

So the project manager needs to periodically assess whether the project is under/over/on budget, ahead/behind/on schedule, and fulfilling the other goals of the project and to assess whether the client is satisfied with the work and deliverables. Additionally, the project manager needs to assess the internal functions of the team and make adjustments if needed.

(Provided by Colin Spence, Project Manager/Partner, Convergent Computing)

In the author's experience, more than 90 percent of the best practices that companies identify come from analysis of the KPIs during the debriefing sessions at the completion of a project. Because of the importance of extracting these best practices, some companies are now training professional facilitators capable of debriefing project teams and capturing the best practices.

1.8 WHAT TO DO WITH A BEST PRACTICE

With the definition that a best practice is an activity that leads to a sustained competitive advantage, it is no wonder that some companies have been reluctant to make their best practices known to the general public. Therefore, what should a company do with its best practices if not publicize them? The most common options available include:

- *Sharing Knowledge Internally Only:* This is accomplished using the company intranet to share information to employees. There may be a separate group within the company responsible for control of the information, perhaps even the PMO. Not all best practices are available to every employee. Some best practices may be password protected, as discussed below.
- *Hidden from All But a Selected Few:* Some companies spend vast amounts of money on the preparation of forms, guidelines, templates, and checklists for project management. These documents are viewed as both company-proprietary information and best practices and are provided to only a select few on a need-to-know basis. An example of a "restricted" best practice might be specialized forms and templates for project approval where information contained within may be company-sensitive financial data or the company's position on profitability and market share.
- *Advertise to Your Customers:* In this approach, companies may develop a best practices brochure to market their achievements and may also maintain an extensive best practices library that is shared with their customers after contract award. In this case, best practices are viewed as competitive weapons.

Even though companies collect best practices, not all best practices are shared outside of the company even during benchmarking studies where all parties are expected to share information. Students often ask why textbooks do not include more information on detailed best practices such as forms and templates. One company commented to the author:

> We must have spent at least $1 million over the last several years developing an extensive template on how to evaluate the risks associated with transitioning a project from engineering to manufacturing. Our company would not be happy giving this template to everyone who wants to purchase a book for $85. Some best practices templates are common knowledge and we would certainly share this information. But we view the transitioning risk template as proprietary knowledge not to be shared.

1.9 CRITICAL QUESTIONS

There are several questions that must be addressed before an activity is recognized as a best practice. Frequently asked questions include:

- Who determines that an activity is a best practice?
- How do you properly evaluate what you think is a best practice to validate that in fact it is a true best practice?
- How do you get executives to recognize that best practices are true value-added activities and should be championed by executive management?
- Who determines when a best practice is no longer a best practice?

Some organizations have committees that have as their primary function the evaluation of potential best practices. Anyone in the company can provide potential best practices data to the committee and the committee in turn does the analysis. Project managers may be members of the committee. Other organizations use the PMO to perform this work. These committees and the PMO most often report to the senior levels of management.

Evaluating whether or not something is a best practice is not time-consuming but it is complex. Simply because someone believes that what he or she is doing is a best practice does not mean that it is in fact a best practice. Some PMOs are currently developing templates and criteria for determining that an activity may qualify as a best practice. Some items that are included in the template might be:

- Is transferable to many projects
- Enables efficient and effective performance that can be measured (i.e., can serve as a metric)
- Enables measurement of possible profitability using the best practice
- Allows an activity to be completed in less time and at a lower cost
- Adds value to both the company and the client
- Can differentiate us from everyone else

One company had two unique characteristics in its best practices template:

- Helps to avoid failure
- If a crisis exists, helps us to get out of a critical situation

Executives must realize that these best practices are, in fact, intellectual property to benefit the entire organization. If the best practice can be quantified, then it is usually easier to convince senior management of its value.

1.10 LEVELS OF BEST PRACTICES

Best practices come from knowledge transfer and can be discovered anywhere within or outside of your organization. This is shown in Figure 1–9.

Figure 1–10 shows various levels of best practices. Each level can have categories within the level. The bottom level is the professional standards level, which would include professional standards as defined by PMI®. The professional standards level contains the greatest number of best practices, but they are more of a general nature than specific and have a low level of complexity.

The industry standards level would identify best practices related to performance within the industry. The automotive industry has established standards and best practices specific to the auto industry.

As we progress to the individual best practices in Figure 1–10, the complexity of the best practices goes from general to very specific applications and, as expected, the quantity of best practices is less. An example of a best practice at each level might be (from general to specific):

- *Professional Standards:* Preparation and use of a risk management plan, including templates, guidelines, forms, and checklists for risk management.

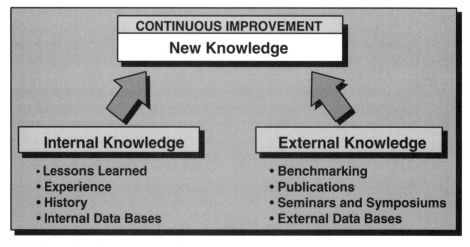

FIGURE 1–9. Knowledge transfer.

FIGURE 1–10. Levels of best practices.

- *Industry Specific:* The risk management plan includes industry best practices such as the best way to transition from engineering to manufacturing.
- *Company Specific:* The risk management plan identifies the roles and interactions of engineering, manufacturing, and quality assurance groups during transition.
- *Project Specific:* The risk management plan identifies the roles and interactions of affected groups as they relate to a specific product/service for a customer.
- *Individual:* The risk management plan identifies the roles and interactions of affected groups based upon their personal tolerance for risk, possibly through the use of a responsibility assignment matrix prepared by the project manager.

Best practices can be extremely useful during strategic planning activities. As shown in Figure 1–11, the bottom two levels may be more useful for project management strategy formulation whereas the top three levels are more appropriate for the execution or implementation of a strategy.

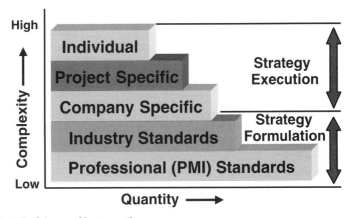

FIGURE 1–11. Usefulness of best practices.

1.11 COMMON BELIEFS

There are several common beliefs concerning best practices that companies have found to be valid. A partial list is:

- Because best practices can be interrelated, the identification of one best practice can lead to the discovery of another best practice, especially in the same category or level of best practices. Best practices may be self-perpetuating.
- Because of the dependencies that can exist between best practices, it is often easier to identify categories for best practices rather than individual best practices.
- Best practices may not be transferable. What works well for one company may not work for another company.
- Even though some best practices seem simplistic and common sense in most companies, the constant reminder and use of these best practices lead to excellence and customer satisfaction.
- Best practices are not limited exclusively to companies in good financial health. Companies that are cash rich can make a $10 million mistake and write it off. But companies that are cash poor are very careful in how they approve projects, monitor performance, and evaluate whether or not to cancel the project.

Care must be taken that the implementation of a best practice does not lead to detrimental results. One company decided that the organization must recognize project management as a profession in order to maximize performance and retain qualified people. A project management career path was created and integrated into the corporate reward system.

Unfortunately the company made a severe mistake. Project managers were given significantly larger salary increases than line managers and workers. People became jealous of the project managers and applied for transfer into project management thinking that the "grass was greener." The company's technical prowess diminished and some people resigned when not given the opportunity to become a project manager.

Sometimes, the implementation of a best practice is done with the best of intentions but the final result either does not meet management's expectations or may even produce an undesirable effect. The undesirable effect may not be apparent for some time. As an example, consider the first best practice in Table 1–4. Several companies are now using traffic light reporting for their projects. One company streamlined its Intranet project

TABLE 1–4. IMPROPER APPLICATION OF BEST PRACTICES

Type of Best Practice	Expected Advantage	Potential Disadvantage
Use of traffic light reporting	Speed and simplicity	Poor accuracy of information
Use of a risk management template/form	Forward looking and accurate	Inability to see all possible risks
Highly detailed WBS	Control, accuracy, and completeness	More control and cost of reporting
Using enterprise project management on all projects	Standardization and consistency	Too expensive on certain projects
Using specialized software	Better decision making	Too much reliance on tools

management methodology to include "traffic light" status reporting. Beside every work package in the work breakdown was a traffic light capable of turning red, yellow, or green. Status reporting was simplified and easy for management to follow. The time spent by executives in status review meetings was significantly reduced and significant cost savings were realized.

Initially, this best practice appeared to be beneficial for the company. However, after a few months, it became apparent that the status of a work package, as seen by a traffic light, was not as accurate as the more expensive written reports. There was also some concern as to who would make the decision on the color of the traffic light. Eventually, the traffic light system was enlarged to include eight colors, and guidelines were established for the decision on the color of the lights. In this case, the company was fortunate enough to identify the disadvantage of the best practice and correct it. Not all disadvantages are easily identified, and those that are may not always be correctable.

There are other reasons why best practices can fail or provide unsatisfactory results. These include:

- Lack of stability, clarity, or understanding of the best practice
- Failure to use best practices correctly
- Identifying a best practice that lacks rigor
- Identifying a best practice based upon erroneous judgment
- Failing to provide value

1.12 BEST PRACTICES LIBRARY

With the premise that project management knowledge and best practices are intellectual property, then how does a company retain this information? The solution is usually the creation of a best practices library. Figure 1–12 shows the three levels of best practices that seem most appropriate for storage in a best practices library.

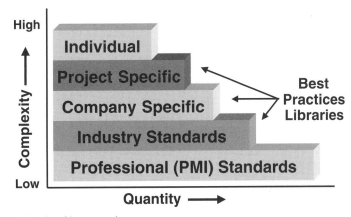

FIGURE 1–12. Levels of best practices.

Figure 1–13 shows the process of creating a best practices library. The bottom level is the discovery and understanding of what is or is not a "potential" best practice. The sources for potential best practices can originate anywhere within the organization.

The next level is the evaluation level to confirm that it is a best practice. The evaluation process can be done by the PMO or a committee but should have involvement by the senior levels of management. The evaluation process is very difficult because a one-time positive occurrence may not reflect a best practice that will be repetitive. There must exist established criteria for the evaluation of a best practice.

Once it is agreed upon that a best practice exists, then it must be classified and stored in some retrieval system such as a company intranet best practices library as was shown for Orange Switzerland. When asked how Orange Switzerland might communicate its best practices in the future, the PMO manager responded:

> Whenever a new best practice is identified, we could communicate it by e-mailing it to the project management community or having a "brown bag" lunch with a short presentation/ explanation.

The approach by Orange Switzerland is excellent because it allows for a more detailed explanation of the best practice as well as providing a means for answering questions. However, each company may have a different approach on how to disseminate this critical intellectual property. As with Orange Switzerland, most companies prefer to make maximum utilization out of the company's Intranet websites. However, some companies simply consider their current forms and templates as the ongoing best practices library. Consider the following examples:

- EDS has a website that lists all of the sanctioned best practices. There are currently 12 best practices listed in the library. The library provides a high-level graphic to depict the relationships of the best practices, a high-level profile of each best practice, and a link to each of the individual best practice websites. All of the best practices are included in a single glossary of terms.

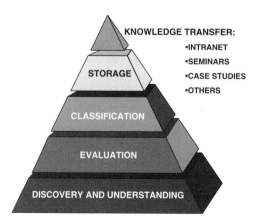

FIGURE 1–13. Creating a best practices library.

The Client Facing Best Practice website identifies best practices by EDS roles, the situation, problem, or opportunity that one is facing, and from the perspectives of the client relationship life cycle. A best practices grid is provided to the employees with a profile of each best practice, an overview presentation to explain the purpose and uses of the best practice, a link to the training materials, and finally a link to the individual best practice web site. (Provided by Doug Bolzman, Consultant Architect, PMP®, ITIL Service Manager, EDS)

- Motorola does not specifically have a best practices library. We do keep a library of all of our standard practices. When a best practice is identified, it is incorporated into the standard practices. We also keep a list of practices that are under review and when they will be reviewed and perhaps enhanced or updated.

  Best practices are institutionalized by being incorporated as formally controlled processes and placed in the iDEN Document Repository (our division's website for processes). Additionally, training is provided for new processes though our PMO group. Semimonthly all-hands meetings are used to inform the project manager community of changes in our baseline processes. Each project also is required to hold a lessons-learned forum, with a cross-discipline invite list, prior to being allowed to be closed out. (Provided by Tama McBride, PMP®, Program Manager, Motorola)

- Yes we have a best practices library and no we do not. Currently we are process and template driven. What could be considered as a library is what is currently in use. We have not formally archived past processes, however, we do encounter customers that are used to a certain method or process that we have centrally abandoned and that insist on these methods. As the customer is always right, we tend to accommodate their comfort in familiarity but casually introduce the changes.

  We task the teams to bring to light any ideas or practices that they consider an improvement. We have the mindsets that, if you bring a problem to the table, bring an idea that you think may resolve or lessen the impact. Internally we consider ourselves, from the highest rank to the lowest rank, the best people to solve the problem. Most all process is driven from daily working activities and from those that perform them. We encourage change and throughout the process communicate openly and freely without regard to the management level present. (Provided by Kelly Workman, PMP®, Senior Manager Field Service Engineering at etalk)

Figure 1–12 showed the levels of best practices, but the classification system for storage purposes can be significantly different. Figure 1–14 shows a typical classification system for a best practices library.

The purpose for creating a best practices library is to transfer knowledge to the employees. The knowledge can be transferred through the company Intranet, seminars on best practices, and case studies. Some companies require that the project team prepare case studies on lessons learned and best practices before the team is disbanded. These companies then use the case studies in company-sponsored seminars. Best practices and lessons learned must be communicated to the entire organization. The problem is determining how to do it effectively. Bill Gasikowski, Senior Project Manager, Global Services at Nortel Networks, comments on Nortel's approach to this issue:

Nortel maintains a centralized repository of all project management–related processes, procedures, and tools, including those that are considered to be "best practice." Project managers often provide examples of forms/templates that have proven successful in the management of their projects, enabling them to be shared with other project managers in

Effectiveness and Efficiency

Future Business

Technology Advances

Satisfaction

Project Management

FIGURE 1–14. Best practices library.

the organization. Best practices are communicated to the project management community through regular communications as well as training.

Another critical problem is best practices overload. One company started up a best practices library and, after a few years, had amassed what it considered to be hundreds of best practices. Nobody bothered to reevaluate whether or not all of these were still best practices. After reevaluation had taken place, it was determined that less than one-third of these were still regarded as best practices. Some were no longer best practices, others needed to be updated, and others had to be replaced with newer best practices.

1.13 BEST PRACTICES IN ACTION: SATYAM

In later chapters, we will discuss project management methodologies and the fact that these methodologies contain business processes as well as project management processes. When projects are debriefed, whether it is at the end of a life-cycle phase or the end of the project, the result can be the identification of business best practices as well as project management best practices. Therefore, best practices libraries can and do contain best practices that affect the entire business, not merely project management. When a company becomes good at capturing best practices, the result is often the creation of a knowledge base or project management knowledge base. According to Satyam[4]:

4. Satyam material has been graciously provided by Dr. Subhash C. Rastogi, Head, Project Management Center of Excellence, Satyam Learning Center; Anu Khendry, Principal Consultant, Corporate Quality; and Rajkumar Periaswamy, Principal Applications, Satyam Computer Services, Hyderabad India.

Satyam's Project Knowledge Base (PKB) contains experiences from past and current projects. This knowledge is leveraged by other projects during project planning and execution.

Satyam's PKB consists of the following:

- Best practices
- Lessons learned
- Risks encountered and successful risk mitigation/handling strategies
- Process database, with organization metrics baselines calculated every quarter for the past five years from closed project data
- Information on tools used in the projects—benefits and other feedback
- Sample documents, for example, new processes and templates created in the project
- Project data and metrics analysis
- Estimation sheet(s)
- Reuse repository (managed through reuse repository site)

Using an online PKB tool, the following activities are done:

- Project teams submit their inputs; a tool provides mail triggers to the teams for contribution.
- A software engineering process group reviews and approves the inputs, with feedback from project associates where required.
- All associates can query for content retrieval, without a sign-on.
- The software engineering process group regularly reviews the content and analyzes its usage by the associates.

There are many conferences and forums where best practices are discussed and shared. Examples of such forums are:

- Annual conferences with a large global audience from across the company, conducted via videocons and telecons
  - Satyam technology review
- Monthly publications
  - Newsletters from business units
- Intranet sites
  - PKB
  - xSell
  - KWindow

There is a single *integrated Web-based* eSupport Services for all associates covering services such as:

- *Personal:* like Payrolls, leaves, insurance, ID cards, service awards, e-mail, business cards, stock options
- *Telecom and Network Access:* New requests, track request
- *Appraisals:* Annual, after each project
- *Best Practices:* Repository, PKB
- *Business Travel:* Domestic and international travel plan, hotel/taxi/travel ticket booking requests, expense reporting, status tracking

- *Tele/Video Conferencing:* Bookings, reservations, cancellations
- *eBuddy:* Networking with other associates, anywhere in the world
- *Facilities Booking:* Office space, training labs, classrooms, conference rooms, residential complexes, holiday homes, transit houses
- *Idea Junction:* Submitting improvement ideas for rewards
- *Procurement:* Submitting RFPs, RFQs, tracking status
- *Reimbursements:* Claims, advances, history
- *Resume Management:* Hot Jobs, referrals
- *Satyam Club:* Events, membership
- *SLC Online:* Learning calendar, project managers portal
- *Surveys:* Various employees surveys
- *Visa and Work Permit:* Services

1.14 BEST PRACTICES IN ACTION: DFCU FINANCIAL

One of the greatest pleasures in being a project management educator is reading about success stories in project management, especially when the story discusses how all of the pieces of the puzzle eventually come together. Such was the case with DFCU Financial. Elizabeth Hershey, PMP®, Vice President Delivery Channel Support with DFCU Financial, describes the evolutionary process of project management and best practices within her company. Elizabeth Hershey and DFCU Financial graciously provided the remainder of this section.

> At $1.7 billion in assets, DFCU Financial Federal Credit Union is the largest credit union in Michigan and among the top 40 largest in the nation. With a 246 percent increase in net income since 2000, DFCU Financial has never done better, and effective project implementation has played a key role. At the root of this success story is a lesson in how to leverage what is best about your corporate culture.
>
> Rolling back the clock to late 1997, I had just volunteered to be the Y2K project manager—the potential scope, scale, and risk associated with this project scared most folks away. And with some justification—this was not a company known for its project successes. We made it through very well, however, and it taught me a lot about the DFCU Financial culture. We did not have a fancy methodology. We did not have business unit managers who were used to being formally and actively involved in projects. We did not even have many information technology (IT) resources that were used to being personally responsible for specific deliverables. What we did have, however, was a shared core value to outstanding service—to doing whatever was necessary to get the job done well. It was amazing to me how effective that value was when combined with a well-chosen sampling of formal project management techniques.
>
> Having tasted project management success, we attempted to establish a formal project management methodology—the theory being that if a little formal project management worked well, lots more would be better. In spite of its bureaucratic beauty, this methodology did not ensure a successful core system conversion in mid-2000. We were back to the drawing board concerning project management and were facing a daunting list of required projects.

With the appointment of a new president in late 2000, DFCU Financial's executive team began to change. It did not take long for the new team to assess the cultural balance sheet. On the debit side, we faced several cultural challenges directly affecting project success:

- Lack of accountability for project execution
- Poor strategic planning and tactical prioritization
- Projects controlled almost exclusively by IT
- Project management overly bureaucratic
- Limited empowerment

On the plus side, our greatest strength was still our strong service culture. Tasked with analyzing the company's value proposition in the market place, senior vice president of marketing, Lee Ann Mares, made the following observations: "Through the stories that surfaced in focus groups with members and employees, it became very clear that this organization's legacy was extraordinary service. Confirming that the DFCU brand was all about service was the easy part. Making that generality accessible and actionable was tough. How do you break a high-minded concept like *outstanding service* into things that people can relate to in their day-to-day jobs? We came up with three crisp, clear guiding principles: Make their day, make it easy, and be an expert. Interestingly enough, these simple rules have not only given us a common language, but have helped us to keep moving the bar higher in so many ways. We then worked with line employees from across the organization to elaborate further on the principles. The result was a list of 13 brand actions—things each of us can do to provide outstanding service (Table 1–5)."

While we were busy defining our brand, we were also, of course, executing projects. Since 2000, we have improved our operational efficiency through countless process improvement projects. We have replaced several key subsystems. We have launched new products and services. We have opened new branches. We have also gotten better and better at project execution, due in large part to several specific changes we made in how we handle projects. When we look closer at what these changes were, it is striking how remarkably congruent they are with our guiding principles and brand actions. As simple as it may sound, we have gotten better at project management by truly living our brand.

Brand Action—Responsibility

Project control was one of the first things changed. Historically, the IT department exclusively controlled most projects. The company's project managers even reported to the chief information officer (CIO). As chief financial officer, Eric Schornhorst comments, "Most projects had weak or missing sponsorship on the business side. To better establish project responsibility, we moved the project managers out of IT, and we now assign them to work with a business unit manager for large-scale projects only. The project managers play more of an administrative and facilitating role, with the business unit manager actually providing project leadership." Our current leadership curriculum, which all managers must complete, includes a very basic project management course, laying the foundation for further professional development in this area.

TABLE 1–5. DFCU FINANCIAL BRAND ACTIONS

	Make their day	*Make it easy*	*Be an expert*
Voice	We recognize team members as the key to the company's success, and each team member's role, contributions, and voice are valued.		
Promise	Our brand promise and its guiding principles are the foundation of DFCU Financial's uncompromising level of service. The promise and principles are the common goals we share and must be known and owned by all of us.		
Goals	We communicate company objectives and key initiatives to all team members, and it is everyone's responsibility to know them.		
Clarity	To create a participative working environment, we each have the right to clearly define job expectations, training, and resources to support job function and a voice in the planning and implementation of our work.		
Teamwork	We have the responsibility to create a teamwork environment, supporting each other to meet the needs of our members.		
Protect	We have the responsibility to protect the assets and information of the company and our members.		
Respect	We are team members serving members, and as professionals, we treat our members and each other with respect.		
Responsibility	We take responsibility to own issues and complaints until they are resolved or we find an appropriate resource to own them.		
Empowerment	We are empowered with defined expectations for addressing and resolving member issues.		
Attitude	We will bring a positive, "can-do" attitude to work each day—it is my job!		
Quality	We will use service quality standards in every interaction with our members or other departments to ensure satisfaction, loyalty, and retention.		
Image	We take pride in and support our professional image by following dress code guidelines.		
Pride	We will be ambassadors for DFCU Financial by speaking positively about the company and communicate comments and concerns to the appropriate source.		

Guiding Principle—Make It Easy

With project ownership more clearly established, we also simplified our project planning and tracking process. We now track all large corporate and divisional projects on a single spreadsheet that the executive team reviews monthly (see Table 1–6 for the report headers). Project priority is tied directly to our strategic initiatives. Our limited resources are applied to the most impact and most critical projects. Eric Schornhorst comments, "Simplifying project management forms and processes has enabled us to focus more on identifying potential roadblocks and issues. We are much better at managing project risk."

Brand Action—Goals

Chief Information Officer Vince Pittiglio recalls the legacy issue of IT overcommitment: "Without effective strategic and tactical planning, we used to manage more of a project wish list than a true portfolio of key projects. We in IT would put our list of key infrastructure projects together each year. As the year progressed, individual managers would add new projects to our list. Often, many of these projects had little to do with what we were really trying to achieve strategically. We had more projects than we could do effectively, and to be honest, we often prioritized projects based on IT's convenience, rather than on what was best for the organization and our members." Focusing on key initiatives has made it possible to say "no" to low-priority projects that are non–value addition or simply not in our members' best interest. And the current measuring stick for project success is not merely whether the IT portion of the project was completed, but rather that the project met its larger objectives and contributed to the company's success as a whole.

TABLE 1–6. DFCU FINANCIAL CORPORATE PROJECTS LIST REPORT HEADERS

Priority	1 = Board reported and/or top priority
	2 = High priority
	3 = Corporate priority, but can be delayed
	4 = Business unit focused or completed as time permits
Project	Project name
Description	Brief entry, especially for new initiatives
Requirements	R = Required
document	Y = Received
status	N/A = Not needed
Status	Phase (discovery, development, implementation) and percentage completed for current phase
Business	Business unit manager who owns the project
owner	
Project	Person assigned to this role
manager	
Projected	Year/quarter targeted for delivery
delivery time	
Resources	Functional areas or specific staff involved
Project notes	Brief narrative on major upcoming milestones or issues

Brand Action—Teamwork

Historically, DFCU Financial was a strong functional organization. Cross-departmental collaboration was rare and occurred only under very specific conditions. This cultural dynamic did not provide an optimal environment for projects. The monthly project review meeting brings together the entire executive team to discuss all current and upcoming projects. The team decides which projects are in the best interest of the organization as a whole. This critical collaboration has contributed to building much more effective, cross-functional project teams. We are developing a good sense of when a specific team or department needs to get involved in a project. We also have a much better understanding of the concept that we will succeed or fail together. We are working together better than ever.

Brand Action—Empowerment

As chief operating officer, Jerry Brandman points out, "our employees have always been positive and pleasant. But our employees were never encouraged to speak their minds, especially to management. This often had a direct negative impact on projects—people foresaw issues, but felt it was not their place to sound the alarm. A lot of the fear related to not wanting to get others 'in trouble.' We have been trying to make it comfortable for people to raise issues. If the emperor is naked, we want to hear about it! To make people visualize the obligation they have to speak up, I ask them to imagine they are riding on a train and that they believe they know something that could put the trip in jeopardy. They have an obligation to pull the cord and stop the train. This has not been easy for people, but we are making headway every day."

Brand Action—Quality

At DFCU Financial project implementation in the past followed more of the big-bang approach—implement everything all at once to everyone. When the planets aligned, success was possible. More often than not, however, things were not so smooth. Jerry Brandman comments, "You have to have a process for rolling things out to your public. You also need to test the waters with a small-scale pilot whenever possible. This allows you to tweak and adjust your project in light of real feedback." Employees all have accounts at DFCU Financial, so we have a convenient pilot audience. Recent projects such as ATM-to-debit-card conversions and the introduction of e-statements have all been piloted with employees prior to launching them to the entire membership.

Bottom line, the most significant best practice at DFCU Financial has been to be true to our core cultural value of providing extraordinary service. As we were working on defining this value and finding ways to make it actionable, we were also making changes to the way we approach project management that were very well aligned with our values. Our commitment to living our brand has helped us to:

- Move project responsibility from IT to the business units
- Simplify project management forms and processes
- Use project review meetings to set priorities and allocate resources more effectively
- Break down organizational barriers and encourage input on projects from individuals across the organization
- Improve project success through pilots and feedback

As president and CEO, Mark Shobe summarizes, "good things happen when you have integrity, when you do what you say you are going to do. The improvements we have made in handling projects have rather naturally come out of our collective commitment to really live up to our brand promise. Have we made a lot of progress in how we manage projects? Yes. Is everything where we want it to be? Not yet. Are we moving in the right direction? You bet. And we have a real good road map to get there."

1.15 BEST PRACTICES IN ACTION: TWO DEGREES

Sometimes, as little as one best practice can have a very favorable impact on a company's business as well as relationships with clients. And, with proper analysis, this one best practice could lead to the discovery of other best practices. This is particularly true in the software industry. As an example, the following section was provided by Leigh Gower, PMP®, Senior Project Manager, Two Degrees.

Best Practice in Multisystem Release Management— Integrated Mock Deployment Exercises

Background
The basic foundation for both project management and software development methodologies is initiation or concept development, requirements and system development, testing and production implementation, and support. Many companies are learning the lesson that cutting time in requirements and planning ultimately costs more money in later project phases when issues are not identified early enough. This has allowed many organizations to build strong software development strategies for their individual platform technologies. Where a number of companies seem to break down and ultimately lose the benefits of this maturity is at the integration points for their various systems. The "silo" approach to system development is still affecting companies that have not yet reached the maturity to successfully integrate their collective project efforts.

As more companies rely on integrated systems architectures to fully support their existing business processes, there is not only an emerging need to continue to mature these systems to support the directional needs of the enterprise but also an underlying need to keep all systems stable in order to support existing customers and ongoing business needs. Many companies put a lot of time and energy into carefully selecting and planning for future project efforts in order to optimize the use of their systems for sustained company growth and profits, yet still face challenges at implementation. Despite the careful planning and dedication to thorough requirements definition and development, many companies still approach the production implementation planning and execution of these projects as an inevitable outcome if all phases of testing are executed successfully.

Best Practice Recommendation

Most project managers and project team members who have participated in an integrated test execution using multiple systems can name a variety of pitfalls from data management across applications to configuration issues between systems, and so on. Rarely does the setup and initial execution of an integrated test phase involving multiple applications proceed successfully without complications. Given the many variables that need to be in sync between applications for any multisystem functionality to implement successfully, we have learned the benefits of fully integrated mock deployment exercises, requiring every application involved in a particular release to execute all tasks on their short interval schedules and provide results that verify the expected results in both estimating durations for the tasks and validating expected results.

Fully integrated mock deployment exercises, which take the execution of a release through the execution and validation stages all the way through a roll-back execution should any application implementation fail, has the potential for being as critical to the execution of a successful project as careful and precise requirements identification. In this age of 24×7 account access via the Web, most companies have performance metrics requiring a specific percentage of "up time" for their systems that service their customers and staff. Multiapplication releases not only have the potential to affect the viability of the functionality and data in these systems in and around a release execution but also affect the up-time statistics for any company as often it is necessary to disable access to all applications while the release implementation is underway.

The steps necessary to execute a successful integrated mock deployment exercise are the same as those used for any other project. Identify the scope and purpose of the exercise, define the requirements and success criteria, work with the tasks and durations for individual applications to document the integrated short interval schedule, plan for the staff and systems necessary to support the execution, exercise execution itself and closeout which involves the identification of lessons learned and project successes that can be carried forward to enhance the planning for production night implementation. Essentially, like many other life-cycle phases, the mock deployment exercise is best approached as a project within a project. In implementing this best practice, each company needs to take into consideration the cost-versus-benefit analysis of such an undertaking.

1.16 HALIFAX COMMUNITY HEALTH SYSTEMS

Previously we discussed the importance of having a structured approach for the capturing of best practices. Halifax Community Health Systems has a structured process for capturing best practices. As stated by Nancy Jeffreys, Portfolio and Program Manager at Halifax Community Health Systems:

> Halifax Community Health Systems uses SMART goals as our measure of success. At the beginning of each project, we meet with our sponsor and project team to define what they want to achieve as a result of the project. We work through what the SMART goals will be. When the project is completed, we should go back and measure the outcome of the project with the original SMART goals. In some instances we have completed this review, but in the larger projects, time has not passed long enough to measure the goals.
>
> At the beginning of each fiscal year, the manager and senior project managers meet to discuss the enterprise project management office (EPMO) goals for the year. From these goals, we determine what the success factors are for each goal. These success factors are tied into the individual project management goals for the year. They are used during the employee reviews for performance indicators. All goals and performance indicators are tied together so everyone is working toward the same goals and performance indicators.
>
> We believe that our customers determine the success of our projects and of our office. At the end of each project we do two things:
>
> 1. We send out a survey about their perception of how well the project was conducted and to rate the project manager.
> 2. At the end of each project, we have a "lessons-learned" meeting where we discuss what success factors should be used in future projects. The template appears in Table 1–7. The EPMO team meets for an internal meeting biweekly. The lessons learned are shared at those meetings for everyone to discuss. At the beginning of each project, we go back to the lessons learned from previous projects to ensure we carry the success factors forward to the new project.

1.17 BEST PRACTICES IN ACTION: DTE ENERGY

Another example of the process by which best practices can be captured is seen at DTE Energy. The following material was provided by Joseph C. Thomas, PMP®, Senior Project Manager, Software Engineering, Methods, and Staffing, and Steve Baker, PMP®, CCP, Principal Analyst, Process and Skills Organization at DTE Energy:

> In 2002, the Information Technology Services (ITS) Organization at DTE Energy initiated an effort to collect and document best practices for project management. Our intent was to publish, communicate, and ensure these best practices were adopted across the culture. We believed this approach would lead to continuous improvement opportunities resulting in higher quality, more timely, and less expensive software-based business solutions.
>
> Rather than describe the ideal state of project management as we could envision it, we decided to describe the current state as it was being practiced by project managers in the organization. The goal was to establish a baseline set of standards that we knew project managers could meet because we were already doing them.
>
> We formed a small team of our most experienced project managers and IT leaders. This team drew upon its recent project experiences to identify a set of best practices. While not every project manager uniformly followed them, the best practices represented the

TABLE 1–7. BEST PRACTICES/LESSONS-LEARNED TEMPLATE

Purpose: The purpose of this policy is to identify processes, tasks, and methodologies from projects completed that can contribute to the success of future projects.

Scope: This policy applies to all project managers and all PMO projects.

Policy: Project managers must complete a lessons-learned review after the project Go Live and before the project is completed. Information is gathered throughout the project from the project manager, core team, and vendor. At the end of the project, these are accumulated into a document that is presented to the team for their review. The lessons should be positive statements that can be used as success factors or risks in future projects. Each project's lessons learned will be accumulated in an EPMO lessons-learned document. The lessons-learned document should be reviewed with the EPMO team to decide what action needs to be taken to incorporate success factors or risks into future projects. These lessons will be added to the EPMO lessons-learned document.

Procedure:

- At the beginning of a project, a blank lessons-learned template should be saved in the project file.
- As issues, risks, or successes arise that should be considered in future projects, they should be documented in the lessons-learned document.
- At the end of the project, a senior project manager will send out the accumulated lessons-learned document to the core team.
- A senior project manager will lead a lessons-learned discussion during the final core team meeting.
- The meeting notes are reviewed with the project manager for that project.
- Lessons from that project will be added to the EPMO lessons-learned document by the project manager.
- The EPMO team will review any new lessons to determine how they can be incorporated into future projects. Should new policies/procedures be developed? Are there items that need to be added to the standard contract? What else can the EPMO do to make the next project successful based on the lessons of this project?
- Any changes to any documents, policies, procedures, or processes will be noted on the EPMO lessons-learned document.
- Prior to the start of a new project, the project manager should review the EPMO lessons-learned document to incorporate the lessons in the new project.
- Any contract must include all of the relevant EPMO lessons learned.

highest common denominator rather than the lowest. We knew that these were feasible since they represented practical experiences of our most successful project managers, and they also characterized the practices we wanted applied consistently across all projects. In this way, the bar was low enough to be achievable but high enough to be a meaningful improvement for most of the projects.

The team agreed to describe the best practices in terms of "what" rather than "how." We wanted to avoid the difficult and time-consuming task of defining detailed procedures with formal documentation. Rather, we described what project managers needed to do and the artifacts that project managers needed to produce. This provided the practicing project managers with some degree of flexibility in the methods (the how) they employed to produce the results (the what).

We published the best practices in a hundred-page "Project Management Standards and Guidelines" manual (see the table of contents in Table 1–8) and also posted them on our Solution Delivery Process Center (SDPC) Intranet website (see the screen shot, Figure 1–15). We included references to other resources such as standard forms, templates, and procedures that already existed.

The SDPC is our process asset library containing scores of high-level role and process descriptions, easy-to-access templates and examples, and links to various resources from other departments across ITS. We designed our digital library to be usable for a variety of perspectives, including role based ("I am a..."), milestone based ("We are at. . ."), artifact based ("I need a. . ."), and so on.

TABLE 1–8. PROJECT MANAGEMENT STANDARDS AND GUIDELINES

Software Engineering, Methods, and Staffing Project Management Standards and Guidelines

CONTENTS

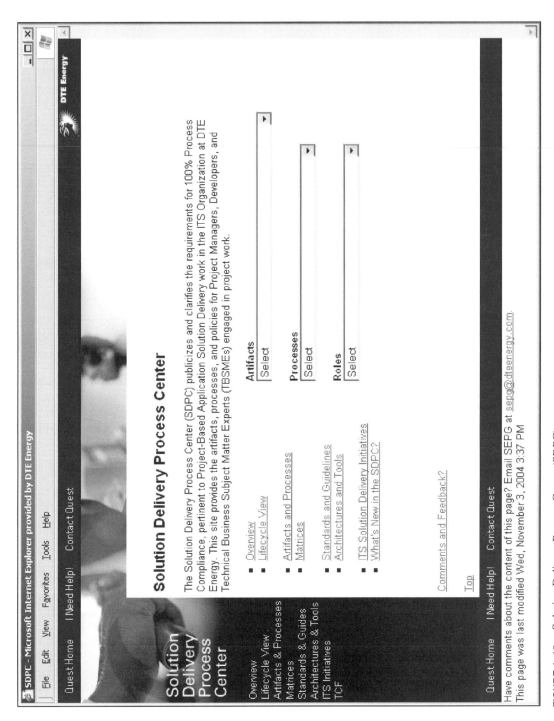

FIGURE 1–15. Solution Delivery Process Center (SDPC).

47

We launched the standards and guidelines materials and the SDPC library with a diverse communication strategy, targeting the right message to the right audience at the right time. We included a feedback process to ensure the evolution and applicability of the standards over time. This continuous improvement process includes (a) an inbound e-mail account for receiving comments, suggestions, and ideas; (b) a review and update process including roles and milestones; and (c) timely updates to the SDPC and targeted printings of the standards and guidelines manual.

As a way to capture our lessons learned from each project, we adopted the after action review (AAR) process. Every project conducts an AAR upon completion, and we seek improvements to and innovations beyond our existing processes and templates. We institutionalize these improvements within our evolving standards and guidelines and the SDPC library. We solved our lessons-learned dilemma (best practices were dutifully archived but rarely referenced) by incorporating each discovery within our standards and guidelines.

Standards and guidelines, in and of themselves, are a means to an end. We found that simply publishing and communicating them is not enough to meaningfully impact our culture. To that end, we instituted a quality management group (QMG) staffed with a small, diverse team of experts. The QMG both *enables* our projects with consulting services and education and *ensures* our projects are in compliance with published standards and guidelines. With five inspection milestones, the QMG demonstrates our organizational commitment to best practices and continuous improvement.

1.18 BEST PRACTICES IN ACTION: AMONTIS

The development of OPM3™ by the PMI has provided companies with the framework for developing organizational maturity in project management. Alexander Matthey, PMP®, Amontis Consulting AG Group Associate—Switzerland, discusses project management best practices and the relationship with OPM3™:

OPM3™ Boosts Competitiveness of a Mobile Phone Operator in Switzerland: First Commercial Implementation of OPM3™ in the World

The Early Initiative
At first, the mandate was to identify a project management training curricula that could respond to the project managers' expectations and which could experience relief from some of the operational problems. But, it was evident that training alone could not be beneficial unless based on a broader perspective of project management education that would include the harmonization trend and address the need of a continuous development of knowledge and skills in the perspective of a project manager's career.

The Choice of OPM3™
The characteristics of OPM3™ retained by the PMO at this mobile phone operator have driven the choice: an organizational maturity evaluation based on a comprehensive and broad set of organizational project management best practices, the support of well-defined improvement paths to progress, and the availability of key performance indicators to follow up on the progress.

An integrated approach that suited the internal needs was perceivable in OPM3™: the presence of the domains of program and portfolio management (addressed by the organization strategy layer) besides the project management domain and the establishment of the stages approach (standardization, measurement, control, and continuous improvement) across the domains and obviously the five process groups of the project management domain (IPECC).

The existence of those three dimensions and the staged approach allowed this organization to design a practical learning curve and boost the organization to a higher maturity in project management? In the first phase of the project, it was decided to improve, the project management domain.

The Project Context

The project was moving along three axes: the educational program, the definition of a project manager's competency model, and project manager's career development.

In that context, Figure 1-16 shows the interaction between the OPM3™ model steps and the full educational program.

For the mobile phone operator it was not known yet which operational tasks needed to be organized, how the assessment information would be collected and analyzed, and how findings would be translated into improvement recommendations. So the organization relied on competent and specialized consultants for OPM3™ to constitute a group of internal assessors.

There were multiple constraints that the company had to take into consideration:

● *Schedule:* It was imperative to begin training on OPM3™ in early January 2004 if the education project was to be completed by March 2004.
● *Resources:* Candidates to the assessment training and assessment exercise had to be representative of the various divisions and be partially relieved from their current tasks at short notice.

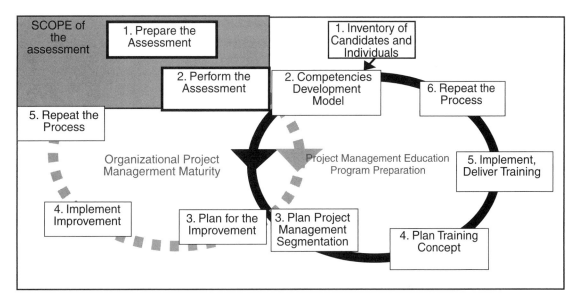

FIGURE 1–16. OPM3™ steps and educational program steps.

- *Planning:* It was necessary to plan and communicate involvement estimates even though nobody could see beyond the three-day training sessions.
- *Organization Environment:* Misunderstandings and therefore fears of the assessment objective (was it about people assessment or project assessment?) when other audits (CMMI™ level 2 of the IT department) had been completed a few weeks earlier. Indeed the replacement of the term *assessment* with *interview* became a condition.

The Implementation Approach

The Assessment Preparation
Preparing the assessment implied extensive communication effort to overcome major resistance during the assessment, which translated into:

- Multiple meetings with functional managers to get the availability of the assessors
- Ad hoc presentations for critical situations to overcome concerns, bring clarification, show the benefits of the assessment, and distance the assessment from previous audits
- Documentation generation to facilitate the assessor's understanding of OPM3™ as most of them were not used to the PMBOK® Guide terminology and standard
- Documentation generation addressed to interviewees and their managers to officially inform them about the assessment session's objectives and procedure and the feedback communication mechanism that would follow

Among the other preparation activities, a fundamental one concerned the assessment questionnaires. Four questionnaires were created covering each of the following areas:

- Project management best practices
- Program management best practices
- Portfolio management best practices
- Support areas best practices

The questionnaires were written based on OPM3™ database contents, strictly following the model but turning each best practice into an easy-to-understand question. The questionnaires were also organized on the best practice basis rather than on the SMCIs (standardized, measurable, controlled, and continuously improved), although these were addressed, with the advantages of reducing to one-fourth the length of the questionnaire, encouraging the assessors, and pleasing the interviewees.

A significant effort in preparing the questionnaires derived from the fact that the OPM3™ documentation did not provide a functionality allowing the best practices list or the support area list to be placed in a file and printed.

The Assessors' Preparation
The assessors' training involved 12 internal people for three days in a workshop that also addressed the next assessment planning and organization: what to assess, how to assess, which risks to consider and how to mitigate, how to collect and analyze the assessment data, and so on. The workshop also included a simulation assessment session.

To overcome the obvious difficulty of most of the assessors, a one-day course on the PMBOK® Guide organized ad hoc has been successful and has encouraged the assessors that run the "interviews."

The trainers were then placed into four teams and it was decided that each assessment session would involve two team members. Assessors were also provided an administrative guidelines document to harmonize the assessment sessions across the teams with scripts on how to start a session, how to answer to most probable questions, how to invite the interviewees, and how to terminate the session.

The assessment operations flow illustrated in Figure 1–17 has been followed 32 times as there have been 32 project management evaluation sessions in the form of interviews of project managers and some line managers. It is worth noting that the assessment has included various vice presidents to check their individual expectations and complete the link between the strategic and operational layers.

Assssment Data Processing and Results
The assessment answers were coded to ensure confidentiality, cleaned, formatted, and consolidated. A significant effort has been spent on those operational activities before storing the data in a database.

The data analysis looked at the following aspects:

● The project management maturity status of the five process groups (initiating, planning, executing, controlling, and closing)
● The project management maturity status per process per division
● The program management maturity status per division

The general findings have shown that there were variances within the divisions in terms of project management practices which could be explained by the lack of a common methodical approach. In essence, the overall maturity in project management was revealed as slightly below 20 percent.

Process-based views and division-based views were produced for the assessed projects and some interesting comments expressed by the interviewees were collected. Besides providing statistical data, the collected information, as it was structured, showed the link between the assessment questionnaires, the definition of needs, and the establishment of real educational requirements.

Those links were necessary to convince executive management that the final report had a substantial basis and that the recommendations were answering "field" needs.

Those results were presented to the executives during individual meetings. This became an opportunity to discuss relevance of an educational program on project management for their specific goals, debate the inevitable connection that exists between strategy and projects, and seek how to best achieve the link.

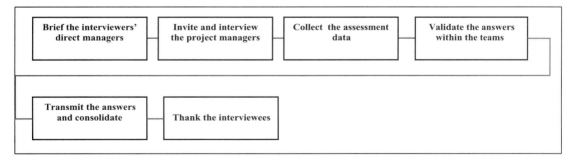

FIGURE 1–17. Assessment flow.

Boosting Project Management

With those findings assessed, the next step was to choose and follow a roadmap of initiatives that would target an improvement in project management practices—roll out a training. The initiatives included:

- Identifying the community of practitioners (not only project managers)
- Defining a strategic education program that would bring high visibility of the early improvements
- Introducing the concept of project managers' career.

Indeed, with the support of the community, it became possible to "advertize" and start educating a majority of practitioners through internal forums organized by the PMO or single topics to debate at small business lunches or just communicating progress and news. The strategic approach to education was needed to introduce improvements, despite the impossibility of involving all practitioners, and to start capitalizing on education investments, becoming free from continuous external support. And the concept of a project management career could only benefit meeting such a target.

The education program was developed on a three-year basis (Figure 1–18) to move project management practices from individual initiatives (status) to a structured approach within the various divisions (phase 1) to harmonized practices at the company level (phase 2).

Such training is to be supported by a competencies development program to ensure individual skills growth and to accommodate the needs of a career for a responsible and accountable project manager.

The innovative approach that followed (Figure 1–19) is the involvement of all the stakeholders in the learning process, thus improving the entire project team's performances (visibility), ensuring commitment from all concerned parties to the use of the taught practices (continuity), and introducing those practices across the company through the project teams (divulgence).

This is what I call a good practice in action. I'm happy to have been able to initiate and drive this process.

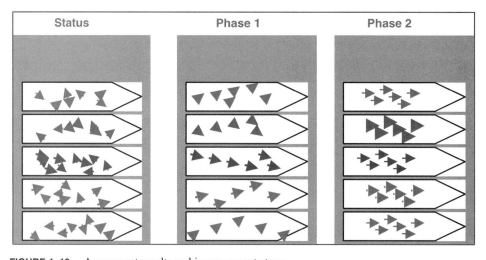

FIGURE 1–18. Assessment results and improvement steps.

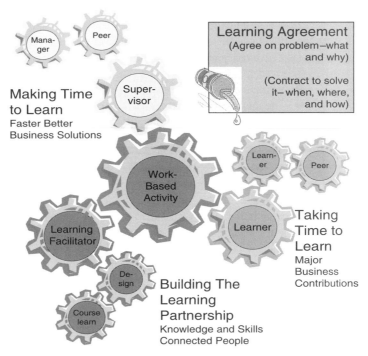

FIGURE 1–19. Educational program implementation model.

1.19 BEST PRACTICES IN ACTION: COMPUTER ASSOCIATES (CA)[5]

Since the publication of *Advanced Project Management: Best Practices on Implementation,* in 2004, much progress has been made to the standardization of intellectual material, policies, processes and procedures within the CA Technology Services organization. As the organization responsible for the enablement of our solutions, CA Technology Services recognized early on that in order to be successful we needed a system of capturing and housing best practices, sharing lessons learned, and making this information available to everyone. One of the fastest ways to get better is to be better.

The Best Practices Library (BPL) was established several years ago as a central repository for storing methods that consisted of a project management methodology (PMM) and various product implementation procedures and templates. Since its inception, the Best Practices Library has evolved into a system hosting repeatable processes that are continually reviewed and fine tuned. Methods range from assessments to solution implementations to optimization services to a project management methodology.

---

5. This section was provided by Linda H. Hickman, PMP®, Manager, Worldwide PMO, and Robert J. H. Zuurdeeg, CKM, ITIL, Manager, Knowledge Architecture

CA Technology Services is an evolving organization, showing strong services growth year over year while improving customer satisfaction and profitability. This is in part due to the BPL. In order to keep the BPL viable, processes have been established to monitor the usage and verify value of its content:

- All methodologies are reviewed (and tuned as needed) on a 4 month basis.
- The method review process was expanded to include additional project data.
- A monthly usage report identifies trends and areas needing attention/focus.
- A all-inclusive zip file was added for easy download of all methodology information.
- Surveys and focus groups were established to guide BPL web site improvements.
- Consistency of template use was improved.
- Methodology baselines were refined.

With the initiative to certify all of our project managers to the industry recognized certification of PMP,[6] the PMM needed to undergo some changes as well. The PMM is now more in line with PMI's PMBOK® Guide and terminology. For example, we now refer to a project management plan rather than a project charter.[7] Additional improvements include:

- Global and regional review boards consisting of cross functional teams have been established for reviewing and maintaining policies and procedures in CA's Engagement Management Model as well as templates in the PMM.
- All major PM documents are included in a single zip file to facilitate usability and ensure currency of versioning.
- PM guides and techniques have been added.
- A recognition category for exceptional PM documents has been added to the BPL to highlight exemplary use of templates and to provide ideas for others.
- Non-English PM documents are now available for most widely used languages.

It is also recognized within the IT industry that no two companies in the world have the same IT infrastructure. So while the BPL provides the best practice for implementing a solution, there is some fine tuning of the methodology that may be needed to address each customer's environment. To help the project team fine tune the methodology, they need access to additional, relevant information. To that end, the Technical Knowledge Library (TKL) was established. The TKL is CA's global repository of managed knowledge, supporting CA and CA partners alike.

The knowledge artifacts in the TKL come from the architects, consultants and project managers who are documenting lessons learned. While this knowledge is certainly used in the regular review of the best practice methods, there may be detailed or specific knowledge that is not appropriate in the method. But retaining the knowledge for re-use is important.

---

6. CA TS requires all its project management personnel to be PMP® certified. This worldwide effort began in 2003 and now places us at the 96% compliance rate.
7. For additional information on CA's BPL, please see Harold Kerzner, *Advanced Project Management: Best Practices in Implementation,* New York: John Wiley & Sons, 2004

So the document's author (the owner of the intellectual capital, IC) submits it to the TKL, which initiates a workflow that ensures content is accurate and that format and readability are addressed before being published. The IC owner is required to review their submission every 4 months for continued value to all TKL users.

Now that we have these "portals" into our intellectual capital, we have begun streamlining our existing project planning and delivery procedures and templates. One of our biggest successes has been the generation of a solution architecture overview and a solution architecture specification.

A critical aspect of any project to be successful is that it be properly scoped so that objectives are clearly understood and expectations can be set. *Scoping a project* is defined as gathering all of the relevant project information so that the statement of work (SOW) will correctly identify the solution required by the customer, as well as the project timeframe, resources, and cost.

To ensure this relevant information is collected, CA Technology Services has developed the solution architecture overview (SAO). This template pulls together information critical during the early stages of discovery that are usually assumed but never documented for all to agree upon. The SAO is used to identify:

- Business problem
- Current environment
- Proposed solution
- Impact on process, people and technology
- Quality attributes
- Project activities and milestones
- Solution metrics

The SAO is shared with the customer during its creation and just before the SOW is generated. Before any expectation about price is set, consensus is obtained on what it is the customer wants, what it will take to get it done, and how the customer will know we did what was asked. This ensures we are proposing the right solution to the given business need(s).

Once the project starts, the SAO is converted into a solution architecture specification (SAS). The SAS contains all of the SAO content and will be updated to reflect actual project activities and timeframes. At completion of the project the SAS has captured:

- SAO content (objectives, solution metrics, etc.)
- Final WBS and effort
- Validation of solution metrics
- Best practice commentary

By using the SAO/SAS process, the project manager and project team can ensure they understand the project objective(s) and have the means to ensure they are met, within defined timeframes and budget. This results in a win-win scenario.

How do all of these pieces work together to ensure that best practices and the latest knowledge is being leveraged for every project? Figure 1–20 below summarizes preproject planning with resources utilized, project delivery, and postproject review.

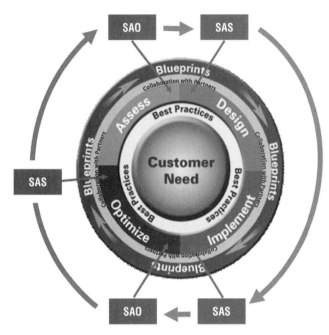

Assess:
Evaluate the condition of an IT environment, to identify and deliver recommendations for areas of improvement based on a standard methodology and approach

Design:
Create requirements based, best practices tested reference architecture that integrates the three critical components of EIM solutions – Process, People and Technology

Implement:
Leverage proven experience and best practices to ensure implementations that accelerate time to value of IT investments

Optimize:
Maximize and optimize the investment in IT by ensuring that the existing technology is fully utilized

FIGURE 1–20.   CA Technology services delivery methodology. Reprinted with permission from Computer Associates, © 2004 Computer Associates International, Inc. (CA).

With proven technology, repeatable processes, and growing libraries of documented intellectual property, CA Technology Services is quickly harnessing the future. No matter the industry and no matter the technological environment, best practices have played a major role in keeping CA Technology Services ahead of the solution delivery curve. Keeping the field teams and management personnel involved in the evolution of best practices has allowed us to structure an exceptional process for collection, review, and continuous improvement of our best practices and methods. CA Technology Services stands proud in its efforts to enable technology.

1.20 PM-ELITE: BEST PRACTICE IN SOFTWARE PM AT INFOSYS[8]

Introduction

Unlike the very poor success rate of IT projects reported by famous CHAOS research, almost 96% of projects executed by Infosys are completed within agreed schedule. Moreover, the level of customer satisfaction is very high, which is reflected in terms of over 90% repeat business on a rapidly growing revenue base for Infosys. Such superior results achieved on a sustained basis in the challenging en-

8. This section was provided by Anoop Kumar, Program Manager, SEPG, Infosys Technologies Limited and Aman Kumar Singhal, Program Manager, SEPG Infosys Technologies Limited.

vironment of global delivery and increasing client expectations are primarily due to a set of institutionalized processes and best practices. Some of these are listed below:

- Best-in-class process framework
- Integrated systems for governance
- Enabling and certifications
- Focus on metrics
- Domain flavors
- Senior management commitment
- Knowledge management

Best-in-Class Process Framework

The project management process in Infosys has evolved over a period of time by assimilating the practices from various world class models and methodologies such as ISO 9001:2000, CMM, CMMI, PMI, Prince 2 etc. Infosys is the first organization in the world to have been assessed at CMMI Level 5, covering the complete operations distributed at offshore and onsite locations in an integrated way.

The project management process is well-defined and implemented covering various aspects of the life cycle such as phases, activities, tasks, entry criteria, inputs, exit criteria, outputs, measurements, tools/systems, reference models, and knowledge assets.

Integrated Systems for Governance

To ensure consistence implementation of processes and practices, Infosys has created an integrated suite of applications and systems to automate the complete value chain.

All client/prospect interactions are tracked in a client relationship model (CRM) system to keep a tab of the business opportunities. Once firmed up, detailed proposal is submitted, and its details are managed in proposal-tracking systems. Upon finalization of the proposal, contract-related information flows into the contact management system. This becomes the basis for project creation. Detailed project plans are created covering various aspects like process plan, risk management plan, resource plan, communication & infrastructure plan, training plan, project goals and improvement strategies etc.

Based on the approved plan, a project budget is created and resources are allocated. During execution, project performance is tracked and analyzed using a balanced set of well-defined metrics. Performance details are rolled up to provide required information to the stakeholders on need-to-know basis. Billing activities are triggered at the specified intervals using the information from tracking systems. This provides inputs for revenue & costs analysis and accounts receivable tracking.

All these systems are developed in-house and integrated with each other seamlessly. Figure 1–21 shows the schematic representation of integrated project management (IPM) used to manage projects in Infosys.

Enabling and Certifications

Infosys has launched a unique enabling and certification program for developing IT project management professionals. This initiative is aimed at enabling and certifying Infoscions as the best-in-class project managers in the IT industry.

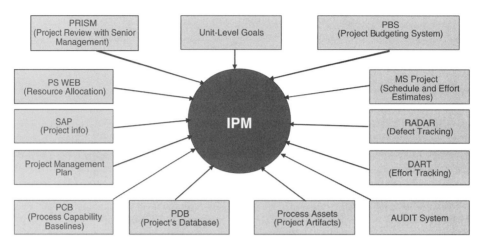

FIGURE 1–21. An integrated project management environment. IPM will provide a dashboard of the project performance to the Project Manager. Easy access to project information across the organization. Rollup of performance and quality of data in a timely and focused form to all levels of management.

This Certification enables and evaluates project managers at two levels of project management competency: *foundation* and *advanced.*

The certification provides a bridge between the concepts of project/program management and its implementation in practice.

Unique Value Proposition

- By practitioners for practitioners—focused on application of concepts
- Project/program management tailored to IT specific needs
- Includes behavioral skills
- Covers Infosys business model and work ethics
- Multiple levels of certifications—mapped as per various roles requirements
- Leverages best practices from within the organization and industry

An enabling program for **PM Elite (Foundation)** consisting of study material, online practice tests, help desk support and references for further readings is also a part of the offering. The enabling effort required from each participant is about 70–90 hours over an 8-week period. The final examination is conducted online for 2 hours in a classroom environment.

A team of over 150 experienced project management practitioners and senior executives across various units were involved in developing this certification.

Focus on Metrics and Measurements   Infosys is driven by a fact-based decision making culture. The organizational measurement program is designed to meet the information needs of all stakeholders (as shown in Figure 1–22 below). While this metric tracking is done at operational level, a balanced score card methodology is in practice at the senior management level to facilitate goal flow-down. This ensures customer satisfaction beyond just meeting these operational targets.

Senior Management Commitment

A formal system exists for reviewing the performance of projects by the members from senior management. Executive leadership spends around 20% of their effort towards this. The Chairman & Chief Mentor reviews projects on fortnightly basis. Potential execution and business risks are identified through formal assessment mechanisms and senior management provides necessary support to mitigate these risks & ensure customer satisfaction. Action items and review comments are tracked to closure, and learning from these projects becomes one of the key inputs for process improvement. Different level of management team members are involved for reviews at different frequency, depending upon the size, strategic nature, and importance of the customers.

Domain Flavors

Over the years, Infosys has tailored its project management processes to suit IT-specific projects. The relevant tools and techniques have been incorporated at various project life-cycle stages to support project management activities. Some of the world-class frameworks like CMM, CMMI, and PCMM have helped us a lot in improving maturity of our project management processes.

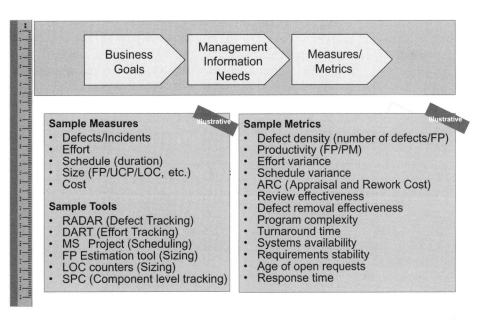

FIGURE 1–22. Organizational measurement program. FP: function points, UCP: use case points, LOC: lines of code, SPC: statistical process control.

The following list highlights some areas where domain flavor have brought tremendous benefits in project management:

- Global delivery model for IT projects
- Infosys vision, values, and governance
- Estimation
- Configuration management
- Statistical process control
- Quality management/quality assurance
- Risk based project management
- Requirements change management
- Geography specific focus areas

Knowledge Management (KM)   The salient features of the KM program include:

- KM process integrated with business workflow and specific projects—"KM in projects"
- Project primes identified at project level
- Facilitated by the KM champions, senior managers and process consultants networks
- Use of metrics to ascertain business benefits
- Re-use opportunity to improve productivity
- Process for content publication
- IPR protection, review, grading, and retirement
- Process for administering reward and recognition programs

> Infosys has won the GLOBAL MAKE (most admired knowledge enterprise award for 3 years (2002–2004) in a row and has now entered in the MAKE Hall of Fame.

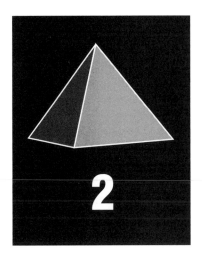

2

From Best Practice to Migraine Headache

2.0 INTRODUCTION

For almost 30 years, project management resided in relatively few industries such as aerospace, defense, and heavy construction. These industries were project-driven and implemented project management mainly to placate customer requests. Project management was considered as something nice to have but not a necessity. As a result, best practices in project management were never really considered as important.

Within the last two decades, project management has evolved into a management process that is mandatory for the long-term survival of the firm. Project management is now a necessity rather than a luxury. Project management permeates all aspects of a business. Companies are now managing their business by projects. Project management has become a competitive weapon. The knowledge learned from project management is treated as intellectual property and PMOs have been established as the guardians of the project management intellectual property, reporting to the senior levels of management, and being given the task of capturing best practices in project management.

As with any new project management activity, benefits are accompanied by disadvantages and potential problems. Some of the problems are small and easy to correct while others are colossal migraine headaches and keep executives awake at night. The majority of the migraine headaches emanate from either a poor understanding of the benefits of project management or having expectations that are set too high. Other potential problems occur when an activity really is not a best practice and detrimental results occur.

2.1 GOOD INTENTIONS BECOMING MIGRAINES

Sometimes, the best intentions can turn into migraine headaches. As an example, one company quickly realized the importance of project management and made it a career path position. This was certainly the right thing to do. Internally, people believed that the company considered project management as a strategic competency and professionalism in project management evolved. Externally, their customers were quite pleased seeing project management as a career path discipline and the business improved.

These good intentions soon turned into problems. To show their support for excellence in project management, the project managers were provided with 14 percent salary increases whereas project team members and line managers received 3–4 percent. Within two years after implementing a project management career path, everyone was trying to become a project manager and climb the project management career path ladder of success, including critical line managers with specialized expertise. Everyone thought that "the grass was greener" in the project manager's yard than in his or her yard. Line managers with critical skills were threatening to resign from the company if they were not given the chance to become project managers. The company eventually corrected the problem by telling everyone that every career path ladder in the company had the same career path opportunities for advancement. The large differential in salary increases disappeared and was replaced by a more equitable plan. However, the damage was done. Team members and line managers felt that the project managers exploited them, and the working relationship suffered. Executives were now faced with the headache of trying to repair the damage.

Figure 2–1 illustrates why many other headaches occur. As project management grows and evolves into a competitive weapon, pressure is placed upon the organization to implement best practices, many of which necessitate the implementation of costly internal control systems for the management of resources, costs, schedules, and quality. The project management systems must be able to handle several projects running concurrently. Likewise, obtaining customer satisfaction is also regarded as a best practice and can come at a price. As the importance of both increases, so do the risks and the headaches.

FIGURE 2–1. Risk growth.

Maintaining parity between customer satisfaction and internal controls is not easy. Spending too much time and money on customer satisfaction could lead to financial disaster on a given project. Spending too much time on internal controls could lead to non-competitiveness.

2.2 ENTERPRISE PROJECT MANAGEMENT METHODOLOGY MIGRAINE

As the importance of project management became apparent, companies recognized the need to develop project management methodologies. Good methodologies are best practices and can lead to sole-source contracting based upon the ability of the methodology to continuously deliver quality results and the faith that the customer has in the methodology. Unfortunately, marketing, manufacturing, information systems, R&D, and engineering may have their own methodology for project management. In one company, this suboptimization was acceptable to management as long as these individual functional areas did not have to work together continuously. Each methodology had its own terminology, lifecycle phases, and gate review processes.

When customers began demanding complete solutions to their business needs rather than products from various functional units, the need to minimize the number of methodologies became apparent. Complete solutions required that several functional units work together. This was regarded by senior management as a necessity, and senior management believed that this would eventually turn into a best practice as well as lead to the discovery of other best practices.

One company had three strategic business units (SBUs), which, because of changing customer demands, now were required to work together because of specific customer solution requirements. Senior management instructed one of the SBUs to take the lead role in condensing all of their functional processes into one enterprise project management (EPM) methodology. After some degree of success became apparent, senior management tried unsuccessfully to get the other two SBUs to implement this EPM methodology that was believed to be a best practice. The arguments provided were "We don't need it," "It doesn't apply to us," and "It wasn't invented here." Reluctantly, the president of the company made it clear to his staff that there was now no choice. Everyone would use the same methodology. The president is now facing the same challenge with globalization of acceptance of the methodology. Now cultural issues become important.

2.3 CUSTOMER SATISFACTION MIGRAINE

Companies have traditionally viewed each customer as a one-time opportunity, and after this customer's needs were met, emphasis was placed upon finding other customers. This is acceptable as long as there exists a large potential customer base. Today, project-driven organizations, namely those that survive on the income from a continuous stream of customer-funded projects, are implementing the "engagement project management" approach. With engagement project management, each potential new customer is approached in a way that is similar to an engagement in marriage where the contractor is soliciting a long-term relationship with the customer rather than a one-shot opportunity. With this approach, contractors are selling not only deliverables and complete solutions but also a willingness to make their EPM methodology compatible with the customer's methodology. To maintain customer satisfaction and hopefully a long-term relationship, customers are requested to provide input on how the contractor's EPM methodology can be extended into their organization. The last life cycle-phase in the EPM methodology used by ABB (Asea, Brown, and Boveri) is called "customer satisfaction management" and is specifically designed to solicit feedback from the customer for long-term customer satisfaction.

This best practice of implementing engagement project management is a powerful best practice because it allows the company to capitalize on its view of project management, namely that project management has evolved into a strategic competency for the firm leading to a sustained competitive advantage. While this approach has merit, it opened a Pandora's box. Customers were now expecting to have a say in the design of the contractor's EPM methodology. One automotive supplier decided to solicit input from one of the Big Three in Detroit when developing its EPM approach. Although this created goodwill and customer satisfaction with one client, it created a severe problem with other clients that had different requirements and different views of project management. How much freedom should a client be given in making recommendations for changes to a contractor's EPM system? Is it a good idea to run the risk of opening Pandora's box for the benefit of customer satisfaction? How much say should a customer have in how a contractor manages projects? What happens if this allows customers to begin telling contractors how to do their job?

2.4 MIGRAINE RESULTING FROM RESPONDING TO CHANGING CUSTOMER REQUIREMENTS

When project management becomes a competitive weapon and eventually leads to a strategic competitive advantage, changes resulting from customer requests must be done quickly. The EPM system must have a process for configuration management for the control of changes. The change control process portion of the EPM system must maintain flexibility. But what happens when customer requirements change to such a degree that corresponding changes to the EPM system must be made, and these changes could lead to detrimental results rather than best practices?

One automotive tier 1 supplier spent years developing an EPM system that was highly regarded by the customers for the development of new products or components. The EPM system was viewed by both the customers and the company as a best practice. But this was about to change. Customers were now trying to save money by working with fewer suppliers. Certain suppliers would be selected to become "solution providers" responsible for major sections or chunks of the car rather than individual components. Several tier 1 suppliers acquired other companies through mergers and acquisitions in order to become component suppliers. The entire EPM system had to be changed and, in many cases, cultural shock occurred. Some of the acquired companies had strong project management cultures and their own best practices, even stronger than the acquirer, while others were clueless about project management. And to make matters even worse, all of these companies were multinational and globalization issues would take center stage. We now had competing best practices.

After years of struggling, success was now at hand for many component suppliers. The mergers and acquisitions were successful and new common sets of best practices were implemented. But once again, customer requirements were about to change. Customers were now contemplating returning to component procurement rather than "solution provider" procurement believing that costs would be lowered. Should this occur across the industry, colossal migraines will appear due to massive restructuring, divestitures, cultural changes, and major changes to the EPM systems. How do contractors convince customers that their actions may be detrimental to the entire industry? Furthermore, some companies that were previously financially successful as chunk or section manufacturers might no longer have the same degree of success as component manufacturers.

2.5 REPORTING LEVEL OF PMO MIGRAINE

Companies have established a PMO as the guardian of project management intellectual property. Included in the responsibilities of a PMO are strategic planning for project management, development of and enhancement to the EPM, maintenance of project management templates, forms and guidelines, portfolio management of projects, mentorship of inexperienced project managers, a hot line for project problem solving, and maintaining a project management best practices library. The PMO becomes the guardian of all of the project management best practices.

While the creation of a PMO is regarded as a best practice for most companies, it places a great deal of intellectual property in the hands of a few, and information is power. And with all of this intellectual property in the hands of three or four people in the PMO, the person to whom the PMO reports could become possibly more powerful than his or her counterparts. What is unfortunate is that the PMO must report to the executive levels of management and there appears to be severe infighting at the executive levels for control of the PMO.

To allay the fears of one executive becoming more powerful than another, companies have created multiple PMOs which are supposedly networked together and sharing information freely. Hewlett-Packard has multiple PMOs all networked together. Exel Corporation has PMOs in the United States, Europe, Asia, Mexico, and Brazil all networked together. Star Alliance has a membership of 15 airlines, each with a PMO and all networked together with the Lufthansa PMO as the lead. These PMOs are successful because information and project management intellectual property are shared freely.

Allowing multiple PMOs to exist may seem like the right thing to do to appease each executive, but in some cases it has created the headaches of project management intellectual property that is no longer centralized. And to make matters worse, what happens if every executive, including multinational executives, each demand their own PMO? This might eventually be viewed as an overmanagement expense, and unless the company can see a return on investment on each PMO, the concept of the PMO might disappear, thus destroying an important best practice because of internal politics.

2.6 CASH FLOW DILEMMA MIGRAINE

For many companies that survive on competitive bidding, the cost of preparing a bid can range from a few thousand dollars to hundreds of thousands. In most cases, project management may not appear until after the contract is awarded. The results can be catastrophic if benefit realization at the end of the project does not match the vision or profit margin expected during proposal preparation or at project initiation. When companies develop an EPM system and the system works well, most companies believe that they can now take on more work. They begin bidding on every possible contract believing that with the EPM system they can accomplish more work in less time and with fewer resources without any sacrifice of quality.

In the summer of 2002, a large, multinational company set up a project management training program in Europe for 50 multinational project managers. The executive vice president spoke for the first 10 minutes of the class and said, "The company is now going to begin turning away work." The project managers were upset over hearing this and needed an explanation. The executive vice president put Figure 2–2 on the screen and made it clear that the company would no longer accept projects where profit margins would eventually be less than 4–6 percent because they were financing the projects for their customers. The company was functioning as a banker for its clients. Benefit realization was not being achieved. To reduce the costs of competitive bidding, the company was responding to proposal requests using estimating databases rather than time-phased labor. The cash flow issue was not being identified until after go-ahead.

While project financing has become an acceptable practice, it does squeeze profits in already highly competitive markets. To maintain profit margins, companies are often forced to disregard what was told to the customer in the proposal and to assign project

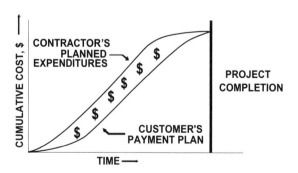

FIGURE 2–2. Spending curve.

resources according to the customer's payment plan rather than the original project schedule provided in the proposal. While this may lead to short-term profitability, it often results in elongated schedules, potential lawsuits, and customer dissatisfaction. The balance between customer satisfaction, long-term client relationships, and profitability is creating a huge headache. The best practice of creating a world-class EPM system can lead to detrimental results if profitability cannot be maintained.

2.7 SCOPE CHANGE DILEMMA MIGRAINE

For companies that require successful competitive bidding for survival, the pot of gold is often the amount of scope changes that occur after go-ahead. The original contract may be underbid in the hope that lucrative customer or contractor-generated scope changes will occur. For maximization of profit, a best practices scope change control process must be part of the EPM system.

Over the years, project managers have been encouraged by their superiors to seek out any and all value-added scope changes to be funded by the customers. But these scope changes are now playing havoc with capacity-planning activities and the assigning of critical resources needed for the scope changes and other projects. As companies mature in project management, the EPM systems become Web based. All individual project schedules are rolled up into a master schedule such that senior management can get a realistic picture of resources committed for the next 90 or 180 days. This allows a company to determine how much additional work it can undertake without overtaxing the existing labor base. And if a resource bottleneck is detected, it should be relatively clear how many additional resources should be hired and in which functional groups.

As capacity planning converts from an art to a science, the problems with obtaining qualified resources for unplanned scope changes grow. Maximization of profits on a particular project may not be in the best interest of the company, especially if the resources can be used more effectively elsewhere in the organization. Organizations today are understaffed believing that it is better to have more work than people rather than more people than work. Executives must find a way to balance the need for added project resources, scope changes, portfolio selection of projects, and the strain on the working relationship between project and line managers. How do executives now convince project managers that scope changes are unnecessary and to forget profit maximization?

2.8 OUTSOURCE OR NOT MIGRAINE

One of the responsibilities of a PMO is debriefing the project team at the completion of the project. This includes capturing lessons learned, identifying opportunities for improving the EPM system, and updating the estimating database. As the estimating database improves, companies realize that they can outsource some project work at a significantly lower cost than performing the same work internally.

While this function can become an important best practice and can save the company some money, there may be detrimental results. A bank received significant negative publicity in local newspapers when it was discovered that the information systems division would be downsized in conjunction with cost-effective outsourcing. Another organization also outsourced its information systems work to such an extent that it had to begin providing its suppliers and contractors with company-proprietary data. Headaches occur when executives must balance short-term profitability with the long-term health of the corporation and community stakeholder needs and expectations.

Best practices are designed to benefit both the company and the workers. When the implementation of best practices leads to loss of employment, the relative importance of best practices can diminish in the eyes of the employees.

2.9 MIGRAINE OF DETERMINING WHEN TO CANCEL A PROJECT

Virtually every EPM system is based upon life-cycle phases. Each life-cycle phase terminates with an end-of-phase gate review meeting designed to function as a go/no-go decision point for proceeding to the next phase. Very few projects seem to be terminated at the early gate review meetings. One reason for this is that project managers do not necessarily provide all of the critical information necessary to make a viable decision. Project managers provide information in forecast reports on the estimated cost at completion and time at completion. What is missing is the expected benefits at completion and this value may be more important than time and cost. While it is understandable that this value may be difficult to obtain during early life-cycle phases, every attempt should be made to present reasonable benefits-at-completion estimates.

If a project comes in late or is over budget, the expected benefits may still be achievable. Likewise, if a project is under budget or ahead of schedule, there may be no reason to believe that the vision at the project's initiation will be met at completion. Intel has initiated a concept called map days where the team maps out its performance to date, including expected benefits at completion.

While good project management methodologies are best practices and provide valuable information for the management of projects, the system must also be capable of providing the necessary information to senior management for critical decision-making. All too often, EPM systems are developed for the benefit of project managers alone rather than for the best interest of the entire company.

2.10 MIGRAINE OF PROVIDING PROJECT AWARDS

Perhaps the biggest headache facing senior management is the establishment of an equitable project award/recognition system that is part of the Wage and Salary Administration Program. Companies have recognized that project management is a team effort and that rewarding project teams may be more beneficial than rewarding individuals. The headache is how to do it effectively.

There are several questions that need to be addressed:

- Who determines the magnitude of each person's contribution to the project's success?
- Should the amount of time spent on the project impact the size of the award?
- Who determines the size of the award?
- Will the award system impact future estimating, especially if the awards are based upon underruns in cost?
- Will the size of the awards impact future personnel selection for projects?
- Will employees migrate to project managers that have a previous history of success and providing large awards?
- Will people migrate away from high-risk projects where rewards may not be forthcoming?
- Will employees avoid assignments to long-term projects?
- Can union employees participate in the project award system?

Providing monetary and nonmonetary recognition is a best practice as long as it is accomplished in an equitable manner. Failure to do so can destroy even the best EPM systems as well as a corporate culture that has taken years to develop.

2.11 MIGRAINE FROM HAVING WRONG CULTURE IN PLACE

Creating the right corporate culture for project management is not easy. However, when a strong corporate culture is in place and it actively supports project management such that other best practices are forthcoming, the culture is very difficult to duplicate in other companies. Some corporate cultures lack cooperation among the players and support well-protected silos. Other cultures are based upon mistrust while yet others foster an atmosphere where it is acceptable to persistently withhold information from management.

A telecommunications company funded more than 20 new product development projects which all had to be completed within a specific quarter to appease Wall Street and provide cash flow to support the dividend. Management persistently overreacted to bad news and information flow to senior management became filtered. The project management methodology was used sparingly for fear that management would recognize early on the seriousness of problems with some of the projects.

Not hearing any bad news, senior management became convinced that the projects were progressing as planned. When it was discovered that more than one project was in serious trouble, management conducted intensive project reviews on all projects. In one day, eight project managers were either relieved of their responsibilities or fired. But the damage was done and the problem was really the culture that had been created. Beheading the bearer of bad news can destroy potentially good project management systems and lower morale.

In another telecommunications company, senior management encouraged creativity and provided the workforce with the freedom to be creative. The workforce was heavily loaded with technical employees with advanced degrees. Employees were expected to spend up to 20 percent of their time coming up with ideas for new products. Unfortunately, this time was being charged back to whatever projects the employees were working on at the time, thus making the cost and schedule portion of the EPM system ineffective.

While management appeared to have good intentions, the results were not what management expected. New products were being developed but the payback period was getting longer and longer while operating costs were increasing. Budgets established during the portfolio selection of projects process were meaningless. To make matters worse, the technical community defined project success as exceeding specifications rather than meeting them. Management on the other hand defined success as commercialization of a product. And given the fact that as many as 50–60 new ideas and projects must be undertaken to have one commercially acceptable success, the cost of new product development was bleeding the company of cash and project management was initially blamed as the culprit. Even the best EPM systems are unable to detect when the work has been completed other than by looking at money consumed and time spent.

It may take years to build up a good culture for project management, but it can be destroyed rapidly through the personal whims of management. A company undertook two high-risk R&D projects. A time frame of 12 months was established for each in hopes of making a technology breakthrough and, even if it could happen, the product would have a shelf life of about 1 year before obsolescence would occur.

Each project had a project sponsor assigned from the executive levels. At the first gate review meeting, both project managers recommended that their projects be terminated. The executive sponsors, in order to save face, ordered the projects to continue to the next gate review rather than terminate the projects while the losses were small. The executives forced the projects to continue on to fruition. The technical breakthroughs occurred 6 months late and virtually no sales occurred with either product. There was only one way the executive sponsors could save face—promote both project managers for successfully developing two new products and then blame marketing and sales for their inability to find customers.

Pulling the plug on projects is never easy. People often view bad news as a personal failure, a sign of weakness, and a blemish on their career path. There must be an understanding that exposing a failure is not a sign of weakness. The lesson is clear: Any executive who always makes the right decision is certainly not making enough decisions and any company where all of the projects are being completed successfully is not working on enough projects and not accepting reasonable risk.

2.12 SOURCES OF SMALLER MIGRAINES

Not all project management headaches lead to migraines. The following list identifies some of the smaller headaches that occurred in various companies but do not necessarily lead to major migraines:

- *Maintaining Original Constraints:* As the project team began working on the project, work began to expand. Some people believed that within every project was a larger project just waiting to be recognized. Having multiple project sponsors all of whom had their own agendas for the project created this problem.

- *Revisions to Original Mission Statement:* At the gate review meetings, project redirection occurred as management rethought its original mission statement. While these types of changes were inevitable, the magnitude of redirections had a devastating effect on the EPM system, portfolio management efforts, and capacity planning.
- *Lack of Metrics:* An IT organization maintained a staff of over 500 employees. At any given time, senior management was unable to establish metrics on whether or not the IT group was overstaffed, understaffed, or just right. Prioritization of resources was being done poorly and resource management became reactive rather than proactive.
- *More Metrics:* in another example, the IT management team, to help identify whether or not projects were being delivered on schedule, recently implemented an IT balanced scorecard for projects. After the first six months of metric gathering, the conclusion was that 85 percent of all projects were delivered on time. From executive management's perspective, this appeared to be misleading, but there was no way to accurately determine whether or not this number was accurate. For example, one executive personally knew that none of his top 5 projects and all 10 of an IT manager's projects were behind schedule. Executive management believed the true challenge would be determining appropriate metrics for measuring a project's schedule, quality, and budget data.
- *Portfolio Management of Projects:* When reviewing project portfolios or individual projects, all of the plans were at different levels of detail and accuracy. For example, some plans included only milestones with key dates while other plans had too much detail. The key issue became "what is the correct balance of information that should be included in a plan and how can all plans provide a consistent level of accuracy across all projects?" Even the term *accuracy* was not consistent across the organization.
- *Prioritization of Projects and Resources:* In one company, there were no mechanisms in place to prioritize projects throughout the organization and this further complicated resource assignment issues in the organization. For example, the CIO had his top 5 projects, one executive had his top 10 projects, and an IT manager had his top 10 projects. Besides having to share project managers and project resources across all of these projects, there was no objective way to determine that the CIO's #3 project was more/less important than an executive's #6 project or an IT manager's #1 project. Therefore, when competing interests developed, subjective decisions were made and it was challenging to determine whether or not the right decision had been made.
- *Shared Accountability for Success and Failure:* The organization's projects traditionally were characterized as single-resource, single-process, and single-platform projects. Now, almost every project was cross team, cross platform, and cross process. This new model had not only increased the complexity and risk for many projects but also required increased accountability by the project team for the success/failure of the project. Unfortunately, the organization's culture and people

still embraced the old model. For example, if one team was successful on its part of a project and another was not, the attitude would be "I am glad I was not the one who caused the project to fail" and "Even though the project failed, I succeeded because I did my part." While there was some merit to this, overall, the culture needed to be changed to support an environment where "If the project succeeds, we all succeed" and vice versa.

- *Measuring Project Results:* Many of the projects that were completed were approved based on process improvements and enhanced efficiency. However, after a process improvement project was completed, there were no programs in place to determine whether or not the improvements were achieved. In fact, because the company was experiencing double-digit growth annually, the executive team questioned whether or not approved process improvements were truly scalable in the long term.

- *Integrating Multiple Methodologies:* Application development teams had adopted the software development methodology (SDM) and agile methodology for software development. Both of these methodologies had excellent approaches for delivering software components that met quality, budget, and schedule objectives. The challenge the organization faced was whether or not components from both of these methodologies could be adapted to projects that were not software development related and, if so, how can this be accomplished? This debate had elevated to upper management for resolution and upper management had been reluctant to make a decision one way or the other. This difference in views on how projects should be managed, regardless of whether or not the project was software development related or not, had led to several different groups lobbying for others to join their efforts to support SDM and Agile for all projects. Overall, the lobbying efforts were not adding value to the organization and were wasted effort by key resources.

- *Organizational Communications:* Although there was a lot of communication about projects throughout the organization, many shortcomings existed with the existing process. For example, one executive stated that when he had his monthly status meeting with his direct reports, he was amazed when a manager was not aware of another manager's project, especially if the project was getting ready to migrate into production. The existing process led many managers to react to projects instead of proactive planning for projects. Additionally, the existing communication process did not facilitate knowledge sharing and coordination across projects or throughout the organization. Instead, the existing communication process facilitated individual silos of communication.

- *Meaning of Words:* A project was initiated from the staff level. The SOW contained numerous open-ended phrases with vague language such as "Develop a world-class control platform with exceptional ergonomics and visual appeal." The project manager and his team interpreted this SOW using their own creativity. There were mostly engineers on the team with no marketing members and the solution ended up being technically strong but a sales/marketing disaster. Months were lost in time to market.

- *Problem with Success:* A project was approved with a team charter that loosely defined the boundaries of the project. During the course of the project, some early successes were realized and word quickly spread throughout the organization. As the project moved forward, certain department managers began "sliding" issues into the project scope using their own interpretation of the SOW, hoping to advance their own agendas with this talented group. The project eventually bogged down and the team became demoralized. Senior management disbanded the group. After this, management had real trouble getting people to participate on project teams.

- *Authority Challenges:* A new cross-functional project team was assembled involving technical experts from numerous departments. The project manager was a consultant from an outside contractor. During the course of this large project, resource conflicts with production schedules began to arise. Inevitably, the line managers began to draw resources away from the project. The consultant promptly reported pending delays due to this action and the staff reiterated the consultant's concerns and the need for the organization to support the project. The struggles continued through the entire length of the project, creating stressful situations for team members as they tried to balance their workloads. The project finished late with significant cost overruns and indirectly caused a great deal of animosity among many of the participants.

- *Open-Ended Deliverables:* A project was launched to redesign and deploy the engineering change management system. The team received strong support throughout its duration. At a project closure meeting with the executive staff, the project manager presented the team's interpretation of the deliverables. Much to his surprise, the staff determined that the deliverables were not complete. In the end, this particular team worked on "spider webs" spawning off of their original SOW for over three years (the original closing presentation took place after nine months). The team was frustrated working on a project that never seemed to have an end and the staff grew impatient with a team they felt was "milking" a job. The project management process at the company came under fire, threatening future efforts and staff support.

- *Cost Overruns:* Soon after a major product renovation project was commissioned, the project manager reported that the cost of completion was grossly understated. Unfortunately, the marketing department, in anticipation of a timely completion, had already gone to the marketplace with a promotion "blitz" and customer expectations were high in anticipation of the product's release. The senior staff was faced with a decision to have a runaway cost issue to complete the project on time or endure loss of face and sales in the marketplace to delay the project's completion.

Despite all of these headaches, project management does work and works well. But is project management falling short of expectations? Some people argue "yes" because project management is not some magical charm that can produce deliverables under all circumstances. Others argue that project management works well and nothing is wrong except that expectations of the executives are overinflated. Project management can succeed or fail, but the intent, commitment, and understanding at the executive levels must be there.

2.13 TEN UGLIES OF PROJECTS[1]

Introduction

Project management methodologies, classes, and books are adequate at explaining the mechanics of running projects and the tools used to do so. Understanding these mechanics is essential, but it is experience that distinguishes successful project managers. More specifically, it is the sum of all of the negative experiences that project managers have in their careers that teaches them what not to do. As Vernon Law explains, "Experience is a hard teacher because she gives the test first, the lesson afterwards."

In my many years of project management experience, I have come across several areas that consistently cause projects to experience difficulties. I call these the "uglies" of projects since these are the things that make projects turn ugly. These are also usually the things that, once recognized, are hard to fix easily.

This section will discuss the 10 project uglies and propose some resolutions. There are definitely other uglies out there, but these 10 are the ones that seem to be the most common and have the biggest impact based on my experience.

The Ten Uglies

Below are the 10 uglies with a description of each and some symptoms that indicate that these uglies may be happening.

1. Lack of Maintained Documentation: Oftentimes when projects are in a crunch, the first thing that gets eliminated is documentation. Sometimes documentation is not created even when projects do have the time. When documentation is created properly, as projects continue to progress, it is a rarity to see the documentation maintained.

Symptoms
- Requirement documents that do not match what was produced
- Technical documents that can not be used to maintain the technology because they are outdated
- No documentation on what decisions were made and why they were made
- No audit trail of changes made

This is a problem since documentation provides the stewardship of the project. By this I mean that future projects and the people maintaining the project once it has been completed need the documentation to understand *what* was created, *why* it was created, and *how* it was created. Otherwise, they wind up falling into the same traps that happened before—in this case "he who ignores history in documentation is doomed to repeat it."

---

1. This section was provided by Kerry R. Wills, PMP®, Director of Portfolio Management, Infrastructure Solutions Division, The Hartford. ©2005 by Kerry R. Wills. Reproduced by permission of Kerry R. Wills.

2. Pile Phenomenon: "What is that under the rug?" is a question often asked toward the end of a project. The mainstream work always gets the primary focus on a project but it is those tangential things that get forgotten or pushed off until "later," at which point there are several piles (swept under the rug) that need to be handled. I call this the "pile phenomenon" because team members think of it as a phenomenon that all this "extra" work has suddenly appeared at the end.

Symptoms
- Any work that gets identified as "we will do this later" but is not on a plan somewhere
- Growing logs (issues, defects, etc.)
- Documentation assumed to be done at the end

There is no "later" accounted for in most project plans, and therefore these items either get dropped or there is a mad rush at the end to finish the work.

3. No Quality at Source: Project team members do not always take on the mantra of "quality at the source." There is sometimes a mentality that "someone else will find the mistakes" rather than a mentality of ownership of quality. Project managers do not always have the ability to review all work, so they must rely on their team members. Therefore, the team members must have the onus to ensure that whatever they put their name on represents their best work.

Symptoms
- Handing off work with errors before reviewing it
- Developing code without testing it
- Not caring about the presentation of work

There are several studies that show that quality issues not found at the source have an exponential cost when found later in the project.

4. Wrong People on the Job: Project roles require the right match of skills and responsibilities. Sometimes a person's skill set does not fit well with the role that he or she has been given. I also find that work ethic is just as important as skills.

Symptoms
- Team members being shown the same things repeatedly
- Consistent missing of dates
- Consistent poor quality

As project managers, all we have are our resources. Not having the right fit for team members will result in working harder than necessary and impacts everyone else on the team who has to pick up the slack. There is also a motivational issue here: When team members are in the wrong roles, they may not feel challenged or feel that they are working to their potential. This has the impact of those persons not giving their best effort, not embodying a solid work ethic when they normally would, feeling underutilized, and so on.

5. Not Involve the Right People: The people who know how to make the project successful are the team members working on the project. Not involving the right team members at the right time can set the project up for failure before it begins.

Symptoms
- Having to make changes to work already completed
- Constant scope changes from the customer
- Lack of team buy-in to estimates
- Lack of ownership of decisions

Not involving the right people up front in a project always results in changes to work. Not involving team members in decisions and estimates causes them to feel like they have no control over their work or the outcomes of the project.

6. Not Having Proper Sponsorship: Projects need internal and customer executive sponsorship to be successful. Sponsors act as tiebreakers and eliminate organizational politics/roadblocks that are holding up the project.

Symptoms
- Inadequate support from different areas of the organization and from customer stakeholders.
- Issues taking very long before being resolved
- Decisions not being made efficiently

Not having proper sponsorship can result in projects "spinning their wheels." Also, when a change effort is involved, not having proper sponsorship can keep impacted employees from buying in to a project (i.e., not cascading the messages from the top down to the "masses").

7. No Rigor around Process: Almost every company uses a methodology for implementing projects. The success of these methodologies depends on the amount of rigor used on the project. Often, processes are not adhered to and projects run awry.

Symptoms
- Incomplete/nonexistent deliverables
- Inconsistencies within the project
- Lack of understanding of the project's big picture
- Lack of repeatable processes ("reinventing the wheel" unnecessarily)

Processes are only as valuable as the rigidity placed on them. In some companies, there are too many project management methodologies used. Some are necessary due to the varying nature of work, but basic project management practices and principles (and even tools, i.e., using Project vs. Excel) could easily be standardized but are not. When one manager has to transition to another, this creates an extra layer of complexity, because a common language is not being used between the two people (it is like trying to interpret someone else's code when they have not followed the standards you have been using).

8. No Community Plan: Project managers spend a significant amount of time on planning, estimating, and scheduling activities. If these results are not shared with team members, then they do not know what they are working toward and cannot manage their own schedules. This includes the communication of goals and items that are a big picture for the team.

Symptoms
- Lack of knowledge about what is due and when it is due
- Missed dates
- Lack of ownership of deliverables
- Deliverables get forgotten

Not having a community plan will result in not having an informed community. Having a shared plan and goals helps to build a cohesiveness and a greater understanding of how the work of each individual fits overall.

9. Not Plan for Rework: Estimation techniques often focus on the time that it takes to create units of work. What usually gets left out is the time spent on rework. By this I mean work that was done incorrectly and needs to be revisited as opposed to scope management. When rework is required, it either takes the place of other work which now comes in late or is pushed off until later (see ugly 2).

Symptoms
- Missed dates
- Poor quality

Never assume that anything is done right the first time.

10. Dates Are Just Numbers: Schedule is a major driver of project success. I am amazed at the number of people who think of dates as "suggestions" rather than deadlines. Because of interdependencies on projects, a missed date early on could ripple through the schedule for the remainder of the project.

Symptoms
- Consistently missed dates
- Items left open for long periods of time
- Incomplete/nonexistent deliverables
- Lack of a sense of urgency on the project team

Without structure around the management of dates, success requires a lot more effort. One other issue here is that of communication—these dates need to be communicated clearly and people must agree that this is their target. Also, they must understand what is on the critical path and what has slack, so if they slip on a critical path item, they know there is an impact on the project or on another project within the same program.

Possible Remedies   Upon analyzing the uglies I observed that they are all interrelated. For example, not having rigor around processes (#7) can result in not having a shared plan (#8), which can result in people not caring about dates (#10), and so on. (See Figure 2–3.)

I also realized that a few remedies could mitigate these uglies. The trick here is to proactively solve them rather than react to them since by the time you realize that there is an ugly, YOUR PROJECT IS ALREADY UGLY.

Proactive Management   Proactive management means spending the appropriate amount of time up front to minimize the number of "fires" that need to get put out later. Proactive management includes the following actions:

- Creation of a detailed plan.
- Always looking at the plan to see what is coming up and preparing for it:
  - Thinking about the upcoming work and running down any issues that may be coming. I think of the team as running a marathon and it is my job to "clear the road" in front of them so they can keep on running.
  - Setting up logistics. Something as trivial as not having a conference room booked in advance can cause a schedule delay.
  - Lining up the appropriate people to be ready when the work comes their way.

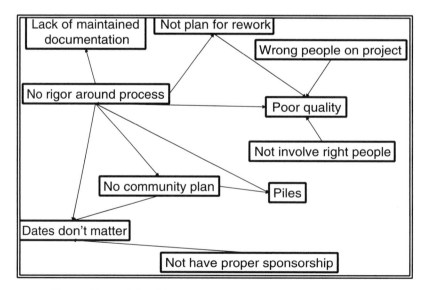

FIGURE 2–3.   Observed interrelationships.

- Know people's vacation schedules.
- Constant replanning as information becomes more available.
- Understanding what is going on with the project. I see so many project managers in the "ivory tower" mode where they find out about things about THEIR project for the first time on a status report. By this time, as much as a week has gone by before the project manager is aware of issues.

There will always be unexpected issues that arise, but proactive management can help to mitigate those things that are controllable. This can be treated as an investment of time, in that you will spend far more time (and money) reacting to problems than you will focusing on ensuring that the process be followed properly. This is difficult for some project managers because it requires the ability to always look ahead of the current state of the project rather than just focusing on the problem of the day. A key element of proactive management is having the ability to make decisions efficiently.

"Do It While You Do It"   Now that you are not reacting to fires, you can focus team members on maintaining their work as they go. This means staying focused on all aspects of the current work and thinking of implications. Characteristics of this include:

- Documenting as work is being done and not at the end. I am sure that this will get the knee-jerk "we don't have time" reaction but I really believe (and have proved) that documenting as you go takes far less time than doing it at the end.
- Thinking of implications as things change on the project. For example, if a document changes, the owner of that document should think about any other deliverables that may be impacted by the change and communicate it to the appropriate person.
- Check all work before passing it on to others
- Use the process/plan as a guideline for what work has to be done. I have heard this referred to as "living the plan."

The result of this technique will be an even distribution of work across the project and minimal spikes at the end. Rather than the notorious "death march," the worst case could be considered an "uncomfortable marathon."

Empower the Team   Project managers must realize that project structures resemble an inverse pyramid where the project manager works FOR the team. It is the team members who do the work on the project, so the project manager's primary role is to support them and address obstacles that may keep them from completing their work. This includes:

- Involving team members in project planning so they can not say that they were just given a deadline by management.
- Ask team members how things are doing and then act on their concerns. Asking for feedback and then doing nothing about it is worse than not asking at all because it suggests an expectation that concerns will be addressed.
- Celebrate the successes of the team with the team members.
- Be honest with the team members.

I am a big fan of W. Edwards Deming, who revolutionized the manufacturing industry. His 14 points of management revolve around empowerment of the team and apply very much to projects. Excerpts are noted below with my opinion of how they relate to project management:

Deming Point	Observation
8. Drive out fear, so that everyone may work effectively for the company.	This means that the "iron fist" technique of project management is not such a great idea. People will be averse to giving their opinions and doing a quality job.
10. Eliminate slogans, exhortations, and targets for the workforce asking for zero defects and new levels of productivity. Such exhortations only create adversarial relationships, as the bulk of the causes of low quality and low productivity belong to the system and thus lie beyond the power of the workforce.	I take this to mean that project managers should not just throw out targets, but rather involve the team members in decisions. It also means that project managers should look at the process for failure and not the team members.
12. Remove barriers that stand between the hourly worker and his (or her) right to pride of workmanship.	This is my marathon metaphor—where project managers need to remove obstacles and let the team members do their work.
13. Institute a vigorous program of education and and self-improvement.	Allow the team members to constantly build their skill sets.

Empowering the team will enable the project manager to share information with the team members and will also enable the team members to feel like they have control over their own work. The result is that each team member becomes accountable for the project.

Results of the Remedies The results of applying these remedies to the uglies are shown below. I call my vision of the new way of doing things the "attractive state" since it attracts people to success.

Ugly Number	Ugly Name	Ugly State Characteristics	Attractive State Characteristics		
			Proactive Management	Do It While You Do It	Empower
1	Maintained documentation	• No idea what decisions were made • Do not know why decisions were made • Cannot rely on accuracy of documents • Cannot use on future projects	• Updated documentation • Documentation will be planned for • Anyone can understand decisions	• Done during the project • No extra work at the end of the project	• Team members will own documentation
2	Piles	• Put off until later • May never get done	• Manageable work • If piles do exist, they will be scheduled in the plan	• Will be worked on as people go, so they should never grow out of control	• Minimized because people will take ownership of work
3	Quality at the source	• No ownership of work • Poor quality • Expensive fixes	• Better quality because you have spent appropriate time upfront	• Quality will be focused on as people do their work rather than assumed at a later time	• Quality will be upheld as people take ownership of work

4	People fit	• Bad project fit	• The ability to recognize resource issues and resolve them before they seriously impact the project • Proper resource fit from the start	• Manage work so resource issues are identified early	• Other team members may take on work for failing fcolleagues
5	People involvement	• Changes after work has been done • No ownership of work • No accountability for	• Involving the right people up front to avoid rework later	• Involve people during work rather than have them react to it later	• Involve people during work rather than have them react to it later. • Empowered team members take ownership for work
6	Sponsorship	• Cannot resolve problems • Caught up in organizational politics	• Engaging stakeholders early will enable their support when really needed	• Rapid and effective decisions as needed	• May be improved due to better understanding of issues
7	Process rigor	• No rigor • Poor quality • Inconsistent work	• Proper rigor is the essence of proactive management • Repeatable processes • Looking ahead will ensure proper attention to process	• Rigor will be followed as team members follow the process • Ensures that process steps are not missed	• Ownership of work will enable better rigor around process
8	Community plan	• No idea what is due and when • Team members do not take accountability for work—the plan is for the project manager manager	• Have the ability to share a plan and goals with the team	• Everyone is working to the same plan and knows where they are going	• Everyone is informed— shared goals • People can manage their own work
9	Rework	• Not planned for • Trade-off between doing other work or fixing issues	• Anticipating areas where may be rework or scope creep and working with key stakeholders early to address those • Planned for	• Rework will be accounted for as the team members work • By staying on top of the project, you will be aware of the magnitude of rework and can replan as needed	• Should be minimized due to motivation and ownership of work
10	Dates	• Dates do not matter • No accountability • Missing deliverables	• Dates (and impacts of missing them) clearly communicated	• Will matter and items will be closed when they are due	• Team members take ownership of dates

Conclusion   Focusing on proactive management, keeping up with work, and em-
                     powering your teams are key to running a successful project. There is
nothing in this section that has not been written of or spoken of hundreds of time before.
Nothing should sound new to a project manager. And yet, we keep seeing the uglies over
and over again. That leads me to a conclusion that it is the application of these concepts
that is the challenge. I find that after I read a good paper or attend a management course,
I have great enthusiasm to try out the new techniques but at the first signs of trouble I re-
vert back to my comfort zone. Therefore, I propose that there is a fourth remedy for the
uglies—being conscious. This is nothing more than being aware of what is going on and
how you are managing your project.

I come to work every morning a little earlier than the rest of the team so I can have
my quiet time and think about what work needs to be done (not just for that day but in the
upcoming days). I also give myself reminders that trigger my "step-back-and-think" mode.
An excellent series that goes into this technique are the "emotional intelligence" books by
Daniel Goleman.

There will always be uglies on your projects, but if you are conscious of them, then
you can identify them when they are happening and you may be able to prevent them from
throwing your projects into chaos. Best of luck.

References
W. E. Deming, *Out of the Crisis: Quality, Productivity and Competitive Position.* Cambridge:
    Cambridge University Press, 1982, 1986.
D. Goleman, *Working with Emotional Intelligence.* New York: Bantam Books, 1998.

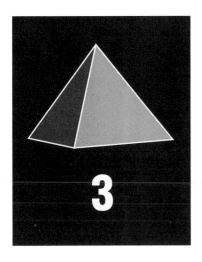

3 Journey to Excellence

3.0 INTRODUCTION

Every company has its own forces, or driving forces as we discussed in Chapter 1, that force the company to embark upon a journey for excellence in project management. Some companies complete the journey in two or three years, while others may require a decade or more. In this chapter, we will discuss the approaches taken by a variety of companies. Each company took a different path, but they all achieved some degree of excellence in project management.

The driving forces for excellence include:

- Capital projects
- Customer expectations
- Competitiveness
- Executive understanding
- New product development
- Efficiency and effectiveness

Even the smallest manufacturing organization can conceivably spend millions of dollars each year on capital projects. Without good estimating, good cost control, and good schedule control, capital projects can strap the organization's cash flow, force the organization to lay off workers because the capital equipment either was not available or was not installed properly, and irritate customers with late shipment of goods. In non-project-driven organizations and manufacturing firms, capital projects are driving forces for maturity.

Customers' expectations can be another driving force. Today, customers expect contractors not only to deliver a quality product or quality services but also to manage this activity using sound project management practices. This includes effective periodic reporting of status, timely reporting of status, and overall effective customer communications. It should be no surprise that low bidders may not be awarded contracts because of poor project management practices on previous projects undertaken for the client.

The third common driving force behind project management is competitiveness. Companies such as Nortel and Hewlett-Packard view project management as a competitive weapon. Project-driven companies that survive on contracts (i.e., income) from external companies market their project management skills through virtually every proposal sent out of house. The difference between winning and losing a contract could very well be based upon a firm's previous project management history of project management successes and failures.

The most common form of competitiveness is when two or more companies are competing for the same work. Contracts have been awarded based upon previous project management performance, assuming that all other factors are equal. A subset of this type of competitiveness is when a firm discovers that outsourcing is cheaper than insourcing. This can easily result in layoffs, disgruntled employees, and poor morale. This creates an environment of internal competition and can prevent an organization from successfully implementing project management.

A fourth driving force toward excellence is executive buy-in. Visible executive support can reduce the impact of many obstacles. Typical obstacles that can be overcome through executive support include:

- Line managers who do not support the project
- Employees who do not support the project
- Employees who believe that project management is just a fad
- Employees who do not understand how the business will benefit
- Employees who do not understand customers' expectations
- Employees who do not understand the executives' decision

Another driving force behind project management is new product development. The development of a new product can take months or years and may well be the main source of the company's income for years to come. The new product development process encompasses the time it takes to develop, commercialize, and introduce new products to the market. By applying the principles of project management to new product development, a company can produce more products in a shorter period of time at lower cost than usual with a potentially high level of quality and still satisfy the needs of the customer.

In certain industries, new product development is a necessity for survival because it can generate a large income stream for years to come. Virtually all companies are involved in one way or another in new product development, but the greatest impact may very well be with the aerospace and defense contractors. For them, new product development and customer satisfaction can lead to multiyear contracts, perhaps for as long as 20 or more years. With product enhancement, the duration can extend even further.

Customers will pay only reasonable prices for new products. Therefore, any methodology for new product development must be integrated with an effective cost management and control system. Aerospace and defense contractors have become experts in earned value measurement systems. The cost overruns we often hear about on new government product development projects are attributed not necessarily to ineffective project management or improper cost control but more to scope changes and enhancements.

Improvement in overall efficiency and effectiveness of the company is difficult. It often requires change in the corporate culture, and culture changes are always painful. The speed at which such changes accelerate the implementation of project management often depends on the size of the organization. The larger the organization, the slower the change.

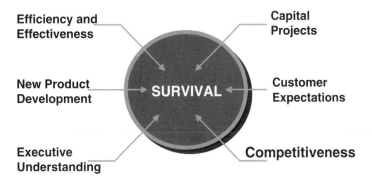

FIGURE 3–1. Components of survival.

Obviously, the most powerful force behind project management excellence is survival. It could be argued that all of the other forces are tangential to survival (see Figure 3–1). In some industries, such as aerospace and defense, poor project management can quickly lead to going out of business. Smaller companies, however, certainly are not immune.

Sometimes, there are additional driving forces:

● Increase in project size mandated by the necessity to grow
● Customers demanding faster implementation
● Customers demanding project management expertise for some degree of assurance of success completion
● Globalization of the organization mandated by the need to grow
● Consistency in execution in order to be treated as a partner rather than as a contractor

3.1 THE LIGHT AT THE END OF THE TUNNEL

Most people seem to believe that the light at the end of the tunnel is the creation of an enterprise project management methodology that is readily accepted across the entire organization and supports the need for survival of the firm. While there may be some merit to this belief, there are other elements that must be considered, as shown in Figure 3–2. Beginning at the top of the triangle, senior management must have a clear vision of how project management will benefit the organization. The two most common visions are for the implementation of project management to provide the company with a sustained competitive advantage and for project management to be viewed internally as a strategic competency.

Once the vision is realized, the next step is to create a mission statement, accompanied by long- and short-term objectives that clearly articulate the necessity for project management. As an example, look at Figure 3–3. In this example, a company may wish to be recognized by its clients as a solution provider rather than as a supplier of products or services. Therefore, the mission might me to develop a customer-supported enterprise project management methodology that provides a continuous stream of successful solutions for the

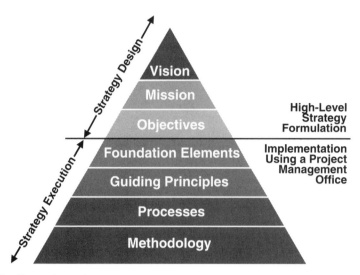

FIGURE 3–2. Enterprise project management.

customers whereby the customers treat the contractor as a strategic partner rather than as just another supplier. The necessity for the enterprise project management methodology may appear in the wording of both the vision statement and the mission statement.

Mission statements can be broken down into near- and long-term objectives. For example, as seen in Figure 3–4, the objectives might begin with the establishment of metrics from which we can identify the CSFs and the KPIs. The CSFs focus on customer satis-

FIGURE 3–3. Identifying the mission.

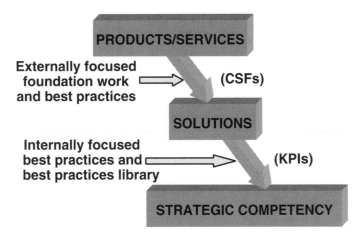

FIGURE 3–4.　Identifying the metrics.

faction metrics within the product, service, or solution. The KPIs are internal measurements of success in the use of the methodology. The CSFs and KPIs are the drivers for project management to become a strategic competency and a competitive advantage. Notice also in Figure 3–4 that the CSFs and KPIs can be based upon best practices.

The top three levels of the triangle in Figure 3–2 represent the design of the project management strategy. The bottom four levels involve the execution of the strategy beginning with the foundation elements. The foundation elements are the long- and short-term factors that must be considered perhaps even before beginning with the development of an enterprise project management methodology (Table 3–1). While it may be argumentative as to which factors are most important, companies seem to have accelerated to excellence in project management when cultural issues are addressed first.

To achieve excellence in project management, one must first understand the driving forces that mandate the need for excellence. Once the forces are identified, it is essential

TABLE 3–1.　FOUNDATION ELEMENTS

Long Term	Short Term
Mission	Primary and secondary processes
Results	Methodology
Logistics	Globalization rollout
Structure	Business case development
Accountability	Tools
Direction	Infrastructure
Trust	
Teamwork	
Culture	

to be able to identify the potential problems and barriers that can prevent successful implementation of project management. Throughout this process, executive involvement is essential. In the following sections, these points will be discussed.

3.2 MOTOROLA

"Motorola has been using project management for well over 20 years, but institutionalized within the last nine years," according to Thomas Dye, Director of Program Management at Motorola. The forces that drove the company to recognize the need to become successful in project management were "increasing complexity of projects coupled with quality problems, schedule and cost overruns, which drove senior management to seek an alternative management solution to what previously existed," stated Thomas.

Thomas Dye has also provided a chronology of what Motorola did to get where it is today as well as some of the problems encountered:

- 1995: Hire a director of project management
- 1996: First hire project managers—formal role definition and shift in responsibilities for scheduling and ship acceptance
- 1998: Formal change control instituted—driven by project managers
- 1998: Stage–gates rolled out and deployed across all projects
- 2000: Deployment of time-tracking tool
- 2001: Deployment of a more formal resource tracking
- 2002: Improved resource planning and tracking
- 2004: Project cost accounting

Initially, program management was viewed as an overhead activity, with engineering managers reluctant to give up program control and status communication. It was only through senior management commitment to formal project management practices that a PMO was created and roles and responsibilities shifted. Full engineering management acceptance did not occur until after several years of project management demonstrating the value of structured program management practices which resulted in consistent on-time product delivery. These include formal, integrated, and complete project scheduling, providing independent cross-functional project oversight, communicating unbiased program status, coordinating cross-functional issue resolution, and the identification and management of program risks. Later, project management responsibilities increased to include other key areas such as customer communications, scope control and change management, cost containment, and resource planning.

Executive support was provided through sponsorship of the development of the program management function. The reporting structure of the function has been carefully kept within an appropriate area of the organization, ensuring independence from undue influences from other functional areas so that objective and independent reporting and support would be provided.

At Motorola, project management is regarded as a profession. According to Thomas Dye, 90 percent of the project managers are PMP®s.

3.3 TEXAS INSTRUMENTS

A critical question facing companies is whether the methodology should be developed prior to establishing a project management culture. Companies often make the fatal mistake of believing that the development of a project management methodology is the solution to their ailments. While this may be true in some circumstances, the excellent companies realize that people execute methodologies and that the best practices in project management might be achieved quicker if the focus is on the people rather than the tools.

Texas Instruments recognized the importance of focusing on people as a way to accelerate project success. Texas Instruments developed a success pyramid for managing global projects. The success pyramid is shown in Figure 3–5. A spokesperson at Texas Instruments describes the development and use of the success pyramid for managing global projects at Texas Instruments:

> By the late 1990s, the business organization for sensors and controls had migrated from localized teams to global teams. I was responsible for managing 5–6 project managers who were in turn managing global teams for NPD (new product development). These teams typically consisted of 6–12 members from North America, Europe, and Asia. Although we were operating in a global business environment, there were many new and unique difficulties that the teams faced. We developed the success pyramid to help these project managers in this task.
>
> Although the message in the pyramid is quite simple, the use of this tool can be very powerful. It is based on the principle of building a pyramid from the bottom to the top. The bottom layer of building blocks is the *foundation* and is called "understanding and trust." The message here is that for a global team to function well, there must be a common bond.

FIGURE 3–5. Texas Instruments success pyramid.

The team members must have trust in one another, and it is up to the project manager to make sure that this bond is established. Within the building blocks at this level, we provided additional details and examples to help the project managers. It is common that some team members may not have ever met prior to the beginning of a project, so this task of building trust is definitely a challenge.

The second level is called "sanctioned direction." This level includes the team charter and mission as well as the formal goals and objectives. Since these are virtual teams that often have little direct face time, the message at this level is for the project manager to secure the approval and support from all the regional managers involved in the project. This step is crucial in avoiding conflicts of priorities from team members at distant locations.

The third level of the pyramid is called "accountability." This level emphasizes the importance of including the values and beliefs from all team members. On global teams, there can be quite a lot of variation in this area. By allowing a voice from all team members, not only can project planning be more complete but also everyone can directly buy into the plan. Project managers using a method of distributed leadership in this phase usually do very well. The secret is to get people to transition from attitude of obligation to a willingness of accepting responsibility.

The next level, called "logistics," is where the team lives for the duration of the project and conducts the day-to-day work. This level includes all of the daily, weekly, and monthly communications and is based on an agreement of the type of development process that will be followed. At Texas Instruments, we have a formal process for NPD projects, and this is usually used for this type of project. The power of the pyramid is that this level of detailed work can go very smoothly, provided there is a solid foundation below it.

Following the execution of the lower levels in the pyramid, we can expect to get good "results," as shown in the fifth level. This is driven in the two areas of internal and external customers. Internal customers may include management or may include business center sites that have financial ownership of the overall project.

Finally, the top level of the pyramid shows the overall goal and is labeled "team success." Our experience has shown that a global team that is successful on a one- to two-year project is often elevated to a higher level of confidence and capability. This success breeds added enthusiasm and positions the team members for bigger and more challenging assignments. The ability of managers to tap into this higher level of capability provides competitive advantage and leverages our ability to achieve success.

At Texas Instruments, the emphasis on culture is a best practice. It is unfortunate that more companies do not realize this.

3.4 EDS

When a company can recognize the driving forces for excellence in project management and understands that project management potentially could be needed for the survival of the firm, good things can happen quickly for the betterment of both the company and its clients. Doug Bolzman, Consultant Architect, PMP®, ITIL Service Manager at EDS, describes the forces affecting project management success at EDS and some of the problems they faced and overcame:

The significant emotional events that we have experienced in client environments are:

- Loss of market share
- Not knowing the baseline timing or budgets for projects, thus not knowing if they are doing good or poorly
- Not having the ability for speed to market
- Understanding that there is much bureaucracy in the organization due to no design of a single project management capability

Doug Bolzman discusses three problems that EDS faced:

Problem 1: Management not knowing or understanding the relevance of full-time, professionally trained and certified project management staff. This problem generated several business symptoms that were removed once the root cause of the problem was eliminated. To remove this problem, management needs to analytically understand all of the roles and responsibilities performed by project management, the deliverables produced, and the time required. Once they understand it is a significant effort, they can start to budget and plan for the role separate from the work at hand.

One manager was convinced that the engineering team was not working at the capacity they should until it was demonstrated that the amount of project management work they were required to perform was over and above their engineering responsibilities. Since the work was distributed to every engineer, their overall output was reduced. The leader of the engineering team demonstrated the roles and the time commitments that were project management related for the executive to assign the role to a full-time project manager. The output of the team was restored to expected levels.

Problem 2: Everyone is overworked, and there is no time to implement a project management discipline. Since this is a common problem, the way to work around this situation is to generate a tactical Project Management Governance Board to determine the standards, approaches, and templates that will be considered "best practice" from previous projects and leveraged to future projects. To not place additional scope or risk to existing projects, they are "grandfathered" from the new standards. As a project charter and team are generated, they are trained and mentored in the new discipline. The Governance Board meets when needed to approve new project management structures and measure conformance by project managers.

Problem 3: Project managers were working at a higher level of maturity than the organization can benefit. Project managers often use all the tools and templates at their disposal to manage a project but are incoherent of the client's level of business maturity. For such cases, the saying goes, "That manager is using 30 pounds of project management to manage a 10-pound project." If the client is in an unstable, ever-changing environment, the project manager spends most of the time formally administering change management, adjusting all of the appropriate costing tools, and does not further the project. To remedy this situation, guidelines must be given to the project managers to balance the level of project management maturity to the client's business environment. This is done while working with the client to demonstrate how the maturity of the business environment costs additional time, money, and resources.

With regard to the role of executives during project management implementation, Doug Bolzman commented:

> Many executives take a mild "management commitment" role during the implementation since project management and framework implementations are foundational capabilities and are not recognized as market facing, revenue generating, or exciting! Usually the executive approves a low budget plan where the majority of resources are absorbed from the organization and will be a motivational speaker at the kickoff meeting. I attended a kickoff meeting last week where the sponsor told the team that he did not expect the effort to be successful or change the culture. The team wondered if the sponsor was providing motivation by instituting a challenge.
>
> Executives understand business language and do not tolerate or listen to project management techno talk. Executives are results oriented, and if the project teams can simply translate the environment into business terms and create a business cast for incremental improvements to provide business value, the executive will be receptive to assist. If the executives are expected to generate the strategy or plan for improvement, or define project management's role within the organization, the implementation will fail. The majority of implementation success comes from the immediate business leaders and the project managers themselves who are tired of the status quo and want to implement improvements.

As for the chronology of events at EDS, Doug Bolzman continues:

> When planning for the implementation of a framework, such as the implementation of a project, change, or release management (all using project management disciplines), we have learned that the organization needs to successfully progress through a series of organizational milestones. An example is shown in Table 3–2. The chronology is similar to a person who decides they need to lose weight. The person first makes the determination due

TABLE 3–2. ORGANIZATIONAL MILESTONES

Milestone	Activity	Value
1. Establish Governance Board structure	Development of all participants' roles and responsibilities for implementing the improvements	• Implementing of a working "best practice" governance structure • All roles integrated and approved
2. Governance assignments	The sponsors (executives) name who will play each role, assigning accountability and authorization	• Executives establish priority through assignments • Everyone is trained in their role; expectations are set
3. Generation of attributes	The attributes describe the requirements, standards, capabilities, and metrics that will be used to define the improvements and measure the results	• Improvement is measurable, not emotional • Team can demonstrate value in business terms
4. Generation of improvement plan	Incremental plans for improvement are generated based on a maturity model or business improvement objectives	• The environment is improved based upon the speed the organization can afford • The plans can be adjusted based on business changes
5. Implementation	Each implementation is a release of the environment, is measured, and demonstrates business value	• Incremental improvements realized • Business invests incrementally, based on need

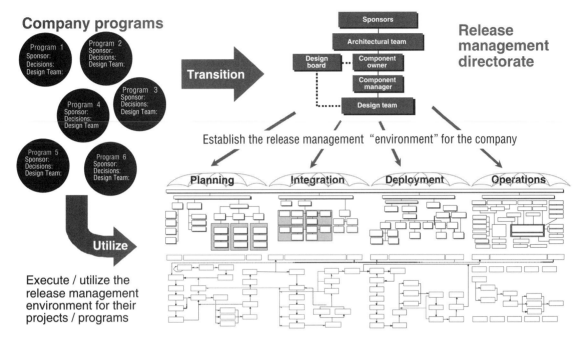

FIGURE 3–6. The transformation.

to an event, such as clothes getting tight, peoples' observations, or health issues. Then the person realizes a cultural change is required, and if they are not willing to change behavior, they will not lose weight. The person has to encounter the "significant emotional event" for them to justify the discomfort of the change of behavior, such as exercising, not eating at night, or changing food types.

For clients, a basic approach is defined and reviewed. Many times the client attempts short cuts but then realizes that every step provides a foundational value for the larger journey. For one client, this approach was implemented seven years ago, is still in place, has generated nine major releases of their change management environment, and has weathered five major corporate reorganizations.

Figure 3–6 reflects how the client needs to transform from a functional to a matrix directorate to establish a common framework and how the programs are then measured for how they conform to the framework.

3.5 EXEL CORPORATION[1]

One of the characteristics of a well-managed company is not only early recognition that excellence in project management is needed but also developing a structured approach to

1. Material on Exel Corporation was graciously provided by Julia Caruso, PMP®, Project Manager, Regional PM Group, Americas; Todd Daily, PMP®, Project Manager, Exel Consolidated Services; Francena Gargaro, PMP®, Director, Regional PM Group, Americas; Phil Trabulsi, Senior Director, Exel Consolidated Services; and Chintee Teo, Director, Regional PM Group, Asia-Pacific.

achieve some degree of maturity and excellence in project management in a reasonable time frame. Any structured approach to implementing project management must be done first and foremost for the benefit of improving the business. This occurred at Exel. According to Phil Trabulsi, Senior Director, Exel Consolidated Services for Exel Corporation:

> Beginning in 1997, Exel set out on a journey to understand the business needs of the organization with regard to projects and how projects were managed. This journey has spanned nearly seven years and has evolved into what Exel, today, calls enterprise project management (EPM), thus developing project management (PM) into a global core competency.
>
> The following list is a summary of major PM changes that have occurred in recent years that indicate a direction leading toward maturity and excellence in PM:
>
> 1. Operations to project-centric mindset
> 2. Defined PM processes and tools
> 3. Defined PM methodology
> 4. Senior management directive for project management and support
> 5. Project management value and maturity awareness and tracking
> 6. Global PM rollout
> 7. Global training curriculum
> 8. Centralized PM center of excellence (EPM group)
> 9. Strong PM marketing and communication efforts
> 10. Establishment of a project manager career path
> 11. Multilingual tools and training

The four phases listed below outline this journey toward PM growth and maturity. See Figure 3–7. Also listed below are the barriers that had to be overcome.

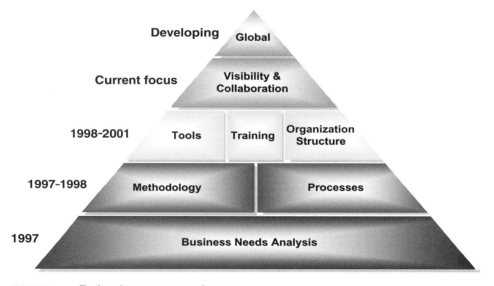

FIGURE 3–7.   Exel project management journey.

Phase I—Business Needs Analysis (1997)

Situation
- Exel is operationally focused
- Poor project execution
- Inconsistent PM approach
- Rely heavily on individual heroics

Barriers
- Perception of the organization by management as an operating company versus a project-centric organization
- No PM expertise demand from customers
- Undefined PM processes, roles, and responsibilities
- Organizational perception of PM as non–value added

Critical Success Factors and Accomplishments
- Senior management directive for development of single, global, business delivery process
- Investment in outside consultancy to facilitate change program over nine-month period
- Project management begins to be perceived as enabler to change
- Informal PMO established as internal thought leadership team
- Assessment and tracking of PM value and maturity

Phase II—Process and Methodology (1997–1998)

Situation
- Exel establishes formal business delivery process (BDP)
- Three Phases (strategy, business delivery, supporting infrastructure)
- Nine steps from pursuit through implementation to closing
- Identified three new focus areas (strategic alignment, business delivery, supporting infrastructure)
- No singular PM methodology established

Barriers
- Multiple organizational "agendas"
- Ad hoc PM approach by department
- Buy-in across business units
- No available proof source for PM
- No reference point for industry

Critical Success Factors and Accomplishments
- Project management process must fit overall BDP
- Simple is better to enable rapid engagement
- Previous project failures utilized to reinforce need for consistent processes across business units/divisions
- Methodology standardized
- Executive sponsorship obtained

Phase III—Tools, Training, and Organizational Structure (1998–2000)

Situation
- Defined PM process with basic tools
- Small PMO—thought leadership focus

- Division-based PM teams forming
- Limited engagement in organization

Barriers
- Identification of internal PM proponents
- Shift to matrix team structure
- Reluctance to invest in PM development
- Quantification of PM value

Critical Success Factors and Accomplishments
- Project management defined as a high priority within the organization.
- Acceptance of project-centric organization
- Appeal to broad audience
- Initial participants highly supportive
- Project management tools and training must connect with all stakeholders and BDP
- Global training curriculum
- Develop KPIs to illustrate progress/value
- Divisional teams responsible for tactical application and implementation
- Centralized PM center of excellence (EPM group)
- Avoidance of mandated tools that may not be globally acceptable/appropriate
- Ensure training of tools prior to release and utilization
- Determine appropriate level of technology that supports processes
- Emphasis on professional certification in PM

Phase IV—Visibility, Collaboration, and Globalization (2000–2003)

Situation
- Well-established business delivery processes
- Global merger/organization
- Geographically and culturally diverse organization
- Varying degrees of PM maturity
- Multi-industry service offerings
- More complex customer expectations
- Track record of reliability and predictability

Barriers
- Geography and time zones
- Culture and languages
- Multicultural project teams
- Global PM visibility
- Geographically dispersed project teams
- Project resource constraints (internal and customer)
- Variations in cultural issues

Critical Success Factors and Accomplishments
- Enterprise PM group established and linked to divisional and regional PMOs
- Enterprise PM focused solely on strategic development, training, tools, processes, and knowledge management
- Strong, global communication and broad marketing efforts
- Centralized knowledge base (e.g., Lotus Notes)
- Collaboration among all divisions/departments via enterprise management software (PlanView) and collaboration software (Lotus SameTime)

- Global collaboration on PM tool development and deployment
- Consistent, multilingual PM tools with standard Exel "look-n-feel"
- Globally consistent PM training curriculum

For growth and maturity in project management to occur in a reasonable time frame, there must exist not only a structured approach, such as the Exel journey shown above, but also visible executive support. This requires that senior management visibly spearhead the journey and define their expectations at journey's end. This was initiated at Exel by Bruce Edwards, CEO. Mr. Edwards provided Exel with a clear definition of excellence in project management. According to Mr. Edwards this included, in no specific order:

1. Project-centric organization
2. Project-based culture
3. Strong organizational and leadership support for project management
4. Matrix team structure
5. Focus on project management skill development and education
6. Emphasis on project management skill track
7. Globally consistent project management training curriculum
8. Globally consistent project management processes and tools
9. Template-based tools versus procedures
10. Multilingual tools and training
11. Acknowledgment and support of advanced certification in project management (PMP, CAPM)
12. Internal PMP and CAPM support programs for associates
13. Strong risk management
14. Project management knowledge sharing
15. Organizational visibility to portfolio of projects and status via enterprise software (PlanView)

One of the reasons behind Exel's success was that Exel viewed its journey to growth and maturity in project management as a strategic planning effort. Todd Daily, PMP®, Project Manager, Exel Consolidated Services, explains the strategic planning process for project management excellence at Exel:

Recently, Exel's EPM group, with guidance from Harold Kerzner's paper *"Strategic planning for Project Management and the Project Office"* [*Project Management Journal,* 2004], has put together a strategic planning matrix for each of the critical activities identified in the paper. Using these identified activities and a few Exel-specific categories, the EPM group conducted a gap analysis of project management (PM) strengths and weaknesses that can be used for planning purposes. See example below for strength/weakness areas:

The critical activities are:

1. Project management information system (PMIS)
2. Project failure information system (PFIS)
3. Dissemination of information

   4. Mentorship
   5. Development of standards and templates
   6. Project management benchmarks
   7. Business case development
   8. Customized training in project management
   9. Stakeholder and relationship management
   10. Continuous improvement
   11. Capacity planning/resource management
   12. Reporting and organizational structure
   13. Internal/functional projects
   14. Project management maturity

An extract from the strategy-planning matrix is illustrated in Table 3–3.

According to Todd Daily, there were significant driving forces that provided indications that excellence in project management was needed:

1. **Increasing project size.** As projects become more complex and involved, the level of control and management is essential to minimize risk and improve quality.
2. **Customer demand for faster implementations.** Exel provides full-service supply chain solutions for our customers that often lead to competing with smaller, niche players. This demands a rapid implementation approach. Project management enables better control, more efficient implementations, and higher quality deliverables.
3. **Customer demand for project management expertise and proficiency.** Today, more and more customers, like Exel, are realizing the importance of project management in their businesses. It is strategically advantageous for Exel to possess project management excellence when being considered as a supply chain solution provider for customers.
4. **Globalization of the organization.** Over the past two years, Exel has completed a significant global merger and a number of strategic acquisitions that have integrated a number of different approaches with regard to project management. As Exel incorporates these new organizations and broadens its service offerings, a consistent, go-to-market project management approach is essential. Geographical and cultural diversity is a key characteristic of Exel's business. With excellence in project management Exel can establish globally diverse project teams, working in any region, with one common project management methodology and a common understanding of all tools. It also enables the delivery of a consistent message to our global customers.
5. **Varying degrees of project management maturity.** Exel is structured in a sector-based (or divisional) format by industry type—for example, automotive, technology, consumer products, health care, retail, and chemical. Based on assessments of each sector, it was apparent there were varying levels of project management maturity by sector. Assessments of each sector enabled Exel to develop an approach to balance project management awareness, knowledge, and expertise.
6. **Senior management mandate for consistent project management processes.**
7. **Shared success stories among and across sectors (lessons learned).**
8. **Management by objectives (MPOs) tied to project management training and advancement.**
9. **Business development and account teams using project management as a selling tool to clients.**

TABLE 3-3. EXEL PROJECT MANAGEMENT: STRATEGIC PLANNING MATRIX

Critical Activities	Description	Kerzner's Guidelines	Exel's Current Status	Rank	Gaps/Suggestions	Risks, Challenges, Next Steps
Project management information system	Process and tools for capturing intellectual information relating to value measurement and risk management	• Company PM Intranet • Project web sites and databases • PMIS/enterprise systems • PM databases	• Campus Interactive • EPM database • PlanView	◖	• More detailed information-gathering tools required	• New version of PlanView • Not standard across the organization • Needs vary by sector
Performance failure information system	Method for gathering project performance information to enhance future project successes	• Lessons-learned activities • Postmortem analysis	• Lessons-learned activities • Failure modes and effects analysis (auto sector) • Operational readiness reviews	◔	• EPM group could conduct lessons learned-activities for projects	• Reluctance to relinquish power by sector • Some information considered confidential and proprietary
Dissemination of information	Communication of critical project management information such as KPIs, CSFs, data, news, and training	KPIs • Line management support • Senior management support • Methodology CSF • Time • Cost • Quality • Scope	• Newsletter • EPM brochure • Press releases • Training • PM process guides • Campus interactive	◕	• Need more line management support • Qualitative information available • Lack of quantitative information	• Continue to market and promote PM aggressively • Work directly with operations for support and to improve line management support (i.e., project reviews)
Mentorship	Project office assumes mentorship role for inexperienced project managers seeking advice and guidance in the practice of project management	• PM guidance and mentorship of functional PM's • Dotted-line reporting structure	• Provide guidance to developing markets (Mexico, S. America, U.K., Asia-Pacific) • Support sector PMs	◔	• More involvement with project teams • Periodic project reviews	• Viewed by some as overstepping bounds of authority • Perceived as watchdog activity • Some sectors don't see EPM as knowledge center
Development of standards and templates	Design and implementation of project management standards and tools that foster teamwork by creating a common "PM" language	• Customized templates, forms, and checklists • Limited formalized policies/procedures • Simple and dynamic • Managed and maintained by project office	• Developed and own PM tools and templates for the organization • Manage updates ensuring consistency across the organization	◕	• Formalized processes, standards, and templates in U.S. • Introduction of tools to Mexico, Latin America, U.K., and Asia	• Acceptance • Adoption • Requires continued "face time" with all project teams • Continue to ensure tools are optimal for our business

99

In the fall of 2003, Exel embarked on a global change management program designed to identify, develop, and instill consistent best practice processes and appropriate behaviors for all customer-related activities throughout every part of the organization. This program was entitled the Exel Way.

Project management has become an essential enabler for Exel in the achievement of its strategic initiatives. The capability to successfully lead, manage, and deliver projects or new operational solutions in a timely and cost-effective manner while adhering to specifications of our customers is core to Exel's delivery approach.

Based on these principles, a project management module team was established, along with six other modules ranging from value proposition through on-going customer relationship management. The project management module focused on global growth and maturity of the discipline. The mission was to further develop and embed Exel's leading project management methodology (DePICT™) across the organization, by leveraging organizational and industry best practices that enable continuous, effective delivery of customer solutions.

By design, each module of the Exel Way program was assigned a sponsor from the executive ranks of the organization and a team of module cosponsors representing all industry sectors and geographic regions. This ensured executive buy-in and participation and served as a means to overcome existing barriers and hurdles in the development and implementation of new practices and procedures.

Bruce Edwards, CEO Americas, sponsored the project management module, with a module team comprised of key project management stakeholders from the Americas, Europe, and Asia.

In early 2004 a comprehensive worldwide survey was conducted among 400 executives, stakeholders, and project management practitioners. The survey results helped establish a baseline on project management maturity within the organization and provide a framework on which to build and enhance new and existing processes. Follow-up interviews were conducted with approximately 100 respondents consisting of key business leaders and practitioners to obtain additional information and clarification.

Based on results obtained in the survey, six guiding principles were identified and used for developing our solution:

1. *Utilize Best Practices:* Apply a comprehensive project management methodology throughout Exel's global businesses that leverages organizational and industry best practices and enables continuous, effective delivery of customer solutions.
2. *Drive Risk Mitigation:* The discipline of recognizing and managing risks before they evolve into bigger problems is at the core of how project management brings value to our business.
3. *Strive for Consistency:* A consistent process to enable reliable execution for our customers and is why project management is part of the Exel Way.
4. *Support the Business Strategy:* Align resources and effort with project priorities as determined by each business unit
5. *Keep It Simple:* Harness knowledge capital gathered across the regions to facilitate the ease of implementation and avoid "reinventing the wheel."
6. *Assure a Cultural Fit:* A scalable and flexible model that can be culturally adopted across all regions and maintain a suitable level of rigor for repeated success.

Further, as a result of these guiding principles and outcomes from the survey, four work streams were created within the project management module to address key subject areas:

1. Awareness and knowledge sharing
2. Methodology, tools, and reporting

3. Training and career development
4. Environment and Structure

Following 18 months of effort, the project management module efforts concluded with a global rollout of initiatives, processes, and tools and an enhanced project management structure for sustaining project management across all areas of Exel.

Key Outcomes and Accomplishments

Some of the key initiatives delivered as a result of the Exel Way project management effort included:

1. A global project management organizational structure compiled of three regional project management offices (Americas, Europe/Middle East and Africa, and Asia-Pacific)
2. An enhanced global project management toolkit and consistent global templates
3. Knowledge-sharing tools and practices, including online databases and a project management portal (currently in development)
4. Enhanced training curriculum that added an advanced project management training course, project management value proposition training for sales and business development teams, online introduction to Exel's project management methodology, IT project delivery training, and enhanced support and sponsorship for advanced certification of candidates through PMI® and Prince2 methodologies
5. Project manager recruiting guidelines and an on-boarding program to better source and retain key project management resources
6. Redefined and formalized project management role profiles to better reflect regional and cultural differences
7. Comprehensive sales support collateral and communications materials
8. A four-volume project management guidebook which includes an executive summary of Exel's project management methodology, an Exel project manager's "Practitioner's Guide," project management tools and templates, and a project management training and career development guide

To date, Exel is approaching 50 certified Project Management Professionals.

Having completed the key development and design phases of the Exel Way project management module, rollout to the global organization will continue throughout 2005.

3.6 HEWLETT-PACKARD

Hewlett-Packard (HP) is a company that has mastered customer expectations. Between 1988 and 1994, revenue at HP doubled. During that period of performance, especially in 1992, Hewlett Packard's Worldwide Customer Support Organization recognized that customer needs were becoming increasingly customized and complex. Customers needed smooth transitions as they were implementing new environments, and they looked to their vendors to provide solutions. Support services were becoming more critical and were viewed as a key decision factor in winning both the product and support orders.

Hewlett-Packard's management made the decision to expand its custom Support Sales Organization and focus support resources on developing maturity and excellence in project management. A new group of dedicated project resources was formed within the support organization and given the charter to become professional project management "experts." The group was and still is composed of individuals who have extensive backgrounds in field service, including support and technical problem management. Hewlett-Packard established an aggressive project management training program as well as an informal "mentor" program where senior project managers would provide guidance and direction for the newly assigned people. In addition to the existing internal training courses, new project management courses were developed. When necessary, these courses were supplemented with external programs that provided comprehensive education on all aspects of project management. Efforts to achieve industry-recognized certification in project management became a critical initiative for the group.

Hewlett-Packard recognized that demonstrating superior project management skills could expand its business. In large, complex solution implementations, project management was viewed as a differentiator in the sales process. Satisfied customers were becoming loyal customers. The net result was additional support and product business for HP. Hewlett-Packard recognized also that its customers either did not have or did not want to tie up their own resources, and HP was able to educate customers in the value of professional project management. Simply stated, if HP has the skills, then why not let HP manage the project?

According to Jim Hansler (PMP®), Project Manager at Hewlett-Packard, the following benefits were obtained:

> First, we are meeting the implementation needs of our customers at a lower cost than they can achieve. Second, we are able to provide our customers a consistent means of implementing and delivering a project through the use of a common set of tools, processes, and project methodologies. Third, we are leveraging additional sales using project management. Our customers now say, "Let HP do it!"

Hewlett-Packard recognized early on that it was no longer in the business of selling only products, but more in the business of providing "solutions" to its customers. In the past, companies like HP provided their customers with a cardboard box (i.e., a product) and the customer had the responsibility to unpack it, inspect it, install it, test it, validate it, and get it up and running. Today, HP sells solutions to its customers whereby HP takes on all of these responsibilities and many more. In the end, the customer is provided with a complete, up-and-running solution without the customer having to commit significant company resources. To do this successfully and on a repetitive basis, HP must also sell its outstanding project management capabilities. In other words, customers expect HP to have superior project management capability to deliver solutions. This is one of the requirements when customers' expectations are the driving force.

Mike Rigodanzo, Senior Vice President, HP Services Operations and Information Technology, believes that:

> In the services industry, how we deliver is as important as what we deliver. Customers expect to maximize their return on IT investments from our collective knowledge and experience when we deliver best-in-class solutions.

The collective knowledge and experience of HP Services is easily accessible in HP Global Method. This integrated set of methodologies is a first step in enabling HP Services to optimize our efficiency in delivering value to our customers. The next step is to know what is available and learn how and when to apply it when delivering to your customers.

HP Global Method is the first step toward a set of best-in-class methodologies to increase the credibility as a trusted partner, reflecting the collective knowledge and expertise of HP Services. This also improves our cost structures by customizing predefined proven approaches, using existing checklists to ensure all the bases are covered and share experiences and learning to improve Global Method.

Hewlett-Packard clearly identifies its project management capabilities in its proposals. The following material is typically included in HP proposals. The material was provided by Ron Kempf, PMP®, Director of PM Competency & Certification at HP Services Engagement:

HP Services' Commitment to Project Management

Why HP Services Project Management

HP Services considers strong project management a key ingredient to providing successful solutions to our customers. Our project managers are seasoned professionals with broad and deep experience in solutions as well as managing projects. Our rigorous business processes make sure you are satisfied. A program roadmap provides an overall architecture of the project life cycle while senior HP Services management conducts regular progress reviews to ensure quality. Our world-class project management methodology combines industry best practices with HP's experience to help keep everything on track. Our knowledge management program enables project managers and technology consultants to put our experience around the globe to work for you.

Project Manager Capability

HP Services has 2500 experienced and qualified project managers throughout the world in 160 countries. Our project managers generally have technical degrees and 12+ years of significant industry experience. We have over 2000 projects active worldwide and manage over 3000 each year. Project sizes range up to $300 million.

As part of the project business infrastructure we have PMOs at worldwide, regional, and country levels to provide support and ensure consistency. HP's goal is to ensure that the highest standards are maintained and to improve both the effective management of our projects and customer satisfaction.

Project Management Processes and Methodology

HP Services uses rigorous processes to manage our programs. The program opportunity roadmap provides an overall architecture for the project lifecycle. It includes the solution and opportunity approval and review (SOAR) process that approves new business as well as conducts implementation progress reviews to ensure quality and resolve problems quickly.

HP Services' project management methodology uses industry best practices with the added value of our experience implemented through Web-based technology to allow quick updates and access throughout the world. It has over 20,000 Web pages of information available to support our project teams. The methodology includes extensive knowledge management databases such as lessons learned and project experience from prior engagements that our project managers can use to help in managing their projects.

3.7 DTE ENERGY

Several maturity models are available in the marketplace to assist companies in their quest for growth, excellence, and success in project management. Table 1–1 from Chapter 1 is one such model. The purpose of the model is simply to provide some sort of structure to the maturity process. Tim Menke, PMP®, Senior Project Manager, Software Engineering, Methods and Staffing, describes the growth process at DTE Energy:

In the year 2000, DTE Energy's Information Technology Services (ITS) Organization initiated a formal drive to increase ITS project management maturity. The primary motivators were to improve cost and schedule predictability on IT projects and to propagate project management successes recently enjoyed in our Year 2000 (Y2K) program and merger with MichCon. We were also striving to (a) propagate positive relations with our business partners, (b) institutionalize capability maturity model (CMM) compliance, and (c) improve our competitive position in response to industry deregulation.

As assessed in 2005, utilizing the survey in Dr. Kerzner's book, *In Search of Excellence in Project Management,* DTE Energy's ITS has:

- Achieved the embryonic stage
- Achieved the executive management stage
- Made significant progress in the line management stage
- Achieved the growth stage
- Achieved the maturity stage

Since 2000, we have accomplished much, including:

- Institutionalized the project management office (PMO), the planning and management table (PMT), and earned value analysis (EVA) entering our sixth year
- Established a community of practice for project managers
- Established project management standards and guidelines
- Developed a project portfolio for ITS
- Established a project management training curriculum to develop project management skills and enable attainment of Project Management Professional (PMP®) certification
- Implemented project management process adherence assessments tied to rewards and compensation
- Continued our commitment to Project Management Institute (PMI®) approaches and CMM key practices
- Established a forum for stakeholder involvement
- Implemented formal job codes and salary ranges for program managers, senior project managers, and project managers
- Implemented a project health check to assess project management process adherence
- Implemented a formal quality assessment process
- Integrated project management and agile software development methodologies

We will focus on much more going forward, including:

- Ensuring conscious alignment of projects with strategic goals
- Continuing efforts to ensure project management methodology scalability
- Increasing collaboration with project management initiatives across the enterprise
- Enhancing project portfolio management capabilities
- Strengthening accountability across organizations and processes to ensure successful project implementation

3.8 QUIXTAR

Sometimes, the quest for excellence in project management begins when new leadership appears in an organization and brings different ideas and ways of managing. Such was the case at Quixtar, as explained by Lynne Allen, PMP®, Project Manager, Quixtar Communications. Lynne Allen describes the evolution of project management at Quixtar:

Company Background

Quixtar is a business opportunity company, offering entrepreneurs the ability to have a business of their own through Quixtar's I-commerce business model. I-commerce empowers *individuals* to market products and manage their own business via the *Internet,* while being compensated by the low-cost, low-risk *independent* business ownership plan and supported by the full-service *infrastructure* of Quixtar.

Since 1999, independent business owners (IBOs) powered by Quixtar have generated more than $4.2 billion in sales at www.quixtar.com plus nearly $320 million for partner stores, earning in excess of $1.37 billion in bonuses and other incentives. Their efforts have propelled Quixtar to be named the number one online retailer in the drug/health and beauty category based on sales and 12th among all e-commerce sites, according to Internet Retailer's *Top 300 Guide.*

Based near Grand Rapids, Michigan, Quixtar currently supports independent businesses in the United States, Canada, Puerto Rico, and various trust territories and independent island nations in the Pacific and Atlantic Oceans and Caribbean Sea. Quixtar Canada headquarters are located in London, Ontario, Canada.

The Need for Project Management

A change in leadership can often bring about a change in the way that organizations get things done. Such was the case with the Quixtar Communications department's adoption of project management (PM).

A new communications director, Beth Dornan, oversaw the department's shift from an internal "service agency" implementing mass communication vehicles to a "strategic partner" delivering more specific communications to targeted audiences. This change in philosophy meant that, rather than merely fulfilling the communication needs of other departments, Communications would now work closely with other areas to create strategies and implement communications tactics that would best help achieve Quixtar's business goals.

"Communications is the gateway by which Quixtar disseminates information and news to all its audiences, including IBOs, customers, and news media," says Beth. "We view our department's evolution as a shift from being all things to all people all the time to delivering the right message to the right audience at the right time."

This philosophical change led to a reevaluation of the role of the account executive (AE) in Communications. The position of AE had existed to implement the direction set by other Quixtar departments. Now that Communications played a part in setting that direction, would there be more value in having people responsible for planning, project managers, rather than people largely responsible for doing, account executives?

Beth asked a member of her management team, Gilann Vail-Boisvenue, to investigate the PM profession. Previously unfamiliar with the field, Gil discovered that it was exactly what Communications needed. The department had always excelled at executing but fallen short at planning. Project management, Gil learned, could help manage budgets, schedules, project scope, workload, and resources.

In addition, PM seemed to support the company's three core values of partnership, achievement, and personal responsibility. It also supported a Quixtar strategic goal to achieve initiatives on time and on budget to successfully impact business drivers like IBO productivity, recruiting, and retention.

The Plan

Gil promptly earned her certification as a Project Management Professional (PMP®) and applied the principles she had learned to craft a three- to five-year plan for transitioning AEs to project managers.

The plan proved to be successful for a number of reasons. First, management and senior management immediately understood the value of PM and supported it. Second, the plan was all about transitioning gradually through step-by-step phases into this new way of operating, rather than forcing the entire concept of PM on the communications group at once.

The plan included the following phases:

Year 1   Control budgets by aligning the department's operating budget with projects and individual teams, develop annual work plans for teams, offer broad-based PM training, and create formal PM job descriptions with salary standards.

Year 2   Control schedules by meeting deadlines, controlling scope, and managing resources; offer focused study groups for PMP® certification; develop PM methodology.

Year 3   Communicate by building reports for upper management. Also, continue to manage resources and finalize a professional procurement group. (*This is the current year.*)

Year 4   Use risk planning and apply lessons learned to new projects.

Year 5   Use quality planning and refine components of five-year plan as needed.

All aspects of the plan are based on the PMBOK® Guide, or Project Management Body of Knowledge. This plan has brought the PM discipline to a level 3 on the PM maturity model within Communications, while PM throughout the rest of Quixtar is at level 1.

Adopting Project Management across the Company

Communications is currently bringing PM to all of Quixtar through a training program designed to educate participants on standard PM processes and documentation. Approximately 140 people completed the program last year, including employees of Quixtar Canada and a sister company's Japanese affiliate.

"In just three short years we've gone from virtually no one at Quixtar knowing anything about PM to hearing many people say things like 'we need to get this project scoped' and 'do we have the money and time?'" says Gil. "Broad-based training helps everyone understand the concepts and the fact that a common language has really taken hold is proof of that understanding."

The PMP®s in Communications also are hosting independent study groups to help other Quixtar employees who want to become certified. The study groups have a 100 percent success rate when it comes to participants passing the certification test and are a major reason that Quixtar now boasts 25 PMP®s across Communications, IT, and Finance. The 13 PMP®s in Communications have full job descriptions and a salary structure built around PM. The PMP®s in other areas, such as IT, have other primary responsibilities like software development and PM is secondary.

A Seven-Step Project Management Methodology

A result of the PM expertise within Quixtar Communications is the creation of a seven-step PM methodology that can be used by any PMP® across the company to effectively manage projects.

The methodology is laid out on the PM website on the corporate intranet and begins with a needs assessment—does the project in question relate to the company's strategic plan? The methodology takes the project through the charter and scope phases, execution and control, and closure.

"We can pair any new PMP® with our seven-step methodology and they can manage projects effectively at Quixtar," says Gil. "There is about a two-month learning curve, but that's mostly to become familiar with our company culture. As long as they know the PMBOK® Guide, they can do projects."

The methodology has been so effective in part because it's very streamlined.

"Many people dislike process and with these seven steps, they don't even know they're in a process," says Gil. "Management often wants to see things get done and how those things get done is up to us. The how is very important because that's where you spend time and money."

The seven-step methodology is also simple and flexible.

"You can use as many or as few of the steps as you like, depending on the complexity of the project," says Gil. "Some projects could be as simple as a scope statement defining the project and the assumptions and constraints. Others could be complicated enough to require a full project plan, including a risk mitigation plan, communication management plan, and tons of other components to ensure success."

Lessons Learned

The success of introducing PM across Quixtar hasn't been without a few bumps along the road. Gil found that those implementing PM practices were at first too rigid, trying to wedge people into static processes and documentation methods.

"It's important to have standards but still be flexible. You don't want people to be so focused on the process that they think they can't do something that makes sense just because it's not the next step in their methodology," says Gil. "It's important to tailor the PM process to each individual project and the people working on it."

In addition to flexibility, reporting has been a success of PM at Quixtar. The project managers use a standard best practices reporting method to communicate project status to management:

- Red light—trouble
- Yellow light—jeopardy
- Green light—all clear

Such simple and effective reporting has helped Communications successfully manage all projects within budget for the past two years.

An aspect of PM at Quixtar currently under review is the control of scope creep.

"Without a working scope management plan, many teams are incapable of meeting their schedules," says Gil. "It's part of the culture around here to always say yes to scope changes, so we've asked management to step in and assess changes to control scope creep."

3.9 CONVERGENT COMPUTING

In the previous sections, we discussed some of the problems that companies face when implementing project management. Some companies believe that education can accelerate the project management learning curve because it is better to learn from the mistakes of other companies than one's own mistakes. While education does not always eliminate the possibility of mistakes, it does accelerate the learning process, especially when executives also participate in and support the learning process. Such was the case at Convergent Computing (CCO).

Anne Walker, Enterprise Project Manager with Convergent Computing, describes her company's experience with project management as well as some of the problems that had to be overcome during implementation:

CCO has been utilizing project management methodologies over 15 years. I have been with CCO going on 9 years and have used project management ongoing since the day I started. I was encouraged to participate in a UC-Berkeley extension project management program that consisted of six courses that we took at night after work. Two of CCO's business owners had already graduated from the program and felt the coursework and results were impressive. Other co-workers were receiving the same encouragement and many enrolled and had support from our managers and the organization. Others in our company have gone through the program on an on-going basis and it truly enhances our abilities to deliver successful projects for our clients.

CCO manages a wide variety of projects and in general each involves our consultants partnering with our clients to best understand their objectives for the project and then delivering them successfully. The project many times will involve employees from different levels within the organization and, in some cases, consultants from other consulting firms. Many times our clients look to our project managers to help train their employees so that they gain experience in managing projects and can then project manage on future projects.

CCO is a medium-sized, privately owned company that partners with our clients who look to CCO for professional and knowledgeable IT consulting services. Staying current on technology and having advanced knowledge of those technologies mean CCO needs to have technical expertise. Our professional services department initially included high-end consultants and engineers who did not have any project management experience or knowledge. Our expertise in IT is what our clients come to us for, so that is a priority throughout the organization. It is our "bread and butter," so to speak, so this made it difficult when consultants were asked to understand project management methodology as well. CCO consultants and engineers tend to be passionate when it comes to IT and have labs at home and enjoy tackling new technology. We look for this skill when we hire and many were not accustomed to identifying the scope of a project, attending decision-making meetings, or having to take a structured approach to testing the technology being implemented. Technical engineers tend to want to get in and fix the problem or take a structured approach to testing the technology being implemented. Technical engineers tend to want to get in and fix the problem or implement the new technology. If a client wanted additional tasks added—and they involved technology—most technical people want to dig in and enjoy taking on the additional challenge. What was missing was someone asking about the scope of the project and whether this was within the scope, would change our deadlines, would impact the budget, and so on. Getting our engineers to understand and work through the objectives of a project as defined by the client was not an easy task.

Many of the consultants and engineers didn't understand why they should have to learn and deal with project management and this made it difficult to get them "on board." Many of them did not want to take the additional time to learn project management methodologies and felt they had enough on their hands just staying knowledgeable with the ever-changing technology. When project managers were assigned to projects and began scheduling kick off meetings or asking for a regular status update, consultants felt they were burdened with additional tasks or asked to attend meetings they didn't see as necessary.

As we added technical writers and project managers to our professional services organization, our sales team had to learn how to help clients understand why a project manager on an IT consulting project was necessary. Many times, clients would agree with our approach in a proposal but would want to cut the project management resource or hours allocated to project management out of the project or process.

I believe CCO has come a long way in "winning over" the engineers and consultants in regards to project management. Some key factors in this are:

- Senior management support.
- Successful project outcomes when project methodology was incorporated into the project.
- The benefits of project management could not be ignored. Multiple engineer projects were running more smoothly, communication improved, people on the team and the client knew where the project was, and our teams were able to respond to situations proactively rather than putting out a "fire" after the fact. As more and more successful projects and happy clients resulted, our professional services engineers and consultants began to expect kickoff meetings and status reports as it made them more successful in their client engagements.
- CCO's own project management expertise and knowledge grew. This reinforced the importance of project management.

Two of the owners of CCO graduated from the UC-Berkeley extension program and encouraged others to participate in the program as well. CCO paid tuition fees for employees who participated in the program and the employees gave up one or two nights a week for two years to complete the program. Executives also worked closely with our sales staff to help them better justify project managers for our consulting services. In delivering our IT consulting services, when a project manager was involved, we inevitably had better success and those projects were delivered on time. We continue to have clients who are very satisfied with what CCO has delivered, especially when we are able to have project management involved in the projects.

3.10 KEYBANK

The growth of project management today applies equally well to so-called non-project-driven organizations as well as project-driven organizations. In some cases, the rate of growth appears quicker than in project-driven organizations. Vicky Bartholomew, IT Communications Specialist, Enterprise Project Management at KeyBank, describes the evolutionary process:

Infrastructure

Key Technology Services first invested in the discipline of project management (PM) in 1996/1997, with an organization formed to develop, document, and teach project methodology. A year later, project methods were evaluated through an initial capability maturity model (CMM) assessment, with the intent to focus on our greatest opportunities for improvement. In 2000, the title of Project Manager was created and individuals were identified across the organization that most closely filled that role. These project managers were organized into five groups—each supporting and reporting through senior technology managers. Three years later, the PMO was formed and included all project managers and methods, tools, and PM quality assurance. Today, PM remains centralized, but aligned to line of business based on business expertise; methods, quality assurance, tools, and portfolio analysis teams make up Key Technology Services' PMO.

The purpose of these changes was to:

- Deliver on project commitments more often through PM skill and enhanced portfolio/project planning
- Improve morale and reduce burnout of line managers (who were filling project manager, application owner, and resource manager roles simultaneously)
- Achieve economies of scale through better PM resource management/reduction of PM bench

We've made tremendous progress on these goals. Since 2000, we have delivered 30 percent more of our projects within cost and schedule commitments, decreased our turnover rate of line managers, and reduced the PM staff by 50 percent.

Today, Enterprise Project Management (EPM) executes five functions: PM talent management, project portfolio analysis, project startup services, software development (SWD) methods and quality assurance, and project tools ownership. Two-thirds of the organization's membership is project managers (project manager is a role with an a eight-step career path ranging from entry level to very senior). The remaining third of the organization is made up of methodologists, process engineers (project coaches), PM tools analysts and technicians, estimators, requirements facilitators, and portfolio analysts. The leader of EPM reports to the chief information officer.

Given the relatively young nature of PM at Key, the organization and project managers have experienced anticipated, yet significant roadblocks to success. Our primary challenges include the newness of our skill set, lack of knowledge about and respect for the role, authority of the role incumbents, our overwhelming desire to meet the needs of the business, and our consensus-based culture.

Specifically, the discipline of PM is still very young at Key. We are working through hiring skilled project managers and leaders and training internal project managers in both the PMBOK® Guide fundamentals and leadership. Also, as the role is relatively new, authority has not come easily to it. Typically, authority has been earned through knowledge of a specific technology or banking business, not discipline in project management. Project managers are working hard to become respected as leaders across the organization.

Another challenge we are working to overcome is our tendency to overcommit to project delivery. In our strong desire to service our lines of business, our associates have optimistically estimated work or estimated work without full understanding of scope and requirements. Today we are focused on improving our planning, monitoring, and statusing practices to provide a better metrics-based understanding of project health. As well, we are moving to a project life-cycle approach in which commitments (scope, schedule, cost) are made only for known work or phases of a project.

The third barrier to reaching our goals stems from our history of consensus-based decision-making. This has slowed project progress and weakened accountability for project success. In an effort to combat this tendency, we are currently undergoing a paradigm shift—centralizing and moving authority from technical owners to project managers.

Cultural elements in support of PM include our business model, management support, and our organization structure. To start, all material work is defined as a project, with a clear starting point, ending deliverable, and scope. Enforcement of our project-based work model comes from the top; senior management also promotes structured software development and PM methods and tools. As well, centralizing project managers within an independent PMO has granted them access to business sponsors and technology management while maintaining their objectivity in project execution.

The next steps in the maturity of our PMO are threefold. First, we are reassessing (using the CMMI framework) our process areas, seeking a better understanding of our areas of focus. Second, we are fortifying our talent management and training program to include professional certification for all EPM associates. Third, we are investing in the planning and maintenance of our project portfolio to better understand and manage to a fixed labor budget and optimize our return on technology investments.

Process

Technology investment and PM policies guide project prioritization decisions and execution. The policies, guidelines, processes, tools, and templates are stored on and shared via the corporate Intranet. Every new EPM associate undergoes approx 30–40 hours training in our PM processes and methods; the curriculum is also tailorable for continuing education for current associates.

PPM at Key consists of three focus areas: planning, project startup, and execution. We'll address them here in that order.

Portfolio analysis is growing in importance at Key. Technology costs are capped for the corporation and distributed to each line of business. Large projects and projects seeking "top of house" funding are reviewed and prioritized by a cross-line of business governance committee. Portfolio managers within Key partner with the lines of business to plan technology project investments appropriate to their portfolio goals and allocations. Portfolio analysts (members of the PMO) assist them in understanding portfolio and project risks and constraints (e.g., resources) while planning and reserving resources.

Projects are scoped, prioritized, and tracked as part of a line-of-business portfolio. Each portfolio is analyzed for type of investment and project health, and the data are used to adjust investments and plan future work. As well, in aggregate, portfolio metrics are used to forecast resource supply and demand. At the detailed level, quarterly cross-organizational pipeline reviews of upcoming projects are held to identify resource needs and constraints.

Key began to apply greater focus on project startup in 2003 with the hiring of requirements facilitators. This function has grown to include support of the project manager in risk assessment, resource capacity and skill, and industry-based estimating. Today, Key has centralized SWD project estimators and requirements facilitators. As well, portfolio analysts partner with project managers and portfolio managers to assess capacity and skill sets of resources available to each upcoming project. Even prior to startup, critical resources (including the project manager, a SWD architect, and business analyst) are "reserved" to ascertain the project is not begun until the company is ready and poised to succeed.

Execution, the purpose of PM, continues to be a focus area for Key. We follow the rational unified process (RUP) for software development, tailoring the processes and artifacts as appropriate for each project. Key applies the RUP best practices of developing iteratively, managing requirements, using component architectures, modeling visually, continuously verifying quality, and managing change to a standard system development life cycle (SDLC), including phases for concept evaluation, inception, elaboration, construction, and transition (including benefit assessment). (See Figure 3–8.)

The PM discipline of the RUP is closely followed; core areas of PM at Key are plan, scope, and change management, and early escalation, based on subjective and objective data, of project issues and risks. Project management processes are aligned with the *Project Management Book of Knowledge* (PMBOK® Guide) to address scope, requirements, quality, risk, change, configuration, test, defect, problem, resource, vendor, plan, and metrics management. Process engineers are assigned to our most difficult and valuable projects to support the project teams through the life cycle of the project.

The primary PM tools in use at Key include an integrated repository of project prioritization, plan, resource management (including skills assessment and tracking), and time-reporting information. This allows us to minimized duplicate data entry and use actual data in the assessment of project and portfolio progress and health. A second, shared repository of project demographic and status report data is also used to communicate across Key the health of our projects.

As part of this status report, Key project managers review cost and schedule milestone "actuals" against plan. Earned value is captured and analyzed against standard tolerance levels for "red/yellow/green"; non–green projects are investigated weekly for corrective action. Project managers also document the subjective assessment of project status, including risk and issues.

3.11 NORTEL

An extension of customers' expectations is stakeholders' expectations. Companies must maintain a delicate balance in trying to satisfy both internal and external customers simultaneously. Jean Claude LeBigre, Vice President of GSM France, Nortel Networks, illustrates this conflict:

> Nortel Networks faces stiff competition in the market and as a by-product of this may face delivery penalties for system-level solutions. The penalties can quickly eat away the profits of a large job. The key to avoiding these penalties is to plan the projects properly and to ensure that realistic scope planning, time, and cost objectives are set.

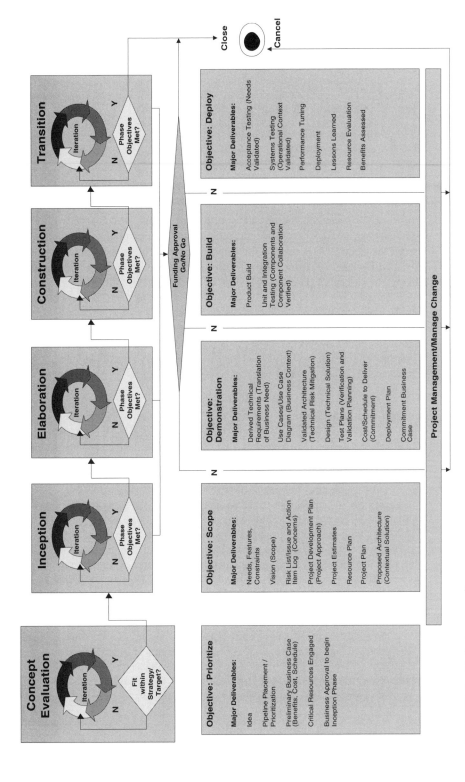

FIGURE 3–8. Project process flow.

Implementing a project on time is extremely important to our customers as they have business partners to satisfy, regulatory obligations to meet, and shareholders who demand a fair return on their investments. The expectations placed on a project manager are significant, and the key to meeting our contractual obligations is the up-front planning of all projects. A project plan available upon contract award derisks the implementation and ensures on-time, on-budget implementations to ensure customer satisfaction.

3.12 HALIFAX COMMUNITY HEALTH SYSTEMS

If the journey to excellence is to be accomplished quickly and correctly, then the organization must assign the best possible people to implementation even if it means hiring from the outside. Because of the importance of project management, there must be highly qualified people at the helm. Such was the case with Halifax Community Health Systems.[2]

In 2002, Halifax Community Health Systems implemented a new health information system across the enterprise. Although there was no formal methodology used, the managers used an informal process to implement the system and the project was a huge success. The manager of information systems was the project manager of the implementation. She was promoted to director. It was because of her leadership and vision that the project management office (PMO) was started.

When she was promoted, her first initiative was to promote a manager (Woody Walker) from within to start the PMO. Portfolio software was purchased (Pacific Edge) and implemented and two project managers (Nancy Jeffreys and Nani Sadowski) were hired. One of the project managers was Six Sigma certified and the other was certified by the Project Management Institute (PMI) as a Project Management Professional (PMP®). The manager earned a Master's Certificate in Project Management.

It was decided that we would use PMI® as the basis of our methodology. We created processes and procedures, templates, and developed project management work flows. All of these were developed as we implemented systems in the hospital.

Right after the project managers were hired and basic methodology was developed, we hired a project analyst to assist with the smaller, IT-related projects (moving communications and network closets, moving department personal computers, printers, etc). As we proved that the methodology was solid and projects were implemented successfully, more departments and executives asked for project managers for their projects. After three years, we now have a manager, two senior project managers, four project managers, and two project analysts.

The most difficult problem we have incurred in this process is that we are sometimes used as an additional management resource for a department instead of performing project management. We have proven that we can complete projects on time and within budget. Departments see that we can get things done, so we are asked to help with day-to-day management activities in a department just to get things accomplished. There have been times

---

2. This section was provided by Nani Sadowski, Manager of the Enterprise Project Management Office; Nancy Jeffreys, Portfolio and Program Manager; and Woody Walker, Director Enterprise Services.

when we get caught up in on-going system support as opposed to projects. This can drain resources.

We have had to spend time training executives and top management one on one as we work through projects. Even though the executives had a lot of exposure to project management during large group meetings, we found that one-on-one meetings with the executives were required to get their buy-in to the process.

The driver within Halifax Community Health Systems was that there were many systems that needed to be implemented. Because we are a growing health care organization, we are constantly moving departments and implementing systems. When we proved that a PMO could successfully complete projects on time and within budget, the need for the services of a project manager grew. Within three years, we became an enterprise project management office to include facility projects and work flow and process improvement initiatives.

According to the job descriptions, project management is a profession within the hospital system. The project managers must have a Bachelor's and a senior project managers must have a Master's and PMP® certification. However, there have been times when we "inherited" people from other departments that may or may not have met the criteria.

3.13 AVALON POWER AND LIGHT

Avalon Power and Light (a disguised case) is a mountain states utility company that, for decades, had functioned as a regional monopoly. All of this changed in 1995 with the beginning of deregulation in public utilities. Emphasis was now being placed on cost cutting and competitiveness.

The Information Systems Division of Avalon was always regarded as a "thorn in the side" of the company. The employees acted as prima donnas and refused to accept any of the principles of project management. Cost-cutting efforts at Avalon brought to the surface the problem that the majority of the work in the Information Systems Division could be outsourced at a significantly cheaper price than performing the work internally. Management believed project management could make the division more competitive, but would employees now be willing to accept the project management approach?

According to a spokesperson for Avalon Power and Light:

Two prior attempts to implement a standard application-development methodology had failed. Although our new director of information systems aggressively supported this third effort by mandating the use of a standard methodology and standard tools, significant obstacles were still present.

The learning curve for the project management methodology was high, resulting in a tendency of the leads to impose their own interpretations on methodology tasks rather than learning the documented explanations. This resulted in an inconsistent interpretation of the methodology, which in turn produced inconsistencies when we tried to use previous estimates in estimating new projects.

The necessity to update project plans in a timely manner was still not universally accepted. Inconsistency in reporting actual hours and finish dates resulted in inaccurate availabilities. Resources were not actually available when indicated on the departmental plan.

Many team leads had not embraced the philosophy behind project management and did not really subscribe to its benefits. They were going through the motions, producing the correct deliverables, but managing their projects intuitively in parallel to the project plan rather than using the project plan to run their projects.

Information systems management did not ask questions that required use of project management in reporting project status. Standard project management metrics were ignored in project status reports in favor of subjective assessments.

The Information Systems Division realized that its existence could very well be based upon how well and how fast it would be able to develop a mature project management system. By 1997, the sense of urgency for maturity in project management had permeated the entire Information Systems Division. When asked what benefits were achieved, the spokesperson remarked:

The perception of structure and the ability to document proposals using techniques recognized outside of our organization has allowed Information Systems to successfully compete against external organizations for application development projects.

Better resource management through elimination of the practice of "hoarding" preferred resources until another project needs staffing has allowed Information Systems to actually do more work with less people.

We are currently defining requirements for a follow-on project to the original project management implementation project. This project will address the lessons learned from our first two years. Training in project management concepts (as opposed to tools training) will be added to the existing curriculum. Increased emphasis will be placed on why it is necessary to accurately record time and task status. An attempt will be made to extend the use of project management to non-application-development areas, such as network communications and technical support. The applicability of our existing methodology to client-server development and Internet application development will be tested. We will also explore additional efficiencies such as direct input of task status by individual team members.

We now offer project management services as an option in our service-level agreements with our corporate "customers." One success story involved a project to implement a new corporate identity in which various components across the corporation were brought together. The project was able to cross department boundaries and maintain an aggressive schedule. The process of defining tasks and estimating their durations resulted in a better understanding of the requirements of the project. This in turn provided accurate estimates that drove significant decisions regarding the scope of the project in light of severe budget pressures. Project decisions tended to be based on sound business alternatives rather than raw intuition.

3.14 ROADWAY

In the spring of 1992, Roadway Express realized that its support systems (specifically information systems) had to be upgraded in order for Roadway Express to be well positioned for the twenty-first century. Mike Wickham, then President of Roadway Express, was a strong believer in continuous change. This was a necessity for his firm, because the rapid changes in technology mandated that reengineering efforts be an ongoing process. Several of the projects to be undertaken required a significantly larger number of resources than past projects had needed. Stronger interfacing between functional departments would also be required.

At the working levels of Roadway Express, knowledge of the principles and tools of project management was minimal at best in 1992. However, at the executive levels, knowledge of project management was excellent. This would prove to be highly beneficial. Roadway Express recognized the need to use project management on a two-year project that had executive visibility and support and that was deemed strategically critical to the company. Although the project required a full-time project manager, the company chose to appoint a line manager who was instructed to manage his line and the project at the same time for two years. The company did not use project management continuously, and the understanding of project management was extremely weak.

After three months, the line manager resigned his appointment as a project manager, citing too much stress and being unable to manage his line effectively while performing project duties. A second line manager was appointed on a part-time basis and, as with his predecessor, he found it necessary to resign as project manager.

The company then assigned a third line manager but this time released her from all line responsibility while managing the project. The project team and selected company personnel were provided with project management training. The president of the company realized the dangers of quick implementation, especially on a project of this magnitude, but was willing to accept the risk.

After three months, the project manager complained that some of her team members were very unhappy with the pressures of project management and were threatening to resign from the company if necessary simply to get away from project management. But when asked about the project status, the project manager stated that the project had met every deliverable and milestone thus far. It was quickly apparent to the president, Mike Wickham, and other officers of the company that project management was functioning as expected. The emphasis now was how to "stroke" the disgruntled employees and convince them of the importance of their work and how much the company appreciated their efforts.

To quell the fears of the employees, the president assumed the role of the project sponsor and made it quite apparent that project management was here to stay at Roadway Express. The president brought in training programs on project management and appeared at each training program.

The reinforcement by the president and his visible support permeated all levels of the company. By June of 1993, less than eight months after the first official use of project management, Roadway Express had climbed further along the ladder to maturity in project management than most other companies accomplish in two to three years due to to the visible support of senior management.

Senior management quickly realized that project management and information systems management could be effectively integrated into a single methodology. Mike Wickham correctly recognized that the quicker he could convince his line managers to support the project management methodology, the quicker they would achieve maturity. According to Mike Wickham, President of Roadway Express at that time (and later Chairman of the Board):

> Project management, no matter how sophisticated or how well trained, cannot function effectively unless all management is committed to a successful project outcome. Before we put our current process in place, we actively involved all those line managers who thought

it was their job to figure out all of the reasons a system would never work! Now, the steering committee says, "This is the project. Get behind it and see that it works." It is a much more efficient use of resources when everyone is focused on the same goal.

3.15 DEFCON CORPORATION

A defense contractor that wishes to remain nameless (we call it Defcon Corporation) had survived for almost 20 years on fixed-price, lump-sum government contracts. A characteristic of a fixed-price contract is that the customer does not audit your books, costs, or perhaps even your project management system. As a result, the company managed its projects rather loosely between 1967 and 1987. As long as deliveries were on time, the capabilities of the project management system were never questioned.

By 1987, the government-subcontracting environment had changed. There were several reasons for this:

- The DoD was undergoing restructuring.
- There were cutbacks in DoD spending, and the cutbacks were predicted to get worse.
- The DoD was giving out more and more cost-reimbursable contracts.
- The DoD was pressuring contractors to restructure from a traditional to product-oriented organizational form.
- The DoD was pressuring contractors to reduce costs, especially the overhead rates.
- The DoD was demanding higher quality products.
- The DoD was now requiring in its proposals that companies demonstrate higher quality project management practices.

Simply to survive, Defcon had to bid on cost-reimbursable contracts. Internally, this mandated two critical changes. First, the organization had to go to more formal rather than informal project management. Second, the organization had to learn how to use and report earned value measurement. In order to be looked upon favorably by the government for the award of a cost-reimbursable contract, a company must have its earned value cost control/reporting system validated by the government.

A manager within one such company that was struggling made the following comments on how "survival" had forced the organization to climb the ladder to maturity over the past 10 years:

> Formal project management began with the award of the first major government program. There was a requirement to report costs by contract line item and to report variances at specific contract levels. A validated system was obtained to give us the flexibility to submit proposals on government programs where cost schedule reporting was a requirement of the RFP (request for proposal).
>
> We have previous experience in PERT (program evaluation and review technique) networking, work breakdown structures, and program office organizations. Management was also used to working in a structured format because of our customer's requirements

for program reviews. After system validation in 1987, it took six months to a year to properly train and develop the skills needed by cost account managers and work package supervisors. As you move along in a program, there is the need to retrain and review project management requirements with the entire organization.

We visited other companies and divisions of our own company that had prior experience in project management. We sent people to seminars and classes held by experts in the field. We conducted internal training classes and wrote policies and procedures to assist employees with the process of project management. Later we purchased canned reporting packages to reduce the cost of internal programming of systems.

We established dedicated teams to a contract/program. We have program office organizations for large programs to follow through and coordinate information to internal management and our customer. We adjusted our systems and reports to meet both our internal and external customers' needs.

Implementation of integrated systems will provide data on a timelier basis. These data will allow management to react quickly to solve the problem and minimize the cost impact.

Project management has allowed us to better understand costs and variances by contract/program. It provides us with timely data and makes tracking of schedule issues, budget issues, and earned values more manageable. Project management has given us visibility into the programs that is useful in implementing cost reductions and process improvements. Having a validated system allows us to remain competitive for bidding on those programs that require formal cost schedule control systems.

3.16 KOMBS ENGINEERING

The company described above was very fortunate to have identified the crises and taken the time to react properly. Some companies are not so fortunate. Consider the Michigan-based Kombs Engineering (name of the company is disguised at company's request).

In June 1993, Kombs Engineering had grown to a company with $25 million in sales. The business base consisted of two contracts with the DoE, one for $15 million and one for $8 million. The remaining $2 million consisted of a variety of smaller jobs for $15,000 to $50,000 each.

The larger contract with the DoE was a five-year contract for $15 million per year. The contract was awarded in 1988 and was up for renewal in 1993. The DoE had made it clear that, although it was very pleased with the technical performance of Kombs, the follow-on contract must go through competitive bidding by law. Marketing intelligence indicated that the DoE intended to spend $10 million per year for five years on the follow-on contract with a tentative award date of October 1993. On June 21, 1993, the solicitation for proposal was received at Kombs. The technical requirements of the proposal request were not considered to be a problem for Kombs. There was no question in anyone's mind that on technical merit alone Kombs would win the contract. The more serious problem was that the DoE required a separate section in the proposal on how Kombs would manage the $10 million/year project as well as a complete description of how the project management system at Kombs functioned.

When Kombs won the original bid in 1988, there had been no project management requirement. All projects at Kombs were accomplished through the traditional organizational structure. Only line managers acted as project leaders.

In July 1993, Kombs hired a consultant to train the entire organization in project management. The consultant also worked closely with the proposal team in responding to the DoE project management requirements. The proposal was submitted to the DoE during the second week of August. In September 1993, the DoE provided Kombs with a list of questions concerning its proposal. More than 95 percent of the questions involved project management. Kombs responded to all questions.

In October 1993, Kombs received notification that it would not be granted the contract. During a postaward conference, the DoE stated that it had no "faith" in the Kombs project management system. Kombs Engineering is no longer in business.

Kombs Engineering is an excellent case study to give students in project management classes. It shows what happens when a subcontractor does not recognize how smart the customer has become in project management. Had Kombs been in close contact with its customers, the company would have had five years rather than one month to develop a mature project management system.

3.17 WILLIAMS MACHINE TOOL COMPANY

The strength of a culture can not only prevent a firm from recognizing that a change is necessary but also block the implementation of the change even after need for it is finally realized. Such was the situation at Williams Machine Tool Company (another disguised case).

For 75 years, the Williams Machine Tool Company had provided quality products to its clients, becoming the third largest U.S.-based machine tool company by 1980. The company was highly profitable and had an extremely low employee turnover rate. Pay and benefits were excellent.

Between 1970 and 1980, the company's profits soared to record levels. The company's success was due to one product line of standard manufacturing machine tools. Williams spent most of its time and effort looking for ways to improve its "bread and butter" product line rather than to develop new products. The product line was so successful that other companies were willing to modify their production lines around these machine tools, rather than asking Williams for major modifications to the machine tools.

By 1980, Williams Company was extremely complacent, expecting this phenomenal success with one product line to continue for 20 to 25 more years. The recession of 1979–1983 forced management to realign its thinking. Cutbacks in production had decreased the demand for the standard machine tools. More and more customers were asking either for major modifications to the standard machine tools or for a completely new product design.

The marketplace was changing and senior management recognized that a new strategic focus was necessary. However, attempts to convince lower-level management and the workforce, especially engineering, of this need were meeting strong resistance. The company's employees, many of them with over 20 years of employment at Williams Company, refused to recognize this change, believing that the glory days of yore would return at the end of the recession.

In 1986, the company was sold to Crock Engineering. Crock had an experienced machine tool division of its own and understood the machine tool business. Williams Company was allowed to operate as a separate entity from 1985 to 1986. By 1986, red ink had appeared on the Williams Company balance sheet. Crock replaced all of the Williams senior managers with its own personnel. Crock then announced to all employees that Williams would become a specialty machine tool manufacturer and the "good old days" would never return. Customer demand for specialty products had increased threefold in just the last 12 months alone. Crock made it clear that employees who would not support this new direction would be replaced.

The new senior management at Williams Company recognized that 85 years of traditional management had come to an end for a company now committed to specialty products. The company culture was about to change, spearheaded by project management, concurrent engineering, and total quality management.

Senior management's commitment to project management was apparent by the time and money spent in educating the employees. Unfortunately, the seasoned 20+ year veterans still would not support the new culture. Recognizing the problems, management provided continuous and visible support for project management in addition to hiring a project management consultant to work with the people. The consultant worked with Williams from 1986 to 1991.

From 1986 to 1991, the Williams Division of Crock Engineering experienced losses in 24 consecutive quarters. The quarter ending March 31, 1992, was the first profitable quarter in over six years. Much of the credit was given to the performance and maturity of the project management system. In May 1992, the Williams Division was sold. More than 80 percent of the employees lost their jobs when the company was relocated over 1500 miles away.

Williams Machine Tool Company did not realize until too late that the business base had changed from production-driven to project-driven. Living in the past is acceptable only if you want to be a historian. But for businesses to survive, especially in a highly competitive environment, they must look ahead and recognize that change is inevitable.

3.18 SWAGELOK COMPANY

One of the common themes throughout this chapter, beginning with Texas Instruments' pyramid of success, has been the importance of culture and people in the journey to excellence in project management. Even when people clearly identify their best practices in project management, roots seem to be always traceable to people and culture. Such was the case at Swagelok Company. According to Matt LoPiccolo, Director of Customer Service & Logistics at Swagelok Company:

> When I think of best practices in project management, sponsorship, project management development, team dynamics, and alignment are what come to mind. It's my experience that a successful project begins when the sponsor, project team, and customer (the ultimate

user of the project deliverables) align their expectations through communication and collaboration.

This alignment begins with the project sponsor. Successful sponsors serve as champions for the business case and take responsibility for creating ownership and accountability of the project deliverables. In addition they support project team development and help clear project obstacles.

Companies with a history of successful projects commit themselves to developing a culture that supports project management skills as a core competency. They focus on training, recognition of project management as a full-time job, promoting lessons learned corporatewide, and continued refinement of project methodology.

Many successful project methodologies share the following components:

- Requirements definition process that involves the customer
- Phase-based methodology with formal reviews
- Change management and financial process controls
- Risk management process
- Communication plan
- Early focus on operational implementation and line of business ownership
- A lessons-learned process integrated into the project's startup and close
- Project value measurement process

One pitfall that often traps people is a belief that a good process will manage a project successfully. Real success stems from good leadership and team-building skills. Well-run projects have a team dynamic that builds on trust between all participants.

Trust is the basis for commitment and open communications that create a collaborative environment that truly allows for alignment of everyone's expectations. The ultimate success of a project is directly proportional to the involvement and enthusiasm of its sponsor, project team, and customer.

3.19 CITY OF CHANDLER, ARIZONA: INFORMATION TECHNOLOGY[3]

Marilyn Delmont, Chief Information Officer, (CIO) states:

> IT Project Management is strategic; it is the methodology that IT uses to move the organization forward not only in technology but also in reengineering business processes while delivering key business goals and objectives. The benefits to any organization, if applied correctly, are HUGE!

Background   The previously agriculture-based city of Chandler, Arizona, experienced a population explosion from 30,000 in 1980 to nearly 237,000 today and continues to expand at a rapid pace. A concurrent shift and expansion to be-

---

3. This section was provided by the IT Group of the City of Chandler, Arizona.

coming a center of technology with the influx of corporations like Intel, Motorola, MTD, Orbital, Microchip, and Avnet has made Chandler one of the focal points of the "Silicon Desert." The growth and shift in culture have presented city management and staff with enormous challenges in providing services and amenities to its citizenry.

The city relies on the, essentially centralized, Information Technology (IT) Division to provide and support its technology requirements. To fulfill its responsibility in supporting a diverse user base with exceptionally diverse needs, IT has grown from 5 employees in 1980 to 51 employees today. Meanwhile, the number of city employees that IT supports has grown from 283 to 1542 during the same time frame.

Culture (The Problem Statement)

Government   The majority of government agencies tend to consist of a number of *fiefdoms*. That is, they become their own entity and build virtual walls around themselves. The art of working together for the greater glory is often sacrificed for fear of losing autonomy and its own segregated budget.

The City   With the high demands placed on the small IT staff, service was waning. Many of the departments were largely dissatisfied with IT's performance. Projects, which had been funded and promised, were slow to get implemented. The coffers were full of project money, which was rolled over from year to year, unused. Some departments began to deal directly with outside vendors to fulfill their needs. Oftentimes, IT was then expected to support technology it was not involved in implementing.

Information Technology   By 2001, IT had gone through many transitions. Staff was qualified and dedicated but was constantly being inundated with requests and demands for services. Juggling the demands of growth, increasing reliance on technology, and the constant changes in technology all within the confines of public-sector budget constraints had taken its toll; staff was weary and demoralized.

Requests for services often went unaddressed or were addressed after lengthy delays. There just weren't enough resources, or project management wasn't savvy enough to accomplish them. The work ethics and technical skills to complete the tasks were present, but staff was disjointed. Due to numerous turnovers in management, detailed expectations, goals, objectives, and policies and procedures were not fully developed or documented.

As with many public-sector and even private-sector organizations, some staff members were resistant to change and some newcomers were overly anxious to impose change in an environment that, by nature, moves relatively slow. Attempts made to formalize procedures often died in infancy because there was no consistent leadership in place to impose them. Frustration levels were up and morale was down.

To adequately manage and support the technology the city's employees relied on, standards needed to be enforced, requests for services needed to be prioritized, and a consistent work flow established, but as a *division* of a department, IT was not the political equal to the other departments and could therefore not implement or enforce any of these necessary components to the extent needed for success.

Incorporation of Project
Management

With the rapid growth of both technology and the city's population and staff, the relatively simple projects to support the user base and incorporate new software had burgeoned into intricate projects involving fiber optics, intercity communications, geographic information systems (GISs), and infrastructure to name but a few.

Although staff members could *conceivably* execute smaller projects, the results were often one dimensional. In other words, they were normally biased to the field the creator had the expertise in and functional only to the extent the staff member had the experience and/or the bandwidth to execute by himself or herself. The solutions could rarely be upgraded, expanded, or integrated and were therefore usually relatively short-lived.

The people managing projects of larger scope, which the city now required due to its size and diversity, needed to have sufficient training, experience, and organizational skills and the position and ability to *manage* the resources. Full-time project managers were needed.

In 2001, an outside vendor was contracted to assist with the interim management of the IT Division. The vendor and staff identified 72 projects in process. These projects lacked a clear understanding of their nature and had little or no documentation, yet the expectations had been made that these projects were viable and would be completed. Clearly, this was not going to happen.

It was decided to "fast-track" an interim project methodology, based on a pared-down version of the vendor's, and reduce the number of projects to a feasible number. IT staff developed documentation on the 12 selected high-priority projects. The remaining 60 projects were canceled and would presumably be resurrected by the sponsors as needed.

It was clear that the new breed of technology projects had to be managed by an experienced project manager. A recommendation was made to restructure the organization to include two project managers that would report to the IT manager. Buy-in was obtained from the city manager and the first two project managers were hired in 2001.

Although this was a definite move in the right direction, assimilating the project managers into IT was met with much resistance from staff. There was resentment toward external personnel being hired at a management-level pay grade and then almost immediately "giving orders" and "taking things over." Managers and supervisors resented giving up valuable resources to work on projects. And there did not seem to be a clear or standard means by which projects were planned or executed.

The Bold (The Vision)

The CIO   As stated by one individual:

> A true leader has the confidence to stand alone, the courage to make tough decisions, and the compassion to listen to the needs of others. He does not set out to be a leader but becomes one by the quality of his actions and the integrity of his intent. In the end, leaders are like eagles—they don't flock; you find them one at a time.

In a bold move, the city reorganized and shifted IT from a division of another department to being a division of the city manager's office and hired its first CIO, Marilyn Delmont, in late 2002. This move not only provided strong leadership for the division but also gave it a direct voice to the city manager.

Mrs. Delmont is definitely not the stereotypical CIO. Having been interviewed and selected from a field of 1400 applicants by both city management and IT staff, she chose to resolve the current injuries by forging ahead rather than dwelling on the past, much like installing a new high-end server rather than continually troubleshooting the old one.

Her ability to ask the right questions and quickly assess a situation and its overall or domino effect on the organization is seldom equaled. But, one of her finest qualities is her vision. She is a taker of calculated, bold moves. One of several bold moves was the formation of the project management office and the appointment of Tyrone Howard to manage it.

Mrs. Delmont took a longer stride, and another bold move, to train every member of IT in the new project management methodology. It was her belief and vision that "in order to be successful, everyone needs to understand how something works, how they are integral to its success, and how it will benefit their careers."

Training was conducted in two groups, each consisting of a blend of managers, project managers, technical staff, and administrative staff. Through the both the instruction and sharing of information, staff now knew how any project they served on would be conducted and they had an understanding of the challenges the project managers faced.

To truly be effective, the PMO and the Human Resources Division collaborated early on to provide project management training to all city staff on an ongoing basis. Additionally, the PMO is developing a customized version of its training for current and future project team members, stakeholders, new IT employees, sponsors, and management. The next step is already underway: The first half of all IT staff has just completed business analysis methodology training. Once again, this is due to the importance the CIO places on everyone being on the same page.

Two-Time Recipient of CIO Magazine's Top-100 Award Marilyn Delmont is the recipient of the 2004 *CIO Magazine's* Agile 100 award, making the City of Chandler only the fourth municipal government to ever win this prestigious award. In 2005, she was again recognized by *CIO Magazine,* this time as one of the Bold & Gold 100. The establishment of the PMO and many of its achievements, contributed to these honors.

PMO Manager Peter F. Drucker states:

> Leadership is not magnetic personality—that can just as well be a glib tongue. It is not "making friends and influencing people"—that is flattery. Leadership is lifting a person's vision to higher sights, the raising of a person's performance to a higher standard, the building of a personality beyond its normal limitations.

Mr. Howard quickly became the *catalyst* and the *enabler.* He had ample education and experience to do the job, but having a strong background in collegiate sports as both participant and coach and his experience as an educator contributed to his being a strong team player, a mentor, and a motivator. However, his greatest attribute in the project management arena is his positive and professional demeanor. His personal affirmation is a classic Vince Lombardi: "You can't dream yourself into character. You must hammer—you must forge—one out for yourself."

Through his leadership example, the PMO team members treat others with mutual respect, continually strive for excellence, and take criticism as an invitation for improvement. It has become a dynamic, agile, and responsive team and it's diversely talented members work as a cohesive unit. As a direct result of this positive and creative environment, numerous tools and models have been developed to assist with the operations and performance of the PMO. Johann Wolfgang von Goethe stated, "Treat people as if they were what they ought to be, and you help them to become what they are capable of being."

Project Management Office   Marilyn Delmont, Chief Information Officer, states, "It normally takes three years to change an organization—we are ahead of schedule."

Prior to Tyrone Howard taking the helm, he was instrumental in the development and formalization of a standard project management methodology for IT. The methodology was derived predominately from one of the major international standards, PMI. Standard templates were developed and put into production. Although there was ample room for individual management styles, the process was the same for every project. Staff, sponsors, stakeholders, and management could now readily follow and contribute to the course of the project.

Under Mr. Howard's leadership, the young PMO has taken flight. Several new project managers were hand selected and were picking up legacy projects where they had been left off. Since many of these projects were already in progress, much of the documentation and the initial steps of the process had to be created after the fact or were grandfathered in. However, the new standard methodology is faithfully adhered to with all new projects and, inasmuch as possible, with legacy projects.

Legacy projects are usually the most difficult to manage. PMO team member Juan Padilla attests to that "projects with past history that failed before have been the most difficult to manage. I can attribute the failure of these projects to broken expectations and lack of trust." It was paramount that the team members have exemplary people skills to assuage the damaged trust and unfailing management skills to carry these projects to successful completion.

In order to build trust, you have to be trustworthy. When sponsors and stakeholders hand their problems and/or visions to someone to turn into reality, they want to trust the person in the director's chair. As Sheneka Coleman so eloquently put it, "When establishing the project management office at the city of Chandler, it was key to develop the right team. We looked for professionals with different strengths but one common underlying value—*honesty*. I believe what has made us so successful is the team's ability to communicate and treat people as equals. The team's ability to work as a cohesive unit and persevere is incredible."

To further develop this cohesive group, it was determined that the PMO itself is a *program*. Rather than divert the efforts of the project managers to managing the PMO program, they appointed a project administrator. This person would tend to the operations of the PMO, such as providing statistics, recording performance, reporting collective status, tracking project progress, addressing PMO issues, and tool and model development.

This dynamic and diverse group has advanced project management within the organization 10-fold. The PMO is now an accepted and fully integrated element of the division and is frequently sought out to provide solutions. Under Mr. Howard's guidance and tutelage and with the full support and forward-thinking vision of the CIO, the PMO is a leader in innovation and communication within IT.

With the creation and utilization of communication and resource tools such as the PMO website and the Eagle's View and performance measurement tools like the quarterly blitz, the PMO matrix, the project tracking and prioritization system, and the ITSP tracking database (which are detailed in subsequent sections), the group has developed a formidable arsenal of tools.

Determined to never become stagnant, additional tools and models are always in various stages of improvement or development. Some of these developments-in-progress are the implementation of project management portfolio software, the creation of the PM Consortium, further development of the *Mutual Fund* model, work flow refinement and automation, DeVry partnership, and improvement of the resource management tool, return on investment (ROI), and actual cost management.[4]

Tools and Models

The PMO relies on a number of tools and tactics to be able to quickly disseminate a large quantity of information in an easily digestible format for any flavor of audience being addressed. Since the majority of the attendees at IT-related presentations and employees that utilize the communications and management tools are technical staff, middle management, and executives, this is particularly applicable. As Marilyn Delmont puts it, "You need to communicate with executives at a different level—they like to see the big-picture—project managers need to paint it."

The painting is usually done in bold colors, since it is well known throughout the industry that individuals retain 10 percent of what they read, 20 percent of what they hear, 30 percent of what they see, 50 percent of what they see and hear, 70 percent of what they talk over with others, and 80 percent of what they use and do in day-to-day life. Additionally, the information is often presented several times, in different formats, since people need to hear messages several times in order to process them.

PMO Website (Communication Tool)   Although a base website was set up by the project management leadership group (PMLG) during the development of project management training and subsequently enhanced by the PMO manager, the site still lacked usability.

With the addition of the project administrator, the PMO was able to further develop and expand the website into a central resource for project management. It is the vehicle for the PMO to provide project status, showcase its accomplishments, share its methodology and templates, track performance, and provide information and how-to's to staff, management, and IT oversight committee members.

---

4. Some of these tools are predecessors to the soon-to-be-implemented project management portfolio software. Redundant tools will be utilized to upload data to the new system and then retired.

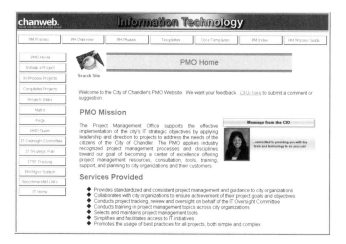

(An example of the PMO website can be viewed at www.tasctaotja.com).

Eagle's View or Eagle's Eye (Communication Tool)   Named after the CIO's penchant for eagles, Eagle's View provides an unparalleled level of communication to IT staff and management. It is a collection of shortcuts directly into the working files of the PMO. This tool is largely utilized *internally* to IT, because it is literally the PMO's shared directory. All current copies of performance and tracking tools are kept there. This was done so staff and management could feel as though they are not just in the communication loop but part of it.

Quarterly Blitz (Performance Measure Tool)   *Merriam-Webster* defines a blitz as an intensive nonmilitary campaign. In the PMO, a blitz is a snapshot in time, a method for measuring performance and successes, and a professional challenge brought forth by setting short-term, lofty goals and beating the industry standard for completing projects. *(And yes, for you war heroes and sports fans, it is also a type of military campaign and a football term.)*

The quarterly blitz starts with each project manager identifying major deliverables due during the upcoming quarter. A commitment is made to accomplish these major deliverables and is graphically charted and presented to the CIO on or as close to the first day of the quarter as possible.

At midquarter, a status meeting is conducted. At this meeting, targets that may not be met are discussed. This keeps the CIO informed and, depending on the severity of the situation, provides the opportunity for a slight modification in priorities, intervention to remove an obstacle, or a decision to leave the situation to the devices of the project manager. Usually, it is the latter.

At the end of each quarterly blitz, the PMO meets with the CIO and presents the results. This is done not as a means of spotlighting slippage but as a "lessons-learned" session. By establishing this challenge, the following benefits were realized:

- Tracks and promotes success
- Provides a performance measure
- Stimulates performance by "raising the bar"
- Communicates productivity internally and externally
- Assists with integrating PMI methodology
- Assists with executive-level planning
- Provides variance control

Due to the success and benefits of the blitz, the PMO has initiated it as one of our standard performance measures. During the PMO's third quarterly blitz, which was initiated on April 1, 2005, 32 major deliverables, referred to as *targets,* were identified and presented to the CIO with a goal of completing them by June 30, 2005. The success rate goal was set at 74 percent.

A status meeting was held on May 18, at which time the status of each target was presented to the CIO. Although 8 targets had already been met, it was believed that 4 targets would not be met.

At the June 30 deadline, 25 targets had been successfully met and 7 targets were not met. This provides the PMO with a 78 percent success rate, a full 4 percent over the 74 percent goal.

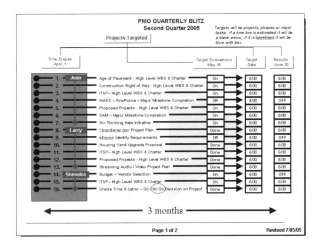

PMO Matrix (Performance/Communication Tool) The PMO matrix was initially utilized as a tool to compile data unearthed during a research effort. To overcome the lack of consistent documentation in the past, the project administrator researched through hundreds of management reports, spreadsheets, and electronic files that had lost continuity and refit them back together—much like making misshapen pieces of a puzzle fit and still look like a picture.

In a determined effort to never lose this revived, historical data or future project-tracking details, the matrix was refined and became a reporting tool and a repository for high-level data that would be loaded into the soon-to-be-implemented project management portfolio software.

A brief, lessons-learned analysis is that project documentation should always be in a centralized location and should always be dated. Secondary copies, other than backups, should not be maintained, as the data are easily desynchronized between copies. This may sound elementary, but an amazing number of organizations encounter the same situation.

PMO Quadrants Sometimes the best tools are the simplest. The PMO quadrant is a testament to that observation. It shows team members and the PMO Manager, at a glance, what is hot and what is not. It is a quick way of tracking major tasks and, since it is validated by the project manager, expeditiously identifying which of them has the priority. It ensures the team is on the same page and it lets each member know when someone else is pressed to meet a deadline and should be given either some space or an offer of assistance.

PMO Operations
Quadrant - 7/15/05

Hot: Quadrant I			Cold: Quadrant III	
Work on Publication Article	PD (7/15)		Citizen Serve Demo – Discuss w/Depts.	LG (1-1/2 month float)
ITOC Revisions Packet	PD (7/18)			
Submit 3rd Quarter Blitz Items	All (7/18)			
Incorporate Final Revisions on Computer Professional's Handbook	PD (7/19)			
Update Website	PD (7/22)			
Establish Update Schedule/Process/Workflow	PD (7/22)			
Consortium	PD (7/22)			

Hot: Has less than a week of float time   Cold: Has less 1 month of float time

No Float ———— **Float**

Warm: Quadrant II			Below Zero: Quadrant IV	
Audit on Project Binders	All (7/22)			
Finalize Mutual Fund Model	TH-PD (7/30)			
Finalize Mutual Fund Weights for Direction	TH (7/30)			
Resource Management Tool	PD (7/30)			

Warm: Has less than 2 weeks float time   Below: Has less greater than 1 month float

Information Technology Strategic Plan (ITSP)

The city acquired the services of Gartner Group, Inc. and developed a five-year strategic plan. Determined to fulfill its pivotal initiatives and not get diverted as most do, the PMO assigned a project manager to each pivotal initiative. Each initiative is managed as a project and/or as a program, depending on its nature.

It was observed and duly noted that it was not only PMO-managed project and programs that contributed to achieving the goals set forth in the ITSP, but the efforts of all IT staff members in the areas of operations, policy and procedures, methods and training were also strong contributors. The PMO devised a means of tracking the work being done in these areas as well as project tracking. This gives a more accurate picture of the progress being made toward the ITSP and makes all the contributing staff members feel their efforts are recognized and valued.

IT Governance

Information Technology Oversight Committee (ITOC) The ITOC was initiated in 1998 to assist in providing guidance and direction to the division by reviewing, approving, and prioritizing IT projects based upon the strategic needs of the city.

The ITOC is comprised of a director, or his or her designated representative, from each department and provides a forum for discussing existing and proposed city IT projects and major operational activities that may impact projects. The goal of the committee is to review, approve, and prioritize all new projects brought before the committee, realign the priority of existing projects based on detailed criteria, and assist with relieving obstacles inhibiting the timely completion of projects. The objective is to be able to aptly utilize IT resources to provide Chandler with IT products and services that best fit the city's expanding and dynamic technology requirements for providing services to its residents.

Historically, it is unclear if the ITOC waned over a period of time, if it never fully gained momentum, or if it was never truly empowered. However, the ITOC is an integral and indispensable element of the governance and overall management of IT projects for the city and it was considered paramount to revive it. It was determined that there was not a clear understanding of the roles and responsibilities and the current scoring tool needed to be replaced to include both *subjective* and *objective* data. The STAIRS model was created and the Project Tracking and Prioritization System developed and implemented to assist in resolving these issues.

The STAIRS Model The STAIRS model is both an acronym and pneumonic to succinctly communicate and promote the understanding and acceptance of the roles and responsibilities of the ITOC and encourage an active and leading role in the management of the organization's projects.

ITOC members are challenged to s̲teer the organization, t̲erminate projects that are no longer viable, a̲ssess and be a̲ware of technology and business challenges, i̲mprove business operations and services by taking a participatory role, r̲ecommend changes and provide ideas, and, most importantly, s̲upport the PMO office and IT in bringing Chandler IT projects in on time, on schedule, on budget, and at the targeted level of quality.

This is the fundamental element of IT governance. It emphasizes that the ITOC does more than simply select projects. Rather, the committee is endowed and empowered to provide the necessary guidance, decision-making, and *steering* of projects to consistently fulfill the strategic needs of the city. The ITOC may reprioritize projects, cancel stagnant projects, place projects on hold, reallocate funds, and remove obstacles to completing projects successfully. These are often tough decisions, but the overall benefit to the city is paramount.

ITOC - Steering Concept Model

To communicate the roles and responsibilities of the committee and encourage an active and lead role in managing IT projects based upon the strategic needs of the City .

Supporting

Recommending

Improving

Assessing/
Awareness

Terminating

Steering

Stairs ('*sters*) – *Structure established to reach a higher elevation or transcend the current level.*

© 2005 City of Chandler

IT Oversight Committee:
"More than just Project Selection"

Definition of STAIRS:

- Steering – Determining direction of city
- Terminating – Based on agreed-upon criteria
- Assessing – Variance reports; Awareness – Staying informed
- Improving – Develop ways to enhance business operations and services through technology, process and people
- Recommending – Areas for improvement
- Supporting – Ensuring that obstacles on projects are removed for project team

Project Tracking and Prioritization System A source of concern within the ITOC and IT was the project approval and prioritization method. Each committee member based the approval and prioritization of projects on the *subjective* scoring of each project in 10 pre-defined categories. Since it was based solely on each committee member's assessment of the project, the prioritization became somewhat diminished as having political or popularity-based undertones.

As the STAIRS model reiterates and encourages full participation in the governance process, the Project Tracking and Prioritization System provides the means to do so. Developed largely by Larry Greenhill and Earl Holland, who endured hundreds of tweaks and changes from multiple sources, the system is a finely honed access database which captures the critical data required to approve and prioritize IT projects and provides it to the ITOC in a consistent, usable format.

One of the key objectives was to eliminate the concern of project selection by favoritism. Although not all *subjective* data could be eliminated, a number of *objective* considerations could be included.

Critical decision points included mandate and compliance issues, project costs, and on-going support costs—both human and financial. *Supporting data* included strategic alignment, *objective* requirements identified by the PMO as necessary to deliver a successful project, and *subjective* criteria identifying the benefits the project would deliver to city residents.

The objective and subjective data collection generated numeric scores that provided automated ranking of proposed IT projects for ITOC approval and prioritization. This information is sent to each committee member, in hard copy and in advance, of ITOC meetings designated to conduct approval and prioritization processes. Each member would then review all the project information prior to the meeting.

During the meeting, the committee would (1) briefly review all project information; (2) accept or change subjective scores for each project; (3) either approve or recommend changes to the list of proposed projects; and (4) accept the ranking of the projects established by objective and subjective scoring or establish a unique prioritization order for project implementation.

Take Flight Model (Explanative Tool)   Tyrone Howard, PMO Manager, states, "Our CIO has encouraged us to use creative ways to simplify the seemingly complex."

To deftly explain the complexities of project management, the analogy of the planning, preparation, and execution of a commercial airline flight was created by the PMO manager. This multidimensional analogy can be utilized to explain virtually any aspect of project management to almost any level of audience.

As Mr. Howard explains it, "Almost everything we need to learn about project management we can learn from airplanes. For instance, the most difficult part of the journey is the takeoff and landing and making sure that the passengers (stakeholders) are on time and on schedule for connecting flights (operations and next projects)."

The following chart shows the correlation between the stages in managing a project and managing a commercial flight:

Project Management	Airplane Analogy
Initiate	Flight plans
Planning	Booking, schedule,
Executing	Flying, communicating with passengers, other planes in the sky, traffic control
Controlling	Radar, correcting, adjusting
Project plans	Flight plans
Issues, variance, risks	Turbulence
Funding, resources	Fuel
Project Management Tracking System	Radar
Governance/steering committee	Traffic control

The Right Formula ("The Right Stuff")

Collin Powell states, "Endeavors succeed or fail because of the people involved. Only by attracting the best people will you accomplish great deeds."

As a lessons-learned analysis, we learned that the right formula is to have support from the executive level and an executive champion plus empowered leadership, the ability to make bold moves and decisions, picking the right people, and unrelentingly providing them with support, effective two-way communication, enthusiasm, challenges, and the right tools (which includes *training*). Last, but not least, make sure everyone is on the same page and documents everything in a single, centralized location. This formula produces an atmosphere where staff feels valued, effective, and accomplished. People who feel valued treat others with mutual respect, which elicits an unparalleled atmosphere of cooperation.

This carries across from the PMO to the management of individual projects. As pointed out by Steve McDonald, "A detailed project plan with all processes and templates in place will not always accomplish the project's goals and objectives. Projects fail or succeed because of the people on the project team. Only by having the right people with both technical skills and people skills will you achieve the best results for your project."

Pamela Des Rosiers states, "The right people, with the right tools, applied appropriately."

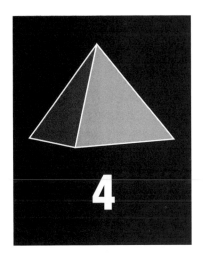

4

Project Management Methodologies

4.0 INTRODUCTION

In Chapter 1 we described the life-cycle phases for achieving maturity in project management. The fourth phase was the growth phase, which included the following:

- Establish life-cycle phases.
- Develop a project management methodology.
- Base the methodology upon effective planning.
- Minimize scope changes.
- Select the appropriate software to support the methodology.

The importance of a good methodology cannot be understated. Not only will it improve your performance during project execution, but it will also allow for better customer relations and customer confidence. Good methodologies can also lead to sole-source procurement contracts.

Creating a workable methodology for project management is no easy task. One of the biggest mistakes made is developing a different methodology for each type of project. Another is failing to integrate the project management methodology and project management tools into a single process, if possible. When companies develop project management methodologies and tools in tandem, two benefits emerge. First, the work is accomplished with fewer scope changes. Second, the processes are designed to create minimal disturbance to ongoing business operations.

This chapter discusses the components of a project management methodology and some of the most widely used project management tools. Detailed examples of methodologies at work are also included.

4.1 EXCELLENCE DEFINED

Excellence in project management is often regarded as a continuous stream of successfully managed projects. Without a project management methodology, repetitive successfully completed projects may be difficult to achieve.

Today, everyone seems to agree somewhat on the necessity for a project management methodology. However, there is still disagreement on the definition of excellence in project management, the same way that companies have different definitions for project success. In this section, we will discuss some of the different definitions of excellence in project management.

Some definitions of excellence can be quite simple and achieve the same purpose as complex definitions. According to Thomas Dye, Director of Program Management at Motorola:

Excellence in project management can be defined as:

- Strict adherence to scheduling practices
- Regular senior management oversight
- Formal requirements change control
- Formal issue and risk tracking
- Formal resource tracking
- Formal cost tracking

According to Colin Spence, Project Manager/Partner at Convergent Computing (CCO):

While CCO does not have a formal definition of "excellence in project management," our project managers or resources tasked with the job of acting as a project manager on a project should seek to achieve the following goals:

- To ensure on-budget, on-time, on-scope delivery of professional services as defined in the proposal or conceptual plan
- To ensure that deliverables are of the highest quality and meet the goals of the project
- To provide strategic oversight of the services delivery process to ensure that all CCO resources are working effectively and efficiently on the project
- To oversee CCO resources to ensure that each is fulfilling the requirements of their role in the client team
- To facilitate communications within the client team and with the client
- To monitor any yellow or red flags in projects and drive toward resolution and escalate if needed
- To develop professional services feedback and performance measurement

Some of the skills that are expected of a CCO project manager include:

- Strong communications and management skills
- Three to five years of project management experience
- Strong organizational skills
- Experience with delivering technology solutions related to the specific project
- Experience with Microsoft Project software

- Knowledge of CCO processes and policies
- Ability to oversee and coordinate multiple resources and activities

Doug Bolzman, Consultant Architect, PMP®, ITIL Service Manager at EDS, discusses his view of excellence in project management:

> Excellence is rated, not by managing the pieces, but by understanding how the pieces fit together, support each other's dependencies, and provide value to the business. If project management only does what it is asked to do, such as manage 300 individual projects in the next quarter, it is providing a low value-added function that basically is the "pack mule" that is needed, but only does what it is asked—and no more. Figures 4–1 and 4–2 demonstrate that if mapping project management to a company's overall release management framework, each project is managed independently with the characteristics shown.
>
> Using the same release framework and the same client requests, project management disciplines can understand the nature of the requirements and provide a valuable service to bundle the same types of requests (projects) to generate a forecast of the work, which will assist the company in balancing its financials, expectations, and resources. This function can be done within the PMO.

At DTE Energy, excellence in project management is defined using the project management methodology. According to Jason Schulist, Manager—Continuous Improvement, Operating Systems Strategy Group:

> DTE Energy leverages a four-gate/nine-step project management model for continuous improvement. (See Figures 4–3 and 4–4.) In gate 1 the project lead clearly defines the metric that will measure the success in the project. In gate 2 of the project, after the ideal state has been defined, the project lead gains approval from the champion confirming not only the appropriate metrics but also the target.

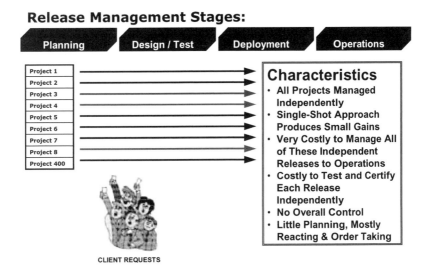

FIGURE 4–1. Release management.

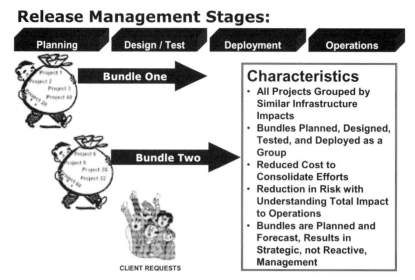

FIGURE 4–2. Bundling requests.

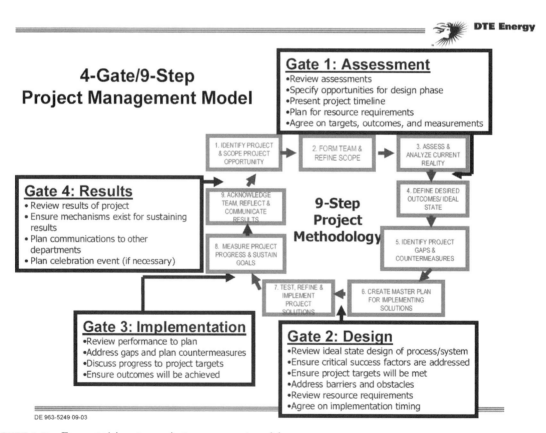

FIGURE 4–3. Four-gate/nine-step project management model.

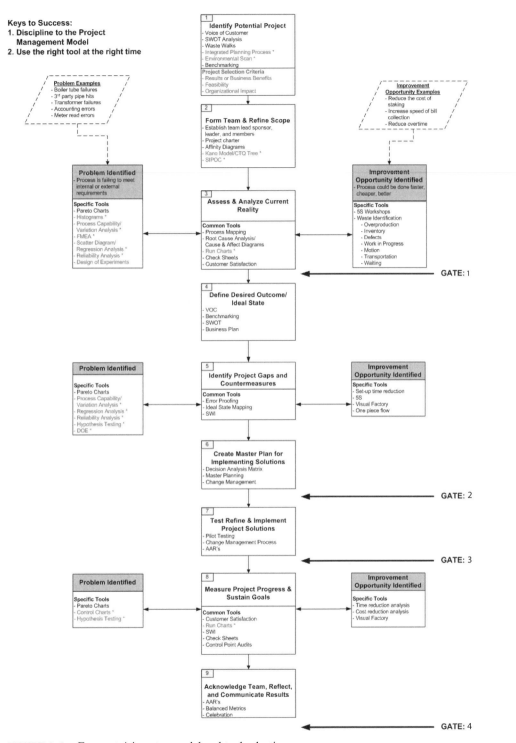

Keys to Success:
1. **Discipline to the Project Management Model**
2. **Use the right tool at the right time**

Problem Examples
- Boiler tube failures
- 3rd party pipe hits
- Transformer failures
- Accounting errors
- Meter read errors

Improvement Opportunity Examples
- Reduce the cost of staking
- Increase speed of bill collection
- Reduce overtime

1 Identify Potential Project
- Voice of Customer
- SWOT Analysis
- Waste Walks
- Integrated Planning Process *
- Environmental Scan *
- Benchmarking
Project Selection Criteria
- Results or Business Benefits
- Feasibility
- Organizational Impact

2 Form Team & Refine Scope
- Establish team lead sponsor, leader, and members
- Project charter
- Affinity Diagrams
- Kano Model/CTQ Tree *
- SIPOC *

Problem Identified
- Process is failing to meet internal or external requirements

Specific Tools
- Pareto Charts
- Histograms *
- Process Capability/ Variation Analysis *
- FMEA *
- Scatter Diagram/ Regression Analysis *
- Reliability Analysis *
- Design of Experiments

Improvement Opportunity Identified
- Process could be done faster, cheaper, better

Specific Tools
- 5S Workshops
- Waste Identification
  - Overproduction
  - Inventory
  - Defects
  - Work in Progress
  - Motion
  - Transportation
  - Waiting

3 Assess & Analyze Current Reality
Common Tools
- Process Mapping
- Root Cause Analysis/ Cause & Affect Diagrams
- Run Charts *
- Check Sheets
- Customer Satisfaction

GATE: 1

4 Define Desired Outcome/ Ideal State
- VOC
- Benchmarking
- SWOT
- Business Plan

Problem Identified

Specific Tools
- Pareto Charts
- Process Capability/ Variation Analysis *
- Regression Analysis *
- Reliability Analysis *
- Hypothesis Testing *
- DOE *

5 Identify Project Gaps and Countermeasures
Common Tools
- Error Proofing
- Ideal State Mapping
- SWI

Improvement Opportunity Identified

Specific Tools
- Set-up time reduction
- 5S
- Visual Factory
- One piece flow

6 Create Master Plan for Implementing Solutions
- Decision Analysis Matrix
- Master Planning
- Change Management

GATE: 2

7 Test Refine & Implement Project Solutions
- Pilot Testing
- Change Management Process
- AAR's

GATE: 3

Problem Identified

Specific Tools
- Pareto Charts
- Control Charts *
- Hypothesis Testing *

8 Measure Project Progress & Sustain Goals
Common Tools
- Customer Satisfaction
- Run Charts *
- SWI
- Check Sheets
- Control Point Audits

Improvement Opportunity Identified

Specific Tools
- Time reduction analysis
- Cost reduction analysis
- Visual Factory

9 Acknowledge Team, Reflect, and Communicate Results
- AAR's
- Balanced Metrics
- Celebration

GATE: 4

FIGURE 4–4. Four-gate/nine-step model and tool selection process map.

> This target for success is maintained throughout the project and the project does not close (gate 4) unless the target is achieved. If the project does not achieve the target through the committed actions, the project reverts to gate 2, where the ideal state is revisited and further actions are determined.

Allan Dutch, PMP®, Senior Project Manager, Software Engineering, Methods and Staffing at DTE Energy, believes that:

> A DTE Energy information technology (IT) project exhibiting success and excellence in project management is one where the project manager directs her or his team much like a conductor directs her or his orchestra. Business value is demonstrable and recognized by the business unit while interactions with support organizations and infrastructure requirements are coordinated smoothly and according to plan.

4.2 RECOGNIZING THE NEED FOR METHODOLOGY DEVELOPMENT

Simply having a project management methodology and following it do not lead to success and excellence in project management. The need for improvements in the system may be critical. External factors can have a strong influence on the success or failure of a company's project management methodology. Change is a given in the current business climate, and there is no sign that the future will be any different. The rapid changes in technology that have driven changes in project management over the past two decades are not likely to subside. Another trend, the increasing sophistication of consumers and clients, is likely to continue, not go away. Cost and quality control have become virtually the same issue in many industries. Other external factors include rapid mergers and acquisitions and real-time communications.

Project management methodologies are organic processes and need to change as the organization changes in response to the ever-evolving business climate. Such changes, however, require that managers on all levels be committed to the changes and develop a vision that calls for the development of project management systems along with the rest of the organization's other business systems.

Today, companies are managing their business by projects. This is true for both non-project-driven and project-driven organizations. Virtually all activities in an organization can be treated as some sort of project. Therefore, it is only fitting that well-managed companies regard a project management methodology as a way to manage the entire business rather than just projects. Business processes and project management processes will be merged together as the project manager is viewed as the manager of part of a business rather than just the manager of a project.

Developing a standard project management methodology is not for every company. For companies with small or short-term projects, such formal systems may not be cost effective or appropriate. However, for companies with large or ongoing projects, developing a workable project management system is mandatory.

For example, a company that manufactures home fixtures had several project development protocols in place. When they decided to begin using project management systematically, the complexity of the company's current methods became apparent. The company had multiple system development methodologies based on the type of project. This became awkward for employees who had to struggle with a different methodology for each project. The company then opted to create a general, all-purpose methodology for all projects. The new methodology had flexibility built into it. According to one spokesman for the company:

> Our project management approach, by design, is not linked to a specific systems development methodology. Because we believe that it is better to use a (standard) systems development methodology than to decide which one to use, we have begun development of a guideline systems development methodology specific for our organization. We have now developed prerequisites for project success. These include:

- A well-patterned methodology
- A clear set of objectives
- Well-understood expectations
- Thorough problem definition

During the late 1980s, merger mania hit the banking community. With the lowering of costs due to economies of scale and the resulting increased competitiveness, the banking community recognized the importance of using project management for mergers and acquisitions. The quicker the combined cultures became one, the less the impact on the corporation's bottom line.

The need for a good methodology became apparent, according to a spokesperson at one bank:

> The intent of this methodology is to make the process of managing projects more effective: from proposal to prioritization to approval through implementation. This methodology is not tailored to specific types or classifications of projects, such as system development efforts or hardware installations. Instead, it is a commonsense approach to assist in prioritizing and implementing successful efforts of any jurisdiction.

In 1996, the Information Services (IS) Division of one bank formed an IS reengineering team to focus on developing and deploying processes and tools associated with project management and system development. The mission of the IS reengineering team was to improve performance of IS projects, resulting in increased productivity, cycle time, quality, and satisfaction of the projects' customers.

According to a spokesperson at the bank, the process began as follows:

> Information from both current and previous methodologies used by the bank was reviewed, and the best practices of all these previous efforts were incorporated into this document. Regardless of the source, project methodology phases are somewhat standard fare. All projects follow the same steps, with the complexity, size, and type of project dictating to what extent the methodology must be followed. What this methodology emphasizes are project controls and the tie of deliverables and controls to accomplishing the goals.

To determine the weaknesses associated with past project management methodologies, the IS reengineering team conducted various focus groups. These focus groups concluded that there was a:

- Lack of management commitment
- Lack of a feedback mechanism for project managers to determine the updates and revisions needed to the methodology
- Lack of adaptable methodologies for the organization
- Lack of training curriculum for project managers on the methodology
- Lack of focus on consistent and periodic communication on the methodology deployment progress
- Lack of focus on the project management tools and techniques

Based on this feedback, the IS reengineering team successfully developed and deployed a project management and system development methodology. Beginning June 1996 through December 1996, the target audience of 300 project managers became aware and applied a project management methodology and standard tool (MS Project).

The bank did an outstanding job of creating a methodology that reflects guidelines rather than policies and provides procedures that can easily be adapted on any project in the bank. Below the selected components of the project management methodology are discussed.

Organizing

With any project, you need to define what needs to be accomplished and decide how the project is going to achieve those objectives. Each project begins with an idea, vision, or business opportunity, a starting point that must be tied to the organization's business objectives. The project charter is the foundation of the project and forms the contract with the parties involved. It includes a statement of business needs, an agreement of what the project is committed to deliver, an identification of project dependencies, the roles and responsibilities of the team members involved, and the standards for how project budget and project management should be approached. The project charter defines the boundaries of the project.

Planning

Once the project boundaries are defined, sufficient information must be gathered to support the goals and objectives and to limit risk and minimize issues. This component of project management should generate sufficient information to clearly establish the deliverables that need to be completed, define the specific tasks that will ensure completion of these deliverables, and outline the proper level of resources. Each deliverable affects whether or not each phase of the project will meet its goals, budget, quality, and schedule. For simplicity sake, some projects take a four-phase approach:

- *Proposal:* Project initiation and definition.
- *Planning:* Project planning and requirements definition.

- *Development:* Requirement development, testing, and training.
- *Implementation:* Rollout of developed requirements for daily operation.

Each phase contains review points to help ensure that project expectations and quality deliverables are achieved. It is important to identify the reviewers for the project as early as possible to ensure the proper balance of involvement from subject matter experts and management.

Managing

Throughout the project, management and control of the process must be maintained. This is the opportunity for the project manager and team to evaluate the project, assess project performance, and control the development of the deliverables. During the project, the following areas should be managed and controlled:

- Evaluate daily progress of project tasks and deliverables by measuring budget, quality, and cycle time.
- Adjust day-to-day project assignments and deliverables in reaction to immediate variances, issues, and problems.
- Proactively resolve project issues and changes to control scope creep.
- Aim for client satisfaction.
- Set up periodic and structured reviews of the deliverables.
- Establish a centralized project control file.

Two essential mechanisms for successfully managing projects are solid status-reporting procedures and issues and change management procedures. Status reporting is necessary for keeping the project on course and in good health. The status report should include the following:

- Major accomplishment to date
- Planned accomplishments for the next period
- Project progress summary:
  - Percent of effort hours consumed
  - Percent of budget costs consumed
  - Percent of project schedule consumed
- Project cost summary (budget versus actual)
- Project issues and concerns
- Impact to project quality
- Management action items

Issues-and-change management protects project momentum while providing flexibility. Project issues are matters that require decisions to be made by the project manager, project team, or management. Management of project issues needs to be defined and properly communicated to the project team to ensure the appropriate level of issue tracking and monitoring. This same principle relates to change management because inevitably the scope of a project will be subject to some type of change. Any change management on the project that impacts the cost, schedule, deliverables, and dependent projects is reported to management. Reporting of issue and change management should be summarized in the status report denoting the number of open and closed items of each. This assists management in evaluating the project health.

Simply having a project management methodology and using it does not lead to maturity and excellence in project management. There must exist a "need" for improving the system toward maturity. Project management systems can change as the organization changes. However, management must be committed to the change and have the vision to let project management systems evolve with the organization.

4.3 CRITICAL COMPONENTS

It is almost impossible to become a world-class company with regard to project management without having a world-class methodology. Companies such as General Motors, Motorola, Ericsson, KeyBank, Johnson Controls Automotive, Lear, ABB, Exel, Computer Associates, and Nortel all have world-class project management methodologies.

The characteristics of a world-class methodology include:

- Maximum of six life-cycle phases
- Life-cycle phases overlap
- End-of-phase gate reviews
- Integration with other processes
- Continuous improvement (i.e., hear the voice of the customer)
- Customer oriented (interface with customer's methodology)
- Companywide acceptance
- Use of templates [level 3 work breakdown structure (WBS)]
- Critical path scheduling (level 3 WBS)
- Simplistic, standard bar chart reporting (standard software)
- Minimization of paperwork

Generally speaking, each life-cycle phase of a project management methodology requires paperwork, control points, and perhaps special administrative requirements. Having too few life-cycle phases is an invitation for disaster, and having too many life-cycle phases may drive up administrative and control costs. Most companies prefer a maximum of six life-cycle phases.

Historically, life-cycle phases were sequential in nature. However, because of the necessity for schedule compression, life-cycle phases today will overlap. The amount of overlap will be dependent upon the magnitude of the risks the project manager will take. The more the overlap, the greater the risk. Mistakes made during overlapping activities are usually more costly to correct than mistakes during sequential activities. Overlapping life-cycle phases requires excellent up-front planning.

End-of-phase gate reviews are critical for control purposes and verification of interim milestones. With overlapping life-cycle phases, there are still gate reviews at the end of each phase, but they are supported by intermediate reviews during the life-cycle phases.

World-class project management methodologies are integrated with other management processes such as change management, risk management, total quality management, and concurrent engineering. This produces a synergistic effect which minimizes paperwork, minimizes the total number of resources committed to the project, and allows the organization to perform capacity planning to determine the maximum workload that the organization can endure.

World-class methodologies are continuously enhanced through key performance indicator (KPI) reviews, lessons-learned updates, benchmarking, and customer recommendations. The methodology itself could become the channel of communication between the customer and contractor. Effective methodologies foster customer trust and minimize customer interference in the project.

Project management methodologies must be easy for workers to use as well as covering most of the situations that can arise on a project. Perhaps the best way is to have the methodology placed in a manual that is user friendly.

Excellent methodologies try to make it easier to plan and schedule projects. This is accomplished by using templates for the top three levels of the WBS. Simply stated, using WBS level 3 templates, standardized reporting with standardized terminology exists. The differences between projects will appear at the lower levels (i.e., levels 4–6) of the WBS. This also leads to a minimization of paperwork.

Today, companies seem to be promoting the use of the project charter concept as a component of a methodology, but not all companies create the project charter at the same point in the project life cycle, as shown in Figure 4–5. The three triangles in Figure 4–5 show possible locations where the charter can be prepared:

● In the first triangle, the charter is prepared immediately after the feasibility study is completed. At this point, the charter contains the results of the feasibility study as well as documentation of any assumptions and constraints that were considered. The charter is then revisited and updated once this project is selected.

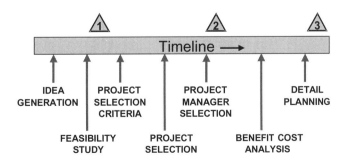

FIGURE 4–5. When to prepare the charter.

- In the second triangle, which seems to be the preferred method, the charter is prepared after the project is selected and the project manager has been assigned. The charter includes the authority granted to the project manager, but for this project only.
- In the third method, the charter is prepared after detail planning is completed. The charter contains the detailed plan. Management will not sign the charter until after detail planning is approved by senior management. Then, and only then, does the company officially sanction the project. Once management signs the charter, the charter becomes a legal agreement between the project manager and all involved line managers as to what deliverables will be met and when.

4.4 PROJECT MANAGEMENT TOOLS

Project management methodologies require software support systems. As little as five years ago, many of the companies described in this book had virtually no project management capabilities. How did these companies implement project management so fast? The answer came with the explosion of personal computer-based software for project planning, estimating, scheduling, and control. These were critical for methodology development.

Until the late 1980s, the project management tools in use were software packages designed for project scheduling. The most prominent were:

- Program evaluation and review technique (PERT)
- Arrow diagramming method (ADM)
- Precedence diagramming method (PDM)

These three networking and scheduling techniques provided project managers with computer capabilities that far surpassed the bar charts and milestone charts that had been in use. The three software programs proved invaluable at the time:

- They formed the basis for all planning and predicting and provided management with the ability to plan for the best possible use of resources to achieve a given goal within schedule and budget constraints.
- They provided visibility and enabled management to control one-of-a-kind programs.
- They helped management handle the uncertainties involved in programs by answering such questions as how time delays influence project completion, where slack exists among elements, and which elements are crucial to meeting the completion date. This feature gave managers a means for evaluating alternatives.
- They provided a basis for obtaining the necessary facts for decision-making.
- They utilized a so-called time network analysis as the basic method of determining manpower, material, and capital requirements as well as providing a means for checking progress.
- They provided the basic structure for reporting information

Unfortunately, scheduling techniques can not replace planning. And scheduling techniques are only as good as the quality of the information that goes into the plan. Criticisms of the three scheduling techniques in the 1980s included the following:

- Time, labor, and intensive effort were required to use them.
- The ability of upper-level management to contribute to decision-making may have been reduced.
- Functional ownership of the estimates was reduced.
- Historical data for estimating time and cost were lost.
- The assumption of uninvited resources was inappropriate.
- The amount of detail required made full use of the scheduling tools inappropriate.

Advancements in the memory capabilities of mainframe computer systems during the 1990s eventually made it possible to overcome many of the deficiencies in the three scheduling techniques being used in project management in the 1970s and 1980s. There emerged an abundance of mainframe software that combined scheduling techniques with both planning and estimating capabilities. Estimating then could include historical databases, which were stored in the mainframe memory files. Computer programs also proved useful in resource allocation. The lessons learned from previous projects could also be stored in historical files. This improved future planning as well as estimating processes.

The drawback was that mainframe project management software packages were very expensive and user unfriendly. The mainframe packages were deemed more appropriate for large projects in aerospace, defense, and large construction. For small and medium-sized companies, the benefits did not warrant the investment.

The effective use of project management software of any kind requires that project teams and managers first understand the principles of project management. All too often, an organization purchases a mainframe package without training its employees in how to use it in the context of project management.

For example, in 1986, a large, nationally recognized hospital purchased a $130,000 mainframe software package. The employees in the hospital's information systems department were told to use the package for planning and reporting the status of all projects. Less than 10 percent of the organization's employees were given any training in project management. Training people in the use of software without first training them in project management principles proved disastrous. The morale of the organization hit an all-time low point and eventually no one even used the expensive software.

Generally speaking, mainframe software packages are more difficult to implement and use than smaller personal computer–based packages. The reason? Mainframe packages require that everyone use the same package, often in the same way. A postmortem study conducted at the hospital identified the following common difficulties during the implementation of its mainframe package:

- Upper-level managers sometimes did not like the reality of the results.
- Upper-level managers did not use the packages for planning, budgeting, and decision-making.

- Day-to-day project planners sometimes did not use the packages for their own projects.
- Some upper-level managers sometimes did not demonstrate support and commitment to training.
- Clear, concise reports were lacking.
- Mainframe packages did not always provide for immediate turnaround of information.
- The hospital had no project management standards in place prior to the implementation of the new software.
- Implementation highlighted the inexperience of some middle managers in project planning and in applying organizational skills.
- Neither the business environment nor the organization's structure supported the hospital project management/planning needs.
- Sufficient/extensive resources (staff, equipment, etc.) were required.
- The business entity did not determine the extent of and appropriate use of the systems within the organization.
- Some employees viewed the system as a substitute for the extensive interpersonal skills required of the project manager.
- Software implementation did not succeed because the hospital's employees did not have sufficient training in project management principles.

Today, project managers have a large array of personal computer–based software available for planning, scheduling, and controlling projects. Packages such as Microsoft Project have almost the same capabilities as mainframe packages. Microsoft Project can import data from other programs for planning and estimating and then facilitate the difficult tasks of tracking and controlling multiple projects.

The simplicity of personal computer–based packages and their user friendliness have been especially valuable in small and medium-sized companies. The packages are so affordable that even the smallest of companies can master project management and adopt a goal of reaching project management excellence.

Clearly, even the most sophisticated software package can never be a substitute for competent project leadership. By themselves, such packages cannot identify or correct task-related problems. But they can be terrific tools for the project manager to use in tracking the many interrelated variables and tasks that come into play in contemporary project management. Specific examples of such capabilities include the following:

- Project data summary; expenditure, timing, and activity data
- Project management and business graphics capabilities
- Data management and reporting capabilities
- Critical-path analyses
- Customized as well as standardized reporting formats
- Multiproject tracking
- Subnetworking
- Impact analysis
- Early-warning systems

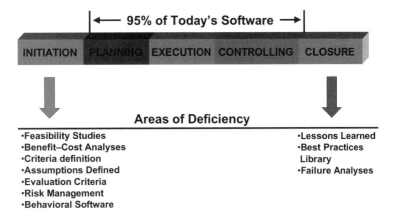

FIGURE 4–6. Project management software.

- Online analyses of recovering alternatives
- Graphical presentations of cost, time, and activity data
- Resource planning and analyses
- Cost and variance analyses
- Multiple calendars
- Resource leveling

Figure 4-6 shows that right now approximately 95 percent of the project management software focus on planning, scheduling, and controlling projects. In the future, we can expect more software to be created for the initiation of a project and the closure of a project.

4.5 GENERAL MOTORS POWERTRAIN GROUP

For companies with small or short-term projects, project management methodologies may not be cost effective or appropriate. For companies with large projects, however, a workable methodology is mandatory. General Motors Powertrain Group is another example of a large company achieving excellence in project management. The company's business is based primarily on internal projects, although some contract projects are taken on for external customers. The size of the group's projects ranges from $100 million to $1.5 billion. Based in Pontiac, Michigan, the GM Powertrain Group has developed and implemented a four-phase project management methodology that has become the core process for its business. The company decided to go to project management in order to get its products out to the market faster. According to Michael Mutchler, former Vice President and Group Executive:

> The primary expectation I have from a product-focused organization is effective execution. This comprehends disciplined and effective product program development, implementation,

and day-to-day operations. Product teams were formed to create an environment in which leaders could gain a better understanding of market and customer needs, to foster systems thinking and cross-functional, interdependent behavior, and to enable all employees to understand their role in executing GM Powertrain strategies and delivering outstanding products. This organizational strategy is aimed at enabling a large organization to be responsive and to deliver quality products that customers want and can afford.

The program management process at GM Powertrain is based upon common templates, checklists, and systems. The following lists several elements that were common across all GM Powertrain programs during the 1990s:

- Charter and contract
- Program team organizational structure with defined roles and responsibilities
- Program plans, timing schedules, and logic networks
- Program-level and part-level tracking systems
- Four-phase product development process
- Change management process

Two critical elements of the GM Powertrain methodology are the program charter and program contract. The program charter defines the scope of the program with measurable objectives, including:

- Business purpose
- Strategic objective
- Results sought from the program
- Engineering and capital budget
- Program timing

The program contract specifies how the program will fulfill the charter. The contract becomes a shared understanding of what the program team will deliver and what the GM Powertrain staff will provide to the team in terms of resources, support, and so on.

4.6 ERICSSON TELECOM AB

General Motors Corporation and the bank are examples of project management methodologies that are internal to the organization (i.e., internal customers). For Ericsson Telecom AB, the problem is more complicated. The majority of Ericsson's projects are for external customers, and Ericsson has divisions all over the world. Can a methodology be developed to satisfy these worldwide constraints?

In 1989, Ericsson Telecom AB developed a project management methodology called PROPS.[1] Though it was initially intended for use at Business Area Public Telecommuni-

---

1. The definition of the acronym PROPS is in Swedish. For simplicity sake, it is referred to as PROPS throughout this book.

cations for technical development projects, it has been applied and appreciated throughout Ericsson worldwide, in all kinds of projects. In the author's opinion, PROPS is one of the most successful methodologies in the world.

New users and new fields of applications have increased the demands on PROPS. Users provide lessons-learned feedback so that their shared experiences can be used to update PROPS. In 1994, a second generation of PROPS was developed, including applications for small projects, concurrent engineering projects, and cross-functional projects and featuring improvements intended to increase quality on projects.

PROPS is generic in nature and can be used in all types of organizations, which strengthens Ericsson's ability to run projects successfully throughout the world. PROPS can be used on all types of projects, including product development, organizational development, construction, marketing, single projects, large and small projects, and cross-functional projects.

PROPS focuses on business, which means devoting all operative activities to customer satisfaction and securing profitability through effective use of company resources. PROPS uses a tollgate concept and project sponsorship to ensure that projects are initiated and procured in a business-oriented manner and that the benefits for the customer as well as for Ericsson are considered.

The PROPS model is extremely generic, which adds flexibility to its application to each project. The four cornerstones of the generic project model are:

- Tollgates
- The project model
- The work models
- Milestones

Tollgates are superordinate decision points in a project at which formal decisions are made concerning the aims and execution of the project, according to a concept held in common throughout the company. In PROPS, five tollgates constitute the backbone of the model. The function and position of the tollgates are standardized for all types of projects. Thus the use of PROPS will ensure that the corporate tollgate model for Ericsson is implemented and applied.

The project sponsor makes the tollgate decision and takes the overall business responsibility for the entire project and its outcome. A tollgate decision must be well prepared. The tollgate decision procedure includes assessment and preparation of an executive summary, which provides the project sponsor with a basis for the decision. The project and its outcome must be evaluated from different aspects: the project's status, its use of resources, and the expected benefit to the customer and to Ericsson. At the five tollgates, the following decisions are made:

- Decision on start of project feasibility study
- Decision on execution of the project
- Decision on continued execution, confirmation of the project or revision of limits, implementation of design
- Decision on making use of the final project results, handover to customer, limited introduction on the market
- Decision on project conclusion

The project model describes which project management activities to perform and which project documents to prepare from the initiation of a prestudy to the project's conclusion. The project sponsor orders the project and makes the tollgate decisions while most of the other activities described in the project model are the responsibility of the project manager. The project model is divided into four phases: prestudy, feasibility study, execution, and conclusion phases.

The purpose of the prestudy phase is to assess feasibility from technical and commercial viewpoints based on the expressed and unexpressed requirements and needs of external and internal customers. During the prestudy phase a set of alternative solutions is formulated. A rough estimate is made of the time schedule and amount of work needed for the project's various implementation alternatives.

The purpose of the feasibility study phase is to form a good basis for the future project and prepare for the successful execution of the project. During the feasibility study, different realization alternatives and their potential consequences are analyzed, as well as their potential capacity to fulfill requirements. The project goals and strategies are defined, project plans are prepared, and the risks involved are assessed. Contract negotiations are initiated, and the project organization is defined at the comprehensive level.

The purpose of the execution phase is to execute the project as planned with respect to time, costs, and characteristics in order to attain the project goals and meet the customer's requirements. Technical work is executed by the line organization according to the processes and working methods that have been decided on. Project work is actively controlled; that is, the project's progress is continuously checked and the necessary action taken to keep the project on track.

The purpose of the conclusion phase is to break up the project organization, to compile a record of the experiences gained, and to see to it that all outstanding matters are taken care of. During the conclusion phase, the resources placed at the project's disposal are phased out, and measures are suggested for improving the project model, the work models, and the processes.

Besides describing the activities that will be performed to arrive at a specific result, the work model also includes definitions of the milestones. However, to get a complete description of the work in a specific project, one or more work models should be defined and linked to the general project model. A work model combined with the general project model is a PROPS application. If there are no suitable work models described for a project, it is the project manager's responsibility to define activities and milestones so that the project plan can be followed and the project actively controlled.

A milestone is an intermediate objective that defines an important, measurable event in the project and represents a result that must be achieved at that point. Milestones link the work models to the project model. Clearly defined milestones are essential for monitoring progress, especially in large and/or long-term projects. Besides providing a way of structuring the time schedule, milestones will give early warning of potential delays. Milestones also help to make the project's progress visible to the project members and the project sponsor. Before each milestone is reached, a milestone review is performed within the project in order to check the results achieved against the milestone criteria. The project manager is responsible for the milestone review.

Ericsson's worldwide success can be partially attributed to the acceptance and use of the PROPS model. Ericsson has shown that success can be achieved with even the simplest of models and without the development of rigid policies and procedures.

4.7 NORTEL

Large companies with multiple product lines can still have a single/standard methodology for project management, but the methodology will have different "process engines." One company that possesses a world-class methodology with multiple engines is Nortel. In 1999, Dave Hudson, Vice President for Time-to-Market Product Development at Nortel Networks, commented:

> Nortel Networks is currently deploying time to market in the product development area. Time to market encompasses the concept of integrated project teams for every substantial product development we undertake. Our project teams use a standard methodology, albeit one with flexibility in the right places. For instance, we use three different "process engines" for the three types of products using the Wheelwright model—derivative products, platform replacements, and breakthrough products. Our methodology uses standard tools, metrics, and executive reporting techniques across all of our R&D projects. Templates and specific best practice examples are available for most steps, along with process guidelines for all steps. We have found senior-level active participation to be necessary and use the concept of a general manager–led team, called the portfolio management team. Their role is to own and direct the evolution of the business unit's portfolio, manage the projects throughout their life cycle using a disciplined "business decision review" process, and, finally, manage the design pipeline (the people resources), including selection of project leaders and project managers and project starts and stops.

4.8 BENEFITS OF A STANDARD METHODOLOGY

For companies that understand the importance of a standard methodology, the benefits are numerous. These benefits can be classified as both short- and long-term benefits. Short-term benefits were described by one company as:

- Decreased cycle time and lower costs
- Realistic plans with greater possibilities of meeting time frames
- Better communications as to "what" is expected from groups and "when"
- Feedback: lessons learned

These short-term benefits focus on KPIs or, simply stated, the execution of project management. Long-term benefits seem to focus more upon critical success factors (CSFs) and customer satisfaction. Long-term benefits of development and execution of a world-class methodology include:

- Faster "time to market" through better scope control
- Lower overall program risk
- Better risk management, which leads to better decision-making
- Greater customer satisfaction and trust, which lead to increased business and expanded responsibilities for the tier 1 suppliers

- Emphasis on customer satisfaction and value-added rather than internal competition between functional groups
- Customer treating the contractor as a "partner" rather than as a commodity
- Contractor assisting the customer during strategic planning activities

Perhaps the largest benefit of a world-class methodology is the acceptance and recognition by your customers. If one of your critically important customers develops its own methodology, that customer could "force" you to accept it and use it in order to remain a supplier. But if you can show that your methodology is superior or equal to the customer's, your methodology will be accepted, and an atmosphere of trust will prevail.

One contractor recently found that its customer had so much faith in and respect for its methodology that the contractor was invited to participate in the customer's strategic planning activities. The contractor found itself treated as a partner rather than as a commodity or just another supplier. This resulted in sole-source procurement contracts for the contractor.

Developing a standard methodology that encompasses the majority of a company's projects and is accepted by the entire organization is a difficult undertaking. The hardest part might very well be making sure that the methodology supports both the corporate culture and the goals and objectives set forth by management. Methodologies that require changes to a corporate culture may not be well accepted by the organization. Non-supportive cultures can destroy even seemingly good project management methodologies.

During the 1980s and 1990s, several consulting companies developed their own project management methodologies, most frequently for information systems projects, and then pressured their clients into purchasing the methodology rather than helping their clients develop a methodology more suited to the clients' needs. Although there may have been some successes, there appeared to be significantly more failures than successes. Previously, we discussed a hospital that purchased a $130,000 project management methodology with the belief that this would be the solution to its information system needs. Unfortunately, senior management made the purchasing decision without consulting the workers who would be using the system. In the end, the package was never used.

Another company purchased a similar package, discovering too late that the package was inflexible and the organization, specifically the corporate culture, would need to change to use the project management methodology effectively. The vendor later admitted that the best results would occur if no changes were made to the methodology.

These types of methodologies are extremely rigid and based on policies and procedures. The ability to custom design the methodology to specific projects and cultures was nonexistent, and eventually these methodologies fell by the wayside—but after the vendors made significant profits. Good methodologies must be flexible.

4.9 SHERWIN-WILLIAMS

There are several ways that a company can develop a methodology for project management. Outsourcing the development process to another company can be beneficial. Some companies have template methodologies that can be used as a basis for developing your own methodology. This can be beneficial if the template methodology has enough flexibility to be adaptable to your organization. The downside is that this approach may have the disadvantage that the end result may not fit the needs of your organization or your company's culture. Hiring outside consultants may improve the situation a little, but the end result may still be the same unfavorable result as well as being more costly. This approach may require keeping contractors on your payroll for a long time such that they can fully understand your culture and the way you do business.

Benchmarking may be effective, but by the time the benchmarking is completed, the company could have begun the development of its own methodology. Another downside risk of benchmarking is that you may not be able to get all of the information you need or the supporting information to make the methodology work for you.

Companies that develop their own methodology internally seem to have greater success, especially if they incorporate their own best practices and lessons learned from other activities. This occurred in companies such as General Motors, Lear, Johnson Controls, Texas Instruments, Exel, Sherwin-Williams, and many other organizations. Rinette Scarso, PMP®, Project Manager, discusses the Sherwin-Williams situation with a case study.

Company Background

The Sherwin-Williams Company is engaged in the manufacture, distribution, and sale of coatings and related products to professional, industrial, commercial, and retail customers primarily in North and South America. The company's Paint Stores Segment consists of 2488 company-operated specialty paint stores. The Consumer Segment develops, manufactures, and distributes a variety of paint, coatings, and related products to third-party customers and the Paint Stores Segment. The Automotive Finishes Segment develops, manufactures, and distributes a variety of motor vehicle finish, refinish, and touch-up products. The International Coatings Segment develops, licenses, manufactures, and distributes a variety of paint, coatings, and related products worldwide. The Administrative Segment (Corporate Division) includes the administrative expenses of the company's and certain consolidated subsidiaries' headquarters sites.

The corporate information technology (IT) department for the Sherwin-Williams Company provides shared services support for the five operating divisions, described above, that make up the organization.

Case Study Background

During the summer of 2002, the corporate IT department engaged in activities surrounding the conversion of international, interstate, intrastate, and local telecommunications services from the company's present voice telecommunications carrier to a new carrier. Project management disciplines and best practices, using a structured project management methodology, were utilized on this project, ultimately leading to a successful project outcome.

The project was implemented using a phased approach consisting of the major phases as described below. The phases were established to include many of the principles stated in the PMBOK® Guide and also included many of the best practices that had been developed previously at The Sherwin-Williams Company. The phases could overlap, if necessary, allowing for a gradual evolvement from one phase to the next. The overlapping also allowed us to accelerate schedules, if need be, but possibly at an additional risk. Project reviews were held at the end of each phase to determine the feasibility of moving forward into the next phase, to make "go/no-go" decisions, to evaluate existing and future risks, and to determine if course corrections are needed.

- *Initiate:* The first phase is the initiate phase where the project team is formed, a project kickoff meeting is held, needs and requirements are identified, and roles and responsibilities are defined.
- *Planning:* The planning phase is the next phase and is regarded by most project managers as the most important phase. Most of the project's effort is expended in the planning phase, and it is believed that the appropriate time and effort invested in this phase ensure the development of a solid foundation for the project. Management wholeheartedly supports the efforts we put forth in this phase because this is where many of our best practices have occurred. Also, a solid foundation in this phase allows for remaining phases of the project to be accomplished more efficiency giving senior management a higher degree of confidence in the ability of our project managers to produce the desired deliverables and meet customer expectations.

   A series of meetings are typically held throughout this phase to identify at the lowest level the project needs, requirements, expectations, processes, and activities/steps for the processes. The results of these meetings are several deliverables, including a needs-and-requirements document, a project plan, a risk management plan, an issue log, and an action item list. Additional documents maintained include quality management and change management plans. Together these documents provide management with an overview of the entire project and the effort involved to accomplish the goal of transitioning services by the target date established by our management.
- *Execution:* The third phase in implementation is execution. This phase is evolved into gradually once the majority of planning has been completed. All activities outlined in the processes during the planning phase come to fruition at this time as actual communication line orders began to take place as well as the installation of equipment where necessary. Services began to be transitioned by division/segment and implementation moved forward aggressively for this project due to a stringent time frame. It is of vital importance that activities in this phase be monitored closely in order to facilitate the proactive identification of issues that may negatively impact the timeline, cost, quality, or resources of the project.

   To facilitate monitoring and control of the project, weekly status meetings were held with the vendor and the project team, as well as short internal daily meetings to review activities planned for each day. Ad hoc meetings also occurred as necessary.
- *Closure:* The final phase of the project is closure. In this phase, there is typically a closure meeting to identify any remaining open issues and to determine the level of client satisfaction. This phase also included any "clean-up" from the project, administrative closeout, the communication of postimplementation support procedures, and a review of lessons learned.

Best practices that worked notably well for The Sherwin-Williams Company included the establishment of success criteria, consisting of project objectives and a needs/requirements analysis, regular communications both within the project team and with stakeholders, dedicated resources, defined roles and responsibilities, knowledge transfer between cross-functional teams, teamwork, the development of a fun, synergistic working environment, and reviewing lessons learned.

One of the best practices in project management is that maturity and excellence in project management can occur quickly when senior management not only actively supports project management but also articulates to the organization their vision of where they expect project management to be in the future. This vision can motivate the organization to excel, and best practices improvements to a project management methodology seem to occur at a rapid rate. Such was the case at The Sherwin-Williams Company. Tom Lucas, Vice President of IT at The Sherwin-Williams Company, comments on his vision for the company:

> The future of project management at The Sherwin-Williams Company includes the integration of project management disciplines and best practices through the establishment of a virtual project management office (PMO), combined with portfolio management techniques to deliver high-value project results on a consistent basis. The Sherwin-Williams Company anticipates that the use of a virtual PMO will not only instill the best practices of project management as core competencies but also aid in the growth of the organization's project management maturity.
>
> We define a virtual PMO as a function that has permanent full-time members at its core. This core group would be responsible for PMO operation and administration crossing all IT operating groups. This core group would be the standards-setting body, provide for best practices identification and sharing, and coordinate the work of the "practicing" project managers, which reside in individual operating groups.
>
> These practicing/virtual project managers would be assigned to the PMO as the project workload requires, and when not attached to the PMO they would reside in the various functional IT work groups to assist with tactical project management within these functions. The intent is to expand and contract PMO resources as you would expand and contract project teams as the workload dictates.
>
> One goal is to unify the goals and objectives of individual departments by applying a universal, yet flexible project management framework in pursuit of better across-the-board results. The Sherwin-Williams Company desires to learn from past successes as well as mistakes, make processes more efficient, and develop people's skills and talents to work more effectively through the establishment of standardized procedures within the company.
>
> In order to complete projects successfully on a consistent basis, The Sherwin-Williams Company realizes the value of establishing a virtual PMO. A virtual PMO will facilitate the alignment of projects with strategic organizational goals and objectives through project portfolio management. PMO best practices will encompass the establishment of standard project management guidelines and templates, centralized communications, training and mentoring of project managers, and a centralized repository for lessons learned.
>
> The Sherwin-Williams Company understands that this undertaking will take time to accomplish based on the current level of project management maturity in the organization and on the fact that the PMO structure will continually evolve over time as the level of project management maturity increases. The Sherwin-Williams Company plans to persevere in its efforts in anticipation of the many benefits that will come as the organization moves up the maturity ladder, including recognition by customers and industry peers.

4.10 ANTARES MANAGEMENT SOLUTIONS

Some companies have found that some of the readily available methodologies that can be purchased or leased have enough flexibility to satisfy their needs. This is particularly true in the IT area. The following information was provided by John Frohlich, Director, Information Systems Development at Antares, and Dan Halicki, Planning Coordinator at Antares:

Introduction

Industry analysts believe that only 19% of IT projects are delivered on time, and fewer are within budget. In response to this problem, various project management approaches have emerged with the primary objective of ensuring project success. The business challenge is to find the proper balance between rigorous methodology requirements and the realities of containing administrative project overhead. More is not always better in the world of project management.

Since 1989, the systems development team of Antares Management Solutions has managed all IT projects by utilizing selected aspects of the Navigator Systems Series methodology originally developed by Ernst & Young (now Cap Gemini Ernst & Young). Navigator was chosen, in large part, because its flexibility and adaptability provided the most customization at a good price. Over the past 14 years, this approach has a solid track record of project successes that have helped Antares to grow and prosper in the competitive world of IT outsourcing.

What, then, are the best practices that Antares has followed to bring the right amount of discipline to its project management approach? The following discusses the techniques and deliverables that constitute the standard project management elements of structure, plan, and control. Additionally, it is important to look beyond the elements of the methodology itself to include the support system that makes it all work, such as executive management buy-in, training, and follow-up activity.

- *Make use of project management concepts and terminology throughout the enterprise, not just in information systems.* Antares uses a strategic planning process that requires collaboration between client management and IT planning to effectively align business vision with technical solutions. To achieve the desired goals, related project proposals are drafted using the standardized project charter format. Consequently, the client management team has a clear idea of how a project is to be defined and structured from the very beginning.
- *Provide ongoing project management training throughout the enterprise.* The term project management can mean different things to different people. An instructor-led class explains how Antares applies the CGE&Y "Navigator Project Management Methodology" to ensure that all project participants, including the customer community, have a common understanding of the process. The class provides instruction and a hands-on workshop on the major components of the project management process, including terms, diagrams, deliverables, charter writing, plans, milestones, and changes.
- *Structure every project in a consistent manner, including scope, responsibilities, risks, and high-level milestones.* Central to the project management process is the creation of the project charter, which documents and formalizes the agreement of all concerned parties, including business sponsors, project manager, and project team members. The charter spells out what will be accomplished, who is responsible for getting it done,

known problems to be addressed, and major milestones to be met. The project plan details out the tasks, time frames, dependencies, and resources needed to deliver the project within agreed-upon time frames and budget.

● *Communicate and update project plans on an ongoing basis using online tools when appropriate.* Once an approved project charter is in place, the project plan becomes the next focus of attention. The plan and the regular status reports that document progress of the plan are the primary communication vehicles for keeping management and staff informed. Since 2000, Antares has instituted an online project status center to keep project planning and status information both current and readily available.

● *Maintain an official project issues list, including who is responsible, what are the potential impacts, and how the issue is being resolved.* As problems arise during the execution of a project, it is vital to maintain an accurate "issues log" to properly document the problems and what is being done to solve them. In project meetings, the log serves as a meaningful tool that not only assures concerned areas that their problems have not been forgotten but also prevents similar problems from recurring. Along with the charter and the regular progress reports, the issues log can be accessed via the online project status center.

● *Use a formal change control process, including an executive steering committee to resolve major changes.* As issues arise that could require additional resources, the nemesis known as "scope creep" can begin to surface and impede a smooth-running project. A formal change control process is essential to help the project manager with the predicament of pleasing the customer or going over budget or missing milestones. For situations that become threatening to the project's ultimate success, the assistance of an executive steering committee can determine the best course of action.

● *Periodically audit the project management process and selected projects to determine how well the methodology is working and to identify opportunities for improvement.* With the establishment of project management standards and the sizable investment in training, it makes sense to step back occasionally and assess if the overall objectives are being met. Where projects ran into difficulty, would a different approach have helped? Where projects went well, what aspects of the project execution ought to be shared by other projects? These are the kinds of questions the audit exercise tries to address.

● *Conclude every major project with an open presentation of the results to share knowledge gained, demonstrate new technology, and gain official closure.* Many organizations rush through the project conclusion phase in order to get on with the next assignment. However, taking the time to fully document accomplishments, outstanding issues, and deferred deliverables is a worthwhile exercise that gives proper credit for successful completions, reduces misunderstandings over omissions and facilitates transitions to follow-up projects, and ensures knowledge transfer useful for future project management success.

Conclusion

One of the major reasons that projects lose control is because project managers operate reactively rather than anticipating possible stumbling blocks. When the stumbling block finally appears, they are hesitant to make effective decisions, which often results in situations that can kill a project. Antares has found that utilizing the eight best practices above the company has been able to foster a more proactive environment in partnership with the customer, resulting in successful project delivery. The outlined approach strikes a balance that requires minimum project overhead while obtaining maximum benefit.

4.11 WESTFIELD GROUP

Developing a project management methodology may not be as complicated as one believes. There are four essential building blocks that, if present, allows for the development of an effective project management methodology in a reasonably short period of time. The four building blocks are:

- Recognition at the executive levels of the need for the methodology
- Executive-level support combined with a clear vision
- Establishing an organization reporting to senior management committed to the development process
- Using the PMBOK® Guide as a starting point for methodology development

Kathy Rhoads, Director, Project Management COE for the Westfield Group, provides us with some insight on the growth of its project management organization and methodology:

> Westfield Insurance recognized that the needs of our customers had changed with regard to information technology and information systems projects. Also, the relationship with our customers had changed. Our customers were now expecting complete solutions to their business needs rather than just products. We needed an organization that was designed to "partner" with our business customers and specialized in providing high-quality business solutions. We replaced our information systems group with a Business Solutions Center (BSC). Senior management's vision for the BSC was to provide solutions to the Westfield Group that would exceed customer expectation. Our focus was on adding value.

> Operational activities include:

- Dedicated support to existing systems
- Answering customers' questions
- Providing technical support

Some high-level accomplishments in building the BSC project management center of excellence (COE) are:

2000:
- Built the technical skills of internal project managers
- Established the beginnings of the Westfield Insurance project
- Project management methodology (PMM)
- Introduced the corporate prioritization process

2001:
- Recruited senior project managers
- Refined the PMM
- Refined the corporate prioritization process, emphasizing executive-level partnerships

2002:
- Established Enterprise Capacity Planning and Prioritization
- Recognition of technically sound and experienced project management team

- Increased successful delivery of projects
- PMM applied more consistently by the project managers and project team members

2003:
- Refined Enterprise Capacity Planning and Prioritization
- Established strategies for maintaining a proficient project management team
- Established continuous improvement strategies for PMM

2004:
- Executed the continuous improvement strategies for PMM

2005:
- Reorganized the structure of the project management COE and program office
- Created a Web version of the PMM

When it came time to develop our PMM, we decided to use the PMBOK® Guide as a guideline to provide some degree of structure to the development process. Figure 4–7 shows the life-cycle phases of our methodology. Within each of these phases, we then identified the activities to be performed and cross-referenced the activities according to the nine process areas of the PMBOK® Guide. This is shown in Figure 4–8. Each of the activities in Figure 4–8 can then be exploded into a flowchart showing the detailed activities needed for accomplishment of the deliverables for this activity. For example, the "project startup process" activity in Figure 4–8 is cross-listed under Human Resource Management. The detailed activities are shown by the flowchart in Figure 4–9.

Kathy Rhoads, Director, Project Management COE, summarizes Westfield Insurance's experience with project management:

> Putting the right building blocks in place created the foundation necessary for moving ahead. Currently, we are experiencing significant increased success in delivery and improved overall results with key business initiatives. Our results validate the need for project management. Increased support from all levels of the organization is evident as key corporate initiatives are led by our staff project managers. We are focusing on continuous improvement and realize a great deal of work remains. Building toward excellence in project management continues at the Westfield Group.

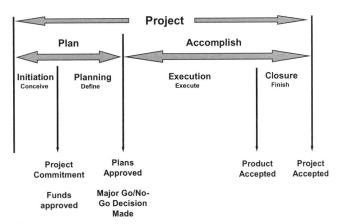

FIGURE 4–7. Life-cycle phases.

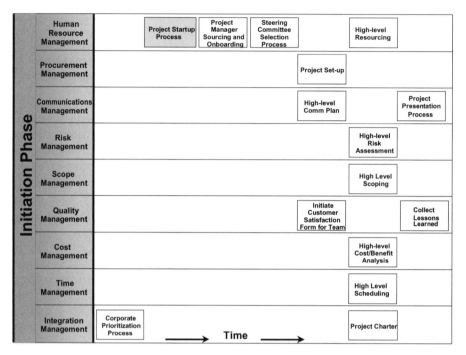

FIGURE 4–8. Initiation phase activities.

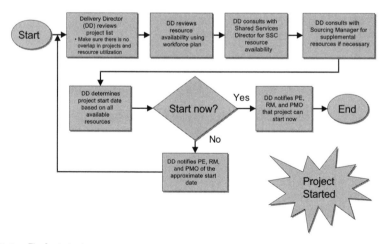

FIGURE 4–9. Project startup process.

4.12 IMPLEMENTING METHODOLOGY

The physical existence of a methodology does not convert itself into a world-class methodology. Methodologies are nothing more than pieces of paper. What converts a standard methodology into a world-class methodology is the culture of the organization and the way the methodology is implemented.

The existence of a world-class methodology does not by itself constitute excellence in project management. The corporatewide acceptance and use of it does lead to excellence. It is through excellence in execution that an average methodology becomes a world-class methodology.

One company developed an outstanding methodology for project management. About one-third of the company used the methodology and recognized its true long-term benefits. The other two-thirds of the company would not support the methodology. The president eventually restructured the organization and mandated the use of the methodology.

The importance of execution cannot be underestimated. One characteristic of companies with world-class project management methodologies is that they have world-class managers throughout their organization.

Rapid development of a world-class methodology mandates an executive champion, not merely an executive sponsor. Executive sponsors are predominantly on an as-needed basis. Executive champions, on the other hand, are hands-on executives who drive the development and implementation of the methodology from the top down. Most companies recognize the need for the executive champion. However, many companies fail to recognize that the executive champion position is a life-long experience. One Detroit company reassigned its executive champion after a few successes were realized using the methodology. As a result, no one was promoting continuous improvement to the methodology.

Good project management methodologies allow you to manage your customers and their expectations. If customers believe in your methodology, then they usually understand it when you tell them that no further scope changes are possible once you enter a specific life-cycle phase. One automotive subcontractor carried the concept of trust to its extreme. The contractor invited the customers to attend the contractor's end-of-phase review meetings. This fostered extreme trust between the customer and the contractor. However, the customer was asked to leave during the last 15 minutes of the end-of-phase review meetings when project finances were being discussed.

Project management methodologies are an "organic" process, which implies that they are subject to changes and improvements. Typical areas of methodology improvement might include:

- Improved interfacing with suppliers
- Improved interfacing with customers
- Better explanation of subprocesses
- Clearer definition of milestones
- Clearer role delineation of senior management
- Recognition of need for additional templates
- Recognition of need for additional metrics

- Template development for steering committee involvement
- Enhancement of the project management guidebook
- Ways to educate customers on how the methodology works
- Ways of shortening baseline review meetings

4.13 CERIDIAN

Bob Ruhala, PMP®, Program Manager, Project Management Center of Excellence at Ceridian, provides insight on how project management implementation can take place[2]:

A project is only approved when the business owner is able to demonstrate how the project outcome directly maps to the strategic objectives of the company. Also, a total-cost-of-ownership template must be completed to provide a return on investment that meets company financial guidelines. Assuming these two key criteria are met and the project is approved, the project's success is then based on meeting the requirements defined by the key stakeholders reflected in the initial requirements review (IRR).

During the planning phase, the project manager is responsible for the project management deliverables consisting of a risk assessment questionnaire, work breakdown structure, and IRR. All these deliverables are created by the individuals identified as the core team and are reviewed for approval at the end of the planning phase by the key stakeholders, primarily the executive sponsor and business owner. The IRR contains the following:

- Business objectives
- Critical success factors
- Technical objectives
- Project organization
- Quality objectives
- Project staffing plan
- Project strategy
- Project assumptions
- Project deliverables
- Project constraints
- Project scope
- Project dependencies (mandatory)
- Project stakeholders
- Project dependencies (discretionary)
- Roles and responsibilities
- Project dependencies and linkages (external)
- Project risks
- Overall milestone schedule
- Project budget

---

2. The remainder of this section is courtesy of Bob Ruhala and Ceridian.

A critical success factor (CSF) for a project is defined by "what the project needs from the executive sponsor and business owner to make the project a success." Examples of these are:

- Trained support resources at the destination locations
- Availability of resources to complete project work at all locations
- Availability of information on existing systems and disaster recovery plans

The CSF is reviewed during the IRR with the key stakeholders. The CSFs are discussed in detail during the initial stage gate review and will continue to be a CSF and/or made an assumption/issue/risk.

The key performance indicators for success throughout the project life cycle are measured by earned value indicators. These indicators are displayed in PlanView, the company's project management and resource utilization tool. These measurements provide a quick snapshot of the health of a project. The project status is available to any stakeholder who has been given access to the project portal in PlanView. The thresholds shown in Figure 4–10 are used.

A minimum of two stage gate reviews are held for each project; however, based on the duration and complexity, significantly more reviews may be necessary. During the reviews any variance to the BCWP, ACWP, SV, CV, EAC, and BAC are explained by the project manager to the stakeholders. In addition to the scheduled reviews, a special management review is conducted by the project manager if the project is 10 days off critical path and/or 15 percent off budget. The guidelines for a special management review can vary based on the agreement of the stakeholders in the IRR.

After the project administrative closure is complete, a customer satisfaction survey is sent to the business owner, executive sponsor, and other key stakeholders. Questions related to communication, quality, and understanding objectives are just a few types of questions that are contained in the survey. Obviously, a key consideration for the success of a project is the completion of all deliverables defined in the IRR. In the customer satisfaction survey result example below, a 3 is considered a successful rating; however, due to other considerations, such as communication, timeliness in handling issues, and/or risks, the rating can fluctuate. The example in Figure 4–11 is an average over a period of 18 months.

Indicator	Description	Red Value Less Than	Yellow Value Between & Including	Green Value Greater Than
Risk	Risk Value/EAC	0.5	0.50–0.25	0.25
Budget	(Baseline Effort—EAC)/ Baseline Effort	-0.25	-0.25 to -0.14	-0.14
SPI	Earned Value / Planned Value	0.75	0.75–0.84	0.84

FIGURE 4–10. Thresholds.

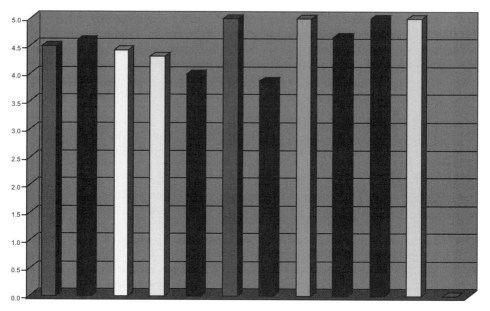

FIGURE 4–11. Executive customer satisfaction.

In an effort to achieve the highest level of proficiency in project management, a "solid foundation" was required within the project management office (PMO). Therefore, the goals below were created for the PMO and achieved in 2003/2004:

● Implement a robust, proactive program management office and environment.
● Implement a robust, proactive process management environment.
● Implement a robust, proactive portfolio management environment.
● Participate in the global community as a world-class project/program management organization.
● Implement and roll out a robust resource management system and process.

Throughout 2005, the environments and processes created as a result of the goals are continuously being improved by Six Sigma initiatives managed by the PMO. All project managers within the PMO are PMP®s and Six Sigma Green Belt certified or they are working toward becoming certified in 2005. In order to continue on the path of project management excellence, ongoing training and exposure to internal/external organizations are constantly in motion.

As a result of the process discipline within the PMO and ongoing training, on a weekly basis project managers are brought together to share lessons learned, share best practices, or present topics that will help increase project management knowledge and effectiveness at running projects successfully. In addition, other department leaders periodically present to educate and share ideas on how we can work together more effectively in a cross-functional nature. The collaboration has been beneficial for not only the PMO but also other departments that either have members involved in projects or are stakeholders on projects that are run by the PMO.

As a result of the process discipline within the PMO, ongoing training, and collaboration between the PMO and other departments, we are viewed as professionals, demonstrated by a comment from Rodney Bowers, Director in Network Services, "The PMO is comprised of talented, experienced people who have many years of project management experience. They are consummate project management professionals who are highly regarded both inside and outside of Ceridian." With feedback like this, the commitment, hard work, and dedication of the PMO members are worthwhile and fulfilling.

4.14 OVERCOMING DEVELOPMENT AND IMPLEMENTATION BARRIERS

Making the decision that the company needs a project management methodology is a lot easier than actually doing it. There are several barriers and problems that surface well after the design and implementation team begins their quest. Typical problem areas include:

- Should we develop our own methodology or benchmark best practices from other companies and try to use their methodology in our company?
- Can we get the entire organization to agree upon a singular methodology for all types of projects or must we have multiple methodologies?
- If we develop multiple methodologies, how easy or difficult will it be for continuous improvement efforts to take place?
- How should we handle a situation where only part of the company sees a benefit in using this methodology and the rest of the company wants to do its own thing?
- How do we convince the employees that project management is a strategic competency and the project management methodology is a process to support this strategic competency?
- For multinational companies, how do we get all worldwide organizations to use the same methodology? Must it be Intranet based?

These are typical questions that plague companies during the methodology development process. These challenges can be overcome, and with great success, as illustrated by the companies identified in the following sections.

4.15 QA

Developing a project management methodology is a lot easier than getting people to accept it and then use it. And sometimes we get it done but without achieving the desired results. The most common reason is that project management methodologies are not aligned with business systems. Brian Sutton has provided his insights on some of the issues related to deploying the methodology[3]:

Deploying and Embedding Project Management Methods

Projects by their nature involve doing things that are new and different. Whenever we embark upon new ways of doing things we inevitably introduce uncertainty, and as uncertainty increases, so does the possibility of error and/or failure. It is not surprising then that projects experience significantly higher error and failure rates than are associated with "business-as-usual" operational management.

When I look at projects in crisis, it is rare for me to find an atmosphere of incompetence. Rather, the norm is that failing projects are staffed by hard-working, well-meaning professionals who, for one reason or another, have been overtaken by events. By contrast, when I look at highly successful projects, rather than the triumph of method, I tend to find individual acts of heroism—cases where a project manager has rescued an ailing project by inspired and sustained brilliance. Yet most of us are not brilliant; indeed most of us need all the help we can get, all of which brings me to the conclusion that for projects to have any chance of success the following conditions must apply:

1. Our people need to understand, live, breathe, and apply well-proven techniques and practices
2. Our organizational processes must be clear, consistently applied, understood by all, and focused on providing management control and alignment with business goals.
3. There must be a clear transparent thread between business strategy and the projects through which that strategy is brought into being. Senior managers must understand their role in project delivery and must provide appropriate steering, advocacy, and championship.

For most organizations this can only be achieved by the adoption and deployment of a project management methodology. Methodologies went out of fashion for a while and even now are sadly much misunderstood and often maligned. Despite their resurgence in popularity, let's be quite clear, a methodology is not and can never be:

1. A panacea or quick fix
2. A cure to all organizational ills
3. An alternative to knowledge, skill, and experience
4. A substitute for management attention

The paradoxical quality of a methodology is that to be successful it needs to be understood, valued, and championed by a management level above that which employs it on a daily basis. To make a real difference, a methodology must go beyond mere guidance on tools and techniques and must encompass project governance structures that reach upward through the organization and ensure alignment between business strategy and project selection. In addition, it must ensure that management decisions that are good for the parts

---

3. Brian Sutton, Director of Learning for QA, is a chartered engineer, a fellow of the Institute of IT Training, a member of the British Computer Society, and a certified IT professional. He holds membership in the PMI® and the APM and is a Prince practitioner. He consults and lectures on project and program management.

are also good for the whole and that the planned business benefits are actually achieved when projects go live.

A common theme across most of the organizations with whom I work is that they are staffed by highly educated, skillful professionals who find themselves trapped within processes that are not aligned with business imperatives and provide conflicting messages about relative priorities. In many cases of project failure the causes of the failure can be traced back to actions or decisions that were taken at or before the start of the project. In these cases the project was doomed from birth. What I find is that a business case may have been created in order to get the cash to launch the project but no measures of success have been articulated, no business metrics of current and desired performance are in place, and no clear benefits realization plan has been produced. A methodology may tell you that metrics and measures are good things to have but only deep organizational commitment will ensure that they are produced and become living documents that guide the conduct and delivery of the project.

We have an abundance of evidence and experience which highlight the key points of failure in projects. We also have a pretty good idea of the practices that we can put in place to ameliorate or eliminate the worst of these issues. What we need is the vision to see that project management can only produce real organizational benefit when we have the professionalism to insist on doing the right things at the right times to an appropriate level of detail and the commitment to ensure that we deliver business benefit rather than disembodied artifacts.

Case Study: Global Industrial Company

We were engaged to facilitate the development and adoption of a consistent project management method to service the global IT community of a large industrial conglomerate. The existing position was that multiple techniques and fragments of methods were being used and pockets of project management excellence existed. However, with an increasing need to complete cross-regional IT implementations, the lack of a single approach was seen as a limit to success. A typical comment from a senior manager was, "We are taking on bigger projects that cross country borders, functional borders so project managers need a different set of skills to what we were currently working with and that are going to be increasingly so."

Some regions employed methods that were no longer supported; some favored the adoption of PMI® best practices, while others were busily adopting the Prince2 method. Overlaying this was a recently developed and widely accepted "stage-and-gate" approach to portfolio management.

The portfolio management method had been put in place to specifically manage the stream of innovation projects that are the lifeblood of organizations of this nature. The approach is shown diagrammatically in Figure 4–12.

In cases like this the purpose of portfolio management is to manage the mix of innovation projects but also, and perhaps most importantly, to manage risk and exposure on the projects that will not be successful. A fundamental principle of an innovation funnel is that to get one good successful project out at the end it may be necessary to put 4–10 ideas in at the start. The funnel manages risk by carefully managing the funding and hence exposure of each project by only committing funds one stage at a time and subjecting the projects to rigorous evaluation and culling. It could be said that the purpose of this project life cycle is to "kill off" projects at the earliest possible stage and thus divert funding to those more likely to offer commercial success.

The stage-and-gate approach is of itself a project life cycle. It provides clear management oversight of the commercial realities of projects throughout their life and is a

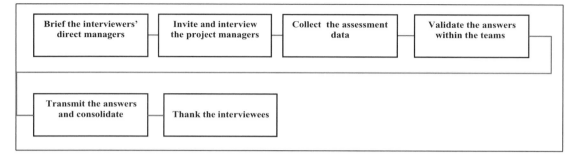

FIGURE 4–12. Portfolio management stage-and-gate model.

great mechanism for managing risk and reward. It is not however a substitute for a project management life cycle as the stage and gate exists to kill projects whereas a project management life cycle is designed to complete projects. Our task was therefore to construct and deploy an effective project management life cycle that could sit alongside and complement the rigor of the portfolio approach.

Toward a Unified Method

When looking to implement change and introduce a method into an organization, it is important to understand where and how failure is occurring and how different root causes respond to different solutions. Generally I find that problems fall into two broad categories, the first being business alignment and the second being consistent technical delivery.

In the case of this company it was perceived that issues existed at both levels. The following comments from senior managers illustrate the broad issues:

● "We don't do projects terribly well. We do lots of projects and quite a lot of them get through to the end but never really deliver in terms of the benefits. The cost savings we thought we would get are not being delivered."
● "To me it's about more than just completing work within a time scale—it's making sure that that work is fully utilized within the business and that it delivers the business results."

Comments like this point to a general weakness in governance. Interestingly, high-level governance had been adopted through the portfolio approach, which focused on business case and viability, but still problems persisted. Typical problems tend to be:

● Poor alignment between project objectives and broader business goals
● Poor business case
● Badly specified project outcomes measured in real business terms
● No benefits realization plan
● Lack of sponsor interest and proactive steering
● Lack of user involvement
● Black box development and launch onto an unsuspecting public
● Scope creep
● Poor risk management and no linkage between project risk and organizational reward
● Lack of devolved authority limits and tolerances from the steering group to the project manager

Interestingly, despite the increased emphasis given by the PMI in its third edition of the PMBOK® Guide, the area of governance remains inadequately covered in best practice. It is however at the heart of the Prince2 method pioneered by the United Kingdom. We therefore recommended the adoption of a three-tier governance structure similar to that espoused by Prince2. In simple form the structure is shown in Figure 4–13. This provides a simple structure that can be adapted and adopted rapidly to suit varying project needs.

We also found a series of management comments that pointed to deficiencies or inconsistencies in the application of project management techniques, namely:

- "We did not have the skills and knowledge to run major programs."
- "There have been a number of programs that have not gone as well as they could have."

Comments such as these point to more prosaic failures. Typically in cases such as this, we might expect to see the following problems:

- Poor definition and/or control of scope
- Poor or inappropriate level of planning
- Poor estimation of the effort required to complete tasks
- Poor allocation or inappropriate use of resources
- Lack of understanding of the nature of risk and poor management of risk
- Uncontrolled or inappropriate change control practices
- Poor or nonexistent reporting of progress against schedule and budget
- Inadequate closure processes
- No learning from experience
- No culture of review or peer review

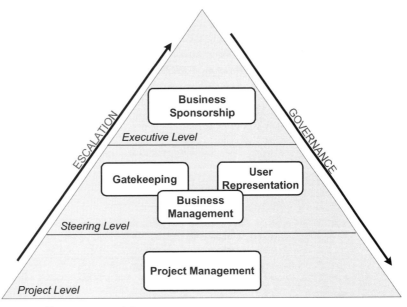

FIGURE 4–13. Governance model.

In these cases the techniques and best practices set out in the PMBOK® Guide can, if applied intelligently and consistently, make a great difference to project delivery. In this case we recommended adoption of the standard five-stage life cycle from the PMBOK® Guide and tailoring the associated techniques, processes, controls, and templates to provide a simple environment within which projects could be managed throughout their life. This is shown in Figure 4–14. The whole method was encapsulated in a new project handbook that ran to just 37 pages. We felt it important that anyone should be able to pick up the method, read it in less than an hour, and fully comprehend why it was structured in the way it was and what business benefit could be accrued through managing projects in this way.

Embedding New Practice

The method and recommended practices were developed through a series of facilitated workshops involving a group of around 20 top professionals drawn from all regions across the company. In this manner the process of consensus building was well on the way to international acceptance within the eight months it took to agree on, develop, and refine the method. The challenge was then how to quickly roll out and scale the practices across the diverse and geographically spread community.

The guiding principle for the design had been to utilize existing best practices wherever possible. This opened the door to the use of generic e-learning materials to convey knowledge of the project management techniques and short face-to-face sessions for the bespoke elements of the method and the company-specific templates. A blended learning program that included classroom training, e-learning, virtual classrooms, bespoke workbooks, and coaching was built and piloted in two regions. The mentors and internal coaches were included to help the transfer of knowledge into practice by providing a focus for the examination of how the new techniques could be deployed within existing projects and programs. The shape of the program is shown in Figure 4–15.

Refinements have been made to the program prior to a planned global rollout across the 3000 strong IT community. During the first six months of 2005 some 200 students from the United States, United Kingdom, Latin America, Europe, Africa, and the Middle East will engage in the program as they work toward an internal accreditation in project management and preparation for the rigorous PMI's PMP® examination. The program is delivered through a comprehensive learning portal that tracks and reports on all aspects of the program and a comprehensive student feedback system has been built into the system to capture detailed student experiences at all stages of the program.

In many ways this was a typical assignment; an organization wished to improve the consistency of its project delivery so that repeatable results could be guaranteed wherever the project was initiated and with whoever was appointed as the project manager. This

FIGURE 4–14. Project management life cycle.

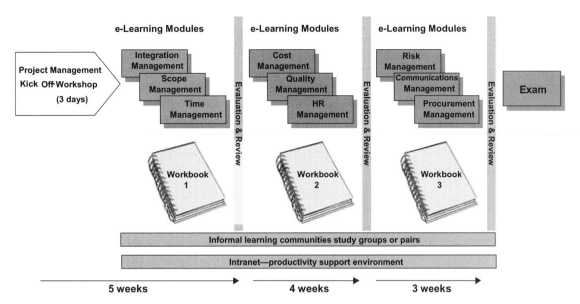

FIGURE 4–15. Typical program format.

level of maturity can only be achieved through the deployment and wide acceptance of a rigorous but flexible project management methodology. Methods however are not a substitute for experience and knowledge. The first step was to fit the method to the culture and the project requirements of the community. The next step was to build consensus in that community that the method was both practical and representative of best practice. Finally a cost-effective method was needed to both roll out use of the method and simultaneously improve the standard of execution of critical project management techniques. I believe that this case is an example of how maturity can be achieved within a global environment.

End Note

This discussion has made a case for the value of deploying simple but internally consistent best practices and methods. We start from the premise that the project management problems that beset organizations have common roots and hence fundamentally similar improvement strategies. The deployment of strong, rigorously applied practices can make a significant difference in the delivery of individual projects, but if an organization is to make real progress in delivering business benefit through its project portfolio, the primary emphasis must be on high-level governance structures and encouraging senior management to steer rather than just observe their critical projects. While the method is inherently good, all methods need to be used intelligently and tailored to suit the criticality, exposure, and risk associated with the project in question. When adopting new practices it should be understood that you are engaged in a process of organizational change. You are changing the way people do their jobs, the knowledge and skills they need to apply to their jobs, the communication and reporting structures related to their jobs, and the way they relate to their colleagues and systems. All of this is both traumatic and potentially destabilizing. The challenges are significant but the rewards are well worthwhile.

4.16 EXEL[4]

Exel was placed in a position of having to develop a methodology that would be global in nature and company Intranet based. Phil Trabulsi, Senior Director, Exel Consolidated Services, describes Exel's project management methodology:

> Exel has an established project management methodology (DePICT™)[5] which was introduced in 1997 based on a detailed assessment of the project management processes. This methodology is based on specific needs of the organization with strong influence from the Project Management Institute's *Project Management Body of Knowledge* (PMBOK® Guide).
>
> The acronym DePICT signifies the five phases of an Exel project: define, plan, implement, control, and transition. Additionally, Exel has a business delivery methodology— The Exel Way™[6] that was introduced to formalize a structured approach to all projects. This is shown in Figure 4–16.
>
> The methodology is Intranet based to some extent. There are two main online sources (internally) that are accessible to the organization with information, tools, and training pertaining to project management and the DePICT methodology. First, Exel has an online, computer-based training program known as Exel Campus which provides a number of training courses in various subjects. This program is accessible to all associates worldwide.
>
> In mid-2002, a project management primer was developed and rolled out. This course provides project management associates and new associates the opportunity to participate in a 30-minute, online tutorial focusing on the core concepts of project management and the Exel methodology.
>
> Second, the enterprise project management (EPM) group manages a database which resides in Lotus Notes and contains the PM toolkit, procedures, training material, guides, and newsletters. It is accessible to all employees and can be linked to their Lotus Notes home page. Finally, an EPM mailbox is set up for all inquiries from project managers company wide and is accessible by all members of the EPM group.
>
> In Exel's case, the methodology is stable and has not undergone any significant modifications in original format. However, concepts, approaches, tools, and training information are revised on a continual basis, based on demands from project managers, customers, and new industry trends. This includes the ongoing enhancement of tools to support efficient and consistent business practices.
>
> Exel receives customer feedback with respect to its project management methodology/ approach through various modes. The most common is direct feedback on project team performance from customers to Exel account owners and customer lessons-learned exercises. In many cases, customers will provide feedback on Exel to various media outlets and industry publications. Today, most lessons-learned exercises are conducted

---

4. Material on Exel Corporation was graciously provided by Julia Caruso, PMP®, Project Manager, Regional PM Group, Americas; Todd Daily, PMP®, Project Manager, Exel Consolidated Services, Ltd.; Francena Gargaro, PMP®, Director, Regional PM Group, Americas; Phil Trabulsi, Senior Director, Exel Consolidated Services, Ltd.; and Chin-tee Teo, Director, Regional PM Group, Asia-Pacific.
5. DePICT is a trademark of Exel plc.
6. The Exel Way is a trademark of Exel plc.

- Business orientation
- Supply chain mapping
- Benchmarking
- Business value drivers
- Opportunity identification

- Current state assessment
- Future state evaluation
- Cost of change
- Risks, sensitivities, contingencies
- Business case

- Project management
- Change management
- Operational realization
- Project back-check
- Continuous improvement

- Detailed testing of solution
- Operational process design
- Implementation planning
- Contingency planning
- Budget development

FIGURE 4–16.   The Exel Way™.

by individual project teams and archived by each specific sector/department. Exel is evaluating methods of collecting, disseminating, and distributing key lessons learned across all sectors.

As companies begin the development of project management methodologies, emphasis seems to be on developing templates first. Exel Corporation has achieved success through its project management templates. According to Todd Daily, PMP®, Project Manager, Exel Consolidated Services:

> Exel uses a project management toolkit comprised of 20 templates that support the phases of a project from initiation through closure. The use of the templates enables the project manager to satisfy the specific needs of his or her project without overburdening them with unnecessary paperwork. These templates have been created in Microsoft Excel and are contained in one individual file, or briefcase, that is transferable and can be easily modified to meet the unique informational requirements of a project. It is macrodriven using navigation buttons for ease of use and contains a glossary with information specific to each tool.
>
> The layout of the toolkit is designed to support Exel's project management methodology DePICT™.[7] Tools specific to each phase are categorized accordingly. DePICT stands for the five phases of a project: define, plan, implement, control, and transition. This is shown in Figure 4–17. Exel has recently strengthened its existing five-phase project management methodology, DePICT, by adding milestone controls and major deliverables. This is shown in Figure 4–18. The DePICT toolkit has also been enhanced, and this appears in Figure 4–19.

---

7. DePICT and ChIPS are trademarks of Exel plc.

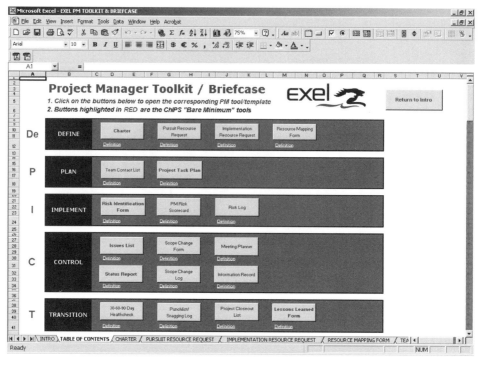

FIGURE 4–17. DePICT's five phases.

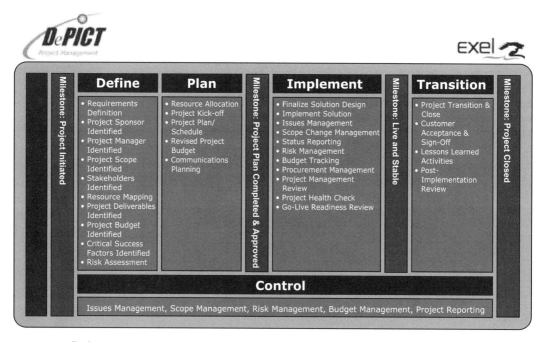

FIGURE 4–18. Project management methodology: key activities and milestones (global).

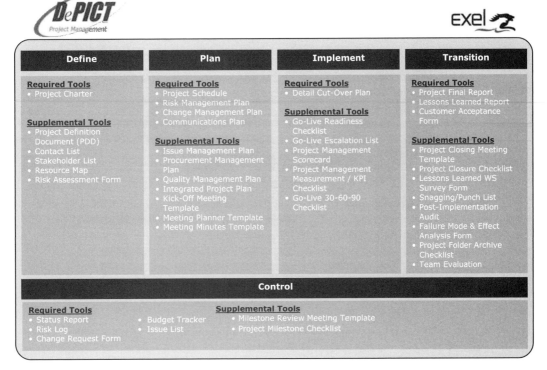

FIGURE 4–19. Project management methodology: toolkit (global)

Additionally, a subset of tools has been identified as the bare-minimum requirement for each project. These are known as the ChIPS™—charter, issues list, project plan, and status report. The use of templates increases understanding of the tool functions, provides a sufficient level of guidance for less experienced project managers, enables flexible/dynamic adaptation to all projects—pursuit or implementation, reduces time, and provides quicker adaptability for associates.

Exel uses templates for all phases of projects. Typical templates appear in Figures 4–20 through 4–25. The two primary types of projects at Exel are pursuit projects, which involve the pursuit of new business via request-for-proposal (RFP) responses and solution design, and implementation projects, which are much larger, involving the implementation and delivery of the designed solution for our clients. Pursuit projects range in length from a couple of weeks to more than a month. Implementation projects can run from a couple of months to more than one year, depending on complexity. IT-specific projects tend to follow a traditional system development life-cycle format with links to general project management tools, such as a charter and issues list. A large implementation project, which usually involves an IT component, may also have system-specific project management tools and templates.

PROJECT CHARTER		
Project Name:		
Project Sponsor:		exel
Customer Name:		
Customer Sponsor:	**Sector/Dept:**	
Project Manager:	**Date:**	
Project Owner:	**Project Number:**	

Executive Summary: (Brief description of situation and need for the project)

Project Objectives:

Project Scope:

Mgt. Approach: (generally descriptional project resource structure-e.g., PM, 2 IT developers, DBA, etc.)

Project Risks:

Assumptions:

Date/Version:	**Attachments:**

FIGURE 4–20. Project charter template.

PROJECT ISSUES LIST

| Project Name: | 0 |
| Project Manager: | 0 |

exel

#	Category/ Function	Issue Description	Issue Origin	Issue Owner	Origin Date	Date Due	Date Completed	Status	Scope Change (Y/N)	Comments

FIGURE 4–21. Project issues list template.

PROJECT TASK PLAN

Project Name:	0
Project Manager:	0
Customer Name:	0
Sector/Dept.:	0
Project Owner:	0
Project Cost Ctr. Code:	

exel

Project Start Date:	
Target Project End Date:	
Actual Project End Date:	

OK	#	Project Task	Resource Name	Start Date:	Target Finish	Duration	Actual Finish	Predecessor

FIGURE 4–22. Project task plan template.

PROJECT STATUS REPORT

Project Name:	0	exel
Project Owner:	0	
From: (Project Manager)	0	
To:		
Reporting Period:		
SUBJECT:		

Functional Area	Status Update

Items in Progress:

#	Task	Responsibility

Major Issues:

#	Event & Resolution	Responsibility

Major Milestones:

Milestone	Date

Distribution:	Attachments:

FIGURE 4–23. Project status report template.

RISK IDENTIFICATION FORM				
Project Name:	0		exel	
Project Manager:	0			
Customer Name:	0			
Sector/Dept:	0	Change Originator:		
Project Owner:	0	Change Request #:		
Risk Event:		Change Request Date:		

Description of Risk Event

Probability of Occurence	High	Medium	Low		Impact	High	Medium	Low

Impact (must be qualifiable)	Budget	Schedule	Customer

Probable Causes

Preventative Steps & Actions

Contingency Plan & Priority	Trigger

Risk Response

FIGURE 4–24. Risk identification template.

						Project Risk log						
Project Name:										exel ⤳		
Project Manager:												
Project Number:												
Customer Name:										Risk Log Controller:		
Sector/Dept.:										Risk Log #:		
Project Owner:										Date:		
No.	Key Risk	Impact 1-3	Prob 1-3	Score	Risk Mitigation Plan (summary)		Risk form no.	By When	Owner(s)	Status		Comment
1												
2												
3												
4												
5												
6												
7												
8												
9												
10												
11												
12												
13												
14												
15												
16												
17												
18												

FIGURE 4–25.   Risk log template.

4.17 HALIFAX COMMUNITY HEALTH SYSTEMS

For almost 30 years during the early evolution of project management, project management methodologies were found predominantly in project-driven companies. Today, both project-driven and non-project-driven companies, including health care, have developed project management methodologies. Nani Sadowski, Manager of the Enterprise Project Management Office (EPMO) at Halifax Community Health Systems, describes the existing methodology:

> The EPMO at Halifax Community Health Systems (HCHS) utilizes PMI methodology as a baseline. The origination of the EPMO began with an astute manager, an experienced PMP, and a Six Sigma certified project manager. While utilizing the PMI methodology as the base, the other management techniques were also incorporated to ensure that a method best suited for our organization was utilized.
>
> The phases that we have incorporated for our projects are:
>
> 1. *Initiation.* Completion and approval of:
>   a. A business case, which includes an executive summary and return on investment.
>   b. A request for proposal (RFP) that includes details of the proposed system. To get to the RFP, we conduct a detailed assessment of the end-use needs, process and work flows, researching vendors, and the technology and contacting other hospitals to determine their best practices. All of these are used to develop the RFP.

      c. A technical requirements review that includes a review of the technology with the proposed vendors to determine if it is compatible with our environment.

2. *Planning*

      d. Develop a project plan, which includes an executive summary, project goals, project scope, impact on operations, assumptions, constraints/risks, completion criteria, project schedule, roles and responsibilities of the sponsors, team, and subject matter experts, project methodology, and a communication plan.

      e. Develop a detailed project schedule with milestones, resources, and dependencies.

      f. Kick off meeting—held with all stakeholders at the beginning of the project.

3. *Execution and Control*

      g. Monitor and control the budget.

      h. Develop and maintain risk assessment document.

      i. Prepare training documentation.

      j. Prepare a communication plan for within the department, within the hospital, and for our patients and general public.

      k. Prepare a detailed activation plan.

      l. Prepare project change requests as needed.

      m. Obtain all signatures at milestones and document any critical decisions.

      n. Prepare contingency plan.

      o. Prepare backup plan

      p. Obtain go-live sign-off.

4. *Completion*

      q. Prepare operational turnover document.

      r. Prepare lessons-learned document and review with team.

      s. Prepare service-level agreement document.

      t. Survey customers.

      u. Obtain final completion sign-off.

The following information is part of a task template that is included in the methodology for HCHS. The template was created for Pacific Edge.

Purpose: The purpose of this policy is to standardize the tasks in Pacific Edge and allow for a checklist of all project documents.

Scope: All project managers should use the task template given below to assign tasks in Pacific Edge to resources.

Policy: There should only be four tasks in the task section. The tasks are consistent with the PMO methodology.

Task Template

1. Initiation
   - Meetings
     - Business case/executive summary
     - Assessment
     - Business case/executive summary
     - Cost spreadsheet
   - Approval

2. Planning
   - RFP/vendor selection/design review
   - Bid specifications
   - Contract review by project manager and executive sponsor
   - Contract review by legal
   - Contract sign-off
   - Cost spreadsheet review
   - Demos/walk-throughs
   - Designing interface specifications
   - Designing the network
   - High-level timeline
   - Risk assessment and management plan
   - Prepare nondisclosure agreement
   - Research, vendor/project
   - RFP/RFI
   - Technical requirements review (integration and network review)
   - Vendor comparison
   - Vendor negotiation
   - Documentation
   - Alerts
   - Budget reconciliation
   - Change requests
   - Communication plan
   - Frequently asked questions
   - Issues list
   - Minutes and agendas
   - Policies and procedure follow-up
   - Project plan document (includes scope)
   - Project schedule
   - Risk assessment
   - Status reports
   - Technical documentation
   - Updating Pacific Edge
   - Work flow processes
3. Execution and Control
   - Implementation
     - Activation plan
     - Communication installation
     - Contingency plan
     - Database configuration
     - Desktop deployment
     - Desktop imaging
     - Dictionary/table building
     - End-user device installation
     - Interface coding

- Network configurations/diagrams
- Printer installation
- Procurement
- Reports
- Server/alerts/background jobs installation
- Security
- Software installation
- Technical documentation
- Testing
  - Back-up/restore testing
  - End-to-end testing
  - Hardware testing
  - Interface testing
  - Parallel testing
  - Report testing
  - Test plan
  - Test scenario spreadsheet/test results
  - Unit testing
  - Volume testing
- Training
  - Application training
  - Training manuals
  - Training plan
  - Train the trainer
  - Technical training

4. Completion
- Operational turnover/sign-off/lessons learned
- Lessons learned
- Service-level agreement
- Sign-off

4.18 ORANGE SWITZERLAND[8]

Orange Switzerland used the concept of systems management to develop its project management systems. A system is composed of interacting parts that operate together to achieve some objective or purpose. A system is intended to "absorb" inputs, process them in some way, and produce outputs that are defined by goals, objectives, or common purposes, as shown in Figure 4–26.

---

8. All information on Orange Switzerland's PMO and project management methodology is provided jointly by Martin Troxler, Director Corporate Quality; Daniel Heller, PMO Manager; and Alexander Matthey, PMP®, former PMO Manager, today Amontis Consulting Group, Associate Partner.

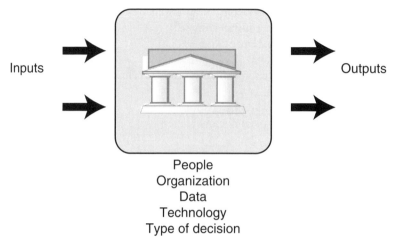

FIGURE 4–26. Systems management model.

Drawing from personal experience, numerous authors' interpretation of what is part of a system, and the specific needs at Orange Switzerland, the PMO team decided on a simple version in which only three major elements, pillars, were retained (Figure 4–27)—the "how" (processes), "by whom" (people, organization), and "with what" (tools and system)—the three pillars of any system, which together contribute to a hopefully effective

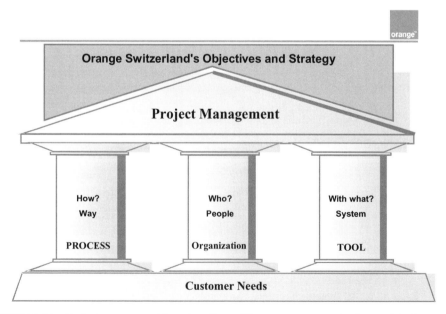

FIGURE 4–27. Project management based on three pillars: process, organization, and tool.

transformation. Conjointly the three pillars foster professional transformation of inputs into outputs. They enable good project management: the input being raw material (needs and tasks), the output achieved objectives. And using this graphic metaphor it seemed easily understandable by all to depict the edifice of this internal system as a temple which lays on the needs it is meant to transform by being controlled by and supporting the corporate strategy.

Process Pillar

The first question is how to do the transformation. In what sequence should a task be executed? At Orange Switzerland we encapsulated all project management knowledge and good practices of our more experienced colleagues or accepted best practices into the process pillar.

We introduced a single corporate project management process (not surprisingly the PMBOK® Guide administered project management life cycle), and made all divisions' project life cycles align with it. It was baptized ADOPT (align decision over project tactics).

The second major constituent of the process pillar at Orange Switzerland is the series of decision meetings between process groups (called phases for simplicity). The most famous gate meeting authorizes a project to start being executed (implemented). It inherited the name PACT (project approval corporate team) since it is composed of the chief executive officer and all vice presidents and is administered by the PMO.

Organization Pillar

This pillar covers a wide spectrum of notions. First are all the project management people at Orange Switzerland. This is shown by the concentric circles in Figure 4–28: the PMO (two full-time people) in the middle surrounded by project managers.

Second is the hierarchical organization in project management—the reporting structures. The aim is to clearly spell out the reporting and responsibility within a matrix organizational structure, where projects range from 100 percent functional type to commando type and different matrix strengths. This is because of the dynamic nature of the organization: Over time (from inception of Orange Switzerland) and with project management maturity the trend was commando → functional → weak matrix → balanced matrix. It is complex when it is a matrix, but when the matrix structure changes, unevenly throughout the company, it's a real challenge.

Third is project management training. For several years there was a fainthearted approach to train project managers, but often this was soon abandoned. There was no PMO to continue the process, and there were no "pillars" of project management. In addition, there was a shift from delivery at the top to blended delivery—classroom plus on-the-job training.

Fourth is the project management competency framework. Training is linked more with organizational development and the responsibility of Human Resources. Good collaboration with Human Resources and the application of PMI's organizational maturity model (OPM3), the first commercial application in the world, allowed us to put this new profession on the corporate map.

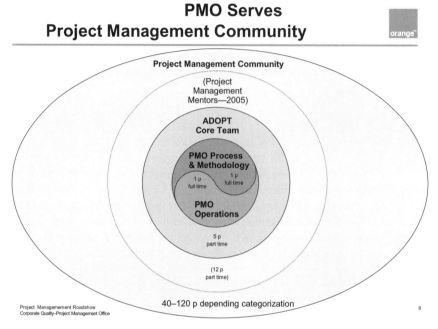

FIGURE 4–28. The PMO.

System Pillar
First, traditionally this is about techniques and tools. When we want to consolidate a company portfolio of 400 projects in parallel, a simple scheduling tool is not adequate. A software product installed some time before the PMO was created, VPMi (Virtual Project Management Intranet, from the U.S.-based VCSOnline) allowed Orange Switzerland to consolidate many of its projects as it provided: high-level definition while uploading from Microsoft projects, risk management, program management, ease of use, easily interfaceable with Artemis (IT project tracking), SAP HR (employees' names), cost effective.

Second, the first set of templates to accompany the project management process was created by the core PMO team in the early days, some common, and some specific. Later during the first training/coaching sessions further templates were developed and adapted as part of the delivery.

Summary
Separately the pillars will not make an organisation successful in project management. None of are sustainable for a long time without the others, so they have to be used in parallel.

In the startup phase, everything was driven by deadlines. Resources were not the issue. The most important thing was to launch services as soon as possible and to acquire as many customers as possible. Therefore people had little time to think about proper methodologies, processes, and so on.

A key factor was to find a way to convince people to follow the process. As soon as we were in a position to tell people that if their project had not followed the process and been approved properly, no money would be released, people started to follow it.

Another problem was and still sometimes is what we call "silo thinking": each division working on its own, which, for example, translated in two separate processes for marketing and another project although both projects were competing for the same resources. When management realized that this was leading to conflict and misunderstanding, it became possible to align the processes and create a single corporate decision body.

Another key factor is the change in people's profile/mindset. People who like working in a startup mode may not always like processes and methodologies. As the company grows, new people who like more structured approaches get hired, which eases the implementation of a project management methodology. This evolution is still in progress and a review of the ADOPT process has been initiated in spring 2005 with objective to streamline the process through increased alignment (decision bodies, templates, etc.) between the divisions.

4.19 ONTARIO PUBLIC SERVICE (OPS)

During the early years of project management, private industry appeared to mature in project management quicker than government agencies primarily because of the profit motive. Today, government agencies have caught up to private industry in the adoption, acceptance, and implementation of project management. Government agencies such as Ontario Public Service (OPS) appear to be on the leading edge of excellence in project management in government agencies.

Adopting and Advancing Project Management in the Public Sector[9]

Why Projects? The importance of project management as a strategic business tool and enabler of change and the need for the development of internal project management capacity have been recognized throughout the OPS.

Projects are a powerful vehicle for enabling transformational change in the OPS, and, with an estimated 10 percent of OPS staff and 30 percent of senior managers engaged in projects at any time, the development of internal OPS strategic project management capacity would support:

- Achievement of government priorities
- Implementation of results-based plans
- Modernization of government
- Knowledge transfer
- Reduced reliance on external consultants

9. The material in this section from the Project Management Excellence Initiative (PMEI), Government of Ontario, has been provided by Lois Bain, Assistant Deputy Minister (A), Centre for Transformation, Innovation and Excellence; Daniel Martyniuk, PMP®, IMBA, Manager, PMEI; and Liberty Velicaria, IMBA, Project Management Consultant, PMEI.

Project Management Excellence Initiative (PMEI)   As a first step toward supporting the development of enterprise-wide project management capacity, the Provincial Government of Ontario launched the PMEI within the Centre for Leadership and Human Resource Management (CFL/HRM), Cabinet Office in July 2002.

In line with its primary goal of supporting the development of strategic project management capacity within the OPS, the initiative recognizes project management as a valued, unique set of skills with specific learning and human resource needs. It aims to build and foster a project culture in the OPS and cultivate knowledge sharing and learning to support best practices and ensure operation at optimum levels.

The specific objectives of the initiative are to:

- Provide corporate support in project management
- Improve the environment for project work by providing planning, learning, and human resource advice and assistance
- Strengthen networking and sharing "right practices" among OPS project leaders and staff

In order to make a positive impact on the project management community and build a strong project management culture within the OPS, PMEI has focused its efforts in three key areas: people, processes, and tools and technology. This is because we define OPS project success to be dependent on having the right *people* who are following the right *processes* and using the right mix of *tools and technology* to get the job done right.

PMEI Supports OPS Project Workers   Recognizing that having the right people is key to project success, PMEI has developed a number of products and services aimed at developing and retaining skilled project management practitioners within the OPS. Specifically, PMEI has:

- Developed and launched the OPS Project Management Learning Framework & Curriculum to facilitate harmonized training, learning, and development
- Fostered a community of practice (OPS Project Management Consultancy Network) to regularly bring together project management practitioners from across the OPS to network and exchange experiences, tips, ideas, and lessons learned
- Initiated a PMO special-interest group bringing together directors, managers, and leads of more than 20 different PMOs from across the OPS to foster collaboration and coordinate efforts and resources
- Established several human resource supports (i.e., PMP certification support, sample job descriptions, resume bank of experienced and qualified individuals)
- Supported recognition of OPS project successes at numerous conferences and forums and through other awards and recognition programs

Our OPS Project Management Learning Framework & Curriculum (as illustrated in Figure 4–29) depicts the importance of having knowledgeable and skilled people at all levels in the project organization structure. Therefore, the courses were designed to meet the unique

FIGURE 4–29. The OPS Project Management Learning Framework & Curriculum.

needs of various audiences, from project staff to project sponsors. Furthermore, all of our courses have been specifically customized for the OPS to reflect the unique challenges and complexities of the public-sector project management environment.

Since the launch of our comprehensive "flag-ship" three-day applied project management course in the summer of 2004, our training sessions have been consistently "selling out" and we are encouraged by the positive feedback and requests for more courses, additional sessions, and dedicated ministry/branch learning events. Much of the success of these courses can be attributed to their "OPS-centric" approach. We have customized the courses with OPS-relevant case studies and focus on teaching the OPS project management approach and using OPS-specific tools that can be actually used the very next day at work. Another factor that has contributed to the success of our courses is the fact that all of our training vendors are registered education providers with PMI®, which allows students to earn professional development units (PDUs) to maintain their PMP® accreditation.

PMEI Promotes Consistent Approach and Provides Advice and Guidance In addition to having the right people "on-board," we realize that they need to follow the right processes in order to maximize the chances of consistent project successes. One of the first steps taken to address that aspect, which is also one of the first steps toward increasing the project management maturity level of the OPS, was the development of a common, standardized project management framework and methodology.

The OPS Integrated Project Management Framework & Methodology (IPMFM) is a customized, corporate approach for the management of projects of various sizes and complexities in the OPS. The OPS IPMFM is based on comprehensive research of global project management best practices in the public and private sectors as well as an extensive review of existing OPS resources relevant to project management. It is closely aligned with PMI's *Guide to the Project Management Body of Knowledge* (it is a derivative of the PMBOK® Guide, 2000 edition) and was developed through extensive OPS-wide consultations with our partners and stakeholders in order to ensure that it aligned with existing OPS policies, directives, business practices, and other corporate initiatives.

Published as an online, user-friendly reference guide with downloadable templates, rather than a rigid prescriptive policy, the OPS IPMFM continues to be updated, improved, and enhanced based on feedback received and lessons learned from real projects. The methodology is generic enough to apply to various types of projects (i.e., information technology systems implementation, policy development, reorganization or business process reengineering, etc.) and scalable so that it can be used for large, complex, enterprise-wide projects or small, ministry, or branch projects. When adopted and consistently applied across the OPS, this common approach to project management helps project workers, at all levels, embrace change and get the right things done right the first time around.

As illustrated by the model in Figure 4–30, the generally accepted project management knowledge areas and processes, as defined by the PMBOK® Guide, form the core of the OPS IPMFM. However, we realize that projects by definition are agents of change, and adoption of project management best practices alone will not necessarily lead to achievement of desired results. That is why we have incorporated a change management process into the model, and its middle ring represents the importance of understanding the

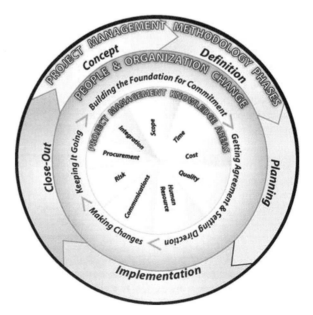

FIGURE 4–30. The OPS integrated project management model.

people and organization change management principles that should be considered and actions required to manage the impact of projects on the people and organizations involved. The outer ring of the model depicts the project life cycle as represented by the five phases of the methodology. The methodology is "integrated" because it brings together project management processes with people and organization change actions as well as existing OPS policies (e.g., management of risk), directives (e.g., procurement), business practices (e.g., records management), and other corporate initiatives (e.g., knowledge management).

One of the key differentiating features of the OPS methodology is the fact that there is a significant focus placed on up-front planning. As illustrated in Figure 4–31, there are three separate phases, concept, definition, and planning, with three separate checkpoints where "go" or "no-go" decisions can take place before implementation. This ensures that attention is paid to such important aspects as proper project scoping and risk planning, and at the same time, sufficient time is spent building the foundation for commitment and getting agreement and setting direction. Furthermore, the keeping-it-going stage of the change management model ensures that, as part of the closeout phase, transition to operations is properly conducted and the changes are institutionalized.

The methodology provides suggested step-by-step guidelines with related tools and templates that can be adopted as a "roadmap" to manage any project carried out in the

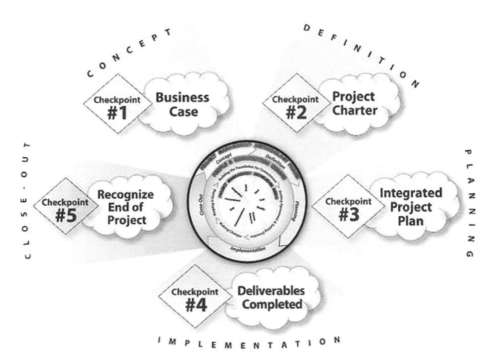

FIGURE 4–31. The OPS integrated project management methodology.

OPS. Furthermore, objectives for each phase are clearly defined, steps and actions to complete each objective are identified, links to available tools and techniques are outlined, and templates to document outputs of each step are provided.

Online PMEI Resources Facilitate Project Success   Finally, in addition to supporting OPS project management practitioners (people) and developing the standardized OPS framework and methodology (processes), PMEI is actively involved in ensuring that the right mix of tools and technology is available to support effective and efficient project delivery.

The OPS IPMFM Intranet website (the home page illustrated in Figure 4–32) is the main vehicle for the provision of readily available tools and resources to OPS project workers across the province. Launched in February 2004, this Web-enabled guide provides easy access to a wide array of readily available resources and acts as a "one-stop project management shop" with easy-to-follow guidelines and more than 100 helpful checklists and templates customized for small- to large-scale projects.

To facilitate the methodology's alignment with corporate policies, procedures, and directives, the Intranet site contains extensive links to other online government documents and resources relevant to project management. For example, project workers following the online guide are encouraged to utilize, where applicable, the linkages to the Ministry of Finance's risk management policy, Management Board Secretariat's accountability and governance di-

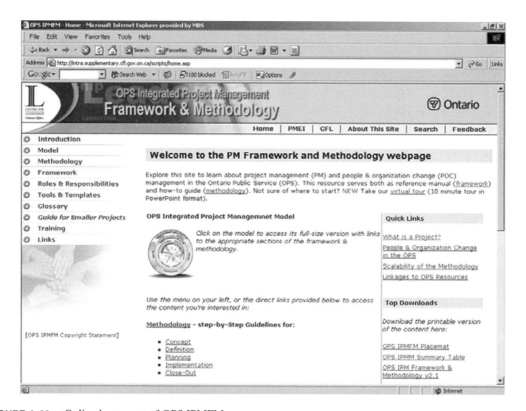

FIGURE 4–32.   Online homepage of OPS IPMFM.

rectives, and the Government of Ontario information technology standards. Extensive links to external project management resources available on the Internet are also provided.

PMEI on the Right Path to Excellence Critical to the ongoing success of the PMEI has been the visible and active executive support, consistent engagement and communications with clients and stakeholders, and continuous improvement of our products and services based on feedback from our community of practice.

PMEI is governed by an executive steering committee that establishes direction and priorities and regularly reviews progress. The steering committee reports to the deputy minister's committee on OPS transformation. This governance structure provides PMEI the high-profile support it needs to take action on issues related to improving project success across the OPS.

Establishing the PMEI has certainly affirmed the importance of communications in project management and change management initiatives. From the outset, we identified the need to communicate with clients and stakeholders in order to successfully introduce and promote the benefits of a common, standardized project management approach. Whether it is through the PMEI courses, one-on-one consultation sessions with OPS project managers, information sessions, presentations, PMEI Intranet site, or PMEI "This Just In . . ." update e-mails, we are constantly reaching out to build and support our community of practice. We are also consistently asking for feedback from our trainers, students, OPS project management practitioners, including those we provide advice and guidance to, and the executive steering committee to ensure that PMEI's products and services are effective and relevant at all levels and throughout the OPS. Accordingly, the PMEI will be conducting its first official OPS client consultations and survey this year to formally obtain feedback, measure the usage of our resources, rate satisfaction, and identify medium- to long-term needs and priorities.

The Government of Ontario's workforce is 60,000 people strong and it is a large and complex environment to navigate. Everyday I meet or speak to someone new from the OPS who was referred to the PMEI by someone who took one of our courses or saw one of our presentations or visited our website. And everyone I speak to is excited about the progress and difference our accomplishments have made.

In reality, the PMEI is no longer an initiative but an essential permanent organization supporting the transformation of the OPS. Through the PMEI, the OPS will continue to build capable and motivated OPS project practitioners to deliver project results that will benefit the people of Ontario.

4.20 CONVERGENT COMPUTING

It is extremely difficult, if not impossible, for information systems consulting organizations to survive in today's business environment without a successful project management methodology. Colin Spence, Project Manager/Partner at Convergent Computing (CCO) describes the methodology in his organization:

> A project manager is to be assigned to all new scoped projects and will work closely with the team members assigned to the project. A project manager's primary responsibility is to ensure that CCO is executing projects on time, on budget, and within scope to fulfill the

obligations outlined in the proposal or scope of work. To this end, the project manager should provide oversight and strategic guidance through the services delivery process.

If the client does not approve funds for a project manager, the technical lead on the project will be expected to fulfill this role and receive assistance "behind the scenes" from a company project manager.

Project management involvement should normally start with approval of the proposal or scope of work (SOW) document(s) as these will be the primary documents that the project manager will use to guide the activities of the resources and to ensure the success of the project and satisfaction of the client. The objectives of the project, SOW, major activities, deliverables, and roles and responsibilities will be monitored as well as overall team effectiveness and progress.

During the project, all primary client deliverables (such as statements of work, consulting documents, project plans, budget reports, as-builts, etc.) should be run through the project manager to ensure our deliverables are consistent with project objectives and of the highest quality.

The project manager should be an escalation point for scope changes or any project flags and will keep the account manager involved in all scope change requests. The project manager will also provide updates on budget and timelines as needed and schedule regular customer satisfaction check point meetings.

A CCO project (using the methodology) is approached as having six distinct steps, as follows:

1. *Project Definition.* This step is designed to allow CCO to determine the scope of the project and sell the client on CCO's abilities. This is typically a "brainstorming" session, with the goal of gathering information rather than CCO recommending a solution.
2. *Internal Strategy.* This step allows CCO to validate the information gathered and craft a strategy for proposing our services. Time is allocated for the CCO team to strategize on the best solution to the client's needs, and a draft of the proposal or statement of work is created.
3. *Proposal.* This step allows CCO to ensure alignment with the client in the areas of budget, roles and responsibilities, goals, and objectives of the project and create the proposal. The draft SOW is delivered/presented to the client and then finalized based on client input. At this point the budget is solidified and the timeline discussed.
4. *Internal Readiness.* This step ensures that all of the internal administrative paperwork is done and that an internal work definition is created if the proposal or SOW does not provide enough information. This phase also ensures that all resources involved in the project understand the SOW to be performed, timeline, and budget.
5. *Project Services Delivery.* The details of this step will vary based on the size and nature of the project and may be split into subphases. Essentially, during this phase, the services are delivered as outlined in the proposal/SOW. There are typically internal team checkpoint meetings as well as customer satisfaction checkpoints with the customer. All deliverables, whether technology implementations, hardware configurations, training services, or documentation, are reviewed by the consultant in charge of the project and the project manager involved with the project.
6. *Sign-Off and Customer Satisfaction.* The final step involves getting the client sign-off indicating the project is complete in their eyes and gathering customer satisfaction information to help CCO improve its services and to set a tone that CCO is committed to high-quality delivery and highly satisfied clients.

There is also a business development step that is typically referred to as step 0 which is required for new clients, to "open the door" and allow CCO the opportunity to meet with the client, which is referred to as step 1.

Note that the activities, resources involved, and level of effort are commensurate with the complexity, strategic importance, and size of the project. So the duration and number of resources involved in each project will vary depending on who the customer is and the nature and complexity of the project.

Figure 4–33 is a flowchart and checklist that outlines the project life cycle created by Colin Spence. The project manager assigned to the project should use this list to ensure that no steps are missed, so check boxes are provided on the form.

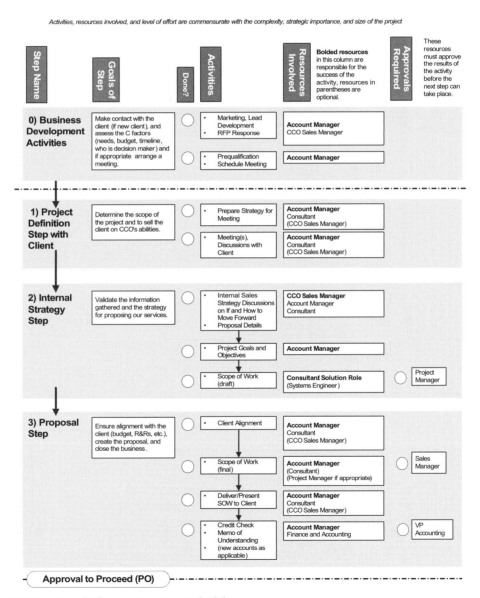

FIGURE 4–33. Project management methodology.

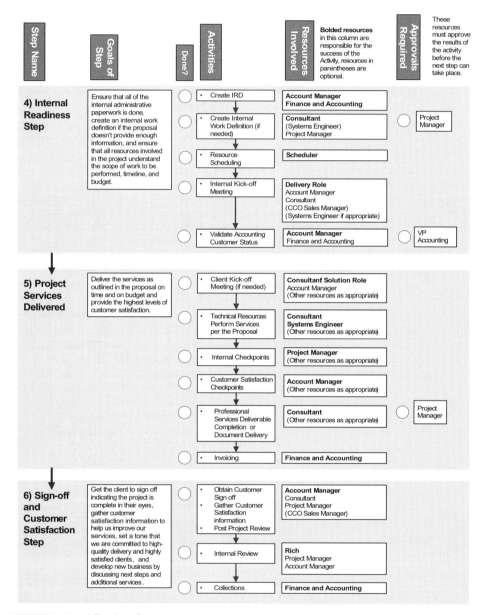

FIGURE 4–33. *(Continued)*

This process of deciding upon the number of life-cycle phases involved many discussions and meetings between the managers. While the final structure seems to deemphasize the actual on-site work that needs to be done, it ensures that the project is well defined, that the right team of people is assembled, and that once the work is done, attention is paid to ensuring that the client is satisfied. CCO management had found through experience that too often resources were being assigned to tasks without a good enough definition of the needs of the client and the exact deliverables the client was expecting. Additionally, there was often not enough assistance provided to the resource or resources in terms of project management support and customer satisfaction suffered as a result.

This phase structure has now been in place close to five years and has drastically improved CCO's ability to provide top-notch professional services.

4.21 EDS

Doug Bolzman, Consultant Architect, PMP®, ITIL Service Manager at EDS, discusses the foundation for a project management methodology:

Many clients have a project management methodology and, in addition, most companies have several methodologies that include project management disciplines. EDS has been successful in integrating the definitive project management method into the other methodologies to allow for leveraging of project management standards and tools without duplication.

EDS has developed a client facing framework called Information Technology Enterprise Management (ITEM). This framework assists clients in mapping their strategic direction into feasible releases. ITEM is a preintegrated framework of three models and a methodology as illustrated in Figure 4–34.

The release management methodology consists of four stages (planning, integration, deployment, and operations). Each stage consists of phases, activities, or tasks, as shown in Table 4–1.

In deciding upon the number of life-cycle phases we used the 9 × 9 rule, as shown in Figure 4–35. If there are more than 9 phases across a stage and more than 9 activities to

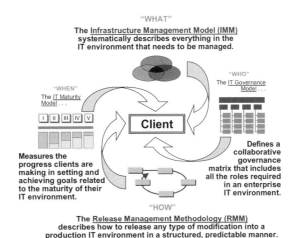

FIGURE 4–34. The EDS ITEM: "An integrated approach to an integrated solution."

TABLE 4–1.   RELEASE METHODOLOGY STAGES

Stage	Description
Planning	The environment that is used to establish and manage the vision and strategic direction of the enterprise IT environment and proactively define the content and schedule of all IT releases. To provide a common means for the client and service providers to clearly and accurately plan the enterprise IT environment and manage all aspects of planning, estimating a release, and setting appropriate client expectations as to what each release will deliver.
Integration	The environment that is used to finalize the design of a planned infrastructure release and perform all of the required testing and client validation, preparing the release to be deployed to the user community. To provide a common means for the client, EDS, and service providers to clearly and accurately validate the accuracy, security, and content of each release and to finalize all development. To provide the client a clear and accurate portrait of the outcome of the release and to set proper expectations of the deployment and operations activities, costs, and schedules.
Deployment	The process that is used by the organization to implement new releases of the enterprise IT design (business, support and technical components) to a target environment. To provide a common means for the client, EDS, and service providers to clearly and accurately schedule, deploy, and turn over to production the updated environment.
Operations	The production environment that is used to sustain and maintain the IT components and configurable items that are part of the enterprise IT environment. To provide a stable IT environment that is required by the IT users to support their business roles and responsibilities.

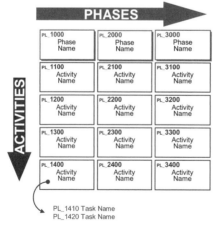

Description:
The sequential hierarchy of events should there be no need to deviate. This demonstrates the highest percentage of occurrence when the process is executed. Main intent for this chart is to expose the tasks subordinate to each activity.

Value:
- Each work element can be identified and mapped internal or external to the component
- All activities divided into tasks (justified)
- All work is represented once (even if executed many times)

Structure:
- All work elements have a unique identifier
  - Phase numbered by the thousands
  - Activity numbered by the hundreds
  - Task numbered by the tens
- All work elements preceded by Component Name Identifier (PL_1000; PL_1100)
- Activity and Task Names kept relatively short; descriptive of work complete, not sentences
- All tasks make up the scope of the activity
- This is NOT a relationship model

FIGURE 4–35.   Activity phase mapping.

each phase (81 total units of work), then the scope will become too large, and our numbering scheme will become unstable.

4.22 DTE ENERGY

Henry Campbell, Principal Analyst, Customer Service Project Management Office at DTE Energy, discusses the growth of project management at DTE Energy:

DTE Energy has created a common approach to ensure projects are implemented in a consistent manner. Prior to 2005, multiple project management methodologies were used throughout the enterprise. Several business units [specifically, customer service (CS), distribution operations (DO), gas operations (GO), operating systems strategy group (OSSG), and information technology services (ITS)] agreed that a "common" approach was needed.

The "common project management process" (See Figure 4–36) was developed utilizing internal and external best practices. The process contains the standard five phases in project management:

1. *Initiation (Phase I).* The Initiation phase includes an assessment of the current state of business and why a change is needed. All projects are initiated with a project charter (Figure 4–37), which contains:
   - Project description and purpose
   - Team members and roles
   - Timeline
   - Case for change
   - Assumptions, risks, and challenges
   - Current-state identification
   - Ideal-state identification
   - Gaps assessment (current and ideal states)
   - Major milestones
   - Metrics (baseline and target)
2. *Planning (Phase II).* The planning phase establishes the desired state of change with an emphasis on process, technical and cultural (re)design. Project managers are given several tools to assist with the overall project planning. One of the tools is the "project plan template" (see Figure 4–38). The template contains a standard planning methodology for customer service projects. It also provides project managers with standard lag and lead times for certain resource intensive tasks. Each project manager customizes the template with respective to their initiative. The project plan template contains:
   - Key project activities
   - Project plan elements (start and finish dates, assigned resources, predecessors, and notes)
   - High-level milestones (macrostones)
3. *Execution and Controlling (Phases III and IV).* The actual process and procedural changes, technical coding, training, and necessary "course corrections" take place during the "execution and controlling" phases. If a project change is required that is related to scope, time, or financial resources, the project manager completes a "change

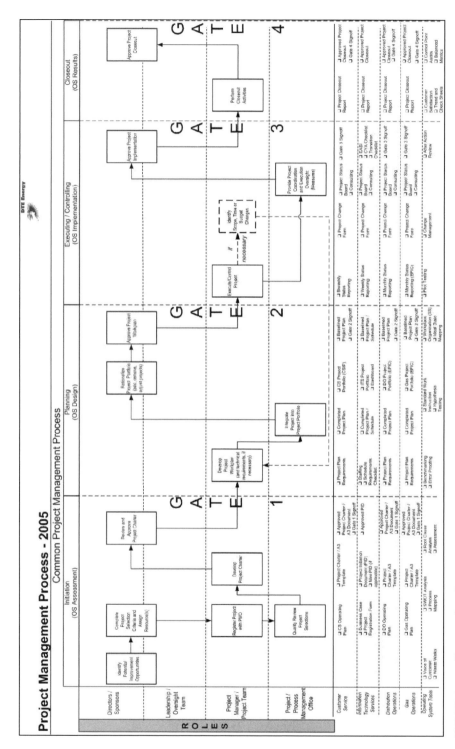

FIGURE 4–36. Integrated project management process.

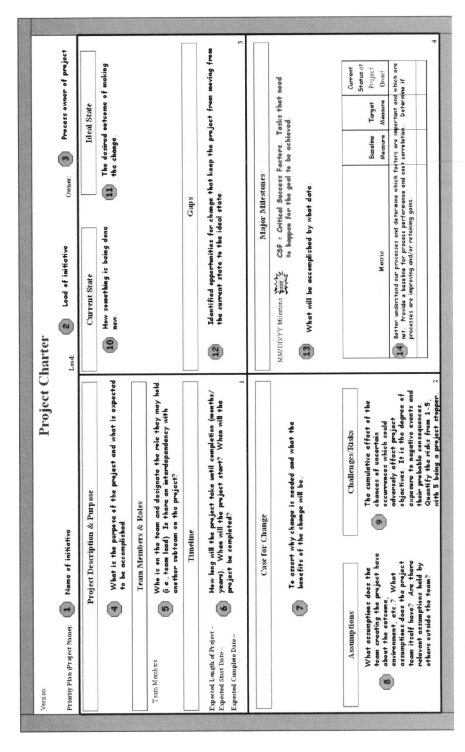

FIGURE 4-37. Project charter template.

ID	ⓘ	Task Name	Duration	Start	Finish	Predecessors	Notes	Resource Names
0		**CS Project Plan Template**	**1 day?**	**1/10/05**	**1/10/05**		This template is to serve as a guide for those individuals managing projects in Customer Service. Tasks, Durations, Dates, Predecessors, and Milestones will vary according to your project.	
1		**Project Administration**	**0 days**	**1/10/05**	**1/10/05**			
2		**Reporting Issues:**	**0 days**	**1/10/05**	**1/10/05**		All issues should have a zero day duration and be numbered numerically (Issue 1, Issue 2 ...)	
3		Issue 1:	0 days	1/1/005	1/1/005			
4		**Initiation / Assessment**	**1 day?**	**1/10/05**	**1/10/05**			
5		Review Project Management Process and Methodology	1 day?	1/1/005	1/1/005		The "2005 Project Management Process and Documentation" folder is located in the CSPM Public folder on the CS Program Management Drive.	
6		Review Operation System Tools to Deploy Throughout Project	1 day?	1/1/005	1/1/005			
7		Identify Project Scope	1 day?	1/1/005	1/1/005			
8		Secure Project Resources / Form Team	1 day?	1/1/005	1/1/005			
9		Assess Current Processes	1 day?	1/1/005	1/1/005			
10		Complete A3 / Project Charter	1 day?	1/1/005	1/1/005		The Ideal State and Gap Analysis does not have to be completely filled out until Gate 2.	
11		**Gate 1 Approval**	**1 day**	**1/1/005**	**1/1/005**			
12								
13		**Planning - Design**	**1 day?**	**1/10/05**	**1/10/05**			
14		Develop Project Workplan	1 day?	1/1/005	1/1/005			
15		*Macrostone: Project Plan Baselined*	*0 days*	*1/10/05*	*1/10/05*			
16		**Process**	**1 day?**	**1/10/05**	**1/10/05**			
17		Define Desired State of Processes	1 day?	1/1/005	1/1/005			
18		Conduct Gap Assessment	1 day?	1/1/005	1/1/005			
19		Develop Countermeaures	1 day?	1/1/005	1/1/005		OSSG Tools: Error Proofing, F.M.E.A, Ideal State Maps, Control Plans	
20		**Technology**	**1 day?**	**1/10/05**	**1/10/05**			
21		Develop Technical Requirements	1 day?	1/1/005	1/1/005			
22		Review Technical Requirements with IT	1 day?	1/1/005	1/1/005			
23		Design (IT)	1 day?	1/1/005	1/1/005			
24		**Gate 2 Approval**	**1 day**	**1/1/005**	**1/1/005**			
25								
26		**Execution / Implementation**	**1 day?**	**1/10/05**	**1/10/05**			
27		**Process**	**1 day?**	**1/10/05**	**1/10/05**			
28		Develop / Modify Processes	1 day?	1/1/005	1/1/005			
29		Develop/Modify Procedures (SW's)	1 day?	1/1/005	1/1/005			

2005 Project Plan Template4 (Detail Gated View).mpp

Page 1

FIGURE 4–38. Project plan template.

request" (Figure 4–39) form. In addition, the project manager provides a bi-weekly status, used to populate the "project status board" (Figure 4–40), which tracks:

- Project information
- Project name and ID
- Project manager name

Customer Service Program Management		Project Change Template	
Request Date	<date>	**Organization**	
Project Manager	<pm name>	***Project Number***	<date>
Project Name	<project name>	***Director/Sponsor***	<date>

Priority	High ☐ Medium ☐ Low ☐	**Business Case Impacted?**	Yes ☐ No ☐
Re-Baseline Required?	Yes ☐ No ☐		

Describe How This Change Impacts the Project o Include affected budget IT dollars o State as change amount and change percent, if possible. For example: Project cost increased by x dollars which represents y percent of approved project cost.	Scope: ☐ _____ Time: ☐ _____ Cost: ☐ _____ Other: ☐ _____
Benefit of Change Request	

Tracking Information—To be completed by Project Management Office

Additional Impact Analysis Required: Yes ☐ No ☐	Review Date: Reviewer:
Issues/Concerns with Change Request:	

Sponsor Approval – To be completed by Project Management Office

Approved ☐ Rejected ☐	Approval Date:
Reason:	
Attachments: *Please attach: (a) revised cost estimate; (b) proposed schedule, as needed.*	

APPROVALS

_____   _____
Project Sponsor   Director of CSPMO

_____
Project Manager

Version 2   Page 1 of 1

FIGURE 4–39. Project change template.

DTE Energy

Customer Service Project Management
Project Status Board (Active Projects)
2/11/2005

	Project Name / Project Manager	Start Date / End Date	% Complete	Gate 1 Sched. Date / Comp. Date	Gate 2 Sched. Date / Comp. Date	Gate 3 Sched. Date / Comp. Date	Gate 4 Sched. Date / Comp. Date	Issues
Credit & Collections	**Project XXX**							
	Project Manager 1							
	Project YYY							
	Project Manager 2							
Data Acquisition								
Customer Billing								
Customer Service Process Management								
Customer Care								
Consumer Affairs								

Project Status Report / Project Plan Submission

Blue	The Project Workplan (Status Update) was not submitted by C.O.B. Friday deadline
Gray	The Project is Complete
Red	4 or more Milestones are past due
Yellow	1 to 3 Milestones are past due or The project has missed a scheduled gate commitment
Orange	Project was not approved, delayed or cancelled

Gate 1 - A3/Charter approved
Gate 2 - Project Work Plan approved
Gate 3 - Project approved for Implementation
Gate 4 - Project Closeout approved

FIGURE 4–40. Project status board.

- Percent complete
- Phase completion (gate approvals)
- Issues

4. *Closeout (Phase V).* During the "closeout" phase, the project manager qualifies the actual project deliverables against the plan. The project is formally closed when the desired targets are attained. The project manager completes the "project closeout report" as part of the closeout process. The closeout report contains:
   - Project summary
   - Objectives achieved
   - Objectives not met

- Measures/metrics
- Lessons learned
- Further actions

Every phase of the common project management process ends with a "gate approval" from the project sponsor. If approval is granted, the project formally moves to the next phase. Where appropriate, each business unit agrees to implement projects utilizing this common approach. While the process is the same across the four business units, the project management procedures are tailored to the needs of each specific department or organization.

4.23 MOTOROLA

Motorola has a project management methodology called Motorola M-gates (stage–gates) that follows the PMBOK® Guide. M. Carmen Paz, Senior Process Manager at Motorola, explains:

M-gates cover all life cycles. M-gates are a framework for planning, managing, and tracking projects across Motorola. Serial gate completion indicates increasing product maturity and ship acceptance readiness. Gates count down from M15 to M0, with our division primarily using M11 through M2. Each gate contains specific criteria required to be completed in order to say that the gate has been achieved.

Major Phases

Business case development (M15–M11)
Portfolio planning (M12–M11)
Project Definition (M10–M7)
Implementation (M6–M4)
Launch & Closeout (M3–M0)
When asked how they arrived at the number of phases or gates, Paz replied:

- *1996–1998.* Motorola's market share and profitability lags behind Ericsson, Nokia, Nortel, and Lucent. Root-cause analysis reveals poor performance in several areas of our processes.
- *1998.* Motorola adopts performance excellence as its new operating model. Performance excellence is comprised of four key components: high-performance business systems, balanced scorecard, reward and recognition, and core process redesign.
- *1999–2000.* Core processes redesigned. M-gates stem from the redesign of two core processes—Marketing and product-line Planning (MPP) and system and product development (SPD). A three-week blitz session with leading process and engineering managers from throughout the corporation defines and finalizes M-gate definition.
- *2000.* Our organization adopts product development M-gates.
- *2001.* M-gates tailored to meet organizational specific needs.

4.24 SAIC/RMA

As can be seen from the companies described in this chapter, they all rely heavily upon information technology for the development and execution of a project management methodology. Done correctly, the result can easily be more efficient operations and a significant cost savings from the use of a system that minimizes paperwork. In addition, good technology makes it easier to perform continuous improvements to the enterprise project management methodology.

Building an IT Foundation for Enterprise Project Management (EPM)[10]

During 2002, the number and scope of IT projects at the U.S. Department of Agriculture (USDA) Risk Management Agency (RMA) were increasing rapidly due to integration of new technology and business requirements. It was clear that a more efficient paradigm would be required in order to assure successful completion with the required levels of program management tracking and control. Since RMA had an established technical relationship with Microsoft, the interest to utilize Microsoft® Project Central and Microsoft Operations Framework (MOF) soon began to take hold.[11]

In early 2003, the RMA administrator and senior staff issued policy and direction regarding the charter leading to the formation of an agency program management office (APMO) and agencywide acceptance of Project Management Institute (PMI)–based standards. This strategically aligned the agency with the USDA and OMB (Office of Management and Budget) guidelines for project management certification requirements for tracking, control, and reporting. From the beginning, since January 2002, Science Applications International Corporation (SAIC) has worked within the RMA Systems Administration Branch (SAB) to perform architecture supportability reviews and scalable IT solutions for successful evolution and migration of Microsoft collaboration products from Microsoft Project Central to the Microsoft Project Server family. Today, RMA SAB is currently utilizing Project Server 2003 in both test and production modes of operations. Project plans that are in their early stages of creation, preliminary cost estimating, and not baselined are examined in the test Project Server environment. This ensures that the production environment is populated with tested and accepted project plans. The enterprise resource pool (ERP) in the test environment matches the production environment ERP by design in order to support cost estimating. Once the preliminary project plan is approved by project management and the sponsor, it is baselined at the kickoff meeting and approved for use in the production Project Server. It is also possible to utilize an ERP with sensitive rate information in an offline mode. In the production Project Server, team resources, and executives have visibility

---

10. The remainder of this section was provided by Mike Martinez, MSSM, PMP, CompTIA IT Project + Principal Systems Engineer Manager, Science Applications International Corporation (michael.ga.martinez@saic.com), and Dennis Stephan, MSSM, Chief, Systems Administration Branch, USDA Risk Management Agency (dennis.stephan@rma.usda.gov).
11. Microsoft, Windows, Project Professional, Project Web Access, MS SQL Server, SharePoint, and SharePoint Portal Server are either registered trademarks or trademarks of Microsoft Corporation in the United States and/or other countries.

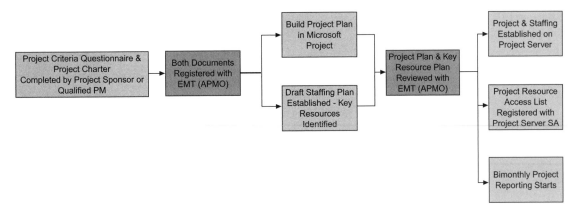

FIGURE 4–41. Adoption process.

to the project plan and use of Project Web Access enterprise-wide to view tasking and progress. Team resources may input actual hours and costs against the accepted baseline, which supports the computations of earned value metrics such as cost variance and schedule variance. Such variances can be used to indicate a red, yellow, or green status indicator per task or rolled up at the phase or project level. Such visual indicators coupled with other information can give management a quick health and status of a project or program (i.e., program of related projects equals portfolio of projects, also called an investment).

Each phase of the EPM evolution has required analysis and definition in areas of project management processes and continued process improvements as a set of enterprise applications were integrated into business processes and work flow. For example, the Figure 4–41 summarizes an adopted process for registering a project leading to publishing a plan on Project Server.

Over the past three years, SAIC has worked to support the RMA PMO policies and SAB IT technical implementation and installation of a flexible and scalable EPM system. Figure 4–42 represents the IT architecture.

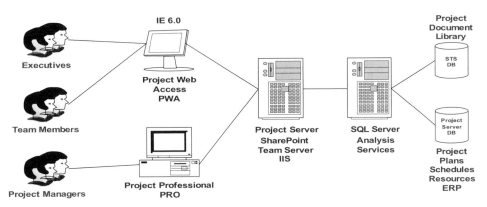

FIGURE 4–42. RMA Microsoft Project Server architecture current.

The design considerations and complexity are not just limited to hardware and software installation, but also require essential training to enable cultural, process, and procedural changes. RMA and SAIC have established a close working relationship with Microsoft and several Microsoft® Gold Certified Partner consultants for targeted areas of installation, testing, and process optimization and tuning enterprise tools. SAIC is a recognized leader in the EPM arena and continues to work with USDA RMA and many vendors to support the evolving EPM system.

The SAB and SAIC team at RMA is utilizing the Project Server security model and designed RMA's resource breakdown structure (RBS) hierarchical system, patterned after the Department of Justice RBS model, to protect cost information, such as rate tables, and control resource allocation. SAIC has further developed custom categories and views to RMA specifications, utilized generic resources (e.g., NetworkEng, SoftwareEng, Manager, etc. . .) for planning purposes on the test server, and exercised the Microsoft® Portfolio Modeler and Microsoft® OLAP Cube capabilities for multiproject analysis. SAIC has been selected and is currently playing a lead role in the implementation of a PMI-based project management system utilizing Project Server to support and provide earned value management reporting within the RMA electronic Written Agreement (eWA) Project. Deliverables of the project will provide processing capabilities to RMA regional, RMA compliance offices, and other nationwide offices across the country. An effective EPM system will facilitate a distributed "real-time" project management model to provide the required tracking, control, and reporting of progress and earned value measurement system (EVMS) metrics to senior management.

Another critical collaboration component of the RMA enterprise architecture was the initial implementation of Microsoft® Windows® SharePoint® services with Project Server and, later, the implementation of SharePoint® Portal Server 2003 to extend enterprise features and management. The local practice was to utilize file servers and Intranets for agency documentation with limited search and organizational capabilities. Today, with SharePoint Portal Server 2003, we have a search engine that allows the users to effectively locate any document, anywhere, anytime! The SharePoint Portal Server has become the official information repository for RMA, and all shared agency documents are required to be on the SharePoint Portal Server for use by federal and contractor staff. This use of technology provides a collaborative, paperless environment that supports the Paperwork Reduction Act of 1995 and the president's e-government (eGov) initiatives.

The RMA SAB utilizes the SharePoint Portal Server to centrally develop, share, and review documents and essential information and maintain document version control for the Integrated Project Team (IPT) of federal employees and contractors.

One of the SAB SharePoint Portal Server home sites provides convenient locations for documents, lists, pictures, events, calendars, announcements, discussions, and links. This facilitates team collaboration in support of SAB IT operations and maintenance (O&M) and project-related activities. New guidance and direction is posted at these SharePoint sites to facilitate and disseminate the flow of information at the national level, as seen in Figure 4–43.

The site illustrated in Figure 4–44 places the enterprise resources on the same page and is an example of a real-world project team site used to facilitate development of deliverables and provide timely management direction.

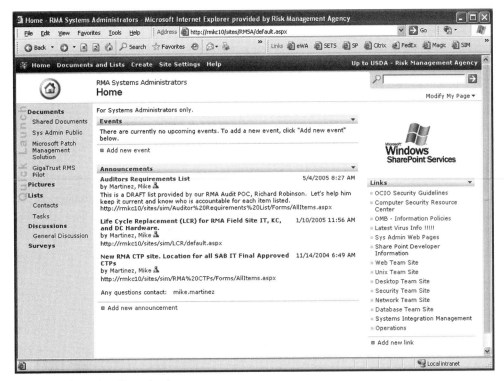

FIGURE 4–43. Information dissemination page.

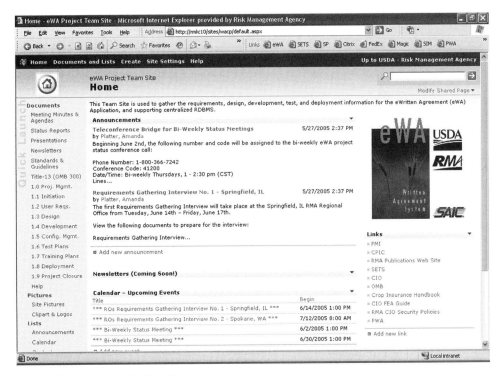

FIGURE 4–44. Information gathering site.

In conclusion, two products from Microsoft provide RMA's essential components to build the IT foundation of an EPM system. The next steps will be reviewing existing procedures and integrating them with the new tools. Developing effective procedures and testing and making IT tool training available to all users is essential to begin the cultural changes required to support the business units of the agency, track metrics, implement controls, and realize expected gains in productivity desired by all organizations.

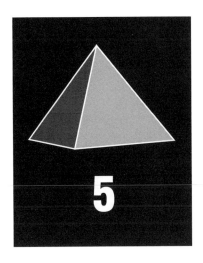

5   **Integrated Processes**

5.0 INTRODUCTION

Companies that have become extremely successful in project management have done so by performing strategic planning for project management. These companies are not happy with just matching the competition. Instead, they opt to exceed the performance of their competitors. To do this on a continuous basis requires processes and methodologies that promote continuous rather than sporadic success.

Figure 5–1 identifies the hexagon of excellence. The six components identified in the hexagon of excellence are the areas where the companies excellent in project management exceed their competitors. Each of these six areas is discussed in Chapters 5–10. We begin with *integrated processes.*

5.1 UNDERSTANDING INTEGRATED MANAGEMENT PROCESSES

As we discussed in Chapter 1, several new management processes since 1985 (e.g., concurrent engineering) have supported the acceptance of project management. The most important complementary management processes and the years they were introduced are listed below:

- 1985: Total quality management (TQM)
- 1990: Concurrent engineering
- 1992: Employee empowerment and self-directed teams
- 1993: Reengineering
- 1994: Life-cycle costing

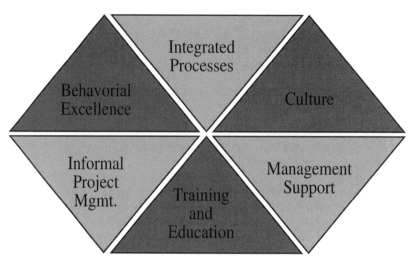

FIGURE 5–1. Six components of excellence. *Source:* Reprinted from H. Ke: *Excellence in Project Management.* New York: Wiley, 1998, p. 14.

- 1995: Change management
- 1996: Risk management
- 1997–1998: Project offices and centers of excellence
- 1999: Colocated teams
- 2000: Multinational teams
- 2001: Maturity models
- 2002: Strategic planning for project management
- 2003: Intranet status reporting
- 2004: Capacity-planning models
- 2005: Six Sigma integration with project management
- 2006: Virtual project management teams

The *integration* of project management with these other management processes is key to achieving excellence. Not every company uses every process all the time. Companies choose the processes that work the best for them. However, whichever processes are selected, they are combined and integrated into the project management methodology. Previously we stated that companies with world-class methodologies employ a single, standard methodology based upon integrated processes. This includes business processes as well as project management–related processes. In the previous chapters, we discussed Motorola's project management methodology. According to M. Carmen Paz, Senior Process Manager at Motorola:

> The M-gates (within Motorola's methodology) integrate all processes, including project and engineering management, quality, risk management, supply chain, outsource management, change control management, prototype manufacturing, and so on. The project man-

ager is responsible for ensuring the project is planned and executed according to the M-gates. The project manager is also responsible for coordinating across all functional groups, including all engineering disciplines, marketing, manufacturing, finance, senior management, quality, and the customer.

The ability to integrate processes is based on which processes the company decides to implement. For example, if a company implemented a stage–gate model for project management, the company might find it an easy task to integrate new processes such as concurrent engineering. The only precondition would be that the new processes were not treated as independent functions but were designed from the onset to be part of a project management system already in place. The four-phase model used by the General Motors Powertrain Group and the PROPS model used at Ericsson Telecom AB readily allow for the assimilation of additional business and management processes.

Previously, we stated that project managers today are viewed as managing part of a business rather than just a project. Therefore, project managers must understand the business and the processes to support the business as well as the processes to support the project. Companies such as Visteon and Johnson Controls understand this quite well and have integrated business processes either into or with their project management methodology.

This chapter discusses each of the management processes listed and how the processes enhance project management. Then we look at how some of the integrated management processes have succeeded using actual case studies.

5.2 EVOLUTION OF COMPLEMENTARY PROJECT MANAGEMENT PROCESSES

Since 1985, several new management processes have evolved parallel to project management. Of these processes, TQM and concurrent engineering are the most relevant. Companies that reach excellence are the quickest to recognize the synergy among the many management options available today. Companies that reach maturity and excellence the quickest are those that recognize that certain processes feed on one another. As an example, consider the seven points listed below. Are these seven concepts part of a project management methodology?

- Teamwork
- Strategic integration
- Continuous improvement
- Respect for people
- Customer focus
- Management by fact
- Structured problem solving

These seven concepts are actually the basis of Sprint's TQM process. They could just as easily have been facets of a project management methodology.

During the 1990s, Kodak taught a course entitled Quality Leadership. The five principles of Kodak's quality leadership program included:

Customer focus	"We will focus on our customers, both internal and external, whose inputs drive the design of products and services. The quality of our products and services is determined solely by these customers."
Management leadership	"We will demonstrate, at all levels, visible leadership in managing by these principles."
Teamwork	"We will work together, combining our ideas and skills to improve the quality of our work. We will reinforce and reward quality improvement contributions."
Analytical approach	"We will use statistical methods to control and improve our processes. Data-based analyses will direct our decisions."
Continuous improvement	"We will actively pursue quality improvement through a continuous cycle that focuses on planning, implementing, and verifying of improvements in key processes."

Had we just looked at the left-hand column we could argue that these are the principles of project management as well. More recently, in 1997, the International Organization for Standardization (ISO) in Geneva, Switzerland, developed the ISO 10006 series, which addresses quality management: guidelines to quality in project management.

Figure 5–2 shows what happens when an organization does not integrate its processes. The result is totally uncoupled processes. Companies with separate methodologies for each process may end up with duplication of effort, possibly duplication of resources, and

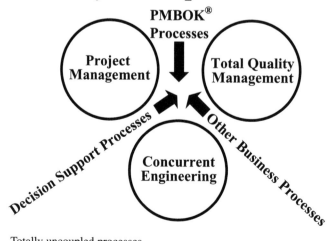

FIGURE 5–2. Totally uncoupled processes.

Partially Integrated Processes

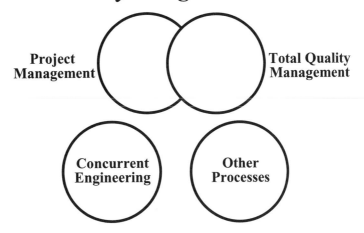

FIGURE 5–3.   Partially integrated processes.

even duplication of facilities. Although there are several processes in Figure 5–2, we will focus on project management, TQM, and concurrent engineering only.

As companies begin recognizing the synergistic effects of putting several of these processes under a single methodology, the first two processes to become partially coupled are project management and TQM, as shown in Figure 5–3. As the benefits of synergy and integration become apparent, organizations choose to integrate all of these processes, as shown in Figure 5–4.

Excellent companies are able to recognize the need for new processes and integrate them quickly into existing management structures. During the early 1990s, integrating project management with TQM and concurrent engineering was emphasized. Since the

Totally Integrated Processes

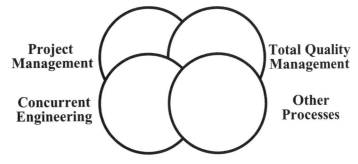

FIGURE 5–4.   Totally integrated processes.

middle 1990s, two other processes have become important in addition: risk management and change management. Neither of these processes is new; it's the emphasis that's new.

During the late 1990s, Steve, formerly Vice President for Product Development at Metzeler Automotive Profile System, described the integrated processes in its methodology:

> Our organization has developed a standard methodology based on global best practices within our organization and on customer requirements and expectations. This methodology also meets the requirements of ISO 9000. Our process incorporates seven gateways that require specific deliverables listed on a single sheet of paper. Some of these deliverables have a procedure and in many cases a defined format. These guidelines, checklists, forms, and procedures are the backbone of our project management structure and also serve to capture lessons learned for the next program. This methodology is incorporated into all aspects of our business systems, including risk management, concurrent engineering, advanced quality planning, feasibility analysis, design review process, and so on.

Clearly, Metzeler sees the integration and compatibility of project management systems and business systems. Another example of integrated processes is the methodology employed by Nortel. During the late 1990s, Bob Mansbridge, Vice President, Supply Chain Management at Nortel Networks, believed:

> Nortel Networks project management is integrated with the supply chain. Project management's role in managing projects is now well understood as a series of integrated processes within the total supply chain pipeline. Total quality management (TQM) in Nortel Networks is defined by pipeline metrics. These metrics have resulted from customer and external views of "best-in-class" achievements. These metrics are layered and provide connected indicators to both the executive and the working levels. The project manager's role is to work with all areas of the supply chain and to optimize the results to the benefit of the project at hand. With a standard process implemented globally, including the monthly review of pipeline metrics by project management and business units, the implementation of "best practices" becomes more controlled, measurable, and meaningful.

Another example of business processes being integrated with project management is in Figure 5–5 (from Symcor, courtesy of Diana Miret, Director, Enterprise Services Management). Notice in this figure that many of the decision points are business decision points in addition to project decision points.

The importance of integrating risk management is finally being recognized. According to Frank T. Anbari, Professor of Project Management, George Washington University:

> By definition, projects are risky endeavors. They aim to create new and unique products, services, and processes that did not exist in the past. Therefore, careful management of project risk is imperative to repeatable success. Quantitative methods play an important role in risk management. There is no substitute for profound knowledge of these tools.

Risk management has been a primary focus among health care organizations for decades, for obvious reasons, as well as financial institutions and the legal profession.

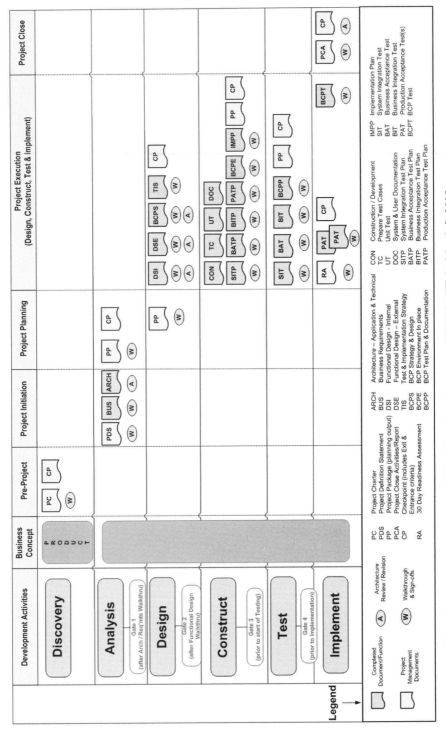

FIGURE 5–5. TS Project Management Stages & SDLC Workflow Diagram - SOX DRAFT 6 - March 2, 2005.

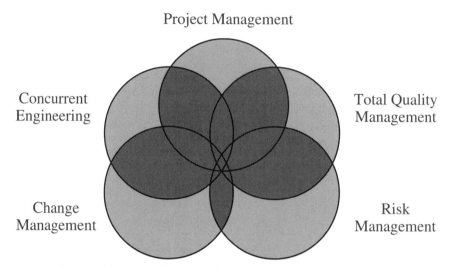

FIGURE 5–6. Integrated processes for twenty-first century.

Today, in organizations of all kinds, risk management keeps us from pushing our problems downstream in the hope of finding an easy solution later on or of the problem simply going away by itself. Change management as a complement to project management is used to control the adverse effects of scope creep: increased costs (sometimes double or triple the original budget) and delayed schedules. With change management processes in place as part of the overall project management system, changes in the scope of the original project can be treated as separate projects or subprojects so that the objectives of the original project are not lost.

Today, excellent companies integrate five main management processes (see Figure 5–6):

- Project management
- Total quality management
- Risk management
- Concurrent engineering
- Change management

Self-managed work teams, employee empowerment, reengineering, and life-cycle costing are also combined with project management in some companies. We briefly discuss these less widely used processes after we have discussed the more commonly used ones.

5.3 CONVERGENT COMPUTING

The importance of integrated processes, especially quality, has become part of all project management methodologies. According to Colin Spence, Project Manager/Partner at Convergent Computing (CCO):

There are steps in the life cycle that ensure these processes are addressed throughout the delivery process. Quality is addressed throughout the life cycle, starting with the attention from the team in crafting a strategy for services delivery in phase 2 and then preparing the statement of work (SOW) document (which is reviewed in draft form with the client in phase 2 and then finalized in phase 3). The SOW contains a section that focuses on any risks to the project and on any special change control processes to be put in place.

Whenever a deliverable is to be provided to the client (e.g., a configured server or deliverable document), the consultant must review it and the project manager must approve it before it can be considered complete. Internal checkpoints are also scheduled by the project manager to allow the team to get together and review progress with the client. This is a critical element in the change control process, and the project manager typically reports project status and any changes required to the client after these meetings.

Typically the success of these additional processes is reviewed in the final customer satisfaction meeting, and the client stakeholders are asked for specific feedback on the success or failure of these processes.

5.4 CIT[1]

The CIT Group has implemented a system development life-cycle (SDLC) methodology known as PMDs, or project management deliverables. The SDLC is a structured approach for development from planning and design to implementation and support. The methodology has a proven series of steps and tasks developers can follow to build quality projects at lower costs and with less risk.

Quality Assurance (QA) is an IT risk management organization within Systems and Technology Services (STS). The organization is dedicated to the introduction, use, and refinement of systems development methodologies for application development. The group also manages the processes surrounding application and infrastructure change control and audit issues resolution for both internal and external auditors. This organization serves the members of STS and all of CIT's business units.

The PMDs have been created to assist project teams in the communication, facilitation, and successful completion of projects. They are based on traditional system development life-cycle methodologies, with customizations based on feedback from STS resources. The responsibility for creating PMDs should be distributed across a variety of project team members based on their roles and responsibilities. All projects require the completion of a "project scope" document, including a methodology compliance assessment. The methodology compliance assessment is a scorecard developed within the IT organization to assess the risk the project may pose to the company. The project manager and STS-QA will determine the appropriate PMDs based on the assessment score and a subsequent discussion regarding project details.

The QA resources dedicated to the PMD methodology work with project managers, developers, business users, and vendors to ensure that project documentation sufficiently

---

1. This section on CIT has been provided by Zephanie Z. Thompson, Project Specialist, The CIT Group, Call Center Technology.

details the management of the project, the gathering of business requirements, the design and development of the solution, the testing of the application and its infrastructure, and the implementation of the solution. Services provided by STS-QA in this area of expertise are outlined below:

- Train developers, project managers, and business analysts on SDLC process, tools, and deliverables
- Organize and lead meetings with senior management to discuss the SDLC process, best practices, and areas for improvement
- Define project-specific deliverables based on evaluation criteria
- Schedule frequent reviews of deliverables with project managers
- Analyze deliverables for completeness and recommend areas for improvement
- Review project plans, requirements documentation, design specifications, test plans, training materials, and so on, to ensure that project teams have satisfactorily addressed business requirements and user needs
- Maintain repository of deliverables and related sign-offs

The QA organization's primary focus is on building strong relationships with the STS community via the provision of various consultative services. Those services include:

- Introducing, evolving, and evaluating project methodology compliance tools and deliverables
- Elevating application code to QA and production environments
- Evaluating, implementing, and maintaining version control systems
- Auditing production environments and some UAT environments
- Building and refining application change control processes
- Facilitating infrastructure change control process
- Managing STS Audit Log

Through these services, STS-QA assists the organization in creating and maintaining valuable information regarding projects, their features/functions, development best practices, and processes/procedures.

Periodically, the QA organization provides training on the methodology, called "PMD Day." During the training, the QA methodology group presents the PMD process and documentation as well as answers any questions from the participants. The STS-QA group encourages all project managers, data owners, STS approvers, and business approvers to attend a PMD session each year.

Phases of PMD Life Cycle The CIT Group has many phases to the PMD life cycle. Below are those phases and definitions of each.

(a) *Phase 1: Project Scope.* The scope represents a high-level look at the project. It includes an application for a project code (which is necessary in STS to spend money) and helps to answer questions such as: What is the problem that the new software or process will solve? What exactly is the solution? At a high level, what is the phase-by-phase approach and timeline for the project? What are the risks associated with the project?

(b) *Phase 2: Functional Requirements Specification.* To provide a highly detailed roadmap for the rest of the project. How does work get done now? How will work be done after the solution is in place? What are the details of the business and technical requirements? What people or technologies might be impacted by the solution? How will we know when the project is complete? How will we manage issues, change, and status reporting? All these questions will be addressed in the requirements specification.

(c) *Phase 3: Technical Architecture Overview.* To provide a set of documents and diagrams that the development team will use to fashion the solution. Infrastructure, application, and database design as other technical considerations are included in the technical architecture.

(d) *Phase 4: Application Design.*

(e) *Phase 5: Application Development.*

(f) *Phase 6: System Integration Testing Development Environment.* To ensure that the solution is as completely tested as possible. The test plan is primarily a translation of the business requirements into testable scripts. Technical testing, such as load testing, is also considered in the plan.

(g) *Phase 7: Elevations Planning.*

(h) *Phase 8: UAT Testing.*

(i) *Phase 9: Deployment/Implementation.* To clearly document approaches to implementation, including installation, documentation, and training. Also, to begin action on service-level agreements.

To keep senior Management in the Methodology loop, QA delivers a monthly methodology status report to the CIO, the CIO's direct reports, the authorized approvers, finance, and audit. Included is a monthly methodology scorecard report. The scorecard serves to provide management with an "at-a-glance" snapshot of the methodological health of the project. Each project that meets certain criteria (methodology score, strategic importance) is listed on the scorecard and rated.

The primary goal of the methodology is to help deliver the best solution and to ensure that the solution has the most prudent level of documentation. It's important to ensure that communication is with the right people (i.e., finance, audit, STS approvers) at the right time and with information that will help you to get the job done.

5.5 TOTAL QUALITY MANAGEMENT

During the past decade, the concept of TQM has revolutionized the operations and manufacturing functions of many companies. Companies have learned quickly that project management principles and systems can be used to support and administer TQM programs, and vice versa. Ultimately excellent companies have completely integrated the two complementary systems.

The emphasis in TQM is on addressing quality issues in total systems. Quality, however, is never an end goal. Total quality management systems run continuously and concurrently in every area in which a company does business. Their goal is to bring to market products of better and better quality and not just of the same quality as last year or the year before.

Total quality management was founded on the principles advocated by W. Edwards Deming, Joseph M. Juran, and Phillip B. Crosby. Deming is famous for his role in turning postwar Japan into a dominant force in the world economy. Total quality management processes are based on Deming's simple plan–do–check–act cycle.

The cycle fits completely with project management principles. To fulfill the goals of any project, first you plan what you're going to do, then you do it. Next, you check on what you did. You fix what didn't work, and then you execute what you set out to do. But the cycle doesn't end with the output. Deming's cycle works as a continuous-improvement system, too. When the project is complete, you examine the lessons learned in its planning and execution. Then you incorporate those lessons into the process and begin the plan–do–check–act cycle all over again on a new project.

Total quality management also is based on three other important elements: customer focus, process thinking, and variation reduction. Does that remind you of project management principles? It should. The plan–do–check–act cycle can be used to identify, validate, and implement best practices in project management.

One of the characteristics of companies that have won the prestigious Malcolm Baldrige Award is that each has an excellent project management system. Companies such as Motorola, Armstrong World Industries, General Motors, Kodak, Xerox, and IBM use integrated TQM and project management systems.

During a live videoconference on the subject, "How to Achieve Maturity in Project Management," Dave Kandt, Group Vice President for Quality and Program Management at Johnson Controls, commented on the reasons behind Johnson Controls' astounding success:

> We came into project management a little differently than some companies. We have combined project management and TQC (total quality control) or total quality management. Our first design and development projects in the mid-1980s led us to believe that our functional departments were working pretty well separately, but we needed to have some systems to bring them together. And, of course, a lot of what project management is about is getting work to flow horizontally through the company. What we did first was to contact Dr. Norman Feigenbaum, who is the granddaddy of TQC in North America, who helped us establish some systems that linked together the whole company. Dr. Feigenbaum looked at quality in the broadest sense: quality of products, quality of systems, quality of deliverables, and, of course, the quality of projects and new product launches. A key part of these systems included project management systems that addressed product introduction and the product introduction process. Integral to this was project management training, which was required to deliver these systems.
>
> We began with our executive office, and once we had explained the principles and philosophies of project management to these people, we moved to the management of plants, engineering managers, analysts, purchasing people, and of course project managers. Only once the foundation was laid did we proceed with actual project management and with defining the role and responsibility so that the entire company would understand

their role in project management once these people began to work. Just the understanding allowed us to move to a matrix organization and eventually to a stand-alone project management department. So how well did that work? Subsequently, since the mid-1980s, we have grown from 2 or 3 projects to roughly 50 in North America and Europe. We have grown from 2 or 3 project managers to 35. I don't believe it would have been possible to manage this growth or bring home this many projects without project management systems and procedures and people with understanding at the highest levels of the company.

In the early 1990s we found that we were having some success in Europe, and we won our first design and development project there. And with that project, we carried to Europe not only project managers and engineering managers who understood these principles but also the systems and training we incorporated in North America. So we had a company wide integrated approach to project management. What we've learned in these last 10 years that is the most important to us, I believe, is that you begin with the systems and the understanding of what you want the various people to do in the company across all functional barriers, then bring in project management training, and last implement project management.

Of course, the people we selected for project management were absolutely critical, and we selected the right people. You mentioned the importance of project managers understanding business, and the people that we put in these positions are very carefully chosen. Typically, they have a technical background, a marketing background, and a business and financial background. It is very hard to find these people, but we find that they have the necessary cross-functional understanding to be able to be successful in this business.

At Johnson Controls, project management and TQM were developed concurrently. Dave Kandt was asked during the same videoconference whether companies must have a solid TQM culture in place before they attempt the development of a project management program. He said:

I don't think that is necessary. The reason why I say that is that companies like Johnson Controls are more the exception than the rule of implementing TQM and project management together. I know companies that were reasonably mature in project management and then ISO 9000 came along, and because they had project management in place in a reasonably mature fashion, it was an easier process for them to implement ISO 9000 and TQM. There is no question that having TQM in place at the same time or even first would make it a little easier, but what we've learned during the recession is that if you want to compete in Europe and you want to follow ISO 9000 guidelines, TQM must be implemented. And using project management as the vehicle for that implementation quite often works quite well.

There is also the question of whether or not successful project management can exist within the ISO 9000 environment. According to Dave Kandt:

Not only is project management consistent with ISO 9000, a lot of the systems that ISO 9000 require are crucial to project management's success. If you don't have a good quality system, engineering change system, and other things that ISO requires, the project manager is going to struggle in trying to accomplish and execute that project. Further, I think it's interesting that companies that are working to install and deploy ISO 9000, if they are being successful, are probably utilizing project management techniques. Each of the different elements of ISO requires training, and sometimes the creation of systems inside the company that can all be scheduled, teams that can be assigned, deliverables that can be established, tracked, and monitored, and reports that go to senior management. That's exactly how we installed TQC at Johnson Controls, and I see ISO 9000 as having a very similar thrust and intent.

5.6 CONCURRENT ENGINEERING

The need to shorten product development time has always plagued U.S. companies. During favorable economic conditions, corporations have deployed massive amounts of resources to address the problem of long development times. During economic downturns, however, not only are resources scarce, but time becomes a critical constraint. Today, the principles of concurrent engineering have been almost universally adopted as the ideal solution to the problem.

Concurrent engineering requires performing the various steps and processes in managing a project in tandem rather than in sequence. This means that engineering, research and development, production, and marketing all are involved at the beginning of a project, before any work has been done. That is not always easy, and it can create risks as the project is carried through. Superior project planning is needed to avoid increasing the level of risk later in the project. The most serious risks are delays in bringing product to market and costs when rework is needed as a result of poor planning. Improved planning is essential to project management, so it is no surprise that excellent companies integrate concurrent engineering and project management systems.

Chrysler (now DaimlerChrysler) Motors used concurrent engineering with project management to go from concept to market with the Viper sports car in less than three years. Concurrent engineering may well be the strongest driving force behind the increased acceptance of modem project management.

5.7 RISK MANAGEMENT

Risk management is an organized means of identifying and measuring risk and developing, selecting, and managing options for handling those risks. Throughout this book, I have emphasized that tomorrow's project managers will need superior business skills in assessing and managing risk. This includes both project risks and business risks. Project managers in the past were not equipped to quantify risks, respond to risks, develop contingency plans, or keep lessons-learned records. They were forced to go to senior managers for advice on what to do when risky situations developed. Now senior managers are empowering project managers to make risk-related decisions, and that requires a project manager with solid business skills as well as technical knowledge.

Preparing a project plan is based on history. Simply stated: What have we learned from the past? Risk management encourages us to look at the future and anticipate what can go wrong, and then to develop contingency strategies to mitigate these risks.

We have performed risk management in the past, but only financial and scheduling risk management. To mitigate a financial risk, we increased the project's budget. To mitigate a scheduling risk, we added more time to the schedule. But in the 1990s, technical risks became critical. Simply adding into the plan more time and money is not the solution to mitigate technical risks. Technical risk management addresses two primary questions:

- Can we develop the technology within the imposed constraints?
- If we do develop the technology, what is the risk of obsolescence, and when might we expect it to occur?

To address these technical risks, effective risk management strategies are needed based upon technical forecasting. On the surface, it might seem that making risk management an integral part of project planning should be relatively easy. Just identify and address risk factors before they get out of hand. Unfortunately, the reverse is likely to be the norm, at least for the foreseeable future.

For years, companies provided lip service to risk management and adopted the attitude that we should simply live with it. Very little was published on how to develop a structure risk management process. The disaster with the Space Shuttle Challenger in January 1986 created a great awakening on the importance of effective risk management.[2]

Risk management today has become so important that companies are establishing separate risk management organizations within the company. However, many companies have been using risk management functional units for years, and yet this concept has gone unnoticed. The following is an overview of the program management methodology of the risk management department of an international manufacturer headquartered in Ohio. This department has been in operation for approximately 25 years.

> The risk management department is part of the financial discipline of the company and ultimately reports to the treasurer, who reports to the chief financial officer. The overall objective of the department is to coordinate the protection of the company's assets. The primary means of meeting that objective is eliminating or reducing potential losses through loss prevention programs. The department works very closely with the internal environmental health and safety department. Additionally, it utilizes outside loss control experts to assist the company's divisions in loss prevention.
>
> One method employed by the company to insure the entire corporation's involvement in the risk management process is to hold its divisions responsible for any specific losses up to a designated self-insured retention level. If there is a significant loss, the division must absorb it and its impact on their bottom-line profit margin. This directly involves the divisions in both loss prevention and claims management. When a claim does occur, risk management maintains regular contact with division personnel to establish protocol on the claim and reserves and ultimate resolution.
>
> The company does purchase insurance above designated retention levels. As with the direct claims, the insurance premiums are allocated to its divisions. These premiums are

---

2. The case study "The Space Shuttle Challenger Disaster" appears in H. Kerzner, *Advanced Project Management: Best Practices on Implementation,* 2nd ed. Wiley: New York, 2004, p. 781.

calculated based upon sales volume and claim loss history, with the most significant per-centage being allocated to claim loss history.

Each of the company's locations must maintain a business continuity plan for its site. This plan is reviewed by risk management and is audited by the internal audit and envi-ronmental health and safety department.

Risk management is an integral part of the corporation's operations as evidenced by its involvement in the due diligence process for acquisitions or divestitures. It is involved at the onset of the process, not at the end, and provides a detailed written report of find-ings as well as an oral presentation to group management.

Customer service is part of the company's corporate charter. Customers served by risk management are the company's divisions. The department's management style with its customers is one of consensus building and not one of mandating. This is exemplified by the company's use of several worker's compensation third-party administrators (TPAs) in states where it is self-insured. Administratively, it would be much easier to utilize one na-tionwide TPA. However, using strong regional TPAs with offices in states where divisions operate provides knowledgeable assistance with specific state laws to the divisions. This approach has worked very well for this company that recognizes the need for the individ-ual state expertise.

The importance of risk management is now apparent worldwide. The principles of risk management can be applied to all aspects of a business, not just projects. Once a company begins using risk management practices, the company can always identify other applica-tions for the risk management processes.

For multinational companies that are project-driven, risk management takes on para-mount importance. Not all companies, especially in undeveloped countries, have an un-derstanding of risk management or its importance. These countries sometimes view risk management as an overmanagement expense on a project.

Consider the following scenario. As your organization gets better and better at project management, your customers begin giving you more and more work. You're now getting contracts for turnkey projects, or complete-solution projects. Before, all you had to do was deliver the product on time and you were through. Now you are responsible for project in-stallation and startup as well, sometimes even for ongoing customer service. Because the customers no longer use their own resources on the project, they worry less about how you're handling your project management system.

Alternatively, you could be working for third world clients who haven't yet developed their own systems. One hundred percent of the risk for such projects is yours, especially as projects grow more complex (see Figure 5–7). Welcome to the twenty-first century!

One subcontractor received a contract to install components in a customer's new plant. The construction of the plant would be completed by a specific date. After construction was completed, the contractor would install the equipment, perform testing, and then start up. The subcontractor would not be allowed to bill for products or services until after a successful startup. There was also a penalty clause for late delivery.

The contractor delivered the components to the customer on time, but the components were placed in a warehouse because plant construction had been delayed. The contractor now had a cash flow problem and potential penalty payments because of external depen-dencies that sat on the critical path. In other words, the contractor's schedule was being

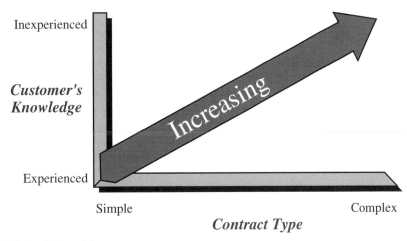

FIGURE 5–7. Future risks.

controlled by actions of others. Had the project manager performed business risk management rather than just technical risk management, these risks could have been reduced.

For the global project manager, risk management takes on a new dimension. What happens if the culture in the country with which you are working neither understands risk management nor has any risk management process? What happens if employees are afraid to surface bad news or identify potential problems? What happens if the project's constraints of time, cost, and quality/performance are meaningless to the local workers?

Even a very simple risk management process is better than having no process at all. Good companies recognize that risk management is part of the value-added chain. Steve Gregerson, formerly Vice President for Product Development at Metzeler Automotive Profile System, believes:

> Risk management is a major value-added function of our project management process. A simple form has been developed with the intent of predicting the likelihood of failure of a program based on its current status. The program team must complete this form for each gateway and report on the risk management in about 20 areas of the program and take countermeasures to mitigate the risk.
>
> In addition, a survey of each member of the program is taken during the gateway review, and any concern which is considered worthy of further analysis is either carried in the team open-issues report or reported in the monthly management reviews or both. I have found that a "gut feeling" of an experienced team member is as good an early-warning system as any.

Keith Rosenau, Chief Engineer and Director of Program Management for Metzeler, continues:

> The improvement process for program management for monthly management reviews now includes senior staff review. Each senior staff member of the attending functional area

is queried for program status and rating. This query requires agreement on the program rating or the lowest rating will be given to the program.

Consulting companies today are under severe pressure to assist their clients with risk management rather than either being an observer or coming on board after the risk management process is completed and not having access to information that could be critical to the success of the project. Brad Ruzicka, Senior Consulting Manager at the StoneBridge Group, explains:

> StoneBridge Group will generally recommend a risk assessment to be performed prior to undertaking projects that meet certain criteria. These criteria include project size, complexity, resource availability, client experience with projects of this type, and client expectations regarding use of new technologies, processes, and/or tools. Our objective in performing the risk assessment is to identify all areas of potential high or medium risk and develop recommendations that will minimize or eliminate the risk. Generally, this approach has been very effective in lowering total project risk.

During the late 1990s, Craig Belton, Vice President for Network Field Operations at Nortel Networks, believed that risk management at the work package level of the work breakdown structure is critical:

> In many areas of Nortel Networks, a risk management qualification is performed as part of the bid response. We are working toward a standard method to perform this risk analysis in order to assess the need for contingency plans. A prerequisite for the risk analysis is the work breakdown structure (WBS) being proposed for the project. Each work package will be examined in terms of potential risk to the planned project time, cost, and quality. The risks are described, impacts and probabilities identified, and the mitigation cost estimated. This assessment of the risk is a quantitative way to identify the contingency plans needed for a project and facilitates the management of these plans during the project implementation.

Hewlett-Packard Services also uses the WBS for risk analysis. Sameh Boutros, Director Americas Engagement PMO for HP Services, states that:

> All projects must go through the SOAR (solution opportunity approval and review) process. Business management reviews projects at the bid stage and at selected points within the project life cycle. A key element of each review is risk analysis and monitoring risk status. A key tool is the WBS. Risk is addressed at the work package level and subjected to the risk planning process. Contingency plans are made and reserves allocated and managed. Because we are invariably competing for business that has to be profitable, risk has to be addressed in detail. If we get it wrong, we either price ourselves out of the bid or have an unprofitable project. Being able to correctly analyze and estimate risk is the key to our business.

One of the major advantages of a project management methodology is that it provides structure to processes such as the risk management process. Risk management templates for project management are an excellent way of providing guidance for workers on how to handle risk management.

5.8 BOEING AIRCRAFT

As companies become successful in project management, risk management becomes a structured process that is performed continuously throughout the life cycle of the project. The two most common factors supporting the need for continuous risk management is how long the project lasts and how much money is at stake. For example, consider Boeing's aircraft projects. Designing and delivering a new plane might require 10 years and a financial investment of more than $5 billion.

Table 5–1 shows the characteristics of risks at Boeing. (The table does not mean to imply that risks are mutually exclusive of each other.) New technologies can appease customers, but production risks increase because the learning curve is lengthened with new technology compared to accepted technology. The learning curve can be lengthened further when features are custom designed for individual customers. In addition, the loss of suppliers over the life of a plane can affect the level of technical and production risk. The relationships among these risks require the use of a risk management matrix and continued risk assessment.

TABLE 5–1. RISK CATEGORIES AT BOEING

Type of Risk	Risk Description	Risk Mitigation Strategy
Financial	Up-front funding and payback period based upon number of planes sold	• Funding by life-cycle phases • Continuous financial risk management • Sharing risks with subcontractors • Risk reevaluation based upon sales commitments
Market	Forecasting customers' expectations on cost, configuration, and amenities based upon a 30- to 40-year life of a plane	• Close customer contact and input • Willingness to custom design per customer • Development of a baseline design that allows for customization
Technical	Because of the long lifetime for a plane, must forecast technology and its impact on cost, safety, reliability, and maintainability	• A structured change management process • Use of proven technology rather than high-risk technology • Parallel product improvement and new product development processes
Production	Coordination of manufacturing and assembly of a large number of subcontractors without impacting cost, schedule, quality, or safety	• Close working relationships with subcontractors • A structured change management process • Lessons learned from other new airplane programs • Use of learning curves

5.9 INTERACTING RISKS: THE SPACE SHUTTLE COLUMBIA DISASTER _____

Sometimes, the importance of risk management does not occur until after a significant disaster appears. When the Space Shuttle Challenger disaster occurred, the marketplace recognized the importance of risk management, especially the need for technical risk management. When the Space Shuttle Columbia disaster occurred, the importance of interacting risks, or the impact that one risk can have on other risks, became important.

The Space Shuttle Columbia Disaster[3]

Few projects start with an explosion. Even fewer start with a deliberate explosion. Yet every time the Space Shuttle is launched into space, five tremendous explosions in the rocket engines are needed to hurl the orbiter into orbit around the earth. In just over 10 minutes, the orbiter vehicle goes from zero miles an hour to over 17,500 miles per hour as it circles the earth.

Shuttle launches are a very dangerous business. The loss of the second Shuttle on February 1, 2003 shocked everyone. It is apparent now that some fuel tank insulation dislodged during liftoff and struck the orbiter during its powered ascent to earth orbit and that the insulation punched a fatal hole in the leading edge of the left wing. This hole allowed super heated gases, about 10,000 degrees Fahrenheit, to melt the left wing during the re-entry phase of the mission. The loss of the orbiter was the result of the loss of the left wing.

Reading through the results of the disaster, one cannot help but conclude how simple and straight forward the project risks can be that are handled by most project managers. As an example, we can consider the writing of software. Writing and delivering computer software has its challenges, but the risks are not on the same scale of a Space Shuttle launch. Even the standard risk response strategies (avoidance, transference, mitigation and acceptance) take on new meanings when accelerating to achieve speeds of over 15,000 mph. For example:

- Avoidance is not possible
- Acceptance has to be active not passive
- Transference is not possible, and
- Mitigation entails a lot of work, and under massive constraints.

For the Space Shuttle, risk analysis is nonlinear but for most software projects, a simple, linear impact analysis may be sufficient. The equation for linear impact analysis can be written as:

$$\text{Risk Impact} = (\text{Risk Probability}) * (\text{Risk Consequence})$$

For a given risk event, there is a probability of the risk occurring and a consequence expressed in some numerical units of the damage done to the project cost, time-line or qual-

---

3. This material is provided by Randall R. Kline, MBA, PMP®, Qualtek Software Development, Inc. Reproduced by Permission of Randall R. Kline.

ity. This is a simple linear equation. If one of the factors on the right side of the equation doubles, the risk impact doubles. For a given set of factors on the right there is one answer, regardless of when the risk occurs. So, based on the equation, impact can be understood and planned for.

Most of the computer software projects have relatively simple functions that either happened or did not happen. The vendor either delivered on time or they did not deliver on time. If a particular "risk" event trigger appeared, then there usually existed a time period, usually in days, when the "risk response" could be initiated. There might be dozens of risks, but each one could be defined and explained with only two or three variables.

This linear approach to risk management had several advantages for computer software projects:

● The risks were understandable and could be explained quite easily.
● Management could understand the process from which a probability and a consequence were obtained.
● There was usually one risk impact for a given risk event.
● No one was aware that one risk event might require dozens of strategies to anticipate all the possible consequences.

One valid argument is that the "risk" of external collisions with the space vehicle as it accelerates to make orbital speed results in a multi-variant, multi-dimensional, non-linear risk function that is very difficult to comprehend, much less manage. This is orders of magnitude more complex than the project risks encountered when managing computer software development projects.

Risk Definitions and Some Terms   For this case study, "risks" and related terms will be defined according to the Project Management Institute's PMBOK® Guide (Project Management Body of Knowledge).

● *Risk:* An uncertain event or condition that, if it occurs, has a positive or negative effect on a project's objectives.

For this discussion, the focus will be on negative risks. This family of negative risks can have detrimental consequences to the successful completion of the project. These risks may not happen, but if they do, we know the consequences will make it difficult to complete the project successfully. The consequences may range from a minor change in the time-line to total project failure. The key here is that for each risk, two variables are needed: probability of occurrence and a measurement.

● *Risk Triggers:* These are indicators that a risk event has happened or is about to happen.
● *Risk Consequence(s):* What could happen if the risk is triggered? Are we going to lose a few dollars, lose our job, or lose an entire business?

To analyze these standard terms, additional terms can be included. These terms are needed to adequately support managing risks that are multi-variant, multi-dimensional, and non-linear risk functions. These additional terms include:

- *Risk Scope:* What parts of the project are impacted if the risk is triggered? Does this risk jeopardize a task, a phase or the entire project? Is the risk confined to one project or an entire portfolio of projects?
- *Risk Response Rules:* Given that the event occurred, and based on available information, what is the best response? Can we derive rules to make intelligent decisions based on the information acquired when the risk event triggers or even the risk events occur?
- *Risk Response Levels:* Based on the variables and the response rules, the level of concern may range from:
  a. No problem
  b. Serious
  c. Nothing is left
- *Risk Time Line:* If the risk event or risk trigger occurs, how much time is available to make a decision about the best response to the risk? Are there two days to make a decision or two seconds?

All we know is if the risk event is "triggered" or occurs, bad things can and will happen. Our goal is to minimize the consequences. Our plan is that by early identification and rigorous analysis of the risks, we will have time to develop a portfolio of responses to minimize the consequences from a risk event.

Background to the Space Shuttle Launch   The three liquid fuel motors consume an amazing quantity of super cooled fuel. The main fuel tank is insulated to insure that the fuel stays hundreds of degrees below the freezing point of water. It is this insulation that had a history of coming off the fuel tank and hitting the orbiter. It most cases, it caused very minor damage to the orbiter because the foam was usually the size of popcorn. In one or two previous launches the foam was able to knock a tile off the orbiter. Fortunately, the orbiter was able to return safely. So for most of the launch team, the news that Columbia had been struck by foam was of minor concern. After all, if the risk was not a major problem in one hundred previous launches, then it could not be a problem in this launch. Reviewing, our linear impact equation:

$$\text{Risk Impact} = (\text{Risk Probability}) * (\text{Risk Consequence})$$

The risk probability was very high but the consequences were always acceptable. Therefore, the conclusion was that it would always be an acceptable risk. This is what happens when there is only one risk consequence for the life of the risk event. People want to believe that the future is just the same history waiting to happen.

Description of What Happens as the Shuttle Re-Enters the Atmosphere   If getting the orbiter into space is one problem, then getting the orbiter back is another problem. Re-entry is a complex set of computer-guided maneuvers to change the speed of the vehicle into heat. And as the heat grows, the speed decreases. Since the metal components of the Shuttle melt around 2,000 degrees Fahrenheit, the leading edges of the orbiter are covered in ceramic tiles that melt at about 3,000 degrees Fahrenheit. The tiles keep the 10,000 degree re-entry heat from penetrating the vehicle. If all goes well, the computers bring the orbiter to a slow enough speed that a human being can land the vehicle.

In Columbia's launch, the foam knocked several of the tiles off the leading edge of the left wing and created a hole where the tiles had been attached. Upon re-entry, the hot gases entered Columbia's left wing and melted the internal structure. When enough of the wing melted, the wing collapsed and the orbiter blew apart.

The Question   What are some of the variables needed to understand the risk of foreign objects colliding with the vehicle from the time the rocket engines start until the rocket engines are jettisoned from the orbiter some ten minutes later?

The Risk Function   Since the linear risk impact equation may not be applicable, what kind of questions should we ask if we are to find a risk impact equation that could work?

Consider what you need to measure and/or track if an object strikes the Shuttle:

(a) What are the attributes of the foreign object?
- What was it that you collided with?
- What is the length, width, thickness?
- What is the mass of the object?
- What is the density of the object?
- How hard is the object?
- How is the mass of the object distributed?
- Is it like a cannon ball, or dumbbells or sheet of paper?

(b) What are the attributes of the collision?
- Where did it hit?
- Were there multiple impact points?
- How much damage was done?
- Can the damage be verified and examined?
- Is this an isolated event or the first of many?
- What was the angle of the collision? Was it a glancing blow or a direct contact?
- Did the object hit and leave the area or is it imbedded in the vehicle?
- Why did you collide with it? Are you off course? Is something coming apart?

(c) What are the attributes of the vehicle?
- How fast was it going at the time of the collision?
- Was it in the middle of a complex maneuver?
- Did the collision damage a component needed in the current phase of the mission?
- Did the collision damage a component needed later in the mission?

This is certainly not an exhaustive list, but it is already orders of magnitude more complex compared to most project managers' experiences in risk management. Unfortunately, the problem is even more complex.

The acceleration of the vehicles adds another dimension to the risk function. A collision with an object at 100 mph is not the same as when the collision occurs when the vehicle is going 200 mph. The damage will not be twice as much as with a linear equation (i.e. if you are going twice as fast, then there will be twice the damage). These risk functions have now become non-linear. The damage caused when the speed doubles may be sixteen times more, not just twice as much. This has a significant impact on how often you track and record the on-going events.

Time is also a critical issue. Time is not on your side in a project that moves this fast. It is not just the fact that the risks are non-linear, but the response envelope is constantly changing. In a vehicle going from zero to 15,000 mph, a lot can happen in a very short time.

Now let's look at what happens to the simple risk-impact equation:

$$\text{Risk Impact} = (\text{Risk Probability}) * (\text{Risk Consequence})$$

One probability for a risk event may be sufficient, but the risk consequences are now a function of many variables that have to be measured before an impact can be computed. Also, the risk consequence may be a non-linear function. This is a much more complex problem than trying to identify one probability and one consequence per risk event.

Conclusions   It may be necessary to compress the risk consequence function into some relatively simple equations and then combine the simple equations into a much more complex mathematical statement. For example, consider the variables of dimensions, weight, and speed. What type of rules can we define to make the **risk impact** easily derived and of value in making responses to the risk?

Rule 1: If the sum of the three dimensions (length + width + height) is less than 30, then the Risk-Level is "10". If the sum of the three dimensions (length + width + height) is more than 30, the Risk-Level is "20".
Rule 2: If the weight is over 500 grams, then the risk-level is multiplied by 1.5.
Rule 3: For every 5 seconds of flight, the risk-level doubles.

This process can be continued on for all relevant variables.

Risk-response-level (RRL) is the sum of the individual risk-levels computed. If the RRL is less than 50, the event is taken as non-critical. If the RRL is less than 100, procedures A, B and C should be initiated, and so on.

This exercise provides us with "rules" to initiate action. There is no discussion or guessing as to the proper response to a "hazardous event." There is no necessity to contact management for "approval" to start further actions. There are no "stare downs" with management to minimize the event for political or other considerations.

The more complicated things get, the more important rules and pre-planned responses become to successfully managing project risk.

Lessons Learned   In reviewing articles on the Space Shuttle events before and after its destruction, several things were learned.

- Debris had hit the Shuttle during its powered ascent in previous launches. Management believed that because there were few problems in the past, the risk impact was known and would not change in the future.

  The lesson learned is not to make the same mistake.
- Risks can be very complex.

  The lesson learned is to study more about risk and how to document the Impact so even managers unfamiliar with risk management concepts can grasp complex impact functions.
- The Shuttle crew never knew the spacecraft was doomed. By the time they were aware of the danger, the Shuttle disintegrated.

  The lesson learned is that life is like that and probably more often than you realize.

References

1. Peter Sprent, *Taking Risks—The Science of Uncertainty,* Penguin Books, 1988
2. Daniel Kehrer, *The Art of Taking Intelligent Risks,* Times Books, 1989
3. William Langewiesche, "Columbia's Last Flight," *The Atlantic Monthly,* November, 2003

5.10 CHANGE MANAGEMENT

Companies use change management to control both internally generated changes and customer-driven changes in the scope of projects. Most companies establish a configuration control board or change control board to regulate changes. For customer-driven changes, the customer participates as a member of the configuration control board. The configuration control board addresses the following four questions at a minimum:

- What is the cost of the change?
- What is the impact of the change on project schedules?
- What added value does the change represent for the customer or end user?
- What are the risks?

The benefit of developing a change management process is that it allows you to manage your customer. When your customer initiates a change request, you must be able to predict immediately the impact of the change on schedule, safety, cost, and technical performance. This information must be transmitted to the customer immediately, especially if your methodology is such that no further changes are possible because of the life-cycle phase you have entered. Educating your customer as to how your methodology works is critical in getting customer buy-in for your recommendations during the scope change process.

Consulting companies must have their own templates for controlling scope changes and must also be knowledgeable with the client's change control process. Brad Ruzicka, Senior Consulting Manager of the StoneBridge Group, explains:

> As a consulting firm, the ability to control changes in scope is extremely important, as we are often asked to provide bids for our services at the outset of a project. As a result, our

standard approach is to define scope, overall approach, deliverables, and budget expectations in our statement of work and obtain agreement from the project sponsor based on examples of similar projects our firm has done in the past. We then agree that any substantive changes to the above over the course of the project will be jointly agreed to by StoneBridge Group and the sponsor, at which point we will produce a revised SOW.

Risk management and change management function together. Risks generate changes that, in turn, create new risks. For example, consider a company in which the project manager is given the responsibility for developing a new product. Management usually establishes a launch date even before the project is started. Management wants the income stream from the project to begin on a certain date to offset the development costs. Project managers view executives as their customers during new project development, but the executives view their customers as the stockholders who expect a revenue stream from the new product. When the launch date is not met, surprises result in heads rolling, usually executive heads first.

In the previous edition of the book, we stated that ABB had developed excellent processes for risk management, so it is understandable that it also has structured change management processes. In companies excellent in project management, risk management and change management occur continuously throughout the life cycle of the project. The impact on product quality, cost, and timing is continuously updated and reported to management as quickly as possible. The goal is always to minimize the number and extent of surprises.

5.11 OTHER MANAGEMENT PROCESSES

Employee empowerment and self-directed work teams took the business world by storm during the early 1990s. With growing emphasis on customer satisfaction, it made sense to empower those closest to the customer—the order service people, nurses, clerks, and so on—to take action in solving customers' complaints. A logical extension of employee empowerment is the self-managed work team. A self-directed work team is a group of employees with given day-to-day responsibility for managing themselves and the work they perform. This includes the responsibility for handling resources and solving problems.

Some call empowerment a basis for the next industrial revolution, and it is true that many internationally known corporations have established self-directed work teams. Such corporations include Esso, Lockheed-Martin, Honeywell, and Weyerhauser. Time will tell whether these concepts turn out to be a trend or only a fad.

Reengineering a corporation is another term for downsizing the organization with the (often unfortunate) belief that the same amount of work can be performed with fewer people, at lower cost, and in a shorter period of time. Because project management proposes getting more done in less time with fewer people, it seems only practical to implement project management as part of reengineering. It still is not certain that downsizing executed at the same time as the implementation of project management works, but project-driven organizations seem to consider it successful.

Life-cycle costing was first used in military organizations. Simply stated, life-cycle costing requires that decisions made during the R&D process be evaluated against the total life-cycle cost of the system. Life-cycle costs are the total cost of the organization for the ownership and acquisition of the product over its full life.

In the future, we can expect numerous other management techniques to appear, and most likely they will all be integrated into the project management methodology.[4]

5.12 JOHNSON CONTROLS

Perhaps one of the best, and most successful methodologies for project management was developed by Johnson Controls, Automotive Group.

Project Management at Johnson Controls[5]

Johnson Controls' *Product Launch System* (PLUS) is the method by which cross-functional teams turn ideas into manufactured products that exceed customers' expectations. Project management methodology provides the framework and impetus that allows PLUS to operate successfully. The following provides some insight into the best practices used by Johnson Controls to ensure successful product launches.

PLUS and The Project Management Body of Knowledge (PMBOK® Guide) The development of PLUS incorporated eight of the nine knowledge areas of project management as defined by the Project Management Institute (PMI®). Organizations interested in utilizing the project management methodology need not include all PMBOK® Guide knowledge areas under one business system; rather, the needs of the organization define the particular knowledge areas for inclusion in a business system. Johnson Controls, for example, chose to incorporate the *procurement management* knowledge area into its Purchasing Operating System (POS).

PLUS and Change PLUS is revised every year in October. This annual change mitigates two key issues: (1) the tendency within large organizations toward inflexibility and (2) change fear or change overload. The continual state of change in the business environment in which Johnson Controls operates necessitates evolution of business systems. The best approach Johnson Controls has found to manage the potential negative effects of change has been to institute annual PLUS updates. The annual updates have eliminated the need for wholesale change and have reduced the anxiety that generally accompanies departure from accepted practices. Change has thus become an accepted part of the organization's culture. Employees and organizational leaders alike have come to expect and request PLUS changes which address emerging needs.

4. For a window into future management techniques, the reader should look at Dinesh Seth and Subhash C. Rastogi, *Global Management Solutions—Demystified.* Singapore:: Thomson Publishers, 2004.
5. The material in this section was provided by David Kandt, Group Vice President, Quality and Program Management, and Terri Pomfret, Director, Program Management Office-Seating Systems.

PLUS and Communication Core to the effective use of PLUS is communication. Johnson Controls has found the best method for communicating PLUS expectations and processes is through multiple media: visual aids, training, and easy-to-find Web-based material. The visual aids (see Figures 5–8 and 5–9) are in the form of banners and pocket reference cards that identify core phase deliverables, deliverable relationships, responsibilities, milestones, and reference document detail. Both types of communication aids have become very popular; the banner can be found in most offices and cubicles, and the card can be found in the pockets (or planners) of most employees and leaders.

Comprehensive PLUS training is available in online self-directed courses and in a classroom environment. The online training is accessible to every employee around the globe. Employees access the training as time permits on an as-needed basis. The major objective for the online training, beyond communicating PLUS' expectations and processes, is easy, immediate, and flexible access. Classroom training, while less immediate and not as easy to access, can be structured to the needs of a particular project team. Employees are encouraged to participate, as project teams, in classroom PLUS training. This type of team training provides a venue for the team to role-play and apply the training to their particular project. Both self-directed and classroom training, although different in their approach, help individuals and teams understand and apply PLUS.

PLUS Applied PLUS is applied to product development projects through cross-functional teamwork. The best practice of ensuring maximization of team meetings effectiveness is a standard simultaneous development team (SDT) meeting methodology. Johnson Controls accumulated the best approaches various teams were utilizing and then combined them into a guideline (see Figure 5–10). The guideline defines expected behavior for SDT members and general meeting efficiency recommendations as well as the agenda framework, time frame, and suggested attendees for five core SDT meetings: tech, timing, finance, launch, and product change. This standardization has helped product development teams stay on track with their projects and provides a regular venue for discussing deliverables and resolving issues.

The venue for discussing project status with business unit leadership is the monthly project review. Project managers are given 15–30 minutes with their leadership to present project status and request executive assistance if needed. To ensure focus on the project deliverables, rather than simply the *hot issue of the day,* project managers use the phase report workbook (see Figure 5–11) to provide status for each core project deliverable. The business unit leadership thus is able to see project progress and/or is altered to issues that may need their intervention.

The workbook was designed to support multiple purposes. First and foremost, it is a working tool used by the SDT to stay cognizant of project deliverables. As such, the workbook is divided into the five PLUS phases that define the required project deliverables and responsibilities that ensure projects will exceed customer expectations. The teams discuss and work through each of these deliverables in their SDT meetings. The workbook also provides reference to supporting forms, work instructions, and guidelines that help teams complete the deliverables. The second purpose of the workbook is to document project status and highlight issues that require business unit leadership intervention. The third purpose is to document phase exit approval.

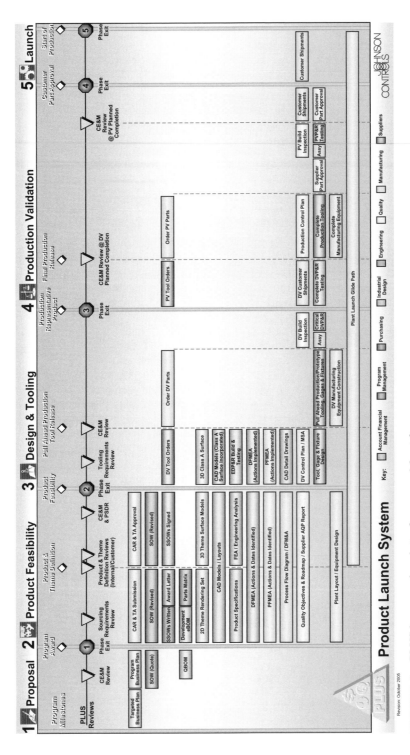

FIGURE 5–8. PLUS banner and pocket reference card front face.

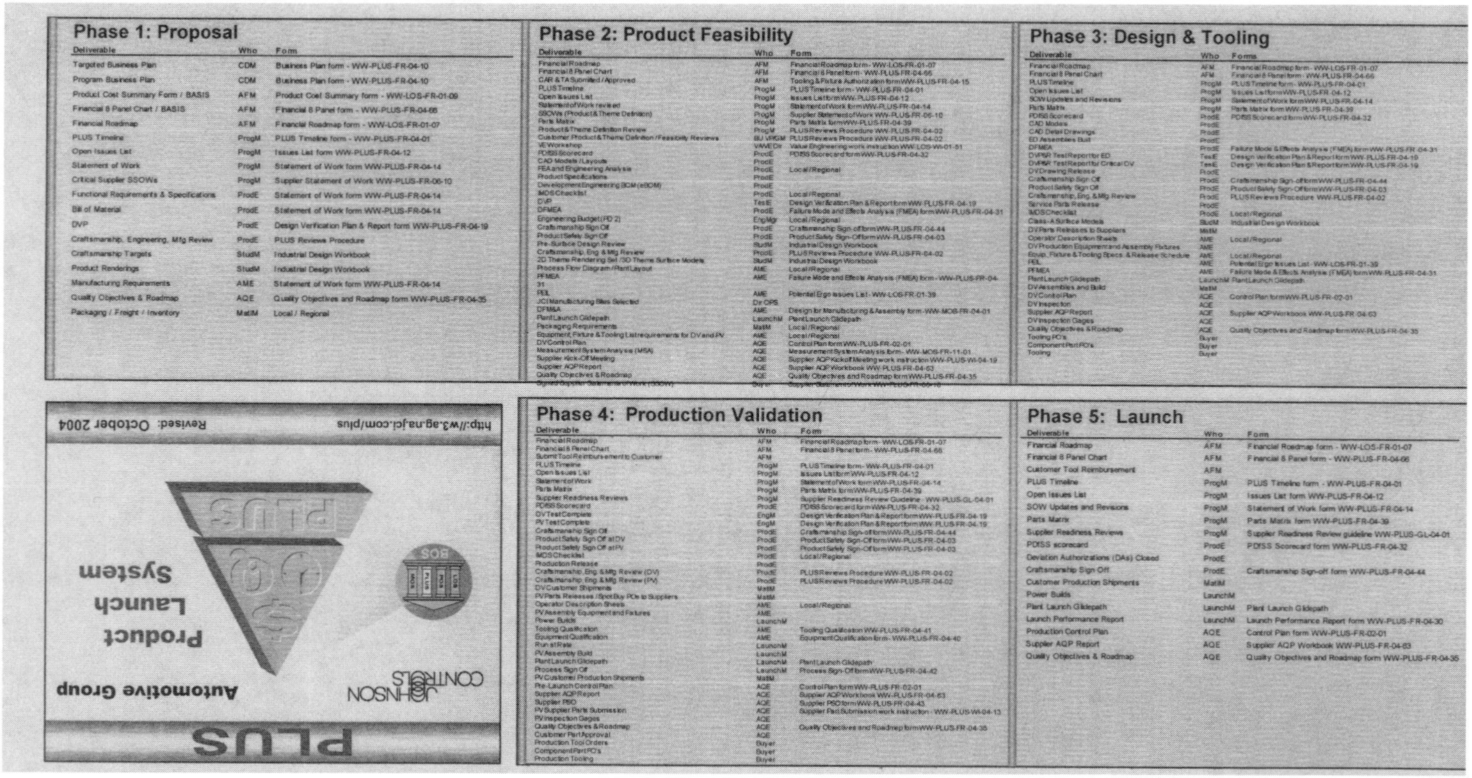
Phase 1: Proposal
Deliverable | Who | Form
Targeted Business Plan | CDM | Business Plan form - WW-PLUS-FR-04-10
Program Business Plan | CDM | Business Plan form - WW-PLUS-FR-04-10
Product Cost Summary Form / BASIS | AFM | Product Cost Summary form - WW-LOS-FR-01-09
Financial 8 Panel Chart / BASIS | AFM | Financial 8 Panel form - WW-PLUS-FR-04-66
Financial Roadmap | AFM | Financial Roadmap form - WW-LOS-FR-01-07
PLUS Timeline | ProgM | PLUS Timeline form - WW-PLUS-FR-04-01
Open Issues List | ProgM | Issues List form WW-PLUS-FR-04-12
Statement of Work | ProgM | Statement of Work form WW-PLUS-FR-04-14
Critical Supplier SSOWs | ProgM | Supplier Statement of Work WW-PLUS-FR-06-10
Functional Requirements & Specifications | ProdE | Statement of Work form WW-PLUS-FR-04-14
Bill of Material | ProdE | Statement of Work form WW-PLUS-FR-04-14
DVP | ProdE | Design Verification Plan & Report form WW-PLUS-FR-04-19
Craftsmanship, Engineering, Mfg Review | ProdE | PLUS Reviews Procedure
Craftsmanship Targets | StudM | Industrial Design Workbook
Product Renderings | StudM | Industrial Design Workbook
Manufacturing Requirements | AME | Statement of Work form WW-PLUS-FR-04-14
Quality Objectives & Roadmap | AQE | Quality Objectives and Roadmap form WW-PLUS-FR-04-35
Packaging / Freight / Inventory | MatlM | Local / Regional
Phase 2: Product Feasibility
Phase 3: Design & Tooling
Phase 4: Production Validation
Phase 5: Launch
Deliverable | Who | Form
Financial Roadmap | AFM | Financial Roadmap form - WW-LOS-FR-01-07
Financial 8 Panel Chart | AFM | Financial 8 Panel form - WW-PLUS-FR-04-66
Customer Tool Reimbursement | AFM
PLUS Timeline | ProgM | PLUS Timeline form - WW-PLUS-FR-04-01
Open Issues List | ProgM | Issues List form WW-PLUS-FR-04-12
SOW Updates and Revisions | ProgM | Statement of Work form WW-PLUS-FR-04-14
Parts Matrix | ProgM | Parts Matrix form WW-PLUS-FR-04-39
Supplier Readiness Reviews | ProgM | Supplier Readiness Review guideline WW-PLUS-GL-04-01
PDISS scorecard | ProdE | PDISS Scorecard form WW-PLUS-FR-04-32
Deviation Authorizations (DAs) Closed | ProdE
Craftsmanship Sign Off | ProdE | Craftsmanship Sign-off form WW-PLUS-FR-04-44
Customer Production Shipments | MatlM
Power Builds | LaunchM
Plant Launch Glidepath | LaunchM | Plant Launch Glidepath
Launch Performance Report | LaunchM | Launch Performance Report form WW-PLUS-FR-04-30
Production Control Plan | AQE | Control Plan form WW-PLUS-FR-02-01
Supplier AQP Report | AQE | Supplier AQP Workbook WW-PLUS-FR-04-63
Quality Objectives & Roadmap | AQE | Quality Objectives and Roadmap form WW-PLUS-FR-04-35
http://w3.ag.na.jci.com/plus
Revised: October 2004
PLUS
Automotive Group
Product Launch System
JOHNSON CONTROLS

FIGURE 5–9. PLUS pocket reference card back face.

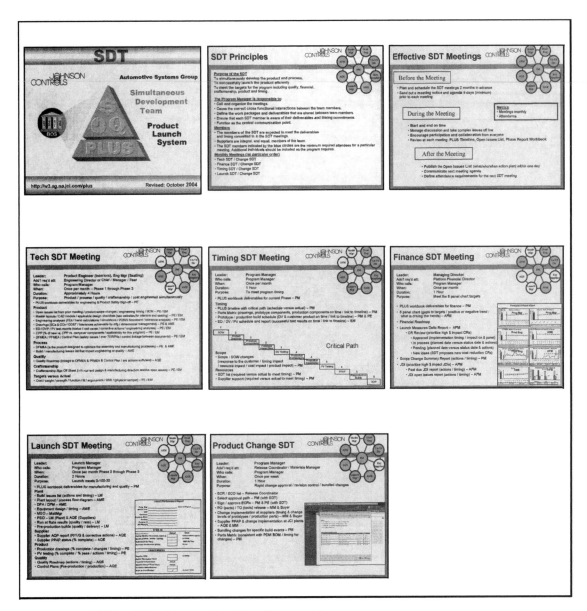

FIGURE 5–10. SDT guideline banner and pocket reference card.

JOHNSON CONTROLS

Phase 1 Report

May-06

Program Manager	
Model Year	
Customer	
Program Name	
Product	
EPIC #	
JCI Plant(s)	
WBP	10
Global VP Lead:	
Global PM Lead:	

	Plan Start	Plan Finish	Actual Finish	WBP
Phase 1 Proposal		22-Mar-04		
Phase 2 Product Feasibility		18-Oct-04		
Product and Theme Definition Review				
CAR & TA Approved				
Phase 3 Design & Tooling		12-Jul-05		-52
Phase 4 Production Validation		20-Mar-06		-16
DV Test Complete				
PV Test Complete				
Customer Part Submission				
Phase 5 Launch		14-Aug-06		5
Start of Production	-	10-Jul-06		0

SDT Schedule	Next Meeting Dates	RYG
Tech SDT		R
Timing SDT		Y
Finance SDT		G
Launch SDT		
Product Change SDT		

Phase 1 Deliverables

Deliverable	Deliverable Requirements	Who	Metrics Yes/No	Risk (RYG)	Problem Statement	Deliverable / Event / Action	Responsible	Due
Account Financial Management								
Targeted Business Plan	Approved plan meets the corporate IRR hurdle rate. Includes phase 1 budget.	CDM						
Program Business Plan	Approved plan with Financial Roadmap meets corporate IRR hurdle rate. Due prior to quote submission.	CDM						
Product Cost Summary Form	Product costs, tooling, capital, ER&D aligned with the SOW assumptions.	AFM						
Financial Roadmap	Identified tasks which meet all financial targets.	AFM						
Program Management								
PLUS Timeline	Critical path identified which achieves internal and customer milestones.	ProgM						
Open Issues List	Problem statement and corrective actions (who, what, when) identifed.	ProgM						
Statement of Work	All program and product assumptions (see SOW checklist); accompanied by Quote.	ProgM						
Phase deliverables confirmed	Required PLUS deliverables for Phases 2-5 are confirmed; Director of Program Mgmt approves deliverable baseline.	ProgM						
Engineering								
Product Specifications/Functional Requirements	Product specifications and functional requirements documented in the SOW.	ProdE						
Bill of Material	Bill of Material documented in the SOW.	ProdE						
Design Validation Plan (DVP)	Test plan and quantities for ED, DV, and PV and documented in the SOW.	ProdE						
Craftsmanship, Engineering and Manufacturing Review (CE&M)	Reviewed Eng & Mfg assumptions prior to SOW/Quote submission. Issues documented in Open Issues List.	EngMgr						
Quote Bill of Material	QBOM "loaded" (not released) in the Product Data Management System.	ProdE						
Industrial Design								
Craftsmanship Targets	Craftsmanship Target Evidence form completed (Reference Industrial Design workbook).	StudM						
Product Renderings	Complete Product Renderings form in the Industrial Design Workbook.	StudM						
Manufacturing								
Manufacturing Requirements	Manufacturing locations and logistics documented in the SOW.	AME						
Quality								
Quality Objectives & Roadmap	Historical product & process quality performance identified.	AQE						
Supply Chain Management								
Packaging / Freight / Inventory	Customer responsible pkg documented in the SOW. Document JCI resp pkg costs in the Prod. Cost Summary.	MatlM						
Baseline Metrics (Measured at Target Phase Exit Date)								
% CPP in SOW	% of total part numbers	EngMgr	%					
% Carry Over in SOW	% of total part numbers	EngMgr	%					
Total new part numbers	Number of new part numbers in program	EngMgr	#					
% SDT Staffing Complete	% of complete staffing	ProgM	%					
% Pull Ahead Production Tooling in SOW	% of total part numbers	EngMgr	%					

All deliverables require a monthly RYG assessment by the SDT.

R	Red = High Risk
Y	Yellow = Medium Risk
G	Green = Low Risk
n/a	Not Applicable

Functional Approval - Phase Exit Deliverable Assessment
(Agrees with the RYG assessment)

Director of Engineering ____ Date
Director of Quality ____ Date
Director of Adv Manuf ____ Date
Director of Finance ____ Date

Phase Exit Deliverable Assessment
(Agree with the deliverable RYG and approve)

Director of Program Management ____ Date
Business Unit VP/General Manager ____ Date

Phase Exit Approval
(All Deliverables Green and Phase Exit approved)

Business Unit VP/General Manager ____ Date
Director of Operations ____ Date

FIGURE 5–11. Phase report workbook—one per PLUS phase.

At the end of each PLUS phase, project managers present their project to executive leadership and request approval to proceed to the next phase in a phase exit review. Ideally, these reviews are a formality assuming the progress of each of the phase deliverables is progressing toward 100 percent completion. From time to time, all deliverables are not complete by the exit due date; fortunately, that does not come as a surprise to the business unit leadership as they have been made aware of the project's progress throughout the phase. For that reason, the project manager and business unit leadership come to the phase exit review with mitigation plans. Occasionally, more aggressive intervention is required.

The executive leadership has made available a standing time slot for presenting *red-flag* issues that require executive involvement. This is an opportunity for project managers to request help or convey assignments to the organization's top leaders. In addition to the red-flag time slot, there is standing time available for presenting major scope changes (internally or externally driven) and acquiring executive support and sponsorship. Such support has allowed Johnson Controls to maximize flexibility and take on appropriate risk, which in turn enables them to achieve the organizational mission.

PLUS Metrics Measuring performance has become a method for ensuring teams concentrate on accomplishing the *right* tasks that enable the project to meet its objectives. It is all too easy for teams, their members, and even their leaders to become distracted on superfluous tasks, that is, not essential to the project objective. For that reason, team metrics align directly with the deliverables identified in the phase report workbook. The metrics are collected monthly and show aggregate status by business unit and by program. In addition to focusing teams on the right tasks, the metrics are used to show trends, which then can be analyzed and addressed.

Project Management Development Johnson Controls' project managers are viewed as *general managers* of their projects. Consequently, they must be versed in a variety of knowledge areas, including project management, problem solving, and Johnson Controls' systems and products:

1. Program management IQ [a shortened version of the PMI® certification curriculum offered by The International Institute for Learning (IIL)]
   - Online self-directed study in PMBOK® Guide methodology
   - Assures all project managers at Johnson Controls have a common understanding of project management principles
2. Program Management Professional (PMP®) certification
   - Certification is encouraged but not required
   - Most members of the PMO are PMP® certified
3. PLUS
   - Online self-directed study in Johnson Controls' product development methodology
   - Verifies all project managers understand PLUS objectives, processes, and milestones
4. Kepner Tregoe
   - Classroom training in a systematic method for solving technical and nontechnical problems

- Provides managers with a tool for solving problems and leading problem-solving efforts

5. Product knowledge
   - Self-directed training coordinated with the manager's PMD (e.g., time spent in a manufacturing plant)

Note: Evidence that project managers have assimilated training knowledge is found in the manner by which their projects function and achieve objectives. Areas that require improvement and additional training are identified as part of the project manager's annual performance evaluation.

PLUS and Suppliers Johnson Controls has learned that, as an organization, it is only as good as its suppliers. Problems suppliers encounter ultimately become Johnson Controls' problems. For that reason, PLUS methodology is generously shared. The PMO also provides suppliers with project management training and mentoring. In some cases Johnson Controls' project managers are *loaned* to suppliers in an effort to jump-start the suppliers' use of project management methods. Johnson Controls is so dedicated to the success of its suppliers that they have a permanent position within the PMO dedicated to supplier support and development.

Closing Remarks As noted in the introduction, Johnson Controls' PLUS, supported by project management methodology, is the system teams utilize to turn ideas into manufactured products that exceed customers' expectations. The aforementioned best practices help Johnson Controls realize the benefits of PLUS.

5.13 VISTEON CORPORATION

Visteon Corporation has developed a project management methodology consisting of a standardized set of processes entitled the *Visteon Business Operating System (VBOS)*. This methodology provides Visteon with a consistent way to plan for and execute deliverables to *meet or exceed customer's expectations.*

Dr. Heinz Pfannschmidt, Executive Vice President and President of Visteon's European and South American Operations, states, "We have defined the operating model, now disciplined execution must rule." Dr. Pfannschmidt goes on to say, "VBOS is our DNA; it truly defines how we will plan, execute, and achieve operational excellence."

The VBOS provides a systemic way to plan, run, and change our business using the plan–do–check–adjust cycle (see Figure 5–12). VBOS characterizes the business processes into three categories:

- *Planning Processes:* How we plan the business.
- *Life-Cycle Processes:* How we run the business, executing the plan.
- *Support Processes:* Processes that enable effective execution and operation of the business.

FIGURE 5–12. Plan–do–check–act cycle.

Planning Processes

Planning processes cover strategic and operational planning. The primary focus is on ensuring strategies are:

- Aligned across functions and consistent with financial objectives
- Global in nature, but reflect regional needs when necessary
- Consistent with Visteon values, leadership standards, and financial targets
- Effectively communicated across functions

Life-Cycle Processes

Commercial success depends on execution of the operating plan through life-cycle disciplines:

- Project leaders and project teams are accountable for delivering results.
- Process discipline is required to ensure we meet customer commitments while providing maximum value from our products and services.

Life-cycle sections include:

Innovation and Commercialization: Describes how we identify and develop new technology and commercialize new systems and products.

Award to Launch: Describes how we identify, pursue, and win new business opportunities and the project management disciplines we utilize to bring products to market.

Delivery and Service: Describes how we support and maintain our customer commitments on an ongoing basis.

Order to Cash: Describes how we receive, fulfill, process, and collect on customer orders.

Source to Pay: Describes materials management processes from sourcing strategy to supplier payment.

Aftermarket "Unique": Describes the integration of aftermarket/service considerations into the mainstream planning and life-cycle processes and develops unique aftermarket/service processes where the mainstream life-cycle processes do not apply.

Support Processes

Support processes provide "enabling" capabilities to the organization. For example:

- Data integrity (e.g., financial, quality)
- Protection of intellectual property
- Systems infrastructure development and performance
- Execution of human resources policies (e.g., staffing, performance planning, etc.)

Below is an overview of VBOS life-cycle processes: innovation and commercialization, award to launch (A2L), and delivery and service. This overview is intended to provide the reader with an understanding of the workings of VBOS and the benefits that are being derived from it.

Innovation and Commercialization *Purpose:* Supporting front-end life-cycle processes from ideation through commercialization.

How Does It Work
- *Innovation Process:* Identifies steps to generate ideas for further potential development actions.
- *Concept Development Process:* Detailed process by which new technology for a system or product concept is defined and developed into an application-ready state.

Benefits
- Mechanism to broaden the base of new ideas
- Keeps the organization focused on product development activities with real commercial value.
- Provides a direct link to the account plan (new business database).
- Engages customer and internal resources upstream.

Award to Launch *Purpose:* Processes focused on supporting the Visteon Product Development System (VPDS) needed to profitably develop and deliver products to any customer's application. A2L starts with pursuit and continues through launch.

How Does it Work
- Identifies steps required to effectively pursue and prepare/submit new business customer proposals
- Details the steps necessary to engage the project team, manage project requirements, work plans, finances, project changes, risks, and quality

- Defines the process for project teams to transition to the required next milestone
- Defines the process to manage the bill of materials
- Defines the process to engage suppliers
- Provides a process to determine cost of purchase parts and raw materials
- Defines the process by which purchased parts are sourced and launched into production
- Details the steps necessary to validate manufacturing process, tooling, and equipment
- Details the process for project teams to assess the successful completion of a project through lessons learned

Benefits

- Provides a consistent, global approach to developing and delivering our products
- Simplifies and clarifies the key processes supporting the VPDS
- Improves project work planning and execution consistently from project to project
- Aligns cross-functional project teams and clarifies roles and responsibilities
- Ensures aftermarket and service are integrated into upfront planning to prevent profit leakage or missed opportunities

Delivery and Service   *Purpose:* Provides consistency in the management of manufacturing resources.

How Does it Work

- Provides processes to ensure our global compliance with environmental regulations and corporate environmental policies
- Provides guidance for a health and safety management system
- Defines the process for inventory control and verification
- Defines the process for operational planning and order fulfillment
- Identifies a common strategy to manage new plant start-ups
- Defines the process for capacity planning
- Details the steps to conduct a make-versus-buy analysis
- Details the steps to establish cost reduction goals and implementation plans
- Reduces waste by simplifying the number of processes and allows sharing of best practices

Benefits

- Standardized, common approach to global manufacturing
- Supports a culture of continuous improvement
- Leverages best practices and lessons learned
- Strongly links delivery and service with other key areas of Visteon's business
- Provides metrics to measure how successfully our processes are working
- Strengthens the link between manufacturing cost reduction and engineering change

To ensure sustainability, Visteon has also developed a *Project Management Handbook* to provide employees with a quick and portable reference guide. Visteon also has developed an extensive project management training curriculum that supports its methodology and provides employees the opportunity to learn and practice using the associated tools in a classroom environment.

5.14 FORD MOTOR CO. ELECTRICAL/ELECTRONIC SYSTEMS ENGINEERING[6]

Ford Motor Co. has revenues of $164.196 billion and 327,531 employees worldwide. The Electrical/Electronic Systems Engineering department develops electrical systems valued at $800 to $1,000 at cost to more than 80 vehicle programs. The department consists of approximately 740 staff resources, with electrical program management teams comprising about 25 engineering resources each.

The Electrical/Electronic Systems Engineering department has four functional engineering areas, each with its own chief engineer:

1. North America Truck,
2. North America Car,
3. Commodity and Application Engineering, and
4. E/E Software and Modeling.

This department is aligned with the product creation mission of Ford—"Great Products . . . More Products . . . Faster"—that outlines the priorities for the department:

- Improve quality,
- Improve quality (intentionally repeated),
- Develop exciting products,
- Achieve competitive cost and revenue, and
- Build relationships.

Additionally, Ford's Electrical/Electronic Systems Engineering department has aligned with the company's key focus areas for department communication and processes. To "intensify communications," the department stresses the following:

- Communicate consistently,
- Focus on vital few priorities,
- Keep the message simple,
- Help people prioritize, and
- Remove barriers.

---

6. Excerpted from APQC's Best Practice Report *Project Management,* which is available for purchase at www.apqc.org/pubs. APQC is an international nonprofit research organization.

The department also emphasizes that each team member should improve working processes by simplifying, stabilizing, standardizing, setting cadence, and sustaining.

By using the above principles across all product development commodities, the department has achieved a reduction in engineering errors, as well as higher engineer engagement.

Overall Best Practices

Examining project management at Ford revealed three best practices.

First is Ford's executive sponsorship of an Electrical/Electronic Systems Engineering project management office. This office standardizes project management and engineering processes across its internal functional areas and the electrical program management team. It also acts as a single governance board for the project management office framework. The department's directors, chiefs, and the electrical business planning and technology office participate in the governance board through weekly project management meetings to provide support and shift priorities as required.

Second, professional project managers consult on the implementation, execution, and maintenance of the project management office, as well as assisting with the transfer of project management knowledge for the organization.

Additionally, the Electrical/Electronic Systems Engineering department has internalized project management as a discipline in engineering and provided training to the entire organization, with follow-up auditing processes in place for implemented projects. It has always been Ford's intent for engineers to develop competencies in the area and build an in-house project management discipline.

Managing Resistance

Transferring the leadership and ownership of project management from professional project managers to the engineering division has allowed further entrenching of the organization's goal of increasing project management maturity and has produced positive results.

Senior level managers in the organization expect 100 percent compliance with the project management tools and methodologies developed by the project management office and approved by the governance board. They approached the changes as sustained continuous improvement and took the time to listen to comments and criticism from the people in the framework, which resulted in less overall resistance than was expected.

Another method used by the Electrical/Electronic Systems Engineering department to counter resistance was to design the project management office framework around stakeholder participation. All organization personnel can participate in the project management office tools and methodology discussions at the management level, as well as the project management office working level meetings. This level of participation in the organization helps build the best practice process.

Driving Consistency in Project Management

Project Definition Electrical/Electronic Systems Engineering project management office acts as the central project manager to standardize projects. The office engages defined projects that usually have a short time frame with a clearly defined scope and a clear allocation of resources. Long-term technical or business planning projects are handled outside of the project management office. Although these projects may interact with the office, it does not directly manage them.

Project Management Organization/Methodology The Electrical/Electronic Systems Engineering department's project management office comprises three levels.

1. **The governance board of executive directors and engineering chiefs**—This small body prioritizes projects according to the corporate scorecard. The group includes two executive directors and four engineering chiefs and sets the tone for the department's overall level of project management excellence.
2. **Stakeholders**—This group includes members of the department that participate either regularly or sporadically in approved projects, usually as subject matter experts. These resources provide technical knowledge regarding the various engineering disciplines and tools.
3. **Professional project managers**—These staff members are from the project management-consulting firm retained by the department. Their duties include participating in cascaded/prioritized projects, developing project execution plans and work plans, performing audit processes, and facilitating team formation and execution of deliverables in a specified time line and scope as approved by the governance board. The professional project managers also developed a change management process for updating existing project management tools on an as-needed basis.

The professional firm of Pcubed Inc. is considered the owner of the project management methodology employed at Ford Motor Company. This methodology is aligned with the Project Management Body of Knowledge (PMBOK), PMI, and PM Berkeley Maturity models, which are the recognized industry standards. The approach comprises three phases.

1. **Discover and define**—The objective during this phase is to assess the overall health and baseline project management process.
2. **Develop and deliver**—The Phase 2 objective is to develop and pilot the recommended solutions to address the needs identified in Phase 1.
3. **Deploy and drive**—The last objective is to ensure solutions are fully implemented across the department.

Project Managers/Teams Five to eight full-time professional project managers staff the Electrical/Electronic Systems Engineering project management office per quarter, depending on the project needs. The project management office reports its general project scope recommendations or issues to the Electrical/Electronic Systems Engineering department business office manager prior to those recommendations/issues being elevated to the governance board review process, where they are then reviewed by directors and engineering chiefs.

The relationship between the project management office and the functional areas is clearly structured, with the project management office as the focal point for all project management processes. The functional teams do not have the authority to influence or overrule the directives managed by the project management office. In 2004 the project management office began to work with the Electrical/Electronic Systems Engineering department to identify resources that will participate in an increased capacity based on the job families for engineers with project management responsibilities.

The composition of a typical Electrical/Electronic Systems Engineering department project team and the corresponding roles and responsibilities include:

- *The project manager*—leads the project execution plan development (This also includes gathering the necessary resources, as well as defining the scope, deliverables and time line for the project.);
- *The stakeholders*—usually subject matter experts who provide feedback about the project deliverables; and
- *The governance board*—reviews the progress of the project and gives the necessary approval or rejections for recommendations.

In some instances, the stakeholders take the lead role, and the project management office acts as coordinator or facilitator.

Currently, the Electrical/Electronic Systems Engineering department identifies resources and potential leaders using the individual development plan, a tool completed by the department's engineers. Resources identified for advance training take on permanent leadership roles in the organization. Some of these resources will have only part-time responsibilities for project management, and others will be used full-time to manage the project management office.

To maintain the structure necessary for consistent project delivery while allowing for changing circumstances, the project management office and the governance board review projects' status monthly and make any necessary recommendations. Stakeholders also meet monthly for change control of project management tools and processes. This is the formal change control process for any methodology improvements to existing projects. The project scope can be modified as necessary to manage changes to the original project assumptions. The suggested revisions are always reviewed by the top two levels of the project management structure (governance board and stakeholder team), and any revisions are taken from their directions.

Ford used the Berkeley Project Management Maturity Model to quantify the needs assessment results across the project management disciplines and the project life cycle. Level one of the Berkeley Maturity Model is the ad hoc stage, where no formal procedures or plans to execute exist and where project management techniques are applied inconsistently, if at all. Level two is the planned stage, where informal and incomplete processes are used and planning and management of projects depends primarily on individuals. Level three is the managed stage, where project management processes demonstrate systematic planning and control and where cross-functional teams are becoming integrated. Level four of the model is the integrated stage. Here, project management processes are formal, integrated, and fully implemented. Lastly, level five is the sustained stage, which involves continuous improvement of the project management processes. At the project management office launch in 2003, the Electrical/Electronic Systems Engineering department had a maturity level rating of 1.85, aligning with the average maturity level of most organizations, which is between level one and two.

At the end of 2003, after the implementation of the project management office and the achievement of an organized approach, an informal review of the organization's processes moved the rating to a level 3. To continue increasing its maturity level in 2004, the department's governance board began internalizing the effort to transfer project management knowledge by using technical maturity models, which provide training models, individual development plans, and core training and education online courses in department project management processes. The goal of the department is to internalize competency and to approach project management internally.

Project Management Strategy   The Electrical/Electronic Systems Engineering department has two primary strategies for selecting project management office projects:

1. Selection based on the corporate scorecard objectives for the given calendar year, and
2. Selection based on the underlining goal of increasing the department's project management maturity.

The project management strategy aligns with the corporate strategic plan by placing top priority on selecting a project based on its ability to meet the corporate scorecard objectives (i.e., improving the product creation process and engineering disciplines). Other criteria can also include the ability to improve work-related efficiency, standardize reports and processes to improve clarity of data for decision making at the senior level, and realign the organization cross-functionally to increase project synergies.

The department's approach to project management has been used to achieve the strategic objectives of the organization in the following ways:

- The project management office had input into the corporate-level development of the engineering quality operating system. The office also had responsibility for building electrical assessment health charts by system and commodity levels, training the Electrical/Electronic Systems Engineering organization to integrate new corporate reporting tools, implementing an auditing process to ensure proper compliance with procedure, and reporting the efficiency of the organization to senior leadership.
- The department worked toward realigning the sourcing process with the finance department, cataloged issues via the engineering quality operating system reporting system, and gained the support of the finance department in a joint partnership to improve the supplier sourcing process.
- The department also maintained continuous improvement projects in product development, such as participating in corporate objectives as they pertain to the processes to improve product creation (e.g. improving time to market and the quality of the product launch).

Resource Assignment Electrical/Electronic Systems Engineering ensures that adequate project resources are devoted to the upfront project phases (project initiation and planning) by defining project execution plans one month prior to the project kick-off. This plan details the scope, time line, and required resources. Once the governance board approves this plan, it ensures sufficient organization resources are enabled, and the project management office matches projects to the skill sets of individual project managers.

To effectively manage geographically dispersed or global project teams, the department uses a clearly defined communication plan including the scope, time line, resources, and the necessary communication tools that can facilitate a global meeting such as eRoom or Pictel. It is also important to form the project team early and clearly define the objectives, as well as outline regular status reporting meetings. Cultural differences that might arise during the project are managed by best practices training. For example, the project leader may make recommendations to the team for specific communication plans, the formality of meetings or conduct, and negotiating work-related differences and scope disagreements.

Project Management Professionalism/Training As discussed previously, advanced project managers in the Electrical/Electronic Systems Engineering department are identified through individual development plans as part of the technical maturity model for project management. Resources identified for advanced training will take on permanent leadership roles in the department, which usually consists of managing projects or the project management office.

Training needs for project managers are also identified by comparing the results of the completed individual personal development plans to the technical maturity model for project management. Resources requiring user/expert level skills will be trained by a variety of sources:

- By the current professional project manager assigned to train them on project management office operations;
- Web-based training or seminar training provided by Ford on core project management disciplines; or
- Specialized courses developed by the department along with Ford Motor Co. on project management processes, tools, and methodologies.

Structuring and Negotiating Project Scope Professional project managers in the project management office initially prepare the project scope based on a discovery phase approach. The scope is outlined in a project execution plan against the project requirements, time line, and resources required. Process changes must go through the formal change control process, as outlined earlier, that begins at the monthly stakeholder meeting. Scope changes related to resources are first reviewed with the manager of electrical technology and operations. The governance board must then review the proposed changes before giving its approval or rejection. An adjustment of resources is then made as necessary to meet the approved changes to the scope.

Maintaining Consistency in Project Management Delivery   Overall, the department identifies a number of important ways that it maintains consistency in project management delivery.

- Project management tools, processes, and methods in the department are standardized.
- The project management office institutionalizes approved new processes through training of the organization.
- The project management office audits the correct use of new tools and processes.
- Monthly change control actions are taken to improve gaps.
- Processes are available to the organization through the use of eRoom documentation storage.
- Ongoing organization training and project management pocket cards for engineers are provided.

Building Project Portfolios by Prioritizing Projects   In Ford's portfolio management approach, projects are ranked based on the priorities identified by the governance board using the corporate scorecard. Initially, the scopes of the various projects are high level, and the project managers review all requested projects and define the scope with the department's business operations manager. In 2004 the organization performed an assessment of this approach and plans to make assessments a biannual process.

Allocation of Resources   As previously outlined, the Electrical/Electronic Systems Engineering department allocates resources to projects based on the project priority, scope, and available resources. If reassignment of resources is necessary because of changes to the project or the personnel, then proposed changes are reviewed and approved by the governance board and department's business office manager. However, the final decision on the prioritization of projects lies with the department's governance board.

The allocation of development funds or resources to different project types, business areas, market sectors, or product lines again depends on the corporate scorecard objectives, areas requiring process improvements, and an increase in the organization's project management maturity level. Organization objectives are cascaded by the governance board to the project management office, which develops high-level project plans that the governance board then reviews for approval. To ensure sufficient resources are available for projects, the governance board conducts monthly reviews to monitor strict adherence to the scope management of projects, as well as manage any over-allocation of resources.

The job of ensuring that low-value projects are terminated before consuming resources is primarily that of the project management office's project manager, governance board, and the Electrical/Electronic Systems Engineering department's business manager. The feedback on value achievement from these sources is provided monthly. Additionally, a periodic formal project management office survey is administered by the Electrical/Electronic Systems Engineering department's business operations planning group to the department to rank the effectiveness and use of project management office tools, processes, and project outcomes. The results of the survey are reviewed with the project management office and the governance board to identify areas of improvement and capture lessons learned.

To enhance ongoing management decisions using the project portfolio, Ford uses the engineering quality operating system reporting system to quantitatively measure the success of program delivery across the North American engineering community, including electrical/electronic commodity and deliverables to the program level. This measurement system is designed to review the history and also present the status of progress across the vehicle programs. The project management office has worked on various projects that have facilitated the communication of these status results in a more streamlined manner to help decision-making capabilities. For example, the Electrical/Electronic Systems Engineering department will prioritize "red issues" and track any red issue closures in a database. These progress reports against the closure of red issues are reviewed as high as the vice president level.

Measuring Project Delivery and End Results

Ford uses the engineering quality operating system to measure the success of its projects in the engineering community. Its integrator reporting system captures the status of projects and can report these findings up to the system and program levels.

Additionally, the metrics or measures used by the project management office are mostly qualitative and can include completed deliverables assigned to the project or feedback by the user community or other outside sources.

The department's business operations planning department manages all financial aspects of the Electrical/Electronic Systems Engineering project cost. The department's business operations planning manager found the project management approach the most cost effective for managing projects in a large organization. This approach has driven 5 percent efficiency in the operating costs for the electrical area of the company.

The collection of project data is managed by the project management office and can come from various sources, such as the engineering quality operating system health charts (project status reports) or work plans. Data integrity is managed by periodic auditing of the functional engineering team's adherence to the organization's tools and processes. The results of the audit are reported to the chief engineers and also posted in the team's specific eRoom for team feedback. The chief engineers examine the auditing reports to drive 100 percent compliance through the organization.

To make data informational and useful, the organization analyzes various types of data with the following frequency:

- Trend analysis of engineering quality operating system health charts is done twice monthly;
- Timing analysis on work plans is conducted monthly and reported to the electrical program management team; and
- Updates to the engineering quality operating system integrator are conducted monthly, but tracking of red issues is conducted on a weekly basis.

Additionally, the following reporting methods or mechanisms are used in the organization:

- The Web-based engineering quality operating system assessment provides red/yellow/green health charts for the commodity and system-level teams;
- Work plans are maintained on eRooms for easy access to project timing data and deliverables; and
- Tracking of red issues conducted via a tracking database and a trend analysis is performed on this data.

Decision makers in the organization act on the reported metric data in different ways. The governance board conducts reviews of the engineering quality operating system red status items across the organization for two hours every week and provides feedback to the managers on action items. The timing reviews are held bimonthly at the system level to review commodity development and testing status. Issues arising from these reviews are elevated to the chief engineers, who actively manage the red issues to green status.

To ensure the project-related measures add value to the organization, the Electrical/Electronic Systems Engineering department can point to improvements in performance. The quality of the red/yellow/green status at various vehicle program milestones has been steadily improving since 2003. The organization acknowledges an effort to minimize projects in the yellow status. Corrective action plans are for the purpose of changing a commodity status to green, not to merely improve it from red to yellow. The Web-based engineering quality operating system assesses milestone deliverables using the red/yellow/green status and provides managers with immediate issue elevation.

Accountability/Authority Because project managers execute governance board approved projects, team members know they are expected to participate and meet project objectives. Project managers are given the authority to elevate issues or roadblocks that arise during the life of the project to the governance board for any needed feedback or assistance. The overall authority granted to project managers is commensurate with their level of accountability.

The roles and responsibilities for project managers are in the process of being mapped into the Ford Electrical/Electronic Systems Engineering job families. At the manager level, however, achievement and technical excellence is [*sic*] recognized and rewarded by senior management.

In terms of future objectives, the project management office has outlined the following effort to continue to improve the Electrical/Electronic Systems Engineering department's project management maturity:

- Develop a technical maturity model for project management to provide training and organizational structure to transfer project management roles and responsibilities and/or competencies,
- Migrate commodity engineering quality operating system assessment summaries to the integrator and audit/coach/mentor commodity teams on the integrator,

- Continue to expand electrical program management teams and commodity-in-a-box tools and processes, and
- Lead electrical work stream development in new product development system.

Greatest Measurement Challenges The primary measurement challenge for Ford's Electrical/Electronic Systems Engineering department was the length of time it took managers to realize that the project management office approach was necessary for project management processes to improve.

As discussed previously, the current auditing processes used by the project management office to measure project delivery typically address quality issues, whereas the project management change control process in the department allows for ongoing improvement to tools and processes, as well as the management of scope changes. Flexibility in these measurement systems has been important in achieving a higher rate of successful project outcomes. Additionally, process-training surveys are conducted with team members after the rolling out of a new process or tool to gather feedback and to identify areas of improvement.

Final Comments and Thoughts

Learning from Project Management Missteps Even with a strong effort to engage personnel, the objectives of the project management office were not initially clearly understood in the Electrical/Electronic Systems Engineering organization. Because most personnel had not previously experienced a working project management office, incorrect assumptions were sometimes made regarding its scope, roles, and responsibilities. It took the project management office some time to get the entire organization aligned on its value and the most effective method for execution of projects. The participation of the stakeholder board was key to the eventual acceptance of the project management office, along with constant communication.

To summarize, the Electrical/Electronic Systems Engineering department's project management office's project execution plans were developed and reviewed and then approved by the governance board to clearly define the quarterly project management office objectives, scope, and resource allocation. These plans were made available to the organization via the eRoom and also reviewed at the manager level. Any overextending of project management resources or changes in project scope are routinely reviewed by the governance board at the monthly status review. After one year, the department had developed an effective working relationship with the project management office and accepted the accompanying project management tools and methodologies.

5.15 SATYAM COMPUTER SERVICES[7]

Quality at Satyam

To satisfy our customers by ensuring that the products and services we provide meet or exceed customer requirements and expectations.

---

7. The material in this section was provided by Anu Khendry, Principal Consultant, Corporate Quality: Rajkumar Periaswamy, Principal Consultant, Enterprise Applications: and Dr. Subhash Rastogi, formerly Head, Project Management Center of Excellence, Satyam Learning Center.

Satyam's quality policy is a testimony to the fact that quality improvement has always been a continuing process at Satyam. (See Figure 5–13.) This reinforces the commitment Satyam as an organization has for the services that it provides to all its customers.

- 2003–2005: CMMI level 5 for eight business units and PCMM level 5 for Pune location
- 2002: Information Security Management Systems (BS7799)
- 2001: Indian Merchant Chambers Ramakrishna Bajaj National Quality Award (equivalent to the Malcolm Baldrige Award)
- 2001: First company worldwide to achieve ISO 9001-2000 certification by BVQI.
- 1999: Tenth organization in the world to have achieved SW-CMM® level 5 rating for all processes across the organization
- 1998: Recertification of ISO 9001-1994 under TickIT scheme
- 1997: First Indian company to get the ITAA certification for Y2K methodology
- 1995: First Indian Company to be certified for ISO 9001-1994 under TickIT scheme by BVQI

Process foundation manifests itself into our customer's confidence in our capabilities thus far and for the future . . .

- True end-to-end IT Services & Consulting partner reflected in our Quality Management System (ISO, SW-CMM, CMMI, ITIL, eSCM)

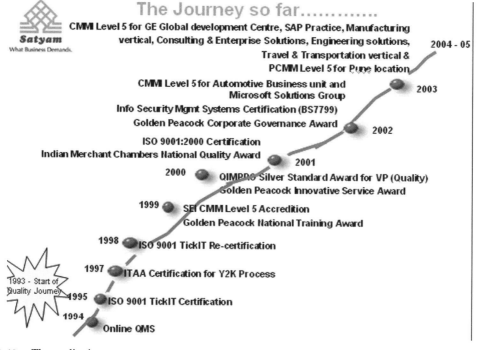

FIGURE 5–13. The quality journey.

- Exceptional growth—Over 17,000 people, 46 countries, 20 development centers
- Increasing customer base—over 370 global organizations with 139 of the Fortune 500
- Increasing repeat business—over 80% of the total turnover
- RightSourcing engagement models to effectively implement the optimal onsite-offsite-offshore combination

Process Quality for Software Projects: Bespoke and Package Applications At Satyam, process focus plays a significant role in the project execution life cycle that includes the project management and technical life cycle. The Web-enabled online Qualify Management System (QMS) QUALIFY has all the processes to enforce and ensure quality (Figure 5–14). The processes are continuously improved based on the periodic audits of the QMS and to keep in tune with the changes forecasted in the business and delivery models.

Projects at Satyam are initiated through a formal initiation process followed by an elaborate planning process. The Web QUANTIFY system facilitates the project initiation and effort capture. This application provides an automated facility for capturing customer purchase orders, work orders, project details, and associated efforts. This also is used for creating billing advice as an input for customer invoice generation.

During the planning phase a suitable methodology based on the nature of the project is selected from QUALIFY and is used to establish the project process. The plan is inspected by the designated inspection team and approved by the project manager as per a predefined process. The quality representative deputed by the corporate quality (strategic support unit) with each business unit plays a significant role in the project plan inspection/review process.

The project planning encompasses the details and plans for:

- Project description and the methodology to be adopted
- Scope of the project along with the scope exclusions and the acceptance criteria

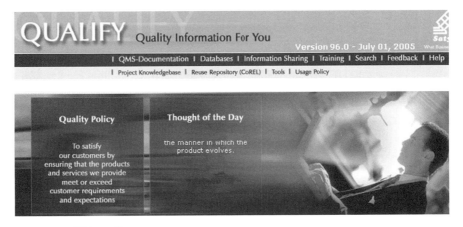

FIGURE 5–14. Web quality management system.

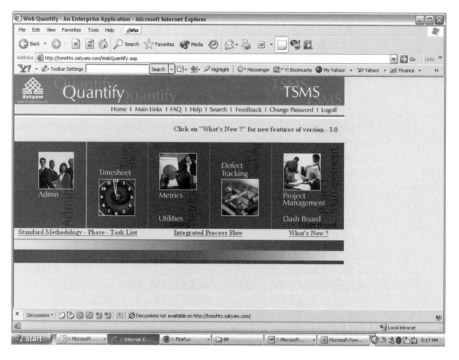

FIGURE 5–14. *(Continued)*

- Software development plan covering project team details, resource requirements, estimation, work management structure, and deliverables
- Software quality assurance plan covering the review plan, defect prevention plan, metrics plan, and details pertaining to the list of quality records
- Configuration management plan
- Project tailoring

All through the project execution, periodic project process-monitoring activities are carried out by the quality representative and the findings are submitted to senior management of the respective business units. (See Figure 5–15.) In addition, quarterly internal quality audits are conducted to ensure conformance to the processes. The audit reports containing the nonconformances are shared with senior management. These reports and findings are also discussed during the management reviews that have been institutionalized across the organization.

The status of each project is monitored and senior management attention is driven through a monthly project maturity index (PMI). The PMI is measured on a scale of 1–5. The index is a derivative of certain metrics parameters, organization norms, and weight age. The PMI is monitored through an online application known as the Quality Cockpit (Figure 5–16).

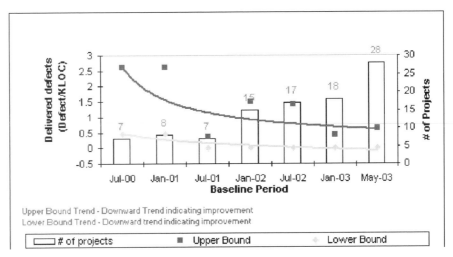

FIGURE 5–15. Delivered defect trend.

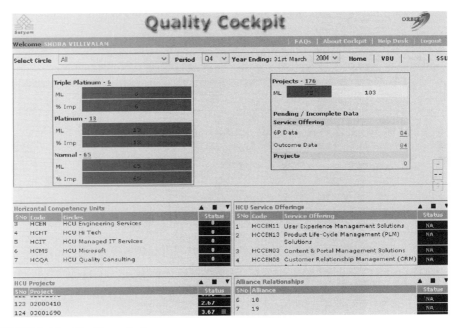

FIGURE 5–16. Quality cockpit.

Process Quality for Support Services: Managed Infrastructure and Internal Infrastructure   The managed IT services group providing IT infrastructure services to compliment the software and packaged application services uses a combination of best practices for IT service management, as shown in Figure 5–17.

Nipuna, Satyam's business process outsourcing unit, has established its process foundations on Carnegie Mellon University's best practices framework for BPO providers called the eSourcing capability model—eSCM-SP Version 2.

Satyam's internal network and systems group has deployed the "remedy system" for incident reporting and tracking that is based on the IT Infrastructure Library's best practices for IT service management (Figure 5–18).

Satyam's QMS is aligned to various quality models such as the ISO, CMM, CMMI, and BS7799 (Figure 5–19). The requirements of all these models are integrated into the common process framework. Satyam has been assessed at CMM level 5 and four of the business units are appraised at CMMI level 5. As per the roadmap for CMMI, the entire organization will be covered by the financial year ending 2006. The People-CMM Initiative is underway and the final assessment is expected to be conducted in April/May 2005.

Apart from the drive on various quality models, Satyam corporate focus for 2003–2004 has been on Organization Business Transformation (ORBIT 5) for raising its business standard to level 5 (Figure 5–20). This initiative addresses "excellence" in "es-

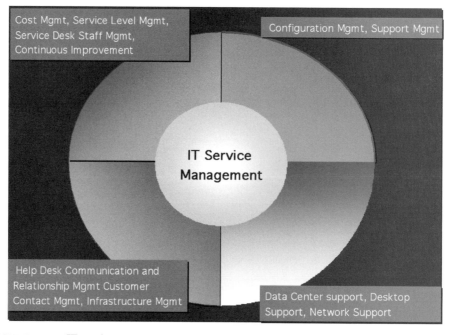

FIGURE 5–17.   IT service management.

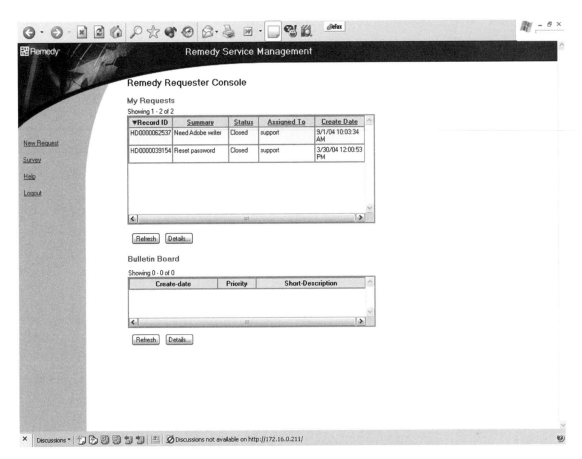

FIGURE 5–18. Remedy service management.

tablishing" the best-in-class service offerings and methodologies and "measuring business outcome" for the same. This initiative is to provide the impetus required for Satyam to help itself establish and sustain one of the top 5 global IT consulting and service provider.

Six Sigma is being used across Satyam as a means to pursue the continuous improvement path for all its organizational processes. Satyam's proprietary Six Sigma methodology is known as iSTRIVE (Figure 5–21). There has been an increased focus on training all the associates on the iSTRIVE methodology as a means of institutionalizing the Six Sigma–based process improvement.

Quality Consulting: Practitioner's Perspective Satyam established its Quality Consulting Division in 2000, in response to requests from some of its major customers to help improve their process capabilities. Satyam's customers were principally interested in adapting Satyam's highly successful processes and methodologies for their own IT organizations. Our first clients were also some of Satyam's largest customers: General Electric,

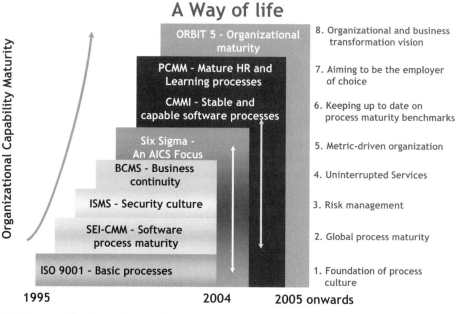

FIGURE 5–19.   Quality and process improvement—Year 2005 onwards.

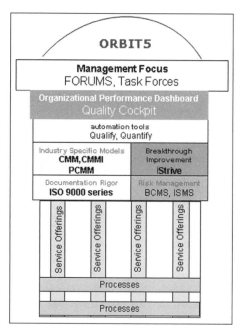

FIGURE 5–20.   Organizational business transformation.

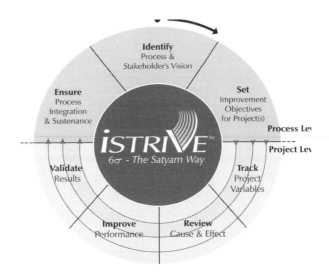

FIGURE 5–21. Satyam six sigma methodology.

Ford, and so on. From that small beginning Satyam's quality consulting has grown into one of the world's largest process-consulting practices.

The practice draws its strength from Satyam's internal efforts to establish world-class quality management systems (Figure 5–22). The current range of offerings from the process-consulting group focuses on the deployment of various process frameworks (ITIL,

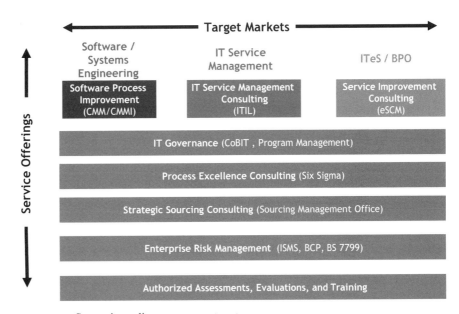

FIGURE 5–22. Satyam's quality management systems.

ISO 9000:2000, BS 7799, SW-CMM®, CMMi®, eSCM[8]) and non-framework-based process improvements.

In Satyam, process improvement is a journey and not the destination . . .

5.16 EDS

Information technology enterprise management (ITEM) integrates all of the project management disciplines along with other IT disciplines such engineering, testing, and model office. Many projects start with a charter and scope that makes a project manager view the work with a definitive start and definitive end. (See Figure 5–23.) If this is applied to the relative stages of a release, they simply stretch the project management process groups across all of the release. That makes the suppliers of the project try to understand if designing and building are part of execution or if deployment of the project is the execution of the project.

As stated in the PMBOK® Guide, project management process groups should be repeated for each release stage. This promotes other project management strategies, such as roll wave planning and resource balancing. With this framework view, other capabilities can be applied to each stage, along with the project management capabilities (Figure 5–24).

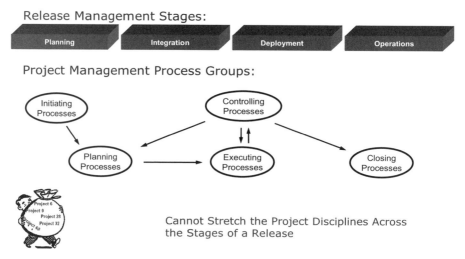

FIGURE 5–23. Typical application of PMBOK®.

---

8. eSCM is a registered service mark of Carnegie Mellon University.

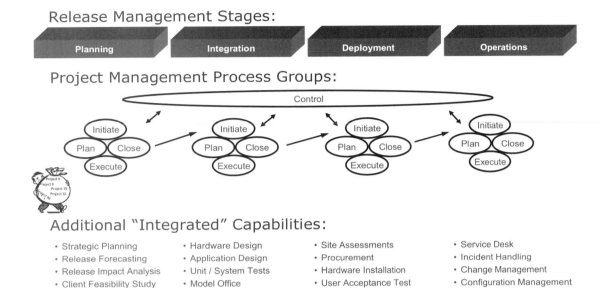

FIGURE 5–24.   Correct application of PMBOK®.

5.17 EARNED VALUE MEASUREMENT

An integral part of most project management methodologies is the ability to perform earned value measurement. Earned value measurement was created so that project managers would manage projects rather than merely monitor results. Even though some companies do not use earned value measurement on a formal basis, core concepts such as variance analysis and reporting are being used. As an example, Keith Kingston, PMP®, Manager of Program Management at Motorola, states:

> Variances to schedule performance are analyzed weekly or biweekly but not as part of a formal earned value approach. Greater than three days of schedule variation on any internal deliverable requires analysis and a mitigation plan. Any variances that impact meeting a customer-required date requires analysis and a mitigation plan.

5.18 DTE ENERGY

One of the characteristics of integrated processes is that it must include an integration with a project management information system capable of reporting earned value measurement. Kizzmett Collins, PMP, Senior Project Manager, Software Engineering, Methods, and Staffing at DTE Energy, describes the integration with earned value measurement:

DTE Energy's ITS Earned Value Analysis Journey

Getting Started

Beginning in 2001, the Information Technology Services' (ITS) project management office (PMO) sponsored several projects that helped to advance and develop earned value analysis (EVA) understanding and knowledge among management and project managers.

The implementation of the Primavera TeamPlay project management suite easily enabled the tracking of EVA metrics for individual projects and project portfolios. Among other sources of education, TeamPlay product training introduced ITS project managers and management to EVA metrics. The PMO developed processes and reports to aid project mangers and management in the analysis and reporting of EVA metrics. ITS contracted Quentin W. Flemming to conduct EVA courses which increased project managers' and ITS management's understanding of EVA.

Reporting EVA Metrics

EVA metrics (such as SPI, CPI, CV, SV, and EAC) are reported weekly in project status reports and in the ITS project portfolio. The project manager provides additional status commentary for variances from target that exceed ± 10 percent.

During the ITS planning and management table (PMT) meetings, project mangers report project status, usually on a monthly basis. The PMT reviews EVA metrics and discusses variances and indicators as warranted. Other triggers that may necessitate a review of the projects' EVA metrics include:

- A project is at 20 percent of original estimated duration.
- A significant phase has ended.
- The project manager presents issues, risks, or changes.

Linking Rewards to EVA CPI Metric

In 2003, the ITS organization began linking rewards to the CPI metric. The CPI metric results are now included in both project manager performance reviews and the ITS organizational scorecard.

The ITS organizational scorecard is tied to the corporate Rewarding Employee Plan (REP). REP pays employees bonuses that are based on achieving the corporate and organizational goals. The ITS organization's CPI metric is the aggregate of the CPI of each project in the project portfolio. As a result, all ITS employees have a monetary stake in the success of each project.

Project manager performance goals include the CPI metric for all projects within their area of responsibility. CPI results greater than 0.95 and less than 1.05 exceed performance expectations. Each project manager's performance review is linked to their merit increase.

Opportunities for Improvement

The ITS organization introduced EVA to the corporation through the ITS scorecard. Both within ITS and across the corporation, further training is needed to expand our shared understanding of EVA. Internally, ITS can take the next step in further understanding what the EVA metrics indicate. For example, we have an opportunity to be more deliberate in allocating dollars elsewhere when a project's CPI indicates cost issues or problems.

5.19 HALIFAX COMMUNITY HEALTH SYSTEMS

Project management methodologies can also be integrated with financial business decision-making. This is illustrated by comments from Woody Walker, Director, Enterprise Services, Halifax Community Heath Systems (HCHS):

> HCHS utilizes ROI (return on investment). We have attached a sample of what we utilize as a five-year forecast. The EPMO assigns projects to a project manager (PM) during the assessment phase. This PM works closely with the requesting executive sponsor to create a task force team or a focus group that they can utilize in order to formalize what is in fact needed. The PM drives the entire process of creating and conducting surveys, performing interviews, creating work low diagrams, and so on. From this as well as research with vendors and reference hospitals, the overall assessment is completed along with the cost estimate. This assessment is then sent through the approval process. Once it is approved as a needed project and all parties agree to move forward and it has gone through our portfolio approval process, the PM fills in the Excel spreadsheet for purchase and lease figures. Then, it is sent to finance for the final ROI. From there, these figures are sent to TAC, SCAC, and the board for final approval. This entire process involves the same PM for consistency and enhanced communications purposes.
>
> When there is a change in the original plan and/or scope, a change management form is filled out by the PM that requires sign-off from the PM, senior PM, sponsor, CIO (if there is impact to cost and/or timeline as well as the executive sponsor if there is a change to cost and/or timeline).

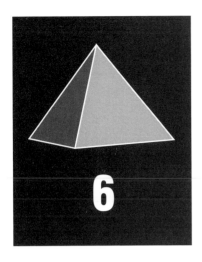

6 Culture

6.0 INTRODUCTION

Perhaps the most significant characteristic of companies that are excellent in project management is their culture. Successful implementation of project management creates an organization and culture that can change rapidly because of the demands of each project and yet adapt quickly to a constantly changing dynamic environment, perhaps at the same time. Successful companies have to cope with change in real time and live with the potential disorder that comes with it.

Change is inevitable in project-driven organizations. As such, excellent companies have come to the realization that competitive success can be achieved only if the organization has achieved a culture that promotes the necessary behavior. Corporate cultures cannot be changed overnight. Years are normally the time frame. Also, if as little as one executive refuses to support a potentially good project management culture, disaster can result.

In the early days of project management, a small aerospace company had to develop a project management culture in order to survive. The change was rapid. Unfortunately, the vice president for engineering refused to buy into the new culture. Prior to the acceptance of project management, the power base in the organization had been engineering. All decisions were either instigated by or approved by engineering. How could the organization get the vice president to buy into the new culture?

The president realized the problem but was stymied for a practical solution. Getting rid of the vice president was one alternative, but not practical because of his previous successes and technical know-how. The corporation was awarded a two-year project that was strategically important to the company. The vice president was then temporarily assigned as the project manager and removed from his position as vice president for engineering. At the completion of the project, the vice president was assigned to fill the newly created position of vice president of project management.

6.1 CREATION OF A CORPORATE CULTURE

Corporate cultures may take a long time to create and put into place but can be torn down overnight. Corporate cultures for project management are based upon organizational behavior, not processes. Corporate cultures reflect the goals, beliefs, and aspirations of senior management. It may take years for the building blocks to be in place for a good culture to exist, but it can be torn down quickly through the personal whims of one executive who refuses to support project management.

Project management cultures can exist within any organizational structure. The speed at which the culture matures, however, may be based upon the size of the company, the size and nature of the projects, and the type of customer, whether it be internal or external. Project management is a culture, not policies and procedures. As a result, it may not be possible to benchmark a project management culture. What works well in one company may not work equally well in another.

Good corporate cultures can also foster better relations with the customer, especially external clients. As an example, one company developed a culture of always being honest in reporting the results of testing accomplished for external customers. The customers, in turn, began treating the contractor as a partner and routinely shared proprietary information so that the customers and the contractor could help each other.

Within the excellent companies, the process of project management evolves into a behavioral culture based upon multiple-boss reporting. The significance of multiple-boss reporting cannot be understated. There is a mistaken belief that project management can be benchmarked from one company to another. Benchmarking is the process of continuously comparing and measuring against an organization anywhere in the world in order to gain information that will help your organization improve its performance and competitive position. Competitive benchmarking is where one benchmarks organizational performance against the performance of competing organizations. Process benchmarking is the benchmarking of discrete processes against organizations with performance leadership in these processes.

Since a project management culture is a behavioral culture, benchmarking works best if we benchmark best practices, which are leadership, management, or operational methods that lead to superior performance. Because of the strong behavioral influence, it is almost impossible to transpose a project management culture from one company to another. What works well in one company may not be appropriate or cost-effective in another company.

Strong cultures can form when project management is viewed as a profession. Ron Kempf, PMP®, Director PM Competency and Certification at HP Services Worldwide Engagement PMO, states that:

> A project management culture is embedded in HP Services. It is recognized as a primary business differentiator. Project managers enjoy high status in the company and have clear development paths to senior levels. A project management professional council with members from worldwide and each regional PMO sets the direction, communicates, and implements programs related to the project management profession. The council focuses on project management development, knowledge sharing, and professional association leadership.
>
> HP Services has a comprehensive Project Management Development Program that covers all aspects of project management training. This world-class program won

Excellence in Practice awards in career development and organizational learning in 2002 from ASTD (American Society for Training and Development), the world's leading resource on workplace learning and performance issues. Every project manager is encouraged to become PMP (Project Management Professional) certified and PMP designation is mandatory for senior project management appointments.

In this example, HP recognized the importance of a good culture for project management and was able to achieve its goal. Unfortunately, not all companies are as successful. When trying to improve project management, senior management often overemphasizes the quantitative components of the project management maturity model and underemphasizes the behavioral component. These mistakes are quite common even in the best management companies.

6.2 CORPORATE VALUES

An important part of the culture in excellent companies is an established set of values that all employees abide by. The values go beyond the normal "standard practice" manuals and morality and ethics in dealing with customers. Ensuring that company values and project management are congruent is vital to the success of any project. In order to ensure this congruence of values, it is important that company goals, objectives, and values be well understood by all members of the project team.

Successful project management can flourish within any structure, no matter how terrible the structure looks on paper, but the culture within the organization must support the four basic values of project management:

- Cooperation
- Teamwork
- Trust
- Effective communication

6.3 TYPES OF CULTURES

There are different types of project management cultures based upon the nature of the business, the amount of trust and cooperation, and the competitive environment. Typical types of cultures include:

- *Cooperative Cultures:* These are based upon trust and effective communication, not only internally but externally as well.
- *Noncooperative Cultures:* In these cultures, mistrust prevails. Employees worry more about themselves and their personal interests than what is best for the team, company, or customer.

- *Competitive Cultures:* These cultures force project teams to compete with one another for valuable corporate resources. In these cultures, project managers often demand that the employees demonstrate more loyalty to the project than to their line manager. This can be disastrous when employees are working on multiple projects at the same time.
- *Isolated Cultures:* These occur when a large organization allows functional units to develop their own project management cultures. This could also result in a culture-within-a-culture environment. This occurs within strategic business units.
- *Fragmented Cultures:* Projects where part of the team is geographically separated from the rest of the team may result in a fragmented culture. Fragmented cultures also occur on multinational projects, where the home office or corporate team may have a strong culture for project management but the foreign team has no sustainable project management culture.

Cooperative cultures thrive on effective communications, trust, and cooperation. Decisions are made based upon the best interest of all of the stakeholders. Executive sponsorship is more passive than active, and very few problems ever go up to the executive levels for resolution. Projects are managed more informally than formally, with minimum documentation, and often with meetings held only as needed. This type of project management culture takes years to achieve and functions well during both favorable and unfavorable economic conditions.

Noncooperative cultures are reflections of senior management's inability to cooperate among themselves and possibly their inability to cooperate with the workforce. Respect is nonexistent. Noncooperative cultures can produce a good deliverable for the customer if you believe that the end justifies the means. However, this culture does not generate the number of project successes achievable with the cooperative culture.

Competitive cultures can be healthy in the short term, especially if there exists an abundance of work. Long-term effects are usually not favorable. An electronics firm would continuously bid on projects that required the cooperation of three departments. Management then implemented the unhealthy decision of allowing each of the three departments to bid on every job. Whichever department would be awarded the contract, the other two departments would be treated as subcontractors.

Management believed that this competitiveness was healthy. Unfortunately, the long-term results were disastrous. The three departments refused to talk to one another and the sharing of information stopped. In order to get the job done for the price quoted, the departments began outsourcing small amounts of work rather than using the other departments, which were more expensive. As more and more work was being outsourced, layoffs occurred. Management now realized the disadvantages of a competitive culture.

6.4 CORPORATE CULTURES AT WORK

Cooperative cultures are based upon trust, communication, cooperation, and teamwork. As a result, the structure of the organization becomes unimportant. Restructuring a company simply to bring in project management will lead to disaster. Companies should be restructured for other reasons, such as getting closer to the customer.

Successful project management can occur within any structure, no matter how bad the structure appears on paper, if the culture within the organization promotes teamwork, cooperation, trust, and effective communications.

Boeing

In the early years of project management, the aerospace and defense contractors set up customer-focused project offices for specific customers such as the Air Force, Army, and Navy. One of the benefits of these project offices was the ability to create a specific working relationship and culture for that customer.

Developing a specific relationship or culture was justified because the projects often lasted for decades. It was like having a culture within a culture. When the projects disappeared and the project office was no longer needed, the culture within that project office might very well disappear as well.

Sometimes, one large project can require a permanent cultural change within a company. Such was the case at Boeing with the decision to design and build the Boeing 777 airplane. The Boeing 777 project would require new technology and a radical change in the way that people would be required to work together. The cultural change would permeate all levels of management, from the highest levels down to the workers on the shop floor. Table 6–1 shows some of the changes that took place.[1]

TABLE 6–1. CHANGES DUE TO BOEING 777 NEW AIRPLANE PROJECT

Situation	Previous New Airplane Projects	Boeing 777
• Executive communications	• Secretive	• Open
• Communication flow	• Vertical	• Horizontal
• Thinking process	• Two dimensional	• Three dimensional
• Decision-making	• Centralized	• Decentralized
• Empowerment	• Managers	• Down to factory workers
• Project managers	• Managers	• Down to nonmanagers
• Problem solving	• Individual	• Team
• Performance reviews (of managers)	• One way	• Three ways
• HR problems focus	• Weak	• Strong
• Meetings style	• Secretive	• Open
• Customer involvement	• Very low	• Very high
• Core values	• End result/quality	• Leadership/participation/ customer satisfaction
• Speed of decisions	• Slow	• Fast
• Life-cycle costing	• Minimal	• Extensive
• Design flexibility	• Minimal	• Extensive

1. Case 28 in H. Kerzner, *Advanced Project Management: Best Practices on Implementation,* 2nd ed. New York, Wiley, 2004, p. 819, provides additional information on the changes that took place.

As project management matures and the project manager is given more and more responsibility, project managers may be given the responsibility for wage and salary administration. However, even excellent companies are still struggling with this new approach. The first problem is that the project manager may not be on the management pay scale in the company but is being given the right to sign performance evaluations.

The second problem is determining what method of evaluation should be used for union employees. This is probably the most serious problem, and the jury hasn't come in yet on what will and will not work. One reason why executives are a little reluctant to implement wage and salary administration that affects project management is because of the union involvement. This dramatically changes the picture, especially if a person on a project team decides that a union worker is considered to be promotable when in fact his or her line manager says, "No, that has to be based upon a union criterion." There is no black-and-white answer for the issue, and most companies have not even addressed the problem yet.

Midwest Corporation (Disguised Company)

The larger the company, the more difficult it is to establish a uniform project management culture across the entire company. Large companies have "pockets" of project management, each of which can mature at a different rate. A large Midwest corporation had one division that was outstanding in project management. The culture was strong, and everyone supported project management. This division won awards and recognition on its ability to manage projects successfully. Yet at the same time, a sister division was approximately five years behind the excellent division in maturity. During an audit of the sister division, the following problem areas were identified:

- Continuous process changes due to new technology
- Not enough time allocated for effort
- Too much outside interference (meetings, delays, etc.)
- Schedules laid out based upon assumptions that eventually change during execution of the project
- Imbalance of workforce
- Differing objectives among groups
- Use of a process that allows for no flexibility to "freelance"
- Inability to openly discuss issues without some people taking technical criticism as personal criticism
- Lack of quality planning, scheduling, and progress tracking
- No resource tracking
- Inheriting someone else's project and finding little or no supporting documentation
- Dealing with contract or agency management
- Changing or expanding project expectations
- Constantly changing deadlines
- Last minute requirements changes
- People on projects having hidden agendas
- Scope of the project is unclear right from the beginning

- Dependence on resources without having control over them
- Finger pointing: "It's not my problem"
- No formal cost-estimating process
- Lack of understanding of a work breakdown structure
- Little or no customer focus
- Duplication of efforts
- Poor or lack of "voice of the customer" input on needs/wants
- Limited abilities of support people
- Lack of management direction
- No product/project champion
- Poorly run meetings
- People do not cooperate easily
- People taking offense at being asked to do the job they are expected to do, while their managers seek only to develop a quality product
- Some tasks without a known duration
- People who want to be involved but do not have the skills needed to solve the problem
- Dependencies: making sure that when specs change, other things that depend on it also change
- Dealing with daily fires without jeopardizing the scheduled work
- Overlapping assignments (three releases at once)
- Not having the right personnel assigned to the teams
- Disappearance of management support
- Work being started in "days from due date" mode, rather than in "as soon as possible" mode
- Turf protection among nonmanagement employees
- Risk management nonexistent
- Project scope creep (incremental changes that are viewed as "small" at the time but that add up to large increments)
- Ineffective communications with overseas activities
- Vague/changing responsibilities (who is driving the bus?)

Large companies tend to favor pockets of project management rather than a companywide culture. However, there are situations where a company must develop a companywide culture to remain competitive. Sometimes it is simply to remain a major competitor; other times it is to become a global company.

6.5 ANDERSON DEVELOPMENT COMPANY

Thus far, we have discussed changing a culture to obtain better project management support. But what happens during joint ventures when cultural clashes occur. What happens when managing multinational projects where culture creates problems? The following case study illustrates the problem and potential solutions.

The NF3 Project: Managing Cultural Differences[2]

Creating Best Practices out of Cultural Clashes   Mitsui Chemicals is one of the largest chemical companies in Japan and is among the largest 25 chemical companies in the world. Headquartered in Japan, Mitsui Chemicals has over 79 consolidated subsidiaries and 97 companies in which they hold equity. Working with so many global companies making up the Mitsui Chemicals Group, the organization has been forced to address how they conduct project management and how they will overcome cultural differences.

A good example has been the global nitrogen trifluoride business. Nitrogen Trifluoride (NF3) is a gas used for etching computer chips, cleaning CVD chambers, and for making LCD panels. In 1990, the Shimonoseki Works began production at their facility in Shimonoseki, Japan. Due to tremendous growth and the need for production in the United States, a decision was made to conduct a technology transfer and build a new plant at their affiliate, Anderson Development Company, located in Adrian, Michigan. This project started in 1996 and was completed in 1997. Along the way, the two organizations had to learn how to adapt their different project management styles to complete the project.

There are many differences between American and Japanese culture as it relates to project management. The differences in project management practices and company values were vast and can be summarized in the table below.

		ADC—American	MCI Shimonoseki— Japanese
Practices	Centralized	Decentralized authority	Centralized authority
	Formalized	Medium level of formalization	High level of formalization
	Hierarchy	Flatter hierarchy	Multiple level hierarchy
Values	Decision making	Individual decision making	Consensual decision making
	Communication	Individually-based	Group-based

Anderson Development Company started out as an entrepreneurial company and still maintains some of that company culture today with a relatively flat hierarchy and medium level of formalization to promote quick decisions. The organization has around 150 employees, and 6 of them were assigned to the NF3 project. In contrast, the Shimonoseki Works project team was embedded with years of large Japanese business practices involving centralized authority with multiple levels of hierarchy. Every decision had to travel the proper hierarchical path and decisions were made by group consensus. Project management was conducted through a very rigid and formalized process, which often meant having many meetings to win support and approval of the initial ideas or project changes at each hierarchy level. Because it was a global project, there were shared accountabilities and multiple reporting requirements. Since it was also a technology transfer, the project was driven by the parent company.

---

2. This material is provided by Scott Tatro, PMP, NF3 Plant Manager & Responsible Care Coordinator, and Jessica Chen, PMP, NF3 Technical Manager & Special Projects Manager, Anderson Development Company. Reproduced by permission.

During the initial construction of the Anderson Development Company NF3 plant, early clashes of these two project management styles hampered the overall schedule of the project. The Mitsui Chemical project manager required the ADC project manager to have frequent meetings, up to 4 per day, to update the project schedule. There was so much time spent in formal reporting, that little progress was being made on the project. A review of the project Gantt chart revealed that the project was falling further behind schedule and budget. To get the project back on track, eventually what emerged was a hybrid of the two project management styles.

To overcome these barriers, the Mitsui and Anderson Development Company needed to find a way to use project management to overcome cultural differences while still satisfying each other's needs. Time was spent listening to and understanding the rigid project management reporting requirements of Mitsui's Project Management system while also understanding the limited resources assigned to the project. With this understanding in place, a hybrid system was developed as shown below:

MCI/ADC-Hybrid

Practices	Centralized	Decentralized authority
	Formalized	High level of formalization include Project Management templates and detailed roles and responsibility manuals
	Hierarchy	Flatter hierarchy
Values	Decision making	Consensual decision making in design phase Individual decision making during implementation phase.
	Communication	Group/individually

In dealing with these multinational cultural issues guidelines had to be created and discussed which addressed the following:

Integration Management
- Clearly defined roles of project sponsor(s), project manager, team members
- Agreement on project management methodology

Scope Management
- Well documented assumptions
- Well documented charter and scope statement

Time Management
- Agreement on working hours (8, 10, 12 hour days, weekends, holidays, etc)
- Local understanding and determination of varying education, experience, and skill level as it relates to assignment of activities
- Understanding of missed milestones and consequences
- Agreement on format for reporting project progress (MS Project, MS Excel, etc)

Cost Management
- Agreement on Yen vs. Dollar currency exchange values and inflation rates

Procurement Management
- Negotiation of local and global procurements items
- Global Customs/shipping issues for declaration and transportation of goods/services

- Authority over specification interpretation

Risk Management
- Understanding of global procurement issues
- Understanding of language barriers
- Understanding of engineering unit conversion and materials of construction

Quality Management
- Understanding of different codes and laws and impact on risks and design requirements
- Differing view of quality and development of agreed upon quality metrics

Human Resource Management
- Differing value/policy systems and skill level sets. Union (Japan) vs. Non-union (America) issues
- Understanding different customs/holidays
- Understanding quantity and quality of resource capabilities internally and externally

Communications Management
- Agreed upon project management communication templates and report timing
- Formal vs. informal communication requirements
- Time zone differences
- Preferred method(s) of communicating (phone, fax, email)
- Overcoming language differences
- Establishing trust

Based on the global project management framework started in 1997, the Anderson Development Company has gone through several additional projects involving expansion of the plant by over 500% in the last 5 years. Mitsui Chemicals and Anderson Development Company continue to share best practices in project management and continuously improve the formalized project management template manuals.

As trust and communication improved between the management teams of Mitsui Chemicals and Anderson Development Company, the groundwork was set to bring the practices and culture of the operational workforce from Mitsui Chemicals to Anderson Development Company and see what practices, if any, would survive the cultural filter.

Mitsui Chemical's commitment to the development of its operational workforce is one of its best practices, and one that was brought to Anderson Development Company (ADC) as part of the technology transfer for its Nitrogen Trifluoride facility starting 1997. This was not, however, without significant effort on the part of all involved. The integration of this best practice in conjunction with project management principles on an operations level proved to have several barriers which had to be gradually overcome in order to achieve the level of success currently seen, namely educational differences, union versus non-union mentalities, and traditional manufacturing roles.

As is common in manufacturing facilities, many of the operators have a high school diploma at best, with typically no education or training beyond the mandatory requirements for OSHA and HAZMAT. Mitsui Chemicals Inc. (MCI), however, has an exemplary training program that requires extensive training in math and chemistry. The requirements are no less for contractors, who must also be trained and pass certification exams to work in specific areas of the facility.

Japanese manufacturing facilities are historically union, as are Mitsui Chemical's facilities. Although the main ADC manufacturing facility in Adrian, MI is located near the heart of automotive (and strongly union) manufacturing bases in Detroit, ADC is actually non-union. The nearby and adjacent manufacturing facilities are also unionized, and ADC itself has shaken off a couple of union movements within its hourly personnel. A general characteristic of unions is that they can promote a separation between the "white hats" and the hourly workforce, drawing a distinct line between what union employees should be empowered or allowed to do versus salaried personnel. Though this delineation can certainly serve a purpose for maintaining rules and regulations, it can be prohibitive to a team-based atmosphere particularly when management is very hands-on. Japanese culture promotes a very strong respect for titles and the roles inherent to them, particularly uniformity—the phrase "the nail that sticks out will be hammered down" is quite applicable. ADC hourly employees were caught between the union mentality and the sudden requirement to empower themselves to make decisions and take on accountability that would have normally been given only to management.

Most significant among the barriers to a successful integration of Mitsui's operational style is the prevalent and accepted tradition of plant management which ties in both of the issues raised above; that "blue collar" employees cannot be given the accountability, authority and responsibility to make decisions that impact production and growth. Operators are usually limited to the basics in training, with the notion that a highly skilled operator is one who is experienced in the process and sticks tightly to the rules. The daily role of an operator can remain fairly unchanged except for the rare upgrade and update of a process, with scant training other than the requirements. Getting involvement from an operator usually comes in the form of process hazard analyses. Otherwise, from a project standpoint the only other objective is to complete the project and pass it off to the manufacturing group as soon as possible. Asking operators not only to be active participants, but also to take on the work breakdown structures or even direct projects is almost unheard of. Even more unusual is the thought that operators with a minimal level of education can take on what is thought to be fairly exclusive even in the engineering field—for example, software programming. Investment in training can be difficult to obtain among the salaried ranks, let alone the idea of sending an operator out of the plant for two weeks. The expense can be greater than that of a salaried person as overtime coverage must also be arranged. Many will justifiably consider this to be a flight risk scenario, as the more highly-trained personnel can either request higher pay, or find a job elsewhere and take the training with them. All in all, a significant change in the mindset of both management and operations is necessary.

The approach to overcoming these barriers was certainly not an overnight process. The technology transfer from Mitsui to Anderson Development Co. at the NF3 plant was a wake-up call to the operators and engineers in terms of expectations and training requirements. Though the primary goal was to have a self-directed workforce, this could not be done without proper long-term and continuous training, the provision of necessary tools, rewards, and, most critically, ownership of the process by the operators. The operators must understand the principles of scope planning, sorting out time, cost, and quality constraints, resource planning, developing and carrying out work breakdown structures, and setting goals and milestones.

Establishing ownership is not just a matter of saying, "Run this plant or else;" it means reinforcing the concept that there is a direct correlation on the plant's performance, daily work activities, and bonus structure tied in to how safely and efficiently the operators perform, and that they have direct impact on their own workload and pay. This shifts away from the attitude that only management or engineering can influence change or improvements, and instead focuses on putting the control and accountability in the hands of the operators.

The operators and contractors at the Mitsui facility must undergo rigorous training and develop a good background in engineering, chemistry, and math-related topics. At ADC, this was not typically a prerequisite. However, as part of the NF3 operator certification program, math, chemistry, and computer-based skills were integrated into the training and examinations. Additional formal training in math was also conducted at the plant. Oral and written exams are periodically administered during the 4–5 month training session which cumulates in a major written exam; the trainee has two chances to get a passing grade. Beyond standard HAZMAT and OSHA-required training, additional on-the-job training includes typical maintenance functions such as valve and instrumentation repair and replacement, quality control/SPC, root cause analysis methodologies such as Kepner-Tregoe™, and troubleshooting, reading and understanding piping and instrument diagrams and project scheduling. With this foundation, areas in which the operators showed talent and the long-term need was recognized as having value by the company proved to be ideal targets for further training and education. This included specialty welding courses, DCS programming, and obtaining and completing degrees. The operators themselves must initially express the interest and desire to receive the extra training, which places the onus upon them to declare their long-term goals and needs and take action to fulfill them. Note that the operators must be given opportunities to use their skills as frequently as possible; not only to maintain those skills but also to prevent frustration or boredom.

Management and engineering also had to undergo changes in appearance, attitude and behavior. The NF3 plant adopted the same principle as that of the Mitsui sister plant in that all personnel wear uniforms, regardless of position. This enables everyone to jump in and participate in all activities, whether it is taking out the trash, running the process, or packaging cylinders. This reinforces the attitude that everyone must be flexible and willing to take on whatever tasks in need of completion, and that rank or title should not be a barrier, nor should it be a buffer to accomplishments. The plant manager can just as easily be found in the control room temporarily substituting for an operator as he can be in a budget review meeting. The plant manager and technical manager also had to be willing to turn over activities in an increasing volume and scope, and to show trust in the capabilities of operations to handle issues. Among the most difficult activities was authorizing operators to proceed with additional training, which required funding and cooperation with other operators in order to provide coverage during their absence.

So, have the diligence, effort, and cost for additional training pay off? Absolutely! A company that shows interest and invests in its employees provides more incentive for people to stay with the company, thus retaining their skills and knowledge about the facility and eliminating costs for hiring and developing new people. On a major project level, operators have been able to present anywhere from 10% to 20% cost savings by taking over and managing specific work breakdown structures, including design, programming, installation, and fabrication. Overall manpower efficiency is increased by taking knowl-edgeable operators and putting them in charge, while reducing the risk of scope changes or errors. In terms of employee retention, none of the operators who received the additional training have left the company. The operators who received DCS programming are now charged with all programming activities, and one of the operators has moved into an Instrumentation Tech position. Some operators who have earned an associate or technical degree have moved into QC roles. The savings on conducting these activities in-house ver-sus the high cost of obtaining an outside programmer has already paid for all of the costs of training. The sense of pride in developing a program or graphic which will be used by the rest of the team, combined with the knowledge of how operators would like to have programs arranged rather than an engineer's or contractor's view of what is acceptable, is also invaluable. Operators with skills in certain types of welding have been able to take over segments or entire work breakdown structures in projects and pre-planned shutdowns. As the operator will ultimately be the one forced to deal with workmanship, they are more apt to be vocal about poor quality, monitoring designs as they are installed, offering sug-gestions for improvements in order to make designs more operator-friendly.

Furthermore, in situations of preplanned maintenance shutdowns, the need for engi-neering and plant management involvement has been nearly eliminated. The team coordi-nator sets up meetings with the necessary parties and establishes daily milestones and objectives for the operators. By setting up communication directly between maintenance and operations, there is less confusion on the prioritization and timing on work orders, bet-ter preparation on the details of the work to be done, and clarification on the roles each group will be performing. In preplanned maintenance shutdowns as well as in projects, there are often large numbers of resources trying to accomplish multiple tasks—usually in a limited space and time frame. Failure to appropriately plan and coordinate all of these resources and activities results in wasted time and therefore additional cost. Integrating project planning principles in top-to-bottom uniformity improves the consistency in plan-ning and again transfers ownership to the operators while reducing man-hours from engi-neering and management in such activities. In so doing, the operations team has been able to successfully reduce the duration of downtime required for preplanned maintenance shutdowns by over 50%.

The benefits to the company in terms of operator development and cost reduction in projects and shutdowns extend beyond. In smaller, resource-constricted facilities such as this nitrogen trifluoride plant, management and engineers often wear multiple hats, partic-ularly when it comes to projects. By freeing these resources up to focus on long-term or other projects and goals, it similarly provides new opportunities and areas for growth that simply would not have been possible before due to time constrictions. The plant manager and I have been able to take on additional responsibilities and projects outside of the im-mediate NF3 facility and expand our roles in the company.

Still under development is a systematic way of rewarding people for ongoing im-provements in daily activities and projects. Mitsui has a system that provides a monetary reward for suggestions that are related to improvements in safety, environmental, quality, and efficiency. If the suggestions are implemented and show actual improvement, addi-tional rewards are provided. On a day-to-day level, operators at Anderson Development Company can freely make suggestions, but must also provide the scope of work, cost and time estimates along with the intended benefits as part of an informal project request. If approved, they often manage the project themselves including ordering materials and doing the actual work. Typically the reward is not a direct monetary bonus, but alternatives such as show or game tickets, gift certificates, or having special meals brought in to the facility for a team luncheon. Obtaining equipment or tools that can make a job more efficient or improve quality is also a good team-based reward.

The bottom line is that by dismissing the notion that only white-collar/management employees can be entrusted with the skills and accountability required for leading projects and endowing blue-collar employees with the training and tools, companies can benefit considerably by involving them and literally handing over the reigns in projects and pre-planned maintenance shutdowns. Providing the incentives in terms of the training, bonuses, and most importantly the opportunity for growth will only increase the likelihood of success in projects.

6.6 PROJECT MANAGEMENT AND CULTURE[3]

Culture, defined as the unsaid artifacts of social behavior, shaped by language, impacts project management on three levels—the culture of the organization, the project management culture, and the culture of the individual participants. An organization's culture drives the general practices of social interaction and business practices and will affect project stakeholder's expectations, communications, and how projects are supported and shaped. The project management culture will affect the quality, execution styles, and deliverables of a project. The participants—from project "owners" to individual contributors—operate in their culture no matter where they are located, affected by the local culture or the culture of their origins, viewing project work and communications through their cultural lens.

Organizations that have a strong culture, often exhibited by very strong beliefs communicated often to their members, will affect projects by overriding project or individual cultural effects. A company's national origin, if very strong in the company, will affect the culture and "ways of working." For example, often a Latin American appointment is a "suggestion" compared to German or Japanese practices. Japanese cultural beliefs about respect drive many of their business practices, affecting negotiation styles, meetings, and communications practices. Project meetings will be handled differently depending on the cultural style of the organization as well as communications and how project deliverables and schedules are handled. In an organization that prizes results at any price, the mantra of ROI or accurate forecasts, budget discipline, and schedule will be drivers for project success. In organizations that prize collegiality or social benefits, delivery, deployment, and participant benefits will be paramount. Understanding the drivers of an organizational

---

3. The section was provided by Bert Potter, PMP®, Project Manager, Nokia.

culture and aligning project practices and deliverables will increase the chance of success and make project management easier.

The project management culture of an organization is often tied to the maturity of the organization and how internal project management practices are communicated. It also affects how project management is organized and recognized by an organization. When project management is an accidental by-product of organizational efforts, the weak project management culture is immature (little or no repeatable results), and poor communication of best practices or any project management practices occurs. Look at the position and importance of project managers and how the organization communicated about project management. Project managers that are recognized for professional efforts and project management skills that are discussed and held out as desired attributes of employees are symptoms of a strong culture and can be a great learning environment as well as a challenge for weak project managers. Strong cultural factors give visibility and well-defined expectations for professional results and behaviors. Cultural statements such as the "we've always done it that way," or the way language is used in communications, will be more direct and explicit in organizations with a strong project management culture—an organizationally specific project management methodology, standard reporting forms, formats, and project templates for project organizations and deliverables—and often will have organization-wide standard tools for project management and reporting.

One key area related to project management and culture for an organization is communication. Critical to this effort is relentlessly defining your terms. Even in the same society, the same organization, and the same culture, the same language can divide. This will affect each phase of the project and its communications and deliverables from initial concepts through delivery, deployment, and close-out. An industry-wide term or project term can be viewed very differently from location to location, and culture exacerbates differences in how people view the components of language that are used to create and manage projects.

At a more basic level, project managers must understand the culture they are working in and how their project participants—stakeholders, contributors, matrixed line managers—will react and affect their project. Individual participant motivations are more understandable if viewed from a cultural lens. In China, large red letters signify blood, and so one should not send an email with a congratulatory message or "thanks" for a good job in large red letters. In one case it caused a negative reaction and the team member was not positively reinforced for good work but rather felt he had done something wrong! The pattern and frequency of communication are important in handling diverse cultures. Informal "hallway" conversations are important to some; frequent formal notes or meetings are important to others. Some cultures prize the praise for an individual, and others want to see praise for the team first. The areas this affects most will be communication and execution as you attempt to correctly and effectively communicate and execute the correct behaviors. Understanding your culture, the most common culture of your project team, and the culture of your team members will help in both communications and execution of projects. Effective project managers will monitor and seek feedback on their communications and practices from team members to gauge how well these are being received and if they are getting the effects, understanding, and behaviors expected.

6.7 ORANGE SWITZERLAND[4]

The start-up phase was globally supporting project-type work, but in a very informal manner. The phase of increased efficiency was marked setting-up standards and formalized methods for project management, together leading to a culture that supports guided, transparent project management, company-wide, with some islands of resistance.

The initial culture was extremely informal. During the company's development from growth to stability other aspects such as company profitability, organizational efficiency, and effectiveness were emerging. Management put coordination and control based on formal project management at the top of the agenda, supporting the development of a company-wide framework. Thus, today Orange Switzerland is applying a formal project management methodology with formal validation and approval gates using standardized tools and documentation.

All divisions manage their own projects by aligning their own project life cycles on the ADOPT (align decisions over project tactics) project management life cycle: the same number of project phases with the same number of decision gates in between. See Figure 6–1.

There is a true cross-divisional verification of the impact of all projects from all divisions on all other divisions.

The employees of Orange Switzerland have always supported project management. Barriers weren't created to overcome working together; barriers appeared when it was required to do things in a different way. To achieve this, formalize the process and render it transparent. Some resistance to those methods translated into a resistance to project management

Creating a pool of competence driving the company-wide change was difficult. It was necessary at first to find a sponsor in the organization who was convinced that developing further project management would create a competitive edge. This was mastered by convincing the manager in the appropriate division, the corporate development office. This vice president allocated the initial resources (people, money) for setting up the core piece, the PMO, which was then in charge of tackling and solving all upcoming barriers.

The barriers were overcome by awareness, adherence, and buy-in. First of all, executives needed to be convinced of the benefits of rolling out a project management approach in the company. Highlighting the benefits, benchmarking, case studies, and pilot projects was extremely useful. The dynamic market pressure was also a very effective catalyst. Some people felt they would lose their autonomy and power if they accepted a formal project management method. Orange Switzerland tried whenever possible to take such aspects into account when developing the methodology. Both management and employees had to be constantly convinced of the benefits of an open and evaluative methodology supported by a permanent communication policy.

Making the project management community aware of the methods and adhere to defined rules presented another challenge. Orange Switzerland overcame it by a well-planned ongoing communication policy: project management forums with the project

---

4. All information on Orange Switzerland's PMO and Project Management methodology is provided jointly by Martin Troxler, Director Corporate Quality; Daniel Heller, PMO Manager; and Alexander Matthey, PMP®, former PMO Manager, today Amontis Consulting Group—Associate Partner.

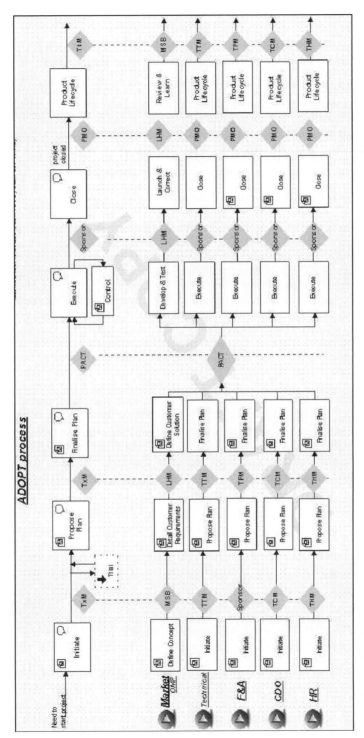

FIGURE 6–1. The ADOPT process mapping.

management community; road shows where project management was presented in a customized way in all divisions and departments; PMO Intranet with link to tools, processes, and documentation as well as a chat room for the project management community.

6.8 MOTOROLA

Keith Kingston, PMP®, Manager of Project Management, describes the culture at Motorola:

> The culture is product oriented. The culture supports project management. There is a certain minimum level of formality to all project management processes between our company and our customer. There are formalized gates and checklists that the project manager and technical leads must adhere to on all projects. However, the degree of formality beyond the minimum standard is typically associated with the complexity of the project. For medium and large projects, we tend to be more formally controlled than for smaller projects and software maintenance releases.
>
> Our customer initially was less formal than we were (a startup company was the main customer). However, as the customer has grown, they hired outside consultants to formalize their processes. In so doing, they have become increasingly more formal and are now enforcing more stringent process and quality requirements on us.

6.9 MCELROY TRANSLATION

Project management cultures are most often designed around the desires and aspirations of senior management. However, the information necessary to transform an existing culture into a project management culture, especially a culture that supports and fosters excellence in project management, also requires input and understanding from all levels of the organization. Tina (Wuelfing) Cargile, PMP®, Project Manager at McElroy Translation Company, describes her experience at McElroy Translation:

> McElroy Translation had been a successful company for decades, primarily working with established clients on fairly routine projects (patent and article translations from foreign languages into English). Procedures that had been developed over the years were performed as they always had been. Deadlines, for the most part, were determined arbitrarily and many projects lingered well beyond their due dates or were subject to sudden acceleration with little explanation. Individual departments operated independently, often unaware of the activities of neighboring departments, and were generally not informed about the procedures, activities, and goals of the sales and operations divisions of the company.
>
> In the 1980s, a rudimentary project management culture began to emerge, involving tracking and oversight of work flow by project coordinators and independent planning and tracking methodologies adopted by individual departments. While this improved internal efficiency within each department and gave management an overview of project activities, there was still little communication between divisions, commitments were made regarding project scope and turnaround without the participation of staff, and line managers were obliged to cope with the specifications and deadlines assigned as best they could.

In the late 1990s, the nature of the translation business began to change rapidly with the advent of globalization as a corporate necessity and subsequent increased client demand for sophisticated, full-service solutions and aggressive turnaround times. As sales in traditional markets began to sag in the early 2000s, the company began to analyze both the increased activity in requests for translation from English into foreign languages and expedited delivery requests and further analyzed internal processes and how the existing business model could be modified to better serve new customer demands.

It was determined that the complexity and variety of the translation and localization needs of clients were not well served by the current operation. Management and sales personnel discussed pending projects with clients in terms of what the client was requesting rather than in terms of what the client needed. This sometimes resulted in the client receiving unusable deliverables (e.g., a translation delivered with encoding incompatible with the client's software or a translation localized for use in Mainland China rather than Taiwan). And while historical best practices had created a series of processes that worked fairly well for standard projects, employees were unable to adapt effectively to unusual requests, often because they had no information regarding the clients' business needs or because the technical requirements involved in providing a requested deliverable had been overlooked. For example, the demand for a cursory edit on a rush patent translation was met with resentment in the editing department and a feeling that management did not care about the integrity of the quality process, since they were unaware that the client planned to use the rough deliverable to decide whether to proceed with further translations of associated patents. Production staff would often be forced to scramble to find a solution when the requested software application and language were incompatible.

After soliciting input from upper managers, project managers, line managers, and employees, it was determined that dissemination of information and improved communication company-wide (including communication between company representatives and clients) had to be improved in order to position McElroy to develop a competitive edge by offering clients solutions rather than products.

A rapid and radical shift in culture and approach took place as a result of this evaluation.

- The most important change was management's decision to invest in the development of proprietary software to enable real-time project activity tracking by all employees, including access to project information, customized reporting, and planning tools, which allowed line managers to more effectively coordinate their staff activities with those of other departments and enabled project managers to efficiently monitor activities and shift focus from information gathering and micromanagement to front-end considerations.
- Making all project materials—including client communications, planning assumptions, estimate information, source files, and so on—available to all employees in electronic form on the shared network made it possible for line staff to independently clarify their understanding of the client's intent and needs. This resulted in an additional value add when remote access to the database system and the network was provided to employees, allowing flexible scheduling to accommodate communication with global vendors and clients beyond the normal workday.
- Independent department network filing and folder structures were merged into a single structure to eliminate redundancy and to make all project materials easily accessible.
- Project managers were involved in the estimate stage to directly engage in problem solving with clients, bringing in technical expertise from line staff when needed, and to ensure that sales personnel had a clear understanding of the internal processes and

challenges that should be considered when discussing projects with clients. Sales personnel were also instructed to probe service requests with questions designed to determine the client's true business need:

1. How would you describe the business problem you are trying to solve?
2. What is the current system in place for addressing translation needs?
3. Please describe content authoring.
4. How will the translations be used?
5. What is your desired output?
6. What resources will be available to the translators? Do you own existing translation memories or terminology glossaries?
7. What are your highest volume and top priority?
8. Please quantify historical and projected translation activity.

(For less complex projects, the simple question "What are you planning to do with the deliverable?" often yields important information that can result in a more effective project plan.)

- Lengthy team meetings on selected projects were replaced with a daily meeting, generally lasting no longer than 15 minutes, reviewing daily and weekly project status, and giving representatives of all departments the opportunity to make suggestions, ask questions, or engage others in problem solving. This activity proved to be particularly valuable when dealing with high-risk projects but also consistently identified solvable problems in more routine projects that previously would not have been discussed in a team setting.
- Project managers established an open-door policy and were encouraged to communicate freely with all staff regarding decisions and assumptions and to incorporate staff feedback into current or future project plans. Management's visible respect for the technical expertise of the employees in the trenches improved morale and trust and often allowed project managers to proactively renegotiate deadlines or staged deliverables.
- Deadlines were assigned to best accommodate client needs and internal workload. Projects were prioritized using a simple coding system, designed to indicate the relative urgency of deadlines and also to indicate where deadline flexibility was possible.
- A dedicated customer service department was created to address client issues, to collect and disseminate information regarding postdelivery problems, and to conduct project postmortems to improve understanding of client needs company-wide.
- Analysis of how information was communicated—between upper management, sales, project management, operations, clients, and accounting—led to the development of electronic shipping procedures and customized electronic reporting that eliminated much of the faxing, copying, shipping, and filing tasks that had previously required the services of a full-time office clerk.

The availability and sharing of information, the emphasis on project management as a company culture, along with upper management's commitment to encouraging teamwork and cooperation have transformed the company, which now enjoys niche status as a vendor of choice for extremely high-risk projects that many agencies must turn away due to turnaround requests, complexity, or the need for customized solutions.

Shelly Orr Priebe, General Manager, McElroy Translation Company, describes the view of the McElroy culture as seen through the eyes of the general manager:

> Leading a company with a rich tradition of stability and financial strength offers undeniable benefits. But what of the potential pitfalls of this enviable market position? The principles of physics too easily apply. How easy it is for a body in motion to remain in motion without changing direction or for a body at rest to remain at rest. But market needs evolve, competition stiffens, trends in offshore sourcing emerge, and technology developments change everything. The challenge at McElroy is to offer clients and employees the best combination of (1) valuing long-term relationships and constancy and (2) competing with the new breed of tech-savvy, "slick" competitors that proliferated on the localization industry landscape in the 1990s.
>
> It would be convenient and "sexy" to laud the many ways that McElroy Translation embraced technology to leapfrog past competitors under a new general manager in 1999. I could write volumes about proprietary technology that was developed and implemented and is continually being improved by internal programmers and systems specialists to better serve the needs of our clients. Technology is fashionable and, admittedly, it has been critical to our ongoing success.
>
> But effective technology use is the by-product of what has mattered most—the emphasis on project management as a company culture, along with upper management's commitment to encouraging teamwork and cooperation. Ideas for change and improvement flow up the organizational chart as often, or more often, than they flow down. Seeing their own good ideas implemented, employees are more vested in achieving overall company goals, instead of just personal or departmental ones. For example, the translation coordination department recently proposed a system for radically decreasing turnaround time for a certain type of project. They were concerned that the "standard procedure" was not realistically addressing the need for a certain market segment. It is exceptional that this initiative for change was generated by the supply side of the company, that is, operations instead of sales or management. These are employees who view the big picture.
>
> Project management must be structured and organized but also be flexible and far reaching. For 15 minutes a day department managers pull together to look each other in the eye and quickly run through the day's priorities and near-term work flow projections. That meeting replaces countless emails and clarifies group priorities, and new ideas are generated there. At that meeting everyone becomes a project manager. Therein lies the key to success.

6.10 HALIFAX COMMUNITY HEALTH SYSTEMS

Nani Sadowski describes the culture change at Halifax Community Health Systems (HCHS):

> HCHS is supportive of project management. This took time to develop and to instill buy-in. It did not start out this way. We continue to "grow the support" as well. This is something that always needs to be cultivated. We are very open to communication as well as feedback. One way we receive the buy-in is by conducting surveys and listing the lessons learned at the end of all projects. Then we conduct follow-up meetings to address any problems. One of the most important keys that we discovered is that all members on the project should be a part of the process and their input valued.

6.11 DTE ENERGY

Tim Menke, PMP®, Senior Project Manager, Software Engineering, Methods and Standing, DTE Energy, describes the culture at DTE Energy:

> The ITS Organization focuses on enabling the business with successful IT projects and on managing by metrics. Support for project management is strongest from upper management and practitioners. Most individual contributors recognize the benefits of project management and therefore adhere to the processes and procedures.
>
> Successes realized through project management in our year 2000 (Y2K) remediation effort and our merger with MichCon were events that strengthened support for project management. This momentum helped tip the scales in favor of project management despite pockets of resistance. We further bolstered project management across the organization by tying rewards to the compliance of project management best practices and the results of earned value analysis (EVA) metrics.
>
> Previously, the PMO focused on traditional "waterfall" project management approaches. For example, we manage our commercial off-the-shelf (COTS) implementation projects using waterfall methods. More recently our PMO increased the focus on emergent agile methodologies. For example, we manage the majority of our application development projects using approaches that better align with our agile software development methodology.
>
> While traditional versus agile development methodologies previously spawned "holy wars" when it came to applying project management methodologies, we have realized significant progress toward recognizing the relative strengths and weaknesses of these approaches. Our discussions now focus on how to best satisfy a particular need, such as scope management, rather than on the relative merits or shortcomings of a given development or project management methodology.
>
> We realized this progress through extensive collaboration between developers, methodologists, and project managers. Rather than mandate a particular approach across the organization, we have chosen instead to select the best approach given the attributes of the project and experience of the practitioners. Our goal is to equip practitioners with skills and tools they can tailor to achieve the best fit for a given project while maintaining a core of minimally required procedures, artifacts, and metrics.

6.12 EDS

Doug Bolzman, Consultant Architect, PMP®, ITIL Service Manager at EDS, believes that:

> In many cases, instituting project management is part of the cultural change required by an organization. When major improvements are needed, the culture is improved by instituting project management and project management cannot depend on the culture being there.
>
> Implementing enterprise wide releases/projects requires the culture to move the organization from a functional to a matrix management, move the delivery from project centric to component centric, and move the planning from tactical (emotional) to strategic (analytical) planning. This level of cultural change needs to be identified, designed, and implemented.

6.13 CONVERGENT COMPUTING

Rich Dorfman, VP Sales and Services, provides a management perspective of Convergent Computing (CCO):

> Culturally, CCO takes a commonsense and value-based approach to business, viewing project management from a similar perspective. Since we're always looking to maximize the consulting value that we provide to clients, we try to avoid overengineering and over-processing activities associated with project management. Practicality speaking, this translates into doing what makes the most sense given situational/scenario-based thinking, therefore balancing our execution around project management (and process) from one situation to the next.
>
> Whereas larger consulting organizations such as PWC, IBM Global Services, and Microsoft Consulting Services tend to have very structured disciplines for project management (often treating their methodology more as a "religion" than a guide), we recognize it's important to manage generic elements associated with project management in order to drive results, elements such as identifying stakeholders, starting with objectives, uncovering constraints, identifying the activities that are time critical, having clearly understood roles and responsibilities, and establishing effective communications. So, culturally we support project management as it relates to these elements; but in most cases, we favor a more informal and practical implementation of them, rather than following the traditional steps and reporting associated with most formalized project management methodologies.
>
> Historically, our focus has its roots in engineering, and our consulting services have been focused more on providing advanced technology expertise and experience rather than project oversight. Management's support for project management was less from the standpoint of project management discipline and more from driving results—the principles inherent in project management. Too often management confused project management with project administration, oversimplifying the role to one that focused almost exclusively to managing project budget and schedule commitments. More often than not, management communicated (in actions and in words) that customers would not pay CCO for project management. So, even where project management time was supposed to be included as a part of CCO's service proposal, it was typically negotiated out of the proposal or not even proposed, because it was assumed the customer would not pay for it. Contributing to the gap, our project managers had a tendency toward thinking about project management in a more formalized way than is culturally our norm while our engineers tended toward focusing in on the technology itself, rather than results. As a result, in most cases the success of the project—project management—rested squarely on the shoulders of the lead consultant, rather than on a dedicated project manager. This history, especially for employees who have worked at CCO for three plus years, left in question management's support for project management.
>
> Over the past year, our business has been steadily shifting from providing technology expertise to helping clients drive measurable business results from the technology they invest in. As our business has evolved, management has recognized that project management takes on increased importance, especially where some of our larger and more profitable clients have attributed project management to be a critical success factor. Yet, because of the past, many employees remain skeptical, and management's more "enlightened" view around project management needs to be continually reinforced and managed, typically on

a case-by-case basis, rather than as a corporate commitment. And, because CCO's philosophy remains significantly different than many other (larger) "high"-tech consulting firms, the enhanced importance management now places on project management is not widely understood.

Because management rarely functions in the role of a project manager but almost always acts as the customer/project sponsor, this divergence in roles creates a challenge for how CCO gets its managers to more actively support project management. Our strategies for working this issue revolve around (1) enhancing team communications so management gets to work more closely with project managers and (2) broadening the responsibility of project management to incorporate program management, relationship building, and business development, in hopes this will do a better job of aligning customer and profit goals with project goals. In the few instances we have tried this approach, we have had very good success combining the roles of project manager and account manager. (3) In addition, where possible, we are trying to replace job titles with job descriptions, so instead of project management, we use a more detailed description of project management that associates value-based activities the project manager will do.

We will continue to look for opportunities to make these kinds of organizational structure changes in the future and increase our commitment to project management. The more we establish a value around project management, the more we will embrace it in the future.

7 Management Support

7.0 INTRODUCTION

As we saw in Chapter 6, senior managers are the architects of corporate culture. They are charged with making sure that their companies' cultures, once accepted, do not come apart. Visible management support is essential to maintaining project management culture.

This chapter examines the importance of management support in the creation and maintenance of project management cultures. Case studies illustrate the vital importance of employee empowerment and the project sponsor's role in the project management system.

7.1 VISIBLE SUPPORT FROM SENIOR MANAGERS

As project sponsors, senior managers provide support and encouragement to the project managers and the rest of the project team. Companies excellent in project management have the following characteristics:

- Senior managers maintain a hands-off approach, but they are available when problems come up.
- Senior managers expect to be supplied with concise project status reports.
- Senior managers practice empowerment.
- Senior managers decentralize project authority and decision-making.
- Senior managers expect project managers and their teams to suggest both alternatives and recommendations for solving problems, not just to identify the problems.

However, there is a fine line between effective sponsorship and overbearing sponsorship. Robert Hershock, former vice president at 3M, said it best:

> Probably the most important thing is that they have to buy in from the top. There has to be leadership from the top, and the top has to be 100 percent supportive of this whole process. If you're a control freak, if you're someone who has high organizational skills and likes to dot all the i's and cross all the t's, this is going to be an uncomfortable process, because basically it's a messy process; you have to have a lot of fault tolerance here. But what management has to do is project the confidence that it has in the teams. It has to set the strategy and the guidelines and then give the teams the empowerment that they need in order to finish their job. The best thing that management can do after training the team is get out of the way.

To ensure their visibility, senior managers need to believe in walk-the-halls management. In this way, every employee will come to recognize the sponsor and realize that it is appropriate to approach the sponsor with questions. Walk-the-halls management also means that executive sponsors keep their doors open. It is important that everyone, including line managers and their employees, feels supported by the sponsor. Keeping an open door can occasionally lead to problems if employees attempt to go around lower-level managers by seeking a higher level of authority. But such instances are infrequent, and the sponsor can easily deflect the problems back to the appropriate manager.

7.2 PROJECT SPONSORSHIP

Executive project sponsors provide guidance for project managers and project teams. They are also responsible for making sure that the line managers who lead functional departments fulfill their commitments of resources to the projects underway. In addition, executive project sponsors maintain communication with customers.

The project sponsor usually is an upper-level manager who, in addition to his or her regular responsibilities, provides ongoing guidance to assigned projects. An executive might take on sponsorship for several concurrent projects. Sometimes, on lower-priority or maintenance projects, a middle-level manager may take on the project sponsor role. One organization I know of even prefers to assign middle managers instead of executives. The company believes this avoids the common problem of lack of line manager buy-in to projects (see Figure 7–1).

In some large, diversified corporations, senior managers do not have adequate time to invest in project sponsorship. In such cases, project sponsorship falls to the level below corporate senior management or to a committee.

Some projects do not need project sponsors. Generally, sponsorship is required on large, complex projects involving a heavy commitment of resources. Large, complex projects also require a sponsor to integrate the activities of the functional lines, to dispel disruptive conflicts, and to maintain strong customer relations.

Consider one example of a project sponsor's support for a project. A project manager who was handling a project in an organization within the federal government decided that

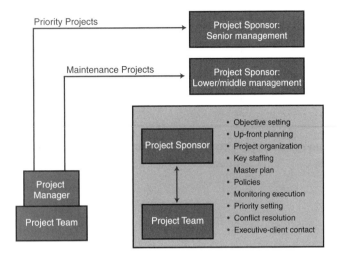

FIGURE 7–1. Roles of project sponsor. *Source:* Reprinted from H. Kerzner, In *Search of Excellence in Project Management.* New York, Wiley, 1998, p. 159.

another position would be needed on his team if the project were to meet its completion deadline. He had already identified a young woman in the company who fit the qualifications he had outlined. But adding another full-time-equivalent position seemed impossible. The size of the government project office was constrained by a unit-manning document that dictated the number of positions available.

The project manager went to the project's executive sponsor for help. The executive sponsor worked with the organization's human resources and personnel management department to add the position requested. Within 30 days, the addition of the new position was approved. Without the sponsor's intervention, it would have taken the organization's bureaucracy months to approve the position, too late to affect the deadline.

In another example, the president of a medium-size manufacturing company wanted to fill the role of sponsor on a special project. The project manager decided to use the president to the project's best advantage. He asked the president/sponsor to handle a critical situation. The president/sponsor flew to the company's headquarters and returned two days later with an authorization for a new tooling the project manager needed. The company ended up saving time on the project, and the project was completed four months earlier than originally scheduled.

Sponsorship by Committee

As companies grow, it sometimes becomes impossible to assign a senior manager to every project, and so committees act in the place of individual project sponsors. In fact, the recent trend has been toward committee sponsorship in many kinds of organizations. A project sponsorship committee usually is made up of a representative from every function of the company: engineering, marketing, and production. Committees may be temporary, when a committee is brought together to sponsor one time-limited project, or permanent, when a standing committee takes on the ongoing project sponsorship of new projects.

For example, General Motors Powertrain had achieved excellence in using committee sponsorship. Two key executives, the vice president of engineering and the vice president of operations, led the Office of Products and Operations, a group formed to oversee the management of all product programs. This group demonstrated visible executive-level program support and commitment to the entire organization. Their roles and responsibilities were to:

- Appoint the project manager and team as part of the charter process
- Address strategic issues
- Approve the program contract and test for sufficiency
- Assure program execution through regularly scheduled reviews with program managers

EDS is also a frequent user of committee sponsorship. According to Gene Panter, Program Manager with EDS:

> EDS executives, in conjunction with key customers, tend to take the role of sponsor for large-scale projects or programs. Sponsors are asked to participate in various checkpoint reviews, assure the acquisition of necessary resources, and provide support in the elimination of barriers that may exist. Large programs tend to have guidance teams in place to provide necessary support and approvals for project teams.
>
> Line managers and functional managers tend to be responsible for working with the project or program manager to identify appropriate human resources for projects. Project or program managers provide the direct management function for the project. EDS is also widely utilizing the concept of a project or program office to provide standards for project tracking, oversight, management, and control support for projects.

Phases of Project Sponsorship

The role of the project sponsor changes over the life cycle of a project. During the planning and initiation phases, the sponsor plays an active role in the following activities:

- Helping the project manager establish the objectives of the project
- Providing guidance to the project manager during the organization and staffing phases
- Explaining to the project manager what environmental or political factors might influence the project's execution
- Establishing the project's priority (working alone or with other company executives) and then informing the project manager about the project's priority in the company and the reason that priority was assigned
- Providing guidance to the project manager in establishing the policies and procedures for the project
- Functioning as the contact point for customers and clients

During the execution phase of a project, the sponsor must be very careful in deciding which problems require his or her guidance. Trying to get involved with every problem that comes up on a project will result in micromanagement. It will also undermine the project manager's authority and make it difficult for the executive to perform his or her regular responsibilities.

For short-term projects of two years or less, it is usually best that the project sponsor assignment is not changed over the duration of the project. For long-term projects of five years, more or less, different sponsors could be assigned for every phase of the project, if necessary. Choosing sponsors from among executives at the same corporate level works best, since sponsorship at the same level creates a "level" playing field, whereas at different levels, favoritism can occur.

Project sponsors need not come from the functional area where the majority of the project work will be completed. Some companies even go so far as assigning sponsors from line functions that have no vested interest in the project. Theoretically, this system promotes impartial decision-making.

Customer Relations

The role of executive project sponsors in customer relations depends on the type of organization (entirely project-driven or partially project-driven) and the type of customer (external or internal). Contractors working on large projects for external customers usually depend on executive project sponsors to keep the clients fully informed of progress on their projects. Customers with multi-million-dollar projects often keep an active eye on how their money is being spent. They are relieved to have an executive sponsor they can turn to for answers.

It is common practice for contractors heavily involved in competitive bidding for contracts to include both the project manager's and the executive project sponsor's resumes in proposals. All things being equal, the resumes may give one contractor a competitive advantage over another.

Customers prefer to have a direct path of communication open to their contractors' executive managers. One contractor identified the functions of the executive project sponsor as:

- Actively participating in the preliminary sales effort and contract negotiations
- Establishing and maintaining high-level client relationships
- Assisting project managers in getting the project underway (planning, staffing, and so forth)
- Maintaining current knowledge of major project activities
- Handling major contractual matters
- Interpreting company policies for project managers
- Helping project managers identify and solve significant problems
- Keeping general managers and client managers advised of significant problems with projects

Decision-Making

Imagine that project management is like car racing. A yellow flag is a warning to watch out for a problem. Yellow flags require action by the project manager or the line manager. There is nothing wrong with informing an executive about a yellow-flag problem as long as the project manager is not looking for the sponsor to solve the problem. Red flags, however, usually do require the sponsor's direct involvement. Red flags indicate problems that may affect the time, cost, and performance parameters of the project. So red flags need to be taken seriously and decisions need to be made collaboratively by the project manager and the project sponsor.

Serious problems sometimes result in serious conflicts. Disagreements between project managers and line managers are not unusual, and they require the thoughtful intervention of the executive project sponsor. First, the sponsor should make sure that the disagreement could not be solved without his or her help. Second, the sponsor needs to gather information from all sides and consider the alternatives being considered. Then, the sponsor must decide whether he or she is qualified to settle the dispute. Often, disputes are of a technical nature and require someone with the appropriate knowledge base to solve them. If the sponsor is unable to solve the problem, he or she will need to identify another source of authority that has the needed technical knowledge. Ultimately, a fair and appropriate solution can be shared by everyone involved. If there were no executive sponsor on the project, the disputing parties would be forced to go up the line of authority until they found a common superior to help them. Having executive project sponsors minimizes the number of people and the amount of time required to settle work disputes.

Strategic Planning   Executives are responsible for performing the company's strategic planning, and project managers are responsible for the operational planning on their assigned projects. Although the thought processes and time frames are different for the two types of planning, the strategic planning skills of executive sponsors can be useful to project managers. For projects that involve process or product development, sponsors can offer a special kind of market surveillance to identify new opportunities that might influence the long-term profitability of the organization. Furthermore, sponsors can gain a lot of strategically important knowledge from lower-level managers and employees. Who else knows better when the organization lacks the skill and knowledge base it needs to take on a new type of product? When the company needs to hire more technically skilled labor? What technical changes are likely to affect their industry?

7.3 EXCELLENCE IN PROJECT SPONSORSHIP

Many companies have achieved excellence in their application of project sponsorship. Radian International depended on single-project sponsors to empower its project managers for decision-making. General Motors proved that sponsorship by committee works. Roadway demonstrated the vital importance of sponsorship training for both sponsorship by a single executive and sponsorship by a committee.

In excellent companies, the role of the sponsor is not to supervise the project manager but to make sure that the best interests of both the customer and the company are recognized. However, as the next two examples reveal, it is seldom possible to make executive decisions that appease everyone.

Franklin Engineering (a pseudonym) had a reputation for developing high-quality, innovative products. Unfortunately, the company paid a high price for its reputation: a large R&D budget. Fewer than 15 percent of the projects initiated by R&D led to the full commercialization of a product and the recovery of the research costs.

The company's senior managers decided to implement a policy that mandated that all R&D project sponsors periodically perform cost–benefit analyses on their projects. When a project's cost–benefit ratio failed to reach the levels prescribed in the policy, the project was canceled for the benefit of the whole company.

Initially, R&D personnel were unhappy to see their projects canceled, but they soon realized that early cancellation was better than investing large amounts in projects that were likely to fail. Eventually, the project managers and team members came to agree that it made no sense to waste resources that could be better used on more successful projects. Within two years, the organization found itself working on more projects with a higher success rate but no addition to the R&D budget.

Another disguised case involves a California-based firm that designs and manufactures computer equipment. Let's call the company Design Solutions. The R&D group and the design group were loaded with talented individuals who believed that they could do the impossible and often did. These two powerful groups had little respect for the project managers and resented schedules because they thought schedules limited their creativity.

In June 1997, the company introduced two new products that made it onto the market barely ahead of the competition. The company had initially planned to introduce them by the end of 1996. The reason for the late releases: Projects had been delayed because of the project teams' desire to exceed the specifications required and not just meet them.

To help the company avoid similar delays in the future, the company decided to assign executive sponsors to every R&D project to make sure that the project teams adhered to standard management practices in the future. Some members of the teams tried to hide their successes with the rationale that they could do better. But the sponsor threatened to dismiss the employees, and they eventually relented.

The lessons in both cases are clear. Executive sponsorship actually can improve existing project management systems to better serve the interests of the company and its customers.

7.4 EMPOWERMENT OF PROJECT MANAGERS

One of the biggest problems with assigning executive sponsors to work beside line managers and project managers is the possibility that the lower-ranking managers will feel threatened with a loss of authority. This problem is real and must be dealt with at the executive level. Frank Jackson, formerly a senior manager at MCI, believes in the idea that information is power:

> We did an audit of the teams to see if we were really making the progress that we thought or were kidding ourselves, and we got a surprising result. When we looked at the audit, we found out that 50 percent of middle management's time was spent in filtering information

up and down the organization. When we had a sponsor, the information went from the team to the sponsor to the operating committee, and this created a real crisis in our middle management area.

MCI has found its solution to this problem. If there is anyone who believes that just going and dropping into a team approach environment is an easy way to move, it's definitely not. Even within the companies that I'm involved with, it's very difficult for managers to give up the authoritative responsibilities that they have had. You just have to move into it, and we've got a system where we communicate within MCI, which is MCI mail. It's an electronic mail system. What it has enabled us to do as a company is bypass levels of management. Sometimes you get bogged down in communications, but it allows you to communicate throughout the ranks without anyone holding back information.

Not only do executives have the ability to drive project management to success, they also have the ability to create an environment that leads to project failure. According to Robert Hershock, former vice president at 3M:

Most of the experiences that I had where projects failed, they failed because of management meddling. Either management wasn't 100 percent committed to the process, or management just bogged the whole process down with reports and a lot of other innuendos. The biggest failures I've seen anytime have been really because of management. Basically, there are two experiences where projects have failed to be successful. One is the management meddling where management cannot give up its decision-making capabilities, constantly going back to the team and saying you're doing this wrong or you're doing that wrong. The other side of it is when the team can't communicate its own objective. When it can't be focused, the scope continuously expands, and you get into project creep. The team just falls apart because it has lost its focus.

Project failure can often be a matter of false perceptions. Most executives believe that they have risen to the top of their organizations as solo performers. It is very difficult for them to change without feeling that they are giving up a tremendous amount of power, which traditionally is vested in the highest level of the company. To change this situation, it may be best to start small. As Frank Jackson observed:

There are so many occasions where senior executives won't go to training and won't listen, but I think the proof is in the pudding. If you want to instill project management teams in your organizations, start small. If the company won't allow you to do it using the Nike theory of just jumping in and doing it, start small and prove to them one step at a time that they can gain success. Hold the team accountable for results—it proves itself.

It is also important for us to remember that executives can have valid reasons for micromanaging. One executive commented on why project management might not be working as planned in his company:

We, the executives, wanted to empower the project managers and they, in turn, would empower their team members to make decisions as they relate to their project or function. Unfortunately, I do not feel that we (the executives) totally support decentralization of decision-making due to political concerns that stem from the lack of confidence we have in our project managers, who are not proactive and who have not demonstrated leadership capabilities.

In most organizations, senior managers start at a point where they trust only their fellow managers. As the project management system improves and a project management culture develops, senior managers come to trust project managers, even though they do not occupy positions high on the organizational chart. Empowerment does not happen overnight. It takes time and, unfortunately, a lot of companies never make it to full project manager empowerment.

7.5 MANAGEMENT SUPPORT AT WORK

Visible executive support is necessary for successful project management and the stability of a project management culture. But there is such a thing as too much visibility for senior managers. Take the following case example, for instance.

Midline Bank   Midline Bank (a pseudonym) is a medium-size bank doing business in a large city in the Northwest. Executives at Midline realized that growth in the banking industry in the near future would be based on mergers and acquisitions and that Midline would need to take an aggressive stance to remain competitive. Financially, Midline was well prepared to acquire other small- and middle-size banks to grow its organization.

The bank's information technology group was given the responsibility of developing an extensive and sophisticated software package to be used in evaluating the financial health of the banks targeted for acquisition. The software package required input from virtually every functional division of Midline. Coordination of the project was expected to be difficult.

Midline's culture was dominated by large, functional empires surrounded by impenetrable walls. The software project was the first in the bank's history to require cooperation and integration among the functional groups. A full-time project manager was assigned to direct the project.

Unfortunately, Midline's executives, managers, and employees knew little about the principles of project management. The executives did, however, recognize the need for executive sponsorship. A steering committee of five executives was assigned to provide support and guidance for the project manager, but none of the five understood project management. As a result, the steering committee interpreted its role as one of continuous daily direction of the project.

Each of the five executive sponsors asked for weekly personal briefings from the project manager, and each sponsor gave conflicting directions. Each executive had his or her own agenda for the project.

By the end of the project's second month, chaos took over. The project manager spent most of his time preparing status reports instead of managing the project. The executives changed the project's requirements frequently, and the organization had no change control process other than the steering committee's approval.

At the end of the fourth month, the project manager resigned and sought employment outside the company. One of the executives from the steering committee then took over the project manager's role, but only on a part-time basis. Ultimately, the project was taken over by two more project managers before it was complete, one year later than planned. The company learned a vital lesson: More sponsorship is not necessarily better than less.

Contractco

Another disguised case involves a Kentucky-based company I'll call Contractco. Contractco is in the business of nuclear fusion testing. The company was in the process of bidding on a contract with the U.S. Department of Energy. The department required that the project manager be identified as part of the company's proposal and that a list of the project manager's duties and responsibilities be included. To impress the Department of Energy, the company assigned both the executive vice president and the vice president of engineering as cosponsors.

The Department of Energy questioned the idea of dual sponsorship. It was apparent to the department that the company did not understand the concept of project sponsorship, because the roles and responsibilities of the two sponsors appeared to overlap. The department also questioned the necessity of having the executive vice president serve as a sponsor.

The contract was eventually awarded to another company. Contractco learned that a company should never underestimate the customer's knowledge of project management or project sponsorship.

Health Care Associates

Health Care Associates (another pseudonym) provides health care management services to both large and small companies in New England. The company partners with a chain of 23 hospitals in New England. More than 600 physicians are part of the professional team, and many of the physicians also serve as line managers at the company's branch offices. The physician-managers maintain their own private clinical practices as well.

It was the company's practice to use boilerplate proposals prepared by the marketing department to solicit new business. If a client were seriously interested in Health Care Associates' services, a customized proposal based on the client's needs would be prepared. Typically, the custom-design process took as long as six months or even a full year.

Health Care Associates wanted to speed up the custom-design proposal process and decided to adopt project management processes to accomplish that goal. In January 1994, the company decided that it could get a step ahead of its competition if it assigned a physician-manager as the project sponsor for every new proposal. The rationale was that the clients would be favorably impressed.

The pilot project for this approach was Sinco Energy (another pseudonym), a Boston-based company with 8600 employees working in 12 cities in New England. Health Care

Associates promised Sinco that the health care package would be ready for implementation no later than June 1994.

The project was completed almost 60 days late and substantially over budget. Health Care Associates' senior managers privately interviewed each of the employees on the Sinco project to identify the cause of the project's failure. The employees had the following observations:

- Although the physicians had been given management training, they had a great deal of difficulty applying the principles of project management. As a result, the physicians ended up playing the role of invisible sponsor instead of actively participating in the project.
- Because they were practicing physicians, the physician sponsors were not fully committed to their role as project sponsors.
- Without strong sponsorship, there was no effective process in place to control scope creep.
- The physicians had not had authority over the line managers, who supplied the resources needed to complete a project successfully.

Health Care Associates' senior managers learned two lessons. First, not every manager is qualified to act as a project sponsor. Second, the project sponsors should be assigned on the basis of their ability to drive the project to success. Impressing the customer is not everything.

7.6 MOTOROLA

Management support is not restricted exclusively to senior management. Line management support is equally crucial for project management to work effectively. Line managers are usually more resistant to project management and often demand proof that project management provides value to the organization before they support the new processes. This problem was identified previously in Exel's journey to excellence in project management and also appeared at Motorola. According to Tama McBride, PMP®, Program Manager at Motorola:

> This (getting line management support) was tough at first. It took years of having PMs provide value to the organization.

Tama McBride believes that today there is "absolutely" management support at Motorola:

> There is always senior management project sponsorship from an array of cross-functional teams. As a matrixed organization, we typically do not have a single management sponsor for a project.

When organizations become mature in project management, sponsorship at the executive levels and at middle management levels becomes minimal and integrated project teams are formed where the integrated or core team is empowered to manage the project with minimal sponsorship other than for critical decisions. These integrated or core teams may or may not include line management. Tama McBride explains why the concept of core teams has become a best practice at Motorola:

> Most project decisions and authority resides in the project core team. The core team is made up of middle- to low-level managers for the different functional areas (marketing, software, electrical, mechanical, manufacturing, system test, program management, quality, etc.) and has the project ownership responsibility. This core team is responsible for reviewing and approving product requirements and committing resources and schedule dates. It also acts as the project change control board and can approve or reject project scope change requests. However, any ship acceptance date changes must be approved by senior management.

7.7 DTE ENERGY

Jason Schulist, Manager, Continuous Improvement, Operating Systems Strategy Group at DTE Energy, comments on project sponsorship:

> The champions of continuous improvement projects that use the four-gate/nine-step methodology shown in Figures 4–3 and 4–4 are primarily vice presidents and directors of DTE Energy. These champions sign off at every gate to approve the results of the process. In some business units, a Master Black Belt also signs off at every gate to ensure that rigorous analysis and the DTE Energy operating system methodology is followed.

7.8 HALIFAX COMMUNITY HEALTH SYSTEMS

Woody Walker, Direct Enterprise Services at Halifax Community Health Systems (HCHS), comments on management support:

> The project office at Halifax Community Health Systems has both executive-level support as well as middle-management-level support. It varies on a project-by-project basis as to whether there will be both. For larger projects as well as high-priority projects, there generally is an executive sponsor as well as a sponsoring manager. In this situation, the sponsoring manager attends all core team meetings (held weekly by the project manager) as well as any meetings surrounding equipment location, milestones, issues, revisions to scope and the sponsor meeting (also a weekly meeting, generally a half hour in length). This manager is also an integral factor in participating in project cost reconciliation and change management. Executive sponsors are involved in a higher level. They sign off on

major milestones and change requests surrounding project scope that have an impact to cost or that create a "red flag" to the project. All projects must be requested by either an executive or a sponsoring manager. These individuals are involved first hand with the overall project approval from the beginning with the approval portfolio process, creation of executive summary, sign-off on all documents, and support while the project itself is being approved through all committees. While the project is underway, the sponsors attend (with the project manager) update meetings as a team that provides progress updates to the executive staff. The sponsors also sign off on all communications that the project manager submits to all internal newsletters and bulletin board postings. If there is not support from the sponsor, then the project will not be worked on by the EPMO.

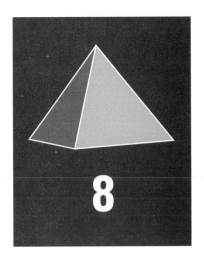

8 Training and Education

8.0 INTRODUCTION

Establishing project management training programs is one of the greatest challenges facing training directors because project management involves numerous complex and interrelated skills (qualitative/behavioral, organizational, and quantitative). In the early days of project management, project managers learned by their own mistakes rather than from the experience of others. Today, companies excellent in project management are offering a corporate curriculum in project management. Effective training supports project management as a profession.

Some large corporations offer more internal courses related to project management than most colleges and universities do. These companies include General Electric, General Motors, Kodak, the National Cryptological School, Ford Motor Company, and USAA. Such companies treat education almost as a religion. Smaller companies have more modest internal training programs and usually send their people to publicly offered training programs.

This chapter discusses processes for identifying the need for training, selecting the students who need training, designing and conducting the training, and measuring training's return on dollars invested.

8.1 TRAINING FOR MODERN PROJECT MANAGEMENT

During the early days of project management, in the late 1950s and throughout the 1960s, training courses concentrated on the advantages and disadvantages of various organizational forms (e.g., matrix, traditional, functional). Executives learned quickly, however, that any organizational structure could be made to work effectively and efficiently when

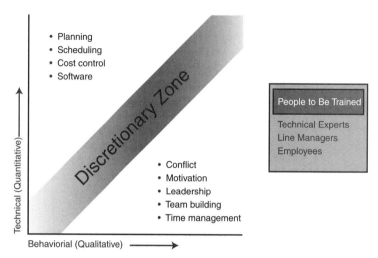

FIGURE 8–1. Types of project management training. *Source:* Reprinted from H. Kerzner, *In Search of Excellence in Project Management.* New York: Wiley, 1998, p. 174.

basic project management is applied. Project management skills based in trust, teamwork, cooperation, and communication can solve the worst structural problems.

Starting with the 1970s, emphasis turned away from organizational structures for project management. The old training programs were replaced with two basic programs:

● Basic project management, which stresses behavioral topics such as multiple reporting relationships, time management, leadership, conflict resolution, negotiation, team building, motivation, and basic management areas such as planning and controlling

● Advanced project management, which stresses scheduling techniques and software packages used for planning and controlling projects

Today's project management training programs include courses on behavioral as well as quantitative subjects. The most important problem facing training managers is how to achieve a workable balance between the two parts of the coursework—behavioral and quantitative (see Figure 8–1). For publicly sponsored training programs, the seminar leaders determine their own comfort levels in the "discretionary zone" between technical and behavioral subject matter. For in-house trainers, however, the balance must be preestablished by the training director on the basis of factors such as which students will be assigned to manage projects, types of projects, and average lengths of projects (see Table 8–1).

8.2 INTERNATIONAL INSTITUTE FOR LEARNING

Given the importance of project management now and in the future, there will certainly be a continuing need for high-quality project management education. E. LaVeme Johnson,

TABLE 8–1. EMPHASES IN VARIOUS TRAINING PROGRAMS

Type of Person Assigned for PM Training (PM Source)	Training Program Emphasis	
	Quantitative/ Technology Skills	Behavior Skills
Training Needed to Function as a Project Manager		
• Technical expert on short-term projects	High	Low
• Technical expert on long-term projects	High	High
• Line manager acting as a part-time project manager	High	Low
• Line manager acting as a full-time project manager	High	Average to high
• Employees experienced in cooperative operations	High	Average to high
• Employees inexperienced in cooperative operations	High	Average to high
Training Needed for General Knowledge		
• Any employees or managers	Average	Average

Source: Reprinted from H. Kerzner, *In Search of Excellence in Project Management.* New York: Wiley, 1998, p. 175.

President and CEO of the International Institute for Learning (IIL), comments on the growth of project management training[1]:

> In the IIL nearly 15-year history we've worked with thousands of companies planning and delivering training to their project managers and helping them to create more effective project management environments. Our clients range across all industries and include large, world-class companies as well as smaller organizations trying to gain an edge through effective programs. With IIL serving our clients' day-to-day needs as well as those that are just emerging on the horizon, we've been in a unique position to participate as project management matured into a full-fledged profession.
>
> From our perspective, courses that were sufficient just a few years ago now fall short. And that's a real sign of progress. The global market and expanding importance of project management has dictated whole new families of courses, much richer content and a flexible range of delivery mechanisms allowing students to learn when and where they need to—in live and virtual classrooms, alone at their desks whether at home or in the office, self-paced or instructor led. It seems that right now learning and technology have come together to offer the project management profession extremely useful tools to keep on building the future.

Evolutionary Years: Learning Trends

Training courses during the 1980s were mostly geared to advancing the project manager's skills. The focus of training was on the basics: the fundamental methodology and the know-how required to pass PMI's Project Management Professional (PMP®) Certification Exam. In response, IIL launched training courses in project management fundamentals and established a comprehensive certification course that allowed individuals to prepare for and successfully pass PMI's PMP® exam. A small variety of books, traditional classroom

---

1. For more information regarding IIL, you can visit the IIL website at www.iil.com.

courses, and software products were made available to those individuals responsible for managing projects in their companies.

Revolutionary Years: Marketplace Trends

In recent years, a far greater variety of companies and industries have recognized the business importance of managing projects more effectively. Compared to previous years, a revolution is emerging. This has become evident in a number of trends:

- The volume of projects is burgeoning as more and more companies run their businesses via projects. Indeed some leading organizations undertake many hundreds of thousands of individual projects each year—some small and simple, others huge and complex.
- The ability to effectively manage projects has become critically important to business, and good project management skills have become a competitive advantage for leading companies.
- As a result of this revolutionary growth, the status and value of the project management professional has grown in importance—having this know-how allows a company to complete projects faster, at lower cost, with greater customer satisfaction, and with more desirable project outcomes.
- Knowledge that was once deemed "nice to have" is now considered "mandatory."
- Today, employees with project management skills expand beyond the PMP. Team members and middle and top management are developing expertise in the subject.
- The complexity and scope of project management methodologies grow to include new skills and new applications.
- A large number of project management–related software programs have been developed to help manage projects (such as Microsoft Project, Primavera, and dozens of others).
- Project management certification has become an even more valuable asset to an individual's career path. As a result, PMI membership grew to over 165,000 by April 2005, a 25 percent annual increase, and the number of registered PMP®s climbed to almost 111,000 for a 39 percent increase over the previous year.
- Heretofore, the project manager's skill set has remained mostly technical. But today we are seeing project managers embrace additional skills: human resources, communications, managerial, and other advanced areas of knowledge.
- Strategic planning for project management has taken on importance. Organizations are now seeking systematic ways to better align project management with business objectives.
- More and more companies are establishing project offices.
- Approaches to project management within an organization remain relatively varied and nonstandardized. There is need to work toward a singular methodology in companies.

Revolutionary Years: Learning Trends

In response to these trends, a far greater variety of courses are available to a broadening number of industries. New methods of learning have been introduced to meet a growing diversity of customer needs. Here are some examples of how IIL has responded to the burgeoning need and established best practices in training and education for project managers:

- IIL has dozens of different course titles in "advanced" areas of knowledge to increase the scope, application, and sophistication of the project manager. Such courses include advanced concepts in risk management, the design and development of a project office, and how to manage multiple projects, just to name a few.

- Courses addressing the "softer" side of project management are now available to hone facilitation skills, interpersonal skills, leadership skills, and other nontechnical areas.
- The growth of project management software applications has demanded new training in how to effectively use these tools. IIL has a comprehensive four-level certification program for Microsoft Project 2003.
- More and more universities are recognizing project management as a part of their degree program. IIL has partnered with the University of Chicago and the University of Southern California to offer project management certificate programs complete with university transcripts and letter grades.
- The way we learn is changing. Employees have less time to devote to classroom study. As a result, in addition to traditional classroom training, IIL now offers innovative technology-based formats—Web-based, "self-paced" training; "virtual" instructor–led courses; hands-on leadership simulation; and online mentoring. Our "virtual" classroom courses are available 24/7 to accommodate the busy professional's needs, budget, and schedule.

A Look into the Crystal Ball: Trends and Learning Responses

It's always a challenge to try and predict the future, but there are some emerging trends that allow us to take a reasonable stab at this. For each of these trends, there will be the need to develop the appropriate learning responses.

- A key competitive factor in companies will be their ability to undertake and effectively manage many, many projects (projects to develop new products and services, get to market faster, reduce costs, improve customer satisfaction, increase sales, and so on). The more well chosen the projects are, the more competitive a company will be in the marketplace (particularly regarding projects to improve products, processes, and customer satisfaction).
- We anticipate a blending of project management methodologies with other proven business strategies (such as Six Sigma, quality management, and risk management). Training in these subjects will similarly become blended.
- Project management will continue to grow in business importance and ultimately become a strategic differentiating factor for remaining competitive.
- Senior management will become more knowledgeable and involved in project management efforts. This will require project management training that meets the unique needs of executives.
- Strategic planning for project management will become a way of life for leading organizations. The role of the "project office" will grow in importance and its existence will become commonplace in companies. Membership will include the highest levels of executive management. Senior management will take leadership of the company's project management efforts.
- An obstacle to participation by upper managers will be their limited experience and training in project management. An essential element will be to provide these managers with experience and training in how to manage project activities within their companies. This training must be tailored to be responsive to the unique needs and business responsibilities of upper management.
- The company's reward and recognition systems will change to stimulate and reinforce project management goals and objectives.

- Training in project management will be expanded to include all levels of the company hierarchy, including the non-PMP. Training will become responsive to the unique needs of this broad array of job functions, levels, and responsibilities.
- The status of the PMP will grow significantly, and the project manager's skills will be both technical and managerial.
- We will witness the establishment of a corporate-level project management executive (chief project management officer).
- Project benchmarking and continuous project improvement will become a way of life in leading organizations. The project management maturity models will play an important role in this regard, as they will help companies identify their strengths, weaknesses, and specific opportunities for improvement.
- The expanding importance of project management will require that more individuals are trained in project management. This in turn will necessitate the development of new and improved methods of delivery. It's likely that Web-based training will play an increasingly important role.
- We will see an order-of-magnitude increase in the number of organizations reaching the higher levels of project management maturity.
- More and more colleges and universities will offer degree programs in project management.

8.3 SCHOOL OF PROJECT MANAGEMENT

Today, project management training and education is a worldwide endeavor. Graduate-level education exists at colleges and universities throughout the world. In addition, during the past 10 years or so, many private organizations have started up with the sole objective of providing high-quality project management education suited to both undergraduate and graduate levels of education. Most of these companies start out with a dream and then cultivate the dream into a story of success. One such success story is the School of Project Management (SPM) in South Africa.[2] According to Dr. Lionel Smalley, President and CEO and the person who formed SPM in March 1989:

> The SPM was established to promote project management training in non-project-driven enterprises primarily in South Africa. From 1980 to 1989, there were only a few project management training courses in South Africa, and these courses appeared to make three fundamental mistakes. First, the project management course was offered by companies that also promoted a multitude of other nonrelated courses, and very little effort was provided to insert quality into the project management course because there appeared to be some concern that project management was just a fad that would soon disappear. Second, the course addressed only the concerns of the project manager rather than the concerns of all of the team players. And third, most training programs at that time focused on how projects should be managed and controlled in mainly project-driven enterprises. The decision to direct attention to product and service enterprises, as well as project-driven en-

---

2. For more information regarding SPM, you can visit the SPM website at www.spm.co.za.

terprises, was based upon research[3] that showed that there was an urgent need for modern-day project management principles and techniques to be applied to all industries, regardless of the type, and that the training programs had to be custom designed for all types of team players rather than just for the project managers. The research also showed that there was a growing need for graduate-level education in project management and that the original belief that project management was simply a fad soon to disappear was incorrect.

The SPM was started with the objective of providing only high-quality project management education for the South African community. The SPM's approach to project management training is focused on the management of projects in association with the use and application of integrated computer-based software packages such as those that would be part of a company's Intranet project management system and the core for the development of a company-wide project management methodology. Training is not purely a technique-based affair. Specialized training is provided for project managers, project team members, and project executives.

For this to become a reality, the SPM had to develop a set of core competencies to satisfy the project management needs of the business community. The core competencies developed by SPM include:

- *Corporate Strategy:* Showing how the environment affects project performance, cost management, and trade-off analysis.
- *Organizational Behavior:* Illustrating the importance of interpersonal relationships, leadership skills, managing conflict situations, and managing cultural diversity.
- *Project Finance:* Showing how to effectively participate in feasibility studies by making decisions based upon IRR values, NPV values, profitability indices, determining payback periods, and the management of risks. Far too many project managers today still are brought on board projects during the detailed planning stage rather than during the feasibility study phase. This is mainly due to a lack of project finance knowledge.
- *Project Negotiations:* Showing how to effectively negotiate for the required resources and/or deliverables. This is extremely important at all management levels and is often downplayed in its importance.
- *Decision Support Systems:* Using linear and goal-programming models to make the "right" decision in order to optimize the required outcome.

The selection of course material, whether it is a new course or enhancements to existing courses, is not a random process. The SPM is in constant communication with industry leaders and executives in both the public and private sectors to make sure that our offerings satisfy their needs. Although we follow the PMBOK® Guide, many of our courses are nontraditional courses based upon the needs of our clients. When they tell us that their needs have changed, such as the result of newly discovered best practices, we immediate include this material in our programs. The SPM also custom designs courses to satisfy the needs of particular clients. As best practices rise to the surface, so will the changes to our offerings.

---

3. By Dr. Smalley for his doctoral thesis completed in 1986 and entitled "Project Management in South Africa."

8.4 IDENTIFYING NEED FOR TRAINING

Identifying the need for training requires that line managers and senior managers recognize two critical factors: first, that training is one of the fastest ways to build project management knowledge in a company and, second, that training should be conducted for the benefit of the corporate bottom line through enhanced efficiency and effectiveness.

Identifying the need for training has become somewhat easier in the past 10 years because of published case studies on the benefits of project management training. The benefits can be classified according to quantitative and qualitative benefits. The quantitative results include:

- Shorter product development time
- Faster, higher-quality decisions
- Lower costs
- Higher profit margins
- Fewer people needed
- Reduction in paperwork
- Improved quality and reliability
- Lower turnover of personnel
- Quicker "best practices" implementation

Qualitative results include:

- Better visibility and focus on results
- Better coordination
- Higher morale
- Accelerated development of managers
- Better control
- Better customer relations
- Better functional support
- Fewer conflicts requiring senior management involvement

Companies are finally realizing that the speed at which the benefits of project management can be achieved is accelerated through proper training.

8.5 SELECTING STUDENTS

Selecting the people to be trained is critical. As we have already seen in a number of case studies, it is usually a mistake to train only the project managers. A thorough understanding of project management and project management skills is needed throughout the organization if project management is to be successful. For example, one automobile subcontractor invested months in training its project managers. Six months later, projects were still coming in late and over budget. The executive vice president finally realized that project management was a team effort rather than an individual responsibility. After that revelation, training was provided for all of the employees who had anything to do with the projects. Virtually overnight, project results improved.

Dave Kandt, Group Vice President, Quality and Program Management at Johnson Controls, explained how his company's training plan was laid out to achieve excellence in project management:

> We began with our executive office, and once we had explained the principles and philosophies of project management to these people, we moved to the managers of plants, engineering managers, cost analysts, purchasing people, and, of course, project managers. Only once the foundation was laid did we proceed with actual project management and with defining the roles and responsibilities so that the entire company would understand its role in project management once these people began to work. Just the understanding allowed us to move to a matrix organization and eventually to a stand-alone project management department.

8.6 FUNDAMENTALS OF PROJECT MANAGEMENT EDUCATION

Twenty years ago, we were somewhat limited as to availability of project management training and education. Emphasis surrounded on-the-job training in hopes that fewer mistakes would be made. Today, we have other types of programs, including:

- University courses
- University seminars
- In-house seminars
- In-house curriculums
- Distance teaming (e-learning)
- Computer-based training (CBT)

With the quantity of literature available today, we have numerous ways to deliver the knowledge. Typical delivery systems include:

- Lectures
- Lectures with discussion
- Exams
- Case studies on external companies
- Case studies on internal projects
- Simulation and role playing

Training managers are currently experimenting with "when to train." The most common choices include:

- *Just-in-Time Training:* This includes training employees immediately prior to assigning them to projects.

- *Exposure Training:* This includes training employees on the core principles just to give them enough knowledge so that they will understand what is happening in project management within the firm.
- *Continuous Learning:* This is training first on basic, then on advanced, topics so that people will continue to grow and mature in project management.
- *Self-Confidence Training:* This is similar to continuous learning but on current state-of-the-art knowledge. This is to reinforce employees' belief that their skills are comparable to those in companies with excellent reputations for project management.

8.7 DESIGNING COURSES AND CONDUCTING TRAINING

Many companies have come to realize that on-the-job training may be less effective than more formal training. On-the-job training virtually forces people to make mistakes as a learning experience, but what are they learning? How to make mistakes? It seems much more efficient to train people to do their jobs the right way from the start.

Project management has become a career path. More and more companies today allow or even require that their employees get project management certification. One company informed its employees that project management certification would be treated the same as a Master's degree in the salary and career-path structure. The cost of the training behind the certification process is only 5 or 10 percent of the cost of a typical Master's degree in business administration program. And certification promises a quicker return on investment (ROI) for the company. Project management certification can also be useful for employees without college degrees; it gives them the opportunity for a second career path within the company.

Linda Kretz of the International Institute for Learning explained what type of project management training worked best in her experience:

> In our experience, we have found that training ahead of time is definitely the better route to go. We have done it the other way with people learning on the job, and that has been a rather terrifying situation at times. When we talk about training, we are not just talking about training. We want our project managers to be certified through the Project Management Institute. We have given our people two years to certify. To that end there is quite a bit of personal study required. I do believe that training from the formal training end is great, and then you can modify that to whatever the need is in-house.

There is also the question of which are better: internally based or publicly held training programs. The answer depends on the nature of the individual company and how many employees need to be trained, how big the training budget is, and how deep the company's internal knowledge base is. If only a few employees at a time need training, it might be effective to send them to a publicly sponsored training course, but if large numbers of employees need training on an ongoing basis, designing and conducting a customized internal training program might be the way to go.

In general, custom-designed courses are the most effective. In excellent companies, course content surveys are conducted at all levels of management. For example, the research and development group of Babcock and Wilcox in Alliance, Ohio, needed a project management training program for 200 engineers. The head of the training department knew that she was not qualified to select core content, and so she sent questionnaires out to executive managers, line managers, and professionals in the organization. The information from the questionnaires was used to develop three separate courses for the audience. At Ford Motor Company, training was broken down into a 2-hour session for executives, a three-day program for project personnel, and a half-day session for overhead personnel.

For internal training courses, choosing the right trainers and speakers is crucial. A company can use trainers currently on staff if they have a solid knowledge of project management, or the trainers can be trained by outside consultants who offer train-the-trainer programs. Either way, trainers from within the company must have the expertise the company needs. Some problems with using internal trainers include the following:

- Internal trainers may not be experienced in all areas of project management.
- Internal trainers may not have up-to-date knowledge of the project management techniques practiced by other companies.
- Internal trainers may have other responsibilities in the company and so may not have adequate time for preparation.
- Internal trainers may not be as dedicated to project management or as skillful as external trainers.

But the knowledge base of internal trainers can be augmented by outside trainers as necessary. In fact, most companies use external speakers and trainers for their internal educational offerings. The best way to select speakers is to seek out recommendations from training directors in other companies and teachers of university-level courses in project management. Another method is contacting speakers' bureaus, but the quality of the speaker's program may not be as high as needed. The most common method for finding speakers is reviewing the brochures of publicly sponsored seminars. Of course, the brochures were created as sales materials, and so the best way to evaluate the seminars is to attend them.

After a potential speaker has been selected, the next step is to check his or her recommendations. Table 8–2 outlines many of the pitfalls involved in choosing speakers for internal training programs and how you can avoid them.

The final step is to evaluate the training materials and presentation the external trainer will use in the classes. The following questions can serve as a checklist:

- Does the speaker use a lot of slides in his or her presentation? Slides can be a problem when students do not have enough light to take notes.
- Does the instructor use transparencies? Have they been prepared professionally? Will the students be given copies of the transparencies?
- Does the speaker make heavy use of chalkboards? Too much chalkboard work usually means too much note taking for the trainees and not enough audiovisual preparation from the speaker.
- Does the speaker use case studies? If he or she does, are the case studies factual? It is best for the company to develop its own case studies and ask the speaker to use those so that the cases will have relevance to the company's business.

TABLE 8–2. COMMON PITFALLS IN HIRING EXTERNAL TRAINERS AND SPEAKERS

Warning Sign	Preventive Step
Speaker professes to be an expert in several different areas.	Verify speaker's credentials. Very few people are experts in several areas. Talk to other companies that have used the speaker.
Speaker's résumé identifies several well-known and highly regarded client organizations.	See whether the speaker has done consulting for any of these companies more than once. Sometimes a speaker does a good job selling himself or herself the first time, but the company refuses to rehire him or her after viewing the first presentation.
Speaker makes a very dramatic first impression and sells himself or herself well. Brief classroom observation confirms your impression.	Being a dynamic speaker does not guarantee that quality information will be presented. Some speakers are so dynamic that the trainees do not realize until too late that "The guy was nice but the information was marginal."
Speaker's résumé shows 10 to 20 years or more experience as a project manager.	Ten to 20 years of experience in a specific industry or company does not mean that the speaker's knowledge is transferable to your company's specific needs or industry. Ask the speaker what types of projects he or she has managed.
Marketing personnel from the speaker's company aggressively show the quality of their company, rather than the quality of the speaker. The client list presented is the company's client list.	You are hiring the speaker, not the marketing representative. Ask to speak or meet with the speaker personally and look at the speaker's client list rather than the parent company's client list.
Speaker promises to custom-design his or her materials to your company's needs.	Demand to see the speaker's custom-designed material at least two weeks before the training program. Also verify the quality and professionalism of view graphs and other materials.

- Are role playing and laboratory experiences planned? They can be valuable aids to learning, but they can also limit class size.
- Are homework and required reading a part of the class? If so, can they be completed before the seminar?

8.8 MEASURING RETURN ON INVESTMENT

The last area of project management training is the determination of the value earned on the dollars invested in training. Chapter 11 is devoted to this process of measuring ROI for training. It is crucial to remember that training should not be performed unless there is a continuous return on dollars for the company. Keep in mind, also, that the speaker's fee is only part of the cost of training. The cost to the company of having employees away from their work during training must be included in the calculation. Some excellent companies hire outside consultants to determine ROI. The consultants base their evaluations on personal interviews, on-the-job assessments, and written surveys.

One company tests trainees before and after training to learn how much knowledge the trainees really gained. Another company hires outside consultants to prepare and interpret posttraining surveys on the value of the specific training received.

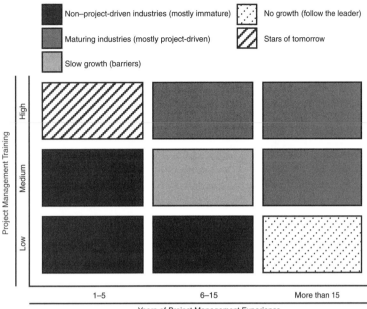

FIGURE 8–2. Amount of training by type of industry and year of project management experience. *Source:* Reprinted from H. Kerzner, *In Search of Excellence in Project Management.* New York: Wiley, 1998, p. 185.

The amount of training needed at any one company depends on two factors: whether the company is project-driven and whether it has practiced project management long enough to have developed a mature project management system. Figure 8–2 shows the amount of project management training offered (including refresher courses) against the number of years in project management. Project-driven organizations offer the most project management training courses, and organizations that have just started implementing project management offer the fewest. That's no surprise. Companies with more than 15 years of experience in applying project management principles show the most variance.

8.9 COMPETENCY MODELS

Twenty years ago, companies prepared job descriptions for project managers to explain roles and responsibilities. Unfortunately, the job descriptions were usually abbreviated and provided very little guidance on what was required for promotion or salary increases. Ten years ago we still emphasized the job description, but it was now supported by coursework, which was often mandatory. By the late 1990s, companies began emphasizing core competency models, which clearly depicted the skills levels needed to be effective as a project manager. Training programs were instituted to support the core competency models. Unfortunately, establishing a core competency model and the accompanying training is no easy task.

8.10 EFFECTIVE TRAINING PROGRAMS

The quality of the project management training and education a company's employees receive is, along with executive buy-in, one of the most important factors in achieving success and ultimately excellence in project management. The training could be for both the employees of the company as well as its suppliers who must interface with the customer's project management methodology. Let's look at some examples of effective training programs.

Hewlett-Packard

Hewlett-Packard is clearly committed to project management training and education. The following material is typically included in HP proposals. The material was provided by Ron Kempf, PMP®, Director of PM Competency and Certification at HP Services Engagement:

Project Management Development

HP Services has a comprehensive project management (PM) development program with courses that cover all aspects of PM training. The program was established in 1995. A standard curriculum with over 25 courses is implemented throughout the world covering project leadership, management, communication, risk management, contracting, managing business performance, scheduling and cost control, and quality. The courses are based on PMI's Project Management Body of Knowledge (PMBOK®). The curriculum also encompasses specialized courses on key HP internal topics, such as the program methodology, as well as essential business and financial management aspects of projects. Over 4000 students complete courses in the PM curriculum each year.

Even the most experienced project managers continue to take courses to strengthen their knowledge and skills. HP Services conducts an intensive weeklong training called Project Management University (PMU) twice a year in each major geography—Americas, Asia/Pacific, and Europe. Over 100 project managers attend each PMU. These events provide project managers with an opportunity to devote concentrated time to study and to exchange knowledge and ideas with other HP project managers from around the world.

All courses taught in HP's PM curriculum are registered in PMI's Registered Education Provider (REP) Program to ensure a consistent basis and oversight. The Project Management Development Program won Excellence in Practice awards in career development and organizational learning in 2002 from ASTD, the world's leading resource on workplace learning and performance issues.

PMP Certification

HP has a well-established program to encourage and support our project managers to achieve certification. HP Services has over 900 individuals who have earned the PMP® (Project Management Professional) certification from PMI®.

PMI Support

HP actively supports the PMI®, a nonprofit organization with more than 100,000 members. PMI® has set standards for PM excellence that are recognized by the industry and our customers worldwide.

HP employees participate on a number of PMI® boards and committees, including the Global Accreditation Center, Research Program Membership Advisory Group, development of the Certified Associate in Project Management (CAPM), development of Certificates of Added Qualification (CAQ) in IT Systems, IT Networks, and Project Management Office, PMBOK® 2000 review, and PMBOK® 2004 Update Team. Many HP employees hold leadership positions in PMI® chapters and special investigation groups (SIGs) throughout the world.

HP sponsored the Monday keynote speaker at the annual PMI® Symposium in October 2002 and was one of the top companies represented at the symposium, with eight papers presented by HP employees.

Exel

Training and education can accelerate the project management maturity process, especially if project management training is accompanied by training on the corporate project management methodology. This approach has been successfully implemented at Exel. According to Francena D. Gargaro, PMP, Director Project and Resource Management, Americas:

> Project management (PM) training is currently not mandatory; however, all sectors are aware of the PM methodology and the training provided. The Enterprise Project Management (EPM) group is responsible for scheduling and conducting the PM training courses. To date, over 1500 associates have been trained in Exel's PM methodology.
>
> Project Management 101 (PMIOI), Exel's introductory PM course, is a two-day, interactive course consisting of lecture, exercises, interactive team activities, and a comprehensive case study. An outside training consultant who is intimately familiar with Exel's business and a certified PMI training provider deliver the course. Members from the EPM group supplement the training with instruction on Exel PM tools, real-world examples, and facilitation of team exercises.
>
> PM101 participants include members of all sectors, company-wide, who have involvement in projects as team members, project managers, sponsors, or business development.
>
> Presently, the PM training programs are trending toward a curriculum-based format. Originally, PM101 was the only, optional PM training offered in-house. Over the past two years, we have expanded the program to include an on-line PM primer, which serves as a precursor to the PM101 course. The PM primer is a 30-minute, online tutorial on the basic concepts of PM and Exel's PM methodology.
>
> Additionally, Exel is in the process of developing the next step in the PM training program—PM201 (Advanced Project Management). It is geared more toward project managers, specifically targeting topics such as managing critical path, risk management, conflict management, customer relationship management, presentation skills, management/ leadership skills, and cost/schedule management.

The PM training curriculum can also lead to certification training, as described by Todd Daily, PMP, Project Manager, Enterprise Project Management, Americas:

> The PM training curriculum does lead to certification training, in some cases. Not everyone who attends PM training or performs the role of project manager pursues formal certification. It is, however, becoming more prominent and recognized within the organization. Today we have 16 certified Project Management Professionals (PMP®) in the U.S. We incorporate information about certification in the PM training courses and our course material follows the PMBOK® Guide approach.

The EPM group provides assistance to candidates within Exel who are interested in pursuing format certification in project management. We have material and processes to guide potential candidates in their pursuit. We also have begun developing assistance for the Certified Associate in Project Management (CAPM) program and have candidates currently pursuing this certification. Internationally, we have candidates pursuing certification in U.K./Europe, Mexico, and Brazil.

Exel Course Listings

- Project Management On-line Primer
- Project Management 101
- Project Management 201 (in development)

Measuring a return on investment in training dollars is not always easy. Sometimes, the returns are more easily identified from a qualitative rather than a quantitative perspective. Francena D. Gargaro, PMP, Director Project and Resource Management, Americas for Exel, believes that:

Current measures are more qualitative than quantitative. Course costs are generally covered by each participant's cost center, along with any associated travel expenses. All course participants, at the end of the class, complete a course and instructor evaluation. Feedback is reviewed, archived, and used to improve the course material and curriculum. Additionally, participants of the course are paired with a "buddy" to incorporate one new project management idea, learned from the course, into their day-to-day job activities and share experiences with their buddy.

Future considerations include a periodic posttraining review with participant's managers/supervisors to evaluate improvements in job performance following the training. That information would then be communicated to the Enterprise Project Management group for tracking and evaluation. This approach is currently being considered but has yet to be implemented.

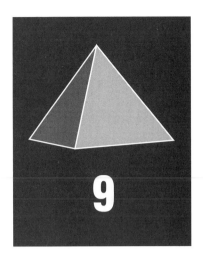

9 Informal Project Management

9.0 INTRODUCTION

Over the past 20 years, the most significant change in project management has been the idea that informal project management does work. In the 1950s and 1960s, the aerospace, defense, and large construction industries were the primary users of project management techniques and tools. Because project management was a relatively new management process, customers of the contractors and subcontractors wanted evidence that the system worked. Documentation of the policies and procedures to be used became part of the written proposal. Formal project management, supported by hundreds of policies, procedures, and forms, became the norm. After all, why would a potential customer be willing to sign a $10 million contract for a project to be managed informally?

This chapter clarifies the difference between informal and formal project management, then discusses the four critical elements of informal project management.

9.1 INFORMAL VERSUS FORMAL PROJECT MANAGEMENT

Formal project management has always been expensive. In the early years, the time and resources spent on preparing written policies and procedures had a purpose: They placated the customer. As project management became established, formal documentation was created mostly for the customer. Contractors began managing more informally, while the customer was still paying for formal project management documentation. Table 9–1 shows the major differences between formal and informal project management. As you can see, the most relevant difference is the amount of paperwork.

TABLE 9–1. FORMAL VERSUS INFORMAL PROJECT MANAGEMENT

Factor	Formal Project Management	Informal Project Management
Project manager's level	High	Low to middle
Project manager's authority	Documented	Implied
Paperwork	Exorbitant	Minimal

Paperwork is expensive. Even a routine handout for a team meeting can cost $500 to $2000 per page to prepare. Executives in excellent companies know that paperwork is expensive. They encourage project teams to communicate without excessive amounts of paper. However, some people are still operating under the mistaken belief that ISO 9000 certification requires massive paperwork.

Figure 9–1 shows the changes in paperwork requirements in project management. The early 1980s marked the heyday for lovers of paper documentation. At that time, the average policies and procedures manual probably cost between $3 million and $5 million to prepare initially and $1 million to $2 million to update yearly over the lifetime of the project. Project managers were buried in forms to complete to the extent that they had very little time left for actually managing the projects. Customers began to complain about the high cost of subcontracting, and the paperwork boom started to fade.

Real cost savings did not materialize until the early 1990s with the growth of concurrent engineering. Concurrent engineering shortened product development times by taking activities that had been done in series and performing them in parallel instead. This change increased the level of risk in each project, which required that project management back away from some of its previous practices. Formal guidelines were replaced by less detailed and more generic checklists.

Policies and procedures represent formality. Checklists represent informality. But informality does not eliminate project paperwork altogether. It reduces paperwork require-

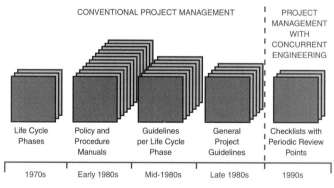

FIGURE 9–1. Evolution of policies, procedures, and guidelines. *Source:* Reprinted from H. Kerzner, *In Search of Excellence in Project Management.* New York: Wiley, 1998, p. 196.

ments to minimally acceptable levels. To move from formality to informality demands a change in organizational culture (see Figure 9–2). The four basic elements of an informal culture are these:

- Trust
- Communication
- Cooperation
- Teamwork

Large companies quite often cannot manage projects on an informal basis although they want to. The larger the company, the greater the tendency for formal project management to take hold. Patty Goyette, Vice President IOC Sales Operations and Customer Service at Nortel Networks, believes that:

> The introduction of enterprise-wide project process and tools standards in Nortel Networks and the use of pipeline metrics (customer-defined, industry standard measures) provides a framework for formal project management. This is necessary given the complexity of telecom projects we undertake and the need for an integrated solution in a short time frame. The Nortel Networks project manager crosses many organizational boundaries to achieve the results demanded by customers in a dynamic environment.

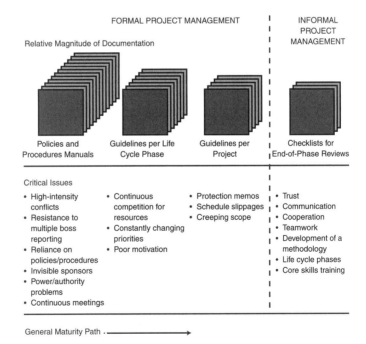

FIGURE 9–2. Evolution of paperwork and change of formality levels. *Source:* Reprinted from H. Kerzner, *In Search of Excellence in Project Management.* New York: Wiley, 1998, p. 198.

Most companies manage either formally or informally. However, if your company is project-driven and has a very strong culture for project management, you may have to manage either formally or informally based upon the needs of your customers. Carl Isenberg, Director of EDS Project Management Consulting, describes this dual approach at EDS:

> Based on the size and scope of a project, formal or informal project management is utilized. Most organizations within EDS have defined thresholds that identify the necessary project management structure. The larger the project (in cost, schedule, and resource requirements), the more strictly the methodology is followed. Smaller projects (such as a modification to a report) require a more cursory approach to the management of that project.
>
> Larger projects require full development of a start-up plan (i.e., the plan for the plan), full-scale planning, execution of the plan and crucial closedown activities to ensure proper project completion, and documentation of lessons learned. These types of projects have a formal project workbook in place (typically in electronic format) to archive project documentation and deliverables. These archives are generally available to be leveraged on future projects that are similar in nature.
>
> The execution of EDS project management methodology is also sometimes dependent on the customer environment and relationship. The contractual nature and/or relationship EDS has with various customers sometimes affect whether project management is done formally or informally. The relationship also affects whose methodology will be used.

9.2 TRUST

Trusting everyone involved in executing a project is critical. You wake up in the morning, get dressed, and climb into your car to go to work. On a typical morning, you operate the foot pedal for your brakes maybe 50 times. You have never met the people who designed the brakes, manufactured the brakes, or installed the brakes. Yet you still give no thought to whether the brakes will work when you need them. No one broadsides you on the way to work. You do not run over anyone. Then you arrive at work and push the button for the elevator. You have never met the people who designed the elevator, manufactured it, installed it, or inspected it. But again you feel perfectly comfortable riding the elevator up to your floor. By the time you get to your office at 8 AM, you have trusted your life to uncounted numbers of people whom you have never even met. Still, you sit down in your office and refuse to trust the person in the next office to make a $50 decision.

Trust is the key to the successful implementation of informal project management. Without it, project managers and project sponsors would need all that paperwork just to make sure that everyone working on their projects was doing the work just as he or she had been instructed. And trust is also key in building a successful relationship between the contractor/subcontractor and the client. Let's look at an example.

Perhaps the best application of informal project management that I have seen occurred several years ago in the Heavy Vehicle Systems Group of Bendix Corporation. Bendix

TABLE 9–2. BENEFITS OF TRUST IN CUSTOMER–CONTRACTOR WORKING RELATIONSHIPS

Without Trust	With Trust
Continuous competitive bidding	Long-term contracts, repeat business, and sole-source contracts
Massive documentation	Minimal documentation
Excessive customer–contractor team meetings	Minimal number of team meetings
Team meetings with documentation	Team meetings without documentation
Sponsorship at executive levels	Sponsorship at middle-management levels

hired a consultant to conduct a three-day training program. The program was custom designed, and during the design phase the consultant asked the vice president and general manager of the division whether he wanted to be trained in formal or informal project management. The vice president opted for informal project management. What was the reason for his decision? The culture of the division was already based on trust. Line managers were not hired solely based on technical expertise. Hiring and promotions were based on how well the new manager would communicate and cooperate with the other line managers and project managers in making decisions in the best interests of both the company and the project.

When the relationship between a customer and a contractor is based on trust, numerous benefits accrue to both parties. The benefits are apparent in companies such as Hewlett-Packard, Computer Associates, and various automobile subcontractors. Table 9–2 shows the benefits.

9.3 COMMUNICATION

In traditional, formal organizations, employees usually claim that communication is poor. Senior managers, however, usually think that communication in their company is just fine. Why the disparity? In most companies, executives are inundated with information communicated to them through frequent meetings and dozens of weekly status reports coming from every functional area of the business. The quality and frequency of information moving down the organizational chart are less consistent, especially in more formal companies. But whether it is a problem with the information flowing up to the executive level or down to the staff, the problem usually originates somewhere upstairs. Senior managers are the usual suspects when it comes to requiring reports and meetings. And many of those reports and meetings are unnecessary and redundant.

Most project managers prefer to communicate verbally and informally. The cost of formal communication can be high. Project communication includes dispensing information on decisions made, work authorizations, negotiations, and project reports. Project managers in excellent companies believe that they spend as much as 90 percent of their time on internal interpersonal communication with their teams. Figure 9–3 illustrates the

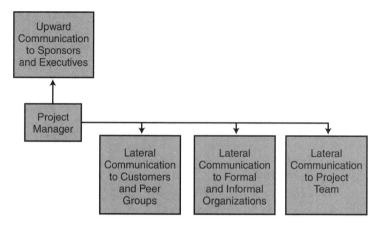

FIGURE 9–3. Internal and external communication channels for project management. *Source:* Reprinted from H. Kerzner, *In Search of Excellence in Project Management.* New York: Wiley, 1998, p. 200.

communication channels used by a typical project manager. In project-driven organizations, project managers may spend most of their time communicating externally to customers and regulatory aencies.

Good project management methodologies promote not only informal project management but also effective communications laterally as well as vertically. The methodology itself functions as a channel of communication. A senior executive at a large financial institution commented on his organization's project management methodology, called Project Management Standards (PMS):

> The PMS guides the project manager through every step of the project. The PMS not only controls the reporting structure but also sets the guidelines for who should be involved in the project itself and the various levels of review. This creates an excellent communication flow between the right people. The communication of a project is one of the most important factors for success. A great plan can only go so far if it is not communicated well.

Most companies believe that a good project management methodology will lead to effective communications, which will allow the firm to manage more informally than formally. The question, of course, is how long it will take to achieve effective communications. With all employees housed under a single roof, the time frame can be short. For global projects, geographical dispersion and cultural differences may mandate decades before effective communication will occur. Even then, there is no guarantee that global projects will ever be managed informally.

Suzanne Zale, Global Program Manager of EDS, emphasized:

> With any global project, communications becomes more complex. It will require much more planning up front. All constituents for buy-in need to be identified early on. In order to leverage existing subject matter, experts conversant with local culture, and suppliers, the need for virtual teams becomes more obvious. This increases the difficulty for effective communications.

The mechanism for communication may also change drastically. Face-to-face conversations or meetings will become more difficult. We tend to rely heavily on electronic communications, such as video and telephone conferencing and electronic mail. The format for communications needs to be standardized and understood up front so that information can be sent out quickly. Communications will also take longer and require more effort because of cultural and time differences.

One of the implied assumptions for informal project management to exist is that the employees understand their organizational structure and their roles and responsibilities within both the organizational and project structure. Forms such as the linear responsibility chart and the responsibility assignment matrix are helpful. Communication tools are not used today with the same frequency as in the 1970s and 1980s.

For multinational projects, the organizational structure, roles, and responsibilities must be clearly delineated. Effective communications is of paramount importance and probably must be accomplished more formally than informally.

Suzanne Zale, Global Program Manager of EDS, stated:

> For any global project, the organizational structure must be clearly defined to minimize any potential misunderstandings. It is best to have a clearcut definition of the organizational chart and roles and responsibilities. Any motivation incentives must also contemplate cultural differences. The drivers and values for different cultures can vary substantially.

The two major communication obstacles that must be overcome when a company truly wants to cultivate an informal culture are what I like to call hernia reports and forensic meetings. Hernia reports result from senior management's belief that that which has not been written has not been said. Although there is some truth to such a belief, the written word comes with a high price tag. We need to consider more than just the time consumed in the preparation of reports and formal memos. There is all the time that recipients spend reading them, as well as all the support time taken up in processing, copying, distributing, and filing them.

Status reports written for management are too long if they need a staple or a paper clip. Project reports greater than 5 or 10 pages often are not even read. In companies excellent in project management, internal project reports answer these three questions as simply as possible:

- Where are we today?
- Where will we end up?
- Are there any problems that require management's involvement?

All of these questions can be answered on one sheet of paper.

The second obstacle is the forensic team meeting. A forensic team meeting is a meeting scheduled to last 30 minutes that actually lasts for more than 3 hours. Forensic meetings are created when senior managers meddle in routine work activities. Even project managers fall into this trap when they present information to management that management should not be dealing with. Such situations are an invitation to disaster.

9.4 COOPERATION

Cooperation is the willingness of individuals to work with others for the benefit of all. It includes the voluntary actions of a team working together toward a favorable result. in companies excellent in project management, cooperation is the norm and takes place without the formal intervention of authority. The team members know the right thing to do, and they do it.

In the average company (or the average group of any kind, for that matter), people learn to cooperate as they get to know each other. That takes time, something usually in short supply for project teams. But companies such as Ericsson Telecom AB, the General Motors Powertrain Group, and Hewlett-Packard create cultures that promote cooperation to the benefit of everyone.

9.5 TEAMWORK

Teamwork is the work performed by people acting together with a spirit of cooperation under the limits of coordination. Some people confuse teamwork with morale, but morale has more to do with attitudes toward work than it has to do with the work itself. Obviously, however, good morale is beneficial to teamwork.

In excellent companies, teamwork has these characteristics:

- Employees and managers share ideas with each other and establish high levels of innovation and creativity in work groups.
- Employees and managers trust each other and are loyal to each other and the company.
- Employees and managers are committed to the work they do and the promises they make.
- Employees and managers share information freely.
- Employees and managers are consistently open and honest with each other.

Making people feel that they are part of a team does not necessarily require a great deal of effort. Consider the situation at the Engineering and Construction Services Division of Dow Chemical Corporation several years ago. Dow Chemical had requested a trainer to develop a project management training course. The trainer interviewed several of the seminar participants before the training program to identify potential problem areas. The biggest problem appeared to be a lack of teamwork. This shortcoming was particularly evident in the drafting department. The drafting department personnel complained that too many changes were being made to the drawings. They simply could not understand the reasons behind all the changes.

The second problem identified, and perhaps the more critical one, was that project managers did not communicate with the drafting department once the drawings were complete. The drafting people had no idea of the status of the projects they were working on, and they did not feel as though they were part of the project team.

During the training program, one of the project managers, who was responsible for constructing a large chemical plant, was asked to explain why so many changes were being made to the drawings on his project. He said, "There are three reasons for the changes.

First, the customers don't always know what they want up front. Second, once we have the preliminary drawings to work with, we build a plastic model of the plant. The model often shows us that equipment needs to be moved for maintenance or safety reasons. Third, sometimes we have to rush into construction well before we have final approval from the Environmental Protection Agency. When the agency finally gives its approval, that approval is often made contingent on making major structural changes to the work already complete." One veteran employee at Dow commented that in his 15 years with the company no one had ever before explained the reasons behind drafting changes.

The solution to the problem of insufficient communication was also easy to repair once it was out in the open. The project managers promised to take monthly snapshots of the progress on building projects and share them with the drafting department. The drafting personnel were delighted and felt more like a part of the project team.

9.6 COLOR-CODED STATUS REPORTING

The use of colors for status reporting, whether it be for printed reports or Intranet-based visual presentations, has grown significantly. Color-coded reports encourage informal project management to take place. Colors can reduce risks by alerting management quickly that a potential problem exists. One company prepared complex status reports but color coded the right-hand margins of each page designed for specific audiences and levels of management. One executive commented that he now reads only those pages that are color coded for him specifically rather than having to search through the entire report. In another company, senior management discovered that color-coded Intranet status reporting allowed senior management to review more information in a timely manner just by focusing on those colors that indicated potential problems. Colors can be used to indicate:

- Status has not been addressed.
- Status is addressed, but no problems exist.
- Project is on course.
- A potential problem might exist in the future.
- A problem definitely exists and is critical.
- No action is to be taken on this problem.
- Activity has been completed.
- Activity is still active and completion date has passed.

9.7 INFORMAL PROJECT MANAGEMENT AT WORK

Let's review two case studies that illustrate informal project management in action.

Polk Lighting

Polk Lighting (a pseudonym) is a $35 million company located in Jacksonville, Florida. The company manufactures lamps, flashlights, and a variety of other lighting instruments. Its business is entirely based in products and services, and the company does not take on contract projects from outside customers. The majority of the company's stock is publicly traded. The president of Polk Lighting has held his position since the company's start-up in 1985.

In 1994, activities at Polk centered on the R&D group, which the president over saw personally, refusing to hire an R&D director. The president believed in informal management for all aspects of the business, but he had a hidden agenda for wanting to use informal project management. Most companies use informal project management to keep costs down as far as possible, but the president of Polk favored informal project management so that he could maintain control of the R&D group. However, if the company were to grow, the president would need to add more management structure, establish tight project budgets, and possibly make project management more formal than it had been. Also, the president would probably be forced to hire an R&D director.

Pressure from the company's stockholders eventually forced the president to allow the company to grow. When growth made it necessary for the president to take on heavier administrative duties, he finally hired a vice president of R&D.

Within a few years, the company's sales doubled, but informal project management was still in place. Although budgets and schedules were established as the company grew, the actual management of the projects and the way teams worked together remained informal.

Boeing Aerospace

Boeing was the prime contractor for the U.S. Air Force's new short-range attack missile (SRAM) and awarded the subcontract for developing the missile's propulsion system to the Thiokol Corporation.

It is generally assumed that communication between large customers and contractors must be formal because of the potential for distrust when contracts are complex and involve billions of dollars. The use of on-site representatives, however, can change a potentially contentious relationship into one of trust and cooperation when informality is introduced into the relationship.

Two employees from Boeing were carefully chosen to be on-site representatives at the Thiokol Corporation to supervise the development of the SRAM's propulsion system. The working relationship between Thiokol's project management office and Boeing's on-site representatives quickly developed into shared trust. Team meetings were held without the exchange of excessive documentation. And each party agreed to cooperate with the other. The Thiokol project manager trusted Boeing's representatives well enough to give them raw data from test results even before Thiokol's engineers could formulate their own opinions on the data. Boeing's representatives in turn promised that they would not relay the raw data to Boeing until Thiokol's engineers were ready to share their results with their own executive sponsors.

The Thiokol–Boeing relationship on this project clearly indicates that informal project management can work between customers and contractors. Large construction contractors have had the same positive results in using informal project management and on-site representatives to rebuild trust and cooperation.

10 Behavioral Excellence

10.0 INTRODUCTION

Previously, we saw that companies excellent in project management strongly emphasize training for behavioral skills. In the past it was thought that project failures were due primarily to poor planning, inaccurate estimating, inefficient scheduling, and lack of cost control. Today, excellent companies realize that project failures have more to do with behavioral shortcomings—poor employee morale, negative human relations, low productivity, and lack of commitment.

This chapter discusses these human factors in the context of situational leadership and conflict resolution. It also provides information on staffing issues in project management. Finally, the chapter offers advice on how to achieve behavioral excellence.

10.1 SITUATIONAL LEADERSHIP

As project management has begun to emphasize behavioral management over technical management, situational leadership has also received more attention. The average size of projects has grown, and so has the size of project teams. Process integration and effective interpersonal relations have also taken on more importance as project teams have gotten larger. Project managers now need to be able to talk with many different functions and departments. There is a contemporary project management proverb that goes something like this: "When researcher talks to researcher, there is 100 percent understanding. When researcher talks to manufacturing, there is 50 percent understanding. When researcher talks to sales, there is zero percent understanding. But the project manager talks to all of them."

Randy Coleman, former senior vice president of the Federal Reserve Bank of Cleveland, emphasizes the importance of tolerance:

> The single most important characteristic necessary in successful project management is tolerance: tolerance of external events and tolerance of people's personalities. Generally, there are two groups here at the Fed—lifers and drifters. You have to handle the two groups differently, but at the same time you have to treat them similarly. You have to bend somewhat for the independents (younger drifters) who have good creative ideas and whom you want to keep, particularly those who take risks. You have to acknowledge that you have some trade-offs to deal with.

A senior project manager in an international accounting firm states how his own leadership style has changed from a traditional to a situational leadership style since becoming a project manager:

> I used to think that there was a certain approach that was best for leadership, but experience has taught me that leadership and personality go together. What works for one person won't work for others. So you must understand enough about the structure of projects and people and then adopt a leadership style that suits your personality so that it comes across as being natural and genuine. It's a blending of a person's experience and personality with his or her style of leadership.

Many companies start applying project management without understanding the fundamental behavioral differences between project managers and line managers. If we assume that the line manager is not also functioning as the project manager, here are the behavioral differences:

- Project managers have to deal with multiple reporting relationships. Line managers report up a single chain of command.
- Project managers have very little real authority. Line managers hold a great deal of authority by virtue of their titles.
- Project managers often provide no input into employee performance reviews. Line managers provide formal input into the performance reviews of their direct reports.
- Project managers are not always on the management compensation ladder. Line managers always are.
- The project manager's position may be temporary. The line manager's position is permanent.
- Project managers sometimes are a lower grade level than the project team members. Line managers usually are paid at a higher grade level than their subordinates.

Several years ago, when Ohio Bell was still a subsidiary of American Telephone and Telegraph, a trainer was hired to conduct a three-day course on project management. During the customization process, the trainer was asked to emphasize planning, scheduling, and controlling and not to bother with the behavioral aspects of project management. At that time, AT&T offered a course on how to become a line supervisor that all of the seminar participants had already taken. In the discussion that followed between the trainer and the course content designers, it became apparent that leadership, motivation, and conflict resolution were being taught from a superior-to-subordinate point of view in AT&T's course. When the course content designers realized from the discussion that project managers provide leadership, motivation, and conflict resolution to employees who do not report directly to them, the trainer was allowed to include project management–related behavioral topics in the seminar.

Organizations must recognize the importance of behavioral factors in working relationships. When they do, they come to understand that project managers should be hired for their overall project management competency, not for their technical knowledge alone. Brian Vannoni, formerly site training manager and principal process engineer at GE Plastics, described his organization's approach to selecting project managers:

> The selection process for getting people involved as project managers is based primarily on their behavioral skills and their skills and abilities as leaders with regard to the other aspects of project management. Some of the professional and full-time project managers have taken senior engineers under their wing, coached and mentored them, so that they learn and pick up the other aspects of project management. But the primary skills that we are looking for are, in fact, the leadership skills.

Project managers who have strong behavioral skills are more likely to involve their teams in decision-making, and shared decision-making is one of the hallmarks of successful project management. Today, project managers are more managers of people than they are managers of technology. According to Robert Hershock, former vice president at 3M:

> The trust, respect, and especially the communications are very, very important. But I think one thing that we have to keep in mind is that a team leader isn't managing technology; he or she is managing people. If you manage the people correctly, the people will manage the technology.

In addition, behaviorally oriented project managers are more likely to delegate responsibility to team members than technically strong project managers. In 1996, Frank Jackson, formerly a senior manager at MCI, said that:

> Team leaders need to have a focus and a commitment to an ultimate objective. You definitely have to have accountability for your team and the outcome of your team. You've got to be able to share the decision-making. You can't single out yourself as the exclusive holder of the right to make decisions. You have got to be able to share that. And lastly again, just to harp on it one more time, is communications. Clear and concise communication throughout the team and both up and down a chain of command is very, very important.

Some organizations prefer to have a project manager with strong behavioral skills acting as the project manager, with technical expertise residing with the project engineer. Other organizations have found the reverse to be effective. Rose Russett, formerly the program management process manager for General Motors Powertrain, stated:

> We usually appoint an individual with a technical background as the program manager and an individual with a business and/or systems background as the program administrator.

This combination of skills seems to complement one another. The various line managers are ultimately responsible for the technical portions of the program, while the key responsibility of the program manager is to provide the integration of all functional deliverables to achieve the objectives of the program. With that in mind, it helps for the program manager to understand the technical issues, but they add their value not by solving specific technical problems but by leading the team through a process that will result in the best solutions for the overall program, not just for the specific functional area. The program administrator, with input from all team members, develops the program plans, identifies the critical path, and regularly communicates this information to the team throughout the life of the program. This information is used to assist with problem solving, decision-making, and risk management.

10.2 CONFLICT RESOLUTION

Opponents of project management claim that the primary reason why some companies avoid changing over to a project management culture is that they fear the conflicts that inevitably accompany change. Conflicts are a way of life in companies with project management cultures. Conflict can occur on any level of the organization, and conflict is usually the result of conflicting objectives. The project manager is a conflict manager. In many organizations, the project managers continually fight fires and handle crises arising from interpersonal and interdepartmental conflicts. They are so busy handling conflicts that they delegate the day-to-day responsibility for running their projects to the project teams. Although this arrangement is not the most effective, it is sometimes necessary, especially after organizational restructuring or after a new project demanding new resources has been initiated.

The ability to handle conflicts requires an understanding of why conflicts occur. We can ask four questions, the answers to which are usually helpful in handling, and possibly preventing, conflicts in a project management environment:

- Do the project's objectives conflict with the objectives of other projects currently in development?
- Why do conflicts occur?
- How can we resolve conflicts?
- Is there anything we can do to anticipate and resolve conflicts before they become serious?

Although conflicts are inevitable, they can be planned for. For example, conflicts can easily develop in a team in which the members do not understand each other's roles and responsibilities. Responsibility charts can be drawn to map out graphically who is responsible for doing what on the project. With the ambiguity of roles and responsibilities gone, the conflict is resolved or future conflict averted.

Resolution means collaboration, and collaboration means that people are willing to rely on each other. Without collaboration, mistrust prevails and progress documentation increases.

The most common types of conflict involve the following:

- Manpower resources
- Equipment and facilities
- Capital expenditures
- Costs
- Technical opinions and trade-offs
- Priorities
- Administrative procedures
- Schedules
- Responsibilities
- Personality clashes

Each of these types of conflict can vary in intensity over the life of the project. The relative intensity can vary as a function of:

- Getting closer to project constraints
- Having met only two constraints instead of three (e.g, time and performance but not cost)
- The project life cycle itself
- The individuals who are in conflict

Conflict can be meaningful in that it results in beneficial outcomes. These meaningful conflicts should be allowed to continue as long as project constraints are not violated and beneficial results accrue. An example of a meaningful conflict might be two technical specialists arguing that each has a better way of solving a problem. The beneficial result would be that each tries to find additional information to support his or her hypothesis.

Some conflicts are inevitable and occur over and over again. For example, consider a raw material and finished goods inventory. Manufacturing wants the largest possible inventory of raw materials on hand to avoid possible production shutdowns. Sales and marketing wants the largest finished goods inventory so that the books took favorable and no cash flow problems are possible.

Consider five methods that project managers can use to resolve conflicts:

- Confrontation
- Compromise
- Facilitation (or smoothing)
- Force (or forcing)
- Withdrawal

Confrontation is probably the most common method used by project managers to resolve conflict. Using confrontation, the project manager faces the conflict directly. With the help of the project manager, the parties in disagreement attempt to persuade one another that their solution to the problem is the most appropriate.

When confrontation does not work, the next approach project managers usually try is compromise. In compromise, each of the parties in conflict agrees to trade-offs or makes concessions until a solution is arrived at that everyone involved can live with. This give-and-take-approach can easily lead to a win–win solution to the conflict.

The third approach to conflict resolution is facilitation. Using facilitation skills, the project manager emphasizes areas of agreement and deemphasizes areas of disagreement. For example, suppose that a project manager said, "We've been arguing about five points, and so far we've reached agreement on the first three. There's no reason why we can't agree on the last two points, is there?" Facilitation of a disagreement does not resolve the conflict. Facilitation downplays the emotional context in which conflicts occur.

Force is also a method of conflict resolution. A project manager uses force when he or she tries to resolve a disagreement by exerting his or her own opinion at the expense of the other people involved. Often, forcing a solution onto the parties in conflict results in a win–lose outcome. Calling in the project sponsor to resolve a conflict is another form of force project managers sometimes use.

The least used and least effective mode of conflict resolution is withdrawal. A project director can simply withdraw from the conflict and leave the situation unresolved. When this method is used, the conflict does not go away and is likely to recur later. Personality conflicts might well be the most difficult conflicts to resolve. Personality conflicts can occur at any time, with anyone, and over anything. Furthermore, they can seem almost impossible to anticipate and plan for.

Let's look at how one company found a way to anticipate and avoid personality conflicts on one of its projects. Foster Defense Group (a pseudonym) was the government contract branch of a Fortune 500 company. The company understood the potentially detrimental effects of personality clashes on its project teams, but it did not like the idea of getting the whole team together to air its dirty laundry. The company found a better solution. The project manager put the names of the project team members on a list. Then he interviewed each of the team members one on one and asked each to identify the names on the list that he or she had had a personality conflict with in the past. The information remained confidential, and the project manager was able to avoid potential conflicts by separating clashing personalities.

If at all possible, the project manager should handle conflict resolution. When the project manager is unable to defuse the conflict, then and only then should the project sponsor be brought in to help solve the problem. Even then, the sponsor should not come in and force a resolution to the conflict. Instead, the sponsor should facilitate further discussion between the project managers and the team members in conflict.

10.3 STAFFING FOR EXCELLENCE

Project manager selection is always an executive-level decision. In excellent companies, however, executives go beyond simply selecting the project manager. They use the selection process to accomplish the following:

- Project managers are brought on board early in the life of the project to assist in outlining the project, setting its objectives, and even planning for marketing and sales. The project manager's role in customer relations becomes increasingly important.

- Executives assign project managers for the life of the project and project termination. Sponsorship can change over the life cycle of the project, but not the project manager.
- Project management is given its own career ladder.
- Project managers given a role in customer relations are also expected to help sell future project management services long before the current project is complete.
- Executives realize that project scope changes are inevitable. The project manager is viewed as a manager of change.

Companies excellent in project management are prepared for crises. Both the project manager and the line managers are encouraged to bring problems to the surface as quickly as possible so that there is time for contingency planning and problem solving. Replacing the project manager is no longer the first solution for problems on a project. Project managers are replaced only when they try to bury problems.

A defense contractor was behind schedule on a project, and the manufacturing team was asked to work extensive overtime to catch up. Two of the manufacturing people, both union employees, used the wrong lot of raw materials to produce a $65,000 piece of equipment needed for the project. The customer was unhappy because of the missed schedules and cost overruns that resulted from having to replace the useless equipment. An inquisition-like meeting was convened and attended by senior executives from both the customer and the contractor, the project manager, and the two manufacturing employees. When the customer's representative asked for an explanation of what had happened, the project manager stood up and said, "I take full responsibility for what happened. Expecting people to work extensive overtime leads to mistakes. I should have been more careful." The meeting was adjourned with no one being blamed. When word spread through the company about what the project manager did to protect the two union employees, everyone pitched in to get the project back on schedule, even working uncompensated overtime.

Human behavior is also a consideration in assigning staff to project teams. Team members should not be assigned to a project solely on the basis of technical knowledge. It has to be recognized that some people simply cannot work effectively in a team environment. For example, the director of research and development at a New England company had an employee, a 50-year-old engineer, who held two Master's degrees in engineering disciplines. He had worked for the previous 20 years on one-person projects. The director reluctantly assigned the engineer to a project team. After years of working alone, the engineer trusted no one's results but his own. He refused to work cooperatively with the other members of the team. He even went so far as redoing all the calculations passed on to him from other engineers on the team.

To solve the problem, the director assigned the engineer to another project on which he supervised two other engineers with less experience. Again, the older engineer tried to do all of the work by himself, even if it meant overtime for him and no work for the others.

Ultimately, the director had to admit that some people are not able to work cooperatively on team projects. The director went back to assigning the engineer to one-person projects on which the engineer's technical abilities would be useful.

Robert Hershock, former vice president at 3M, once observed:

> There are certain people whom you just don't want to put on teams. They are not team players, and they will be disruptive on teams. I think that we have to recognize that and make sure that those people are not part of a team or team members. If you need their expertise, you can bring them in as consultants to the team but you never, never put people like that on the team.
>
> I think the other thing is that I would never, ever eliminate the possibility of anybody being a team member no matter what the management level is. I think if they are properly trained, these people at any level can be participators in a team concept.

In 1996, Frank Jackson, formerly a senior manager at MCI, believed that it was possible to find a team where any individual can contribute:

> People should not be singled out as not being team players. Everyone has got the ability to be on a team and to contribute to a team based on the skills and the personal experiences that they have had. If you move into the team environment one other thing that is very important is that you not hinder communications. Communications is the key to the success of any team and any objective that a team tries to achieve.

One of the critical arguments still being waged in the project management community is whether an employee (even a project manager) should have the right to refuse an assignment. At Minnesota Power and Light, an open project manager position was posted, but nobody applied for the job. The company recognized that the employees probably did not understand what the position's responsibilities were. After more than 80 people were trained in the fundamentals of project management, there were numerous applications for the open position.

It's the kiss of death to assign someone to a project manager's job if that person is not dedicated to the project management process and the accountability it demands.

10.4 VIRTUAL PROJECT TEAMS

Historically, project management was a face-to-face environment where team meetings involved all players meeting together in one room. Today, because of the size and complexity of projects, it is impossible to find all team members located under one roof. Duarte and Snyder define seven types of virtual teams.[1] These are shown in Table 10–1.

Culture and technology can have a major impact on the performance of virtual teams. Duarte and Snyder have identified some of these relationships in Table 10–2.

---

1. D. L. Duarte and N. Tennant Snyder, *Mastering Virtual Teams*. San Francisco: Jossey-Bass, 2001, p. 10. Reproduced by permission of John Wiley & Sons.

TABLE 10–1. TYPES OF VIRTUAL TEAMS

Type of Team	Description
Network	Team membership is diffuse and fluid; members come and go as needed. Team lacks clear boundaries within the organization.
Parallel	Team has clear boundaries and distinct membership. Team works in the short term to develop recommendations for an improvement in a process or system.
Project or product development	Team has fluid membership, clear boundaries, and a defined customer base, technical requirement, and output. Longer-term team task is nonroutine, and the team has decision-making authority.
Work or production	Team has distinct membership and clear boundaries. Members perform regular and outgoing work, usually in one functional area.
Service	Team has distinct membership and supports ongoing customer network activity.
Management	Team has distinct membership and works on a regular basis to lead corporate activities.
Action	Team deals with immediate action, usually in an emergency situation. Membership may be fluid or distinct.

The importance of culture cannot be understated. Duarte and Snyder identify four important points to remember concerning the impact of culture on virtual teams. The four points are[2]:

1. There are national cultures, organizational cultures, functional cultures, and team cultures. They can be sources of competitive advantages for virtual teams that know how to use cultural differences to create synergy. Team leaders and members who understand and are sensitive to cultural differences can create more robust outcomes than can

TABLE 10–2. TECHNOLOGY AND CULTURE

Cultural Factor	Technological Considerations
Power distance	Members from high-power-distance cultures may participate more freely with technologies that are asynchronous and allow anonymous input. These cultures sometimes use technology to indicate status differences between team members.
Uncertainty avoidance	People from cultures with high uncertainty avoidance may be slower adopters of technology. They may also prefer technology that is able to produce more permanent records of discussions and decisions.
Individualism–collectivism	Members from highly collectivistic cultures may prefer face-to-face interactions.
Masculinity–femininity	People from cultures with more "feminine" orientations are more prone to use technology in a nurturing way, especially during team startups.
Context	People from high-context cultures may prefer more information-rich technologies, as well as those that offer opportunities for the feeling of social presence. They may resist using technologies with low social presence to communicate with people they have never met. People from low-context cultures may prefer more asynchronous communications.

Source: D. L Duarte and N. Tennant Snyder, *Mastering Virtual Teams.* San Francisco: Jossey-Bass, 2001, p. 60.

---

2. Duarte and Snyder, ibid., p. 70.

members of homogeneous teams with members who think and act alike. Cultural differences can create distinctive advantages for teams if they are understood and used in positive ways.

2. The most important aspect of understanding and working with cultural differences is to create a team culture in which problems can be surfaced and differences can be discussed in a productive, respectful manner.

3. It is essential to distinguish between problems that result from cultural differences and problems that are performance based.

4. Business practices and business ethics vary in different parts of the world. Virtual teams need to clearly articulate approaches to these that every member understands and abides by.

10.5 REWARDING PROJECT TEAMS

Today, most companies are using project teams. However, there still exist challenges in how to reward project teams for successful performance. The importance of how teams are rewarded is identified by Parker, McAdams, and Zielinski[3]:

> Some organizations are fond of saying, "We're all part of the team, but too often it is merely management-speak. This is especially common in conventional hierarchical organizations; they say the words but don't follow up with significant action. Their employees may read the articles and attend the conferences and come to believe that many companies have turned collaborative. Actually, though, few organizations today are genuinely team-based.
>
> Others who want to quibble point to how they reward or recognize teams with splashy bonuses or profit-sharing plans. But these do not by themselves represent a commitment to teams; they're more like a gift from a rich uncle. If top management believes that only money and a few recognition programs ("team of year" and that sort of thing) reinforce teamwork, they are wrong. These alone do not cause fundamental change in the way people and teams are managed.
>
> But in a few organizations, teaming is a key component of the corporate strategy, involvement with teams is second nature, and collaboration happens without great thought or fanfare. There are natural work groups (teams of people who do the same or similar work in the same location), permanent cross-functional teams, ad hoc project teams, process improvement teams, and real management teams. Involvement just happens.

Why is it so difficult to reward project teams? To answer this question, we must understand what a team is and is not[4]:

> Consider this statement: an organizational unit can act like a team, but a team is not necessarily an organizational unit, at least for describing reward plans. An organizational unit

---

3. G. Parker, J. McAdams, and D. Zielinski, *Rewarding Teams*. San Francisco: Jossey-Bass, 2000, p. 17. Reproduced by permission of John Wiley & Sons.
4. Parker et al., ibid., p. 17.

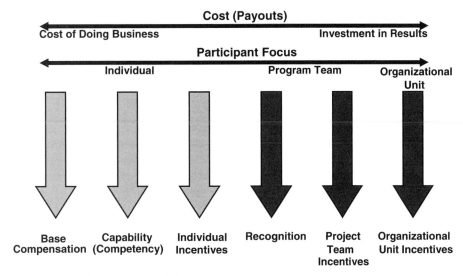

FIGURE 10–1. Reinforcement model.

is just that, a group of employees organized into an identifiable business unit that appears on the organizational chart. They may behave in a spirit of teamwork, but for the purposes of developing reward plans they are not a "team." The organizational unit may be a whole company, a strategic business unit, a division, a department, or a work group.

A "team" is a small group of people allied by a common project and sharing performance objectives. They generally have complementary skills or knowledge and an interdependence that requires that they work together to accomplish their project's objective. Team members hold themselves mutually accountable for their results. These teams are not found on an organization chart.

Incentives are difficult to apply because project teams may not appear on an organizational chart. Figure 10–1 shows the reinforcement model for employees.[5] For project teams, the emphasis is the three arrows on the right-hand side of Figure 10–1.

Project team incentives are important because team members expect appropriate rewards and recognition[6]:

Project teams are usually, but not always, formed by management to tackle specific projects or challenges with a defined time frame—reviewing processes for efficiency or cost-savings recommendations, launching a new software product, or implementing enterprise resource planning systems are just a few examples. In other cases, teams self-form around specific issues or as part of continuous improvement initiatives such as team-based suggestion systems.

---

5. Parker et al., ibid., p. 29.
6. Parker et al., ibid., pp. 38–39.

Project teams can have cross-functional membership or simply be a subset of an existing organizational unit. The person who sponsors the team—its "champion" typically creates an incentive plan with specific objective measures and an award schedule tied to achieving those measures. To qualify as an incentive, the plan must include pre-announced goals, with a "do this, get that" guarantee for teams. The incentive usually varies with the value added by the project.

Project team incentive plans usually have some combination of these basic measures:

- Project Milestones: Hit a milestone, on budget and on time, and all team members earn a defined amount. Although sound in theory, there are inherent problems in tying financial incentives to hitting milestones. Milestones often change for good reason (technological advances, market shifts, other developments) and you don't want the team and management to get into a negotiation on slipping dates to trigger the incentive. Unless milestones are set in stone and reaching them is simply a function of the team doing its normal, everyday job, it's generally best to use recognition-after-the-fact celebration of reaching milestones—rather than tying financial incentives to it.

  Rewards need not always be time-based, such that when the team hits a milestone by a certain date it earns a reward. If, for example, a product development team debugs a new piece of software on time, that's not necessarily a reason to reward it. But if it discovers and solves an unsuspected problem or writes better code before a delivery date, rewards are due.

- Project Completion: All team members earn a defined amount when they complete the project on budget and on time (or to the team champion's quality standards).

- Value Added: This award is a function of the value added by a project, and depends largely on the ability of the organization to create and track objective measures. Examples include reduced turnaround time on customer requests, improved cycle times for product development, cost savings due to new process efficiencies, or incremental profit or market share created by the product or service developed or implemented by the project team.

One warning about project incentive plans: they can be very effective in helping teams stay focused, accomplish goals, and feel like they are rewarded for their hard work, but they tend to be exclusionary. Not everyone can be on a project team. Some employees (team members) will have an opportunity to earn an incentive that others (non-team members) do not. There is a lack of internal equity. One way to address this is to reward core team members with incentives for reaching team goals, and to recognize peripheral players who supported the team, either by offering advice, resources, or a pair of hands, or by covering for project team members back at their regular job.

Some projects are of such strategic importance that you can live with these internal equity problems and non-team members' grousing about exclusionary incentives. Bottom line, though, is this tool should be used cautiously.

Some organizations focus only on cash awards. However, Parker et al. have concluded from their research that noncash awards can work equally well, if not better, than cash awards[7]:

---

7. Parker et al., ibid., pp. 190–191.

Many of our case organizations use non-cash awards because of their staying power. Everyone loves money, but cash payments can lose their motivational impact over time. However, non-cash awards carry trophy value that has great staying power because each time you look at that television set or plaque you are reminded of what you or your team did to earn it. Each of the plans encourages awards that are coveted by the recipients and, therefore, will be memorable.

If you ask employees what they want, they will invariably say cash. But providing it can be difficult if the budget is small or the targeted earnings in an incentive plan are modest. If you pay out more often than annually and take taxes out, the net amount may look pretty small, even cheap. Non-cash awards tend to be more dependent on their symbolic value than their financial value.

Non-cash awards come in all forms: a simple thank-you, a letter of congratulations, time off with pay, a trophy, company merchandise, a plaque, gift certificates, special services, a dinner for two, a free lunch, a credit to a card issued by the company for purchases at local stores, specific items or merchandise, merchandise from an extensive catalogue, travel for business or a vacation with the family, and stock options. Only the creativity and imagination of the plan creators limit the choices.

10.6 KEYS TO BEHAVIORAL EXCELLENCE

There are some distinguishing actions that project managers can take to ensure the successful completion of their projects. These include:

- Insisting on the right to select key project team
- Negotiating for key team members with proven track records in their fields
- Developing commitment and a sense of mission from the outset
- Seeking sufficient authority from the sponsor
- Coordinating and maintaining a good relationship with the client, parent, and team
- Seeking to enhance the public's image of the project
- Having key team members assist in decision-making and problem solving
- Developing realistic cost, schedule, and performance estimates and goals
- Maintaining backup strategies (contingency plans) in anticipation of potential problems
- Providing a team structure that is appropriate, yet flexible and flat
- Going beyond formal authority to maximize its influence over people and key decisions
- Employing a workable set of project planning and control tools
- Avoiding overreliance on one type of control tool
- Stressing the importance of meeting cost, schedule, and performance goals
- Giving priority to achieving the mission or function of the end item
- Keeping changes under control
- Seeking ways to assure job security for effective project team members

Earlier in this book, I claimed that a project cannot be successful unless it is recognized as a project and gains the support of top-level management. Top-level management must be willing to commit company resources and provide the necessary administrative support so that the project becomes part of the company's day-to-day routine of doing business. In addition, the parent organization must develop an atmosphere conducive to good working relationships among the project manager, parent organization, and client organization.

There are actions that top-level management should take to ensure that the organization as a whole supports individual projects and project teams as well as the overall project management system:

- Showing a willingness to coordinate efforts
- Demonstrating a willingness to maintain structural flexibility
- Showing a willingness to adapt to change
- Performing effective strategic planning
- Maintaining rapport
- Putting proper emphasis on past experience
- Providing external buffering
- Communicating promptly and accurately
- Exhibiting enthusiasm
- Recognizing that projects do, in fact, contribute to the capabilities of the whole company

Executive sponsors can take the following actions to make project success more likely:

- Selecting a project manager at an early point in the project who has a proven track record in behavioral skills and technical skills
- Developing clear and workable guidelines for the project manager
- Delegating sufficient authority to the project manager so that she or he can make decisions in conjunction with the project team members
- Demonstrating enthusiasm for and commitment to the project and the project team
- Developing and maintaining short and informal lines of communication
- Avoiding excessive pressure on the project manager to win contracts
- Avoiding arbitrarily slashing or ballooning the project team's cost estimate
- Avoiding "buy-ins"
- Developing close, not meddlesome, working relationships with the principal client contact and the project manager

The client organization can exert a great deal of influence on the behavioral aspects of a project by minimizing team meetings, rapidly responding to requests for information, and simply allowing the contractor to conduct business without interference. The positive actions of client organizations also include:

- Showing a willingness to coordinate efforts
- Maintaining rapport

- Establishing reasonable and specific goals and criteria for success
- Establishing procedures for making changes
- Communicating promptly and accurately
- Committing client resources as needed
- Minimizing red tape
- Providing sufficient authority to the client's representative, especially in decision-making

With these actions as the basic foundation, it should be possible to achieve behavioral success, which includes:

- Encouraging openness and honesty from the start from all participants
- Creating an atmosphere that encourages healthy competition but not cutthroat situations or liar's contests
- Planning for adequate funding to complete the entire project
- Developing a clear understanding of the relative importance of cost, schedule, and technical performance goals
- Developing short and informal lines of communication and a flat organizational structure
- Delegating sufficient authority to the principal client contact and allowing prompt approval or rejection of important project decisions
- Rejecting buy-ins
- Making prompt decisions regarding contract okays or go-aheads
- Developing close working relationships with project participants
- Avoiding arm's-length relationships
- Avoiding excessive reporting schemes
- Making prompt decisions on changes

Companies that are excellent in project management have gone beyond the standard actions as listed previously. These additional actions for excellence include the following:

- The outstanding project manager has these demonstrable qualities:
  - Understands and demonstrates competency as a project manager
  - Works creatively and innovatively in a nontraditional sense only when necessary; does not look for trouble
  - Demonstrates high levels of self-motivation from the start
  - Has a high level of integrity; goes above and beyond politics and gamesmanship
  - Is dedicated to the company and not just the project; is never self-serving
  - Demonstrates humility in leadership
  - Demonstrates strong behavioral integration skills both internally and externally
  - Thinks proactively rather than reactively
  - Is willing to assume a great deal of risk and will spend the appropriate time needed to prepare contingency plans
  - Knows when to handle complexity and when to cut through it; demonstrates tenaciousness and perseverance

- Is willing to help people realize their full potential; tries to bring out the best in people
- Communicates in a timely manner and with confidence rather than despair
- The project manager maintains high standards of performance for self and team, as shown by these approaches:
  - Stresses managerial, operational, and product integrity
  - Conforms to moral codes and acts ethically in dealing with people internally and externally
  - Never withholds information
  - Is quality conscious and cost conscious
  - Discourages politics and gamesmanship; stresses justice and equity
  - Strives for continuous improvement but in a cost-conscious manner
- The outstanding project manager organizes and executes the project in a sound and efficient manner:
  - Informs employees at the project kickoff meeting how they will be evaluated
  - Prefers a flat project organizational structure over a bureaucratic one
  - Develops a project process for handling crises and emergencies quickly and effectively
  - Keeps the project team informed in a timely manner
  - Does not require excessive reporting; creates an atmosphere of trust
  - Defines roles, responsibilities, and accountabilities up front
  - Establishes a change management process that involves the customer
- The outstanding project manager knows how to motivate:
  - Always uses two-way communication
  - Is empathetic with the team and a good listener
  - Involves team members in decision-making; always seeks ideas and solutions; never judges an employee's idea hastily
  - Never dictates
  - Gives credit where credit is due
  - Provides constructive criticism rather than making personal attacks
  - Publicly acknowledges credit when credit is due but delivers criticism privately
  - Makes sure that team members know that they will be held accountable and responsible for their assignments
  - Always maintains an open-door policy; is readily accessible, even for employees with personal problems
  - Takes action quickly on employee grievances; is sensitive to employees' feelings and opinions
  - Allows employees to meet the customers
  - Tries to determine each team member's capabilities and aspirations; always looks for a good match; is concerned about what happens to the employees when the project is over
  - Tries to act as a buffer between the team and administrative/operational problems
- The project manager is ultimately responsible for turning the team into a cohesive and productive group for an open and creative environment. If the project manager succeeds, the team will exhibit the following behaviors:
  - Demonstrates innovation
  - Exchanges information freely

- Is willing to accept risk and invest in new ideas
- Is provided with the necessary tools and processes to execute the project
- Dares to be different; is not satisfied with simply meeting the competition
- Understands the business and the economics of the project
- Tries to make sound business decisions rather than just sound project decisions

10.7 CONVERGENT COMPUTING

One of the biggest challenges facing companies today is making project management a career path. There are two major issues that need to be considered. First, project management must be regarded as a profession. Second, job descriptions must be prepared that differentiate between pay grades of project managers, and this is the difficult part in deciding what should go into each job description. Anne Walker, Enterprise Project Manager at Convergent Computing (CCO), describes her experiences at CCO:

> Project management is regarded as a profession and particularly in our business; IT project management is a specialization. We need to have project managers who understand IT even if only at a high level to be able to manage the teams and projects we are engaged in. This initially has been a difficult combination skill-set to find; however, that is changing. We have dedicated project managers on staff and continue to see their efforts pay off.
>
> I have noticed a change in the past five years with many of our clients. Initially, project management was something they did not want to pay for and expected the engineer or consultant to "manage" the project. While many of our engineers and consultants successfully managed projects and delivered what the client was looking for, the focus was always on the technology or solution being utilized rather than successful project hand-offs, communication, or deliverables such as status reports and documentation. As CCO began implementing more and more project methodology into our projects, clients began to see the benefits of a more structured approach and their expectations about how projects are handled changed. Clients now want to ensure there is a communication plan for a project that is thought out and covers communication to all levels of the organization (if necessary). They want to see design sessions where features and functions are discussed and decisions jointly made about what will stay and what goes. Clients expect a structured testing plan that incorporates prototyping to ensure the technology fits with the business need. I know of a handful of our clients that are actively enrolling their employees in project management courses and looking to the employees to lead projects where in the past they participated but did not lead.
>
> Project managers help facilitate and coordinate the implementation of an IT project and are expected to obtain and maintain project manager certification. Project managers are involved in all phases of the project from obtaining requirements to roll-out and training of end users, all the while maintaining the budget integrity, time constraints, and objectives of the project. Major responsibilities include:
>
> - Validation of the allotted hours and task assignments with each project engineer for a project
> - Providing timelines to CCO's resource manager for engineer assignment(s)
> - Tracking project schedule
>   - Monitoring the project progress by comparing actual versus scheduled timeline
>   - Overseeing adherence to the role and responsibilities section within the scope

- Tracking budget progress
  - Reviewing and monitoring project billable hours as recorded within Timesheet Professional
  - Comparing the billed hours to the scoped hours contained in the project schedule
- Tracking scope
  - Monitoring work progress with an emphasis on the following:
    - Execution of tasks that are within the scope guidelines
    - Managing "scope creep"
- Tracking customer satisfaction
- Insuring customer satisfaction utilizing major task sign-offs and customer surveys
- Monitoring ongoing customer satisfaction (throughout the project)
- Providing status updates and notification of major milestones and issues to account executives

10.8 EDS

Doug Bolzman, Consultant Architect, PMP®, ITIL Service Manager at EDS, discusses the approach at EDS for job descriptions:

> EDS project management roles are found in several job descriptions, along with the project management job family. To manage all of the required roles, each generic role is known as an agent. Table 10–3 provides a breakdown of how we define each agent (i.e.,

TABLE 10–3. JOB DESCRIPTIONS

Section	Description
Agent name and version	The formal name of the role and the version number for that role. As frameworks improve and new technology is implemented, each role may need to be modified, which will be reflected in the version number. This allows for the changes to human resources to be reflected in the project plan, in terms of new training, new skills, new tools, etc.
Agent rational	The business justification for the role, this is where the role is integrated into the overall business environment.
Description	A paragraph that describes the role, authority, and accountability of the role.
Overall responsibilities	High-level responsibilities for the role. For project managers, this includes financial management, scope and schedule management, and resource management.
Component-specific responsibilities	Roles can be broken into specific components of the business environment. This section lists those responsibilities in detail. This allows for several processes to contribute to the development of a single role. These are measurable and the person fulfilling the role is measured against his or her conformance to these responsibilities
Work products	All the deliverables and products that are developed from the roles. These deliverables are integrated and assigned from the overall deliverable list, ensuring that each role is integrated by work products.
Aliases	Since many frameworks or work patterns may identify independent roles or agents, this allows to map this role to other best practices roles.
Comparable job codes	For human resources to function efficiently, this role is mapped to established job codes, so that if more people need to be hired into a role, those job codes can be used as qualified resources. This also helps to integrate the overall human resource family.
Qualifications	List of qualifications—years of experience, training, travel availability—that will contribute to a person successfully implementing the responsibilities of the role.
Skills	Specific skills that are required to fulfill the role, such as language skills, technology skills, business skills.

release manager, network engineer, financial manager). This is used by multiple organizations to manage the overall resource needs, resource balancing, and resource recruiting. As every organization uses the same listing, managing resources becomes more efficient and accurate.

10.9 HARTFORD

Perhaps one of the biggest behavioral challenges facing a project manager, especially a new project manager, is learning how to be proactive rather than reactive. Kerry Wills, discusses this problem.

Proactive Management Capacity Propensity[8]

In today's world Project Managers often get tapped to manage several engagements at once. This usually results in them having just enough time to react to the problems of the day that each project is facing. What they are not doing is spending the time to look ahead on each project to plan for upcoming work, thus resulting in more fires that need to be put out. There used to be an arcade game called "whack-a-mole" where the participant had a mallet and would hit each mole with it when one would pop up. Each time a mole was hit, a new mole would pop up. The cycle of spending time putting out fires and ignoring problems that cause more fires can be thought of as "project whack-a-mole."

It is my experience that proactive management is one of the most effective tools that Project Managers can use to ensure the success of their projects. However, it is a difficult situation to manage several projects while still having enough time to look ahead. I call this ability to spend time looking ahead the "Proactive Management Capacity Propensity" (PMCP). This article will demonstrate the benefits of proactive management, define the PMCP, and propose ways of increasing the PMCP and thus the probability of success on the projects.

Proactive Management

Overview   Project Management involves a lot of planning up-front including work plans, budgets, resource allocations, and so on. The best statistics that I have seen on the accuracy of initial plans says there is a 30% positive or negative variance from the original plans at the end of a project. Therefore, once the plans have been made and the project has started, the Project Manager needs to constantly re-assess the project to understand the impact of the 60% unknowns that will occur.

The dictionary defines proactive as "acting in advance to deal with an expected difficulty." By "acting in advance" a Project Manager has some influence over the control of the unknowns. However, without acting in advance, the impacts of the unknowns will be greater as the Project Manager will be reacting to the problem once it has snowballed.

---

8. The remainder of this section was provided by Kerry R. Wills, PMP®, Director of Portfolio Management, Infrastructure Solutions Division, The Hartford. Reproduced by permission of Kerry R. Wills.

A Metaphor   When I drive into work in the morning, I have a plan and schedule. I leave my house, take certain roads and get to work in forty minutes. If I were to treat driving to work as a Project (having a specific goal with a finite beginning and end), then I have two options to manage my commute [Figure 10–2]:

By *proactively* managing my commute, I watch the news in the morning to see the weather and traffic. Although I had a plan, if there is construction on one of the roads that I normally take, then I can always change that plan and take a different route to ensure that my schedule gets met. If I know that there may be snow then I can leave earlier and give myself more time to get to work. As I am driving, I look ahead in the road to see what is coming up. There may be an accident or potholes that I will want to avoid and this gives me time to switch lanes.

A *reactive* approach to my commute could be assuming that my original plan will work fully. As I get on the highway, if there is construction then I have to sit in it because by the time I realize the impact, I have passed all of the exit ramps. This results in me missing my schedule goal. The same would happen if I walked outside and saw a foot of snow. I now have a chance to scope since I have the added activity of shoveling my driveway and car. Also, if I am a reactive driver, then I don't see the pothole until I have driven over it (which may lead to a budget variance since I now need new axles).

Benefits   The metaphor above demonstrates that reactive management is detrimental to projects because by the time that you realize that there is a problem it usually has a schedule, scope or cost impact. There are several other benefits to proactive management:

- Proactively managing a plan allows the Project Manager to see what activities are coming up and start preparing for them. This could be something as minor as setting up conference rooms for meetings. I have seen situations were tasks were not completed on time because of something as minor as logistics.
- Understanding upcoming activities also allows for the proper resources to be in place. Oftentimes, projects require people from outside of the project team and lin-

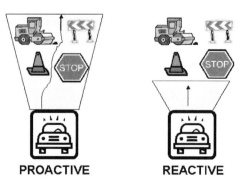

PROACTIVE   **REACTIVE**

FIGURE 10–2.   Driving metaphor.

ing them up are [*sic*] always a challenge. By preparing people in advance, there is a higher probability that they can be ready when needed.

The Relationship

- The Project Manager should constantly be replanning. By looking at all upcoming activities as well as the current ones, it can give a gage of the probability of success which can be managed rather than waiting until the day before something is due to realize that the schedule cannot be met.
- Proactive management also allows time to focus on quality. Reactive management usually is characterized by rushing to fix whatever "mole" has popped up as quickly as possible. This usually means a patch rather than the appropriate fix. By planning for the work appropriately, it can be addressed properly which reduces the probability of rework.
- As previously unidentified work arises, it can be planned for rather than assuming that "we can just take it on."

Proactive management is extremely influential over the probability of success of a project because it allows for replanning and the ability to address problems well before they have a significant impact.

Overview I have observed a relationship between the amount of work that a project manager has and their ability to manage proactively. As Project Managers get more work and more concurrent projects, their ability to manage proactively goes down.

The relationship between Project Manager workload and the ability to manage proactively is shown in Figure 10–3 below. As Project Managers have increased work, they have less capacity to be proactive to and wind up becoming more reactive.

Not all Projects and Project Managers are equal. Some Project Managers can handle several projects well and some projects require more focus than others. I have therefore labeled this factor, the Project Management Capacity Propensity (PMCP). That is, the sum of those qualities that allow a Project Manager to proactively manage projects.

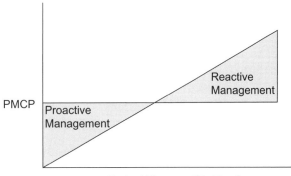

FIGURE 10–3.   Proactivity graph.

PMCP   There are several factors that make up the PMCP that I have outlined below.

Project Manager skill sets have an impact on the PMCP. Having good Time Management and organization techniques can influence how much a PM can focus on looking ahead. A Project Manager who is efficient with their time has the ability to review more upcoming activities and plan for them.

Project Manager expertise of the project is also influential to the PMCP. If the PM is an expert in the business or the project, this may allow for quicker decisions since they will not need to seek out information or clarification (all of which takes away time).

The PMCP is also impacted by team composition. If the Project Manager is on a large project and has several team leads who manage plans, then they have an increased ability to focus on replanning and upcoming work. Also, having team members who are experts in their field will require less focus from the Project Manager.

Increasing the PMCP   The good news about the PMCP is that it can be increased.

Project Managers can look for ways to increase their skillsets through training. There are several books and seminars on time management, prioritization, and organization. Attending these can build the effectiveness of the time spent by the PM on their activities.

The PM can also re-evaluate the team composition. By getting stronger team leads or different team members, the PM can offload some of their work and spend more time focusing on proactive management.

All of these items can increase the PMCP and result in an increased ability to manage proactively. The image below [Figure 10–4] shows how a PMCP increase raises the bar and allows for more proactive management with the same workload.

Conclusion   To proactively manage a project is to increase your probability of being successful. There is a direct correlation between the workload that a PM has and their ability to look ahead. Project Managers do have control over certain aspects that can give them a

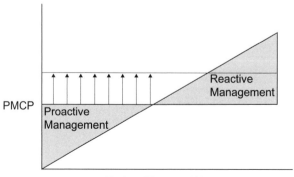

FIGURE 10–4.   Increasing PMCP.

greater ability to focus on proactive management. These items, the PMCP, can be increased through training and having the proper team.

Remember to keep your eyes on the road.

10.10 SYMCOR

Previously, we stated that there was significant complexity in writing job descriptions that differentiated between pay grades. Some companies have replaced job descriptions with competency models while others prefer the easy way out by using project charters. Diana Miret, PMP®, Director, Enterprise Project Management at Symcor, illustrates its solution with three classifications of project management job descriptions:

Diana Miret also provides us with index charts that accompany the job descriptions.

Domain-of-Change Index

Degree of Change	Business Process	Organization	Location	Data	Technology	Application
Minor impact (1)	Automate existing processes	Different procedures	Changed use of existing facilities	Same entities, new attributes	Same products, additional uses	Minor changes to existing applications
Moderate impact (2)	Revised activities in current processes	Different job content	New facilities	New entities	Same products; increased distribution, capacity, workload	Enhancements to existing applications
Major impact (3)	Revised process (process improvement)	Different jobs and organizational structure	Moving work	New data structures	New products	New application
Radical change (4)	New process (process redesign)	Different culture	Moving workers	New data types	New technology types	New application architecture
Score						

Impact	Store	Project Manager Level
Low	0–6	Project leader/project manager I
Moderate	7–14	Project manager II
High	15–24	Project manager III/project director

Additional Information Regarding Domains-of-Change Index

Degree of Change	Business Process
No impact (0)	Supports existing unchanged processes
Minor impact (1)	Automate existing processes: • The processes are not changing; the project will enable/automate the existing processes
Moderate impact (2)	Revised activities in current processes: • Current processes will have different activities to accomplish • Probably results in some modification of policies and procedures
Major impact (3)	Revised process (process improvement) • Change in sequence of processes/processes added or deleted • Results in revision of documentation of process policy • Usually cross functional
Radical change (4)	New process (process redesign) • Final result may be the same (e.g., order) but the journey to get there is totally new • May require process reengineering and creation of documentation of new process • Start with a clean slate

Degree of Change	Business Process
No impact (0)	No impact: • Users would notice no change • Transparent changes
Minor impact (1)	Different procedures: • New steps to follow (e.g., used to send purchase request to a buyer; now sends purchase order directly to warehouse) • Tool change for some processes • Use of existing skills
Moderate impact (2)	Different job content: • Employee has additional/reduced job responsibilities • Tool usage
Major impact (3)	Different jobs and organizational structure: • A new department/organization is necessary to support the business solution • New job descriptions are necessary • Impacts union employees • Elimination of existing support functions
Radical change (4)	Different culture: • The company has a new culture resulting from changes in support systems (e.g., change from supervised work group structure to self-directed; compensation changed from commission basis to customer satisfaction)

Degree of Change	Business Process
No impact (0)	No impact: • No change in existing facilities
Minor impact (1)	Changed use of existing facilities: • Conversion/redesign of existing facilities (e.g., changed receiving area into computer center)
Moderate impact (2)	New facilities: • Addition of new facilities (e.g., new lab, new secure area) • Additional support sites • Addition of a distributed database at a new site
Major impact (3)	Moving work: • Consolidation or decentralization of work (e.g., moving all purchasing to the corporate location, moving databases from central site to regional sites)
Radical change (4)	Moving workers: • Relocation of workers to support the processes

Degree of Change	Business Process
No impact (0)	No impact: • Database/data file requires no change • Data values/content unmodified
Minor impact (1)	Same entities, new attributes: • Adding new data elements to existing entities • Approximately 25% of data values/content of large, critical database modified
Moderate impact (2)	New entities: • Adding a new group of related data elements (e.g., vendor entity with vendor name, vendor address, vendor rating, vendor contact) • Major key change • Approximately 50% of data values/content of large, critical database modified
Major impact (3)	New data structures: • A new data store (e.g., new Oracle database created from an existing database; a totally new data structure such as Oracle, SQL Server) • Consider version/release upgrades • Approximately 75% of data values/content of large, critical database modified
Radical change (4)	New data types: • Use of newer forms of data capture for the system (e.g., video accessible from the PC showing the process of a form of assembly instead of written procedures) • All data values/content of large, critical database modified

Degree of Change	Business Process
No impact (0)	No impact: • Same product/same uses
Minor impact (1)	Same products, additional uses: • Use of other features within the same product (e.g., creating customized reports out of existing tool) • Deployment (e.g., expand the use of a system from initial distribution to scheduled updates/releases) • Project team comfortable with technology • New combination of existing products
Moderate impact (2)	Same products; increased distribution, capacity, workload: • Expanding the installation base of an application • Deployment—add capability for deployment • Improve performance • Consider version change
Major impact (3)	New products: • New product for the project team or application • Significant version change
Radical change (4)	New technology types: • Newer forms of technology transfers • Middleware • Internet (security issues) • Usually represent a change in culture • New technology type for the project team/system/site

Degree of Change	Business Process
No impact (0)	No impact: • No application necessary • Application is not touched
Minor impact (1) (1)	Minor changes to existing applications: • Modifications to existing screens/code • New/changed outputs which use existing data
Moderate impact (2)	Enhancements to existing applications: • New screens/codes which provide added functionality • Consider internal logical changes • New/changed outputs which use new data
Major impact (3)	New application: • Totally new application for the business solution • New functionality within the existing application structure • A subsystem • New COTS package
Radical change (4)	New application architecture: • Rehosting an application (e.g., movement from mainframe to distributed client server)

11

Measuring Return on Investment on Project Management Training Dollars

11.0 INTRODUCTION

For almost three decades, the 1960s through the 1980s, the growth and acceptance of project management were restricted to the aerospace, defense, and heavy construction industries. In virtually all other industries, project management was nice to have but not a necessity. There were very few project management training programs offered in the public marketplace, and those that were offered covered the basics of project management with weak attempts to customize the material to a specific company. The concept of measuring the return on investment (ROI) on training, at least in project management courses, was nonexistent. Within the past 10 years, there have been several studies on quantifying the benefits of project management with some pioneering work on the benefits of project management training.[1–4] There is still a great deal of effort needed, but at least we have recognized the need.

Today, our view of project management education has changed and so has our desire to evaluate ROI on project management training funds. There are several reasons for this:

- Executives realize that training is a basic necessity for companies to grow.
- Employees want training for professional growth and advancement opportunities.

1. W. Ibbs and J. Reginato, *Quantifying the Value of Project Management.* Newton Square, PA: Project Management Institute, 2002.
2. W. Ibbs and Y-H. Kwak, *The Benefits of Project Management.* Newton Square, PA: Project Management Institute, 1997.
3. W. Ibbs, "Measuring Project Management's Value: New Directions for Quantifying PM/ROI®, in *Proceedings of the PMI Research Conference,* June 21–24, 2000, Paris, France.
4. J. Knutson, A three-part series in *PM Network,* January, February, and July 1999.

- Project management is now viewed as a profession rather than a part-time occupation.
- The importance of becoming a PMP® has been increasing.
- There are numerous university programs available leading to MS, MBA, and Ph.D. degrees in project management.
- There are certificate programs in advanced project management concepts where students are provided with electives rather than rigid requirements.
- The pressure to maintain corporate profitability has increased, resulting in less money available for training. Yet more and more training funds are being requested by the workers who desire to become PMP®s and then must accumulate 60 professional development units (PDUs) every three years to remain certified.
- Management realizes that a significant portion of training budgets must be allocated to project management education but it should be allocated for those courses that provide the company with the greatest ROI. The concept of educational ROI is now upon us.

11.1 PROJECT MANAGEMENT BENEFITS

In the early years of project management, primarily in the aerospace and defense industries, studies were done to determine the benefits of project management. In a study by Middleton, the benefits discovered were[5]:

- Better control of projects
- Better customer relations
- Shorter product development time
- Lower program costs
- Improved quality and reliability
- Higher profit margins
- Better control over program security
- Improved coordination among company divisions doing work on the project
- Higher morale and better mission orientation for employees working on the project
- Accelerated development of managers due to breadth of project responsibilities

These benefits were identified by Middleton through surveys and were subjective in nature. No attempt was made to quantify the benefits. At that time, there existed virtually no project management training programs. On-the-job training was the preferred method of learning project management and most people learned from their own mistakes rather than from the mistakes of others.

---

5. C. J. Middleton, "How to Set Up a Project Organization," *Harvard Business Review,* March–April 1967, pp. 73–82.

Today the benefits identified by Middleton still apply and we have added other benefits to the list:

- Accomplishing more work in less time and with few resources
- More efficient and more effective performance
- Increase in business due to customer satisfaction
- A desire for a long term partnership relationship with customers
- Better control of scope changes

Executives wanted all of the benefits described above and they wanted the benefits yesterday. It is true that these benefits could be obtained just by using on-the-job training efforts, but that assumed that time was a luxury rather than a constraint. Furthermore, executives wanted workers to learn from the mistakes of others rather than their own mistakes. Also executives wanted everyone in project management to look for continuous improvement efforts rather than just an occasional best practice.

Not every project management training program focuses on all of these benefits. Some courses focus on one particular benefit while others might focus on a group of benefits. Deciding which benefits you desire is essential in selecting a training course. And if the benefits can be quantified after training is completed, then executives can maximize their ROI on project management training dollars by selecting the proper training organizations.

11.2 GROWTH OF ROI MODELING

In the past several years, the global expansion of ROI modeling has taken hold. The American Society for Training and Development (ASTD) has performed studies on ROI modeling.[6] Throughout the world, professional associations are conducting seminars, workshops, and conferences dedicated to ROI on training. The Japan Management Association (JMA) has published case studies on the ROI process utilized at Texas Instruments, Verizon Communications, Apple Computers, Motorola, Arthur Anderson, Cisco Systems, AT&T, and the U.S. Office of Personnel Management.[7]

A summary of the current status on ROI might be:

- The ROI methodology has been refined over a 25-year period.
- The ROI methodology has been adopted by hundreds of organizations in manufacturing, service, nonprofit, and government settings.
- Thousands of studies are developed each year using the ROI methodology.
- A hundred case studies are published on the ROI methodology.

---

6. J. J. Phillips, *Return on Investment in Training and Performance Improvement Programs,* 2nd ed., Burlington, MA: Butterworth-Heinemann, 2003, Chapter 1. Reprinted with permission from Elsevier. In the opinion of this author, this is by far one of the best, if not the best, text on this subject. The bibliography is current and the examples are real world.
7. Phillips, ibid., p. 9.

- Two thousand individuals have been certified to implement ROI methodologies in their organizations.
- Fourteen books have been published to support the process.
- A 400-member professional network has been formed to share information.[8]

According to the 2001 *Training's* annual report, more than $66 billion was spent on training in 2001. It is therefore little wonder that management treats training with a business mindset, thus justifying the use of ROI measurement. But despite all of the worldwide commitment and documented successes, there is still a very real fear in many companies preventing the use of ROI modeling. Typical arguments are: "It doesn't apply to us"; "We cannot evaluate the benefits quantitatively"; "We don't need it"; "The results are meaningless"; and "It costs too much." These fears create barriers to the implementation of ROI techniques, but most barriers are myths that can be overcome.

In most companies, Human Resources Development (HRD) maintains the lead role in overcoming these fears and performing the ROI studies. The cost of performing these studies on a continuous basis could be as much as 4–5 percent of the HRD budget. Some HRD organizations have trouble justifying this expense. And to make matters worse, the HRD personnel may have a poor understanding of project management.

The salvation in overcoming these fears and designing proper project management training programs could very well be the project management office (PMO). Since the PMO has become the guardian of all project management intellectual property as well as designing project management training courses, the PMO will most likely take the lead role in calculating ROI on project management–related training courses. Members of the PMO might be required to become certified in educational ROI measurement the same way that they are certified as a PMP® or Six Sigma Black Belt.

Another reason for using the PMO is because of the enterprise project management (EPM) methodology. EPM is the integration of various processes such as total quality management, concurrent engineering, continuous improvement, risk management, and scope change control into one project management methodology that is utilized on a company-wide basis. Each of these processes has measurable output that previously may not have been tracked or reported. This has placed additional pressure on the PMO and project management education to develop metrics and measurement for success.

11.3 THE ROI MODEL

Any model used must provide a systematic approach to calculating ROI. It should be prepared on a life-cycle basis or step-by-step approach similar to an EPM methodology. Just like with EPM, there is an essential criterion that must exist for any model to work effectively. A typical list of ROI criteria is:[9]

---

8. Phillips, ibid., p. 11.
9. Phillips, ibid., pp. 18–19.

1. The ROI process must be **simple,** void of complex formulas, lengthy equations, and complicated methodologies. Most ROI attempts have failed with this requirement. In an attempt to obtain statistical perfection and use too many theories, some ROI models have become too complex to understand and use. Consequently, they have not been implemented.

2. The ROI process must be **economical** and must be implemented easily. The process should become a routine part of training and development without requiring significant additional resources. Sampling for ROI calculations and early planning for ROI are often necessary to make progress without adding new staff.

3. The assumptions, methodology, and techniques must be **credible.** Logical, methodical steps are needed to earn the respect of practitioners, senior managers, and researchers. This requires a very practical approach for the process.

4. From a research perspective, the ROI process must be **theoretically sound** and based on generally accepted practices. Unfortunately, this requirement can lead to an extensive, complicated process. Ideally, the process must strike a balance between maintaining a practical and sensible approach and a sound and theoretical basis for the process. This is perhaps one of the greatest challenges to those who have developed models for the ROI process.

5. The ROI process must **account for other factors** that have influenced output variables. One of the most often overlooked issues, isolating the influences of the HRD program, is necessary to build credibility and accuracy within the process. The ROI process should pinpoint the contribution of the training program when compared to the other influences.

6. The ROI process must be appropriate with a **variety of HRD programs.** Some models apply to only a small number of programs such as sales or productivity training. Ideally, the process must be applicable to all types of training and other HRD programs such as career development, organization development, and major change initiatives.

7. The ROI process must have the **flexibility** to be applied on a preprogram basis as well as a post-program basis. In some situations, an estimate of the ROI is required before the actual program is developed. Ideally, the process should be able to adjust to a range of potential time frames.

8. The ROI process must be **applicable with all types of data,** including hard data, which are typically represented as output, quality, costs, and time; and soft data, which include job satisfaction, customer satisfaction, absenteeism, turnover, grievances, and complaints.

9. The ROI process must **include the costs of the program.** The ultimate level of evaluation is to compare the benefits with costs. Although the term ROI has been loosely used to express any benefit of training, an acceptable ROI formula must include costs. Omitting or underestimating costs will only destroy the credibility of the ROI values.

10. The actual calculation must use an **acceptable ROI formula.** This is often the benefits/cost ratio (BCR) or the ROI calculation, expressed as a percent. These formulas compare the actual expenditure for the program with the monetary benefits driven from the program. While other financial terms can be substituted, it is important to use a standard financial calculation in the ROI process.

11. Finally, the ROI process must have a successful **track record** in a variety of applications. In far too many situations, models are created but never successfully applied. An effective ROI process should withstand the wear and tear of implementation and should get the results expected.

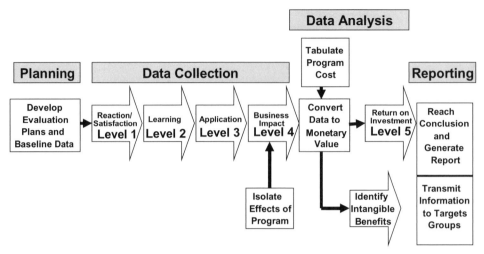

FIGURE 11–1. The ROI model. Adapted from J. J. Phillips, *Return on Investment in Training and Performance Improvement Programs,* 2nd ed. Burlington, MA: Butterworth-Heinemann, 2003 p. 37.

Because these criteria are considered essential, any ROI methodology should meet the vast majority of, if not all, criteria. The bad news is that most ROI processes do not meet these criteria. The good news is that the ROI process presented in Phillips' book meets all of these criteria. The model is shown in Figure 11–1. The definitions of the levels in Figure 11–1 are shown in Table 11–1.

11.4 PLANNING LIFE-CYCLE PHASE

The first life-cycle phase in the ROI model is the development of evaluation plans and baseline data. The evaluation plan is similar to some of the PMBOK® Guide knowledge

TABLE 11–1. DEFINING LEVELS

Level	Description
1: Reaction/satisfaction	Measures the participants' reaction to the program and possibly creates an action plan for implementation of the ideas
2: Learning	Measures specific skills, knowledge, or attitude changes
3: Application	Measures changes in work habit or on-the-job performance as well as application and implementation of knowledge learned
4: Business impact	Measures the impact on the business as a result of implementation of changes
5: Return on investment	Compares monetary benefits with the cost of the training and expressed as a percentage

areas that require a plan as part of the first process step in each knowledge area. The evaluation plan should identify:

- The objective(s) of the program
- The way(s) the objective(s) will be validated
- The target audience
- Assumptions and constraints
- The timing of the program

Objectives for the training program must be clearly defined before ROI modeling can be completed. Table 11–2 identifies typical objectives. The objectives must be clearly defined for each of the five levels of the model. Column 3 in Table 11–2 would be representative of the objectives that a company might have when it registers a participant in a Project Management Certificate Program (PMCP) training course. In this example, the company funding the participant's training might expect the participant to become a PMP® and then assist the organization in developing an EPM methodology based upon the PMBOK® Guide with the expectation that this would lead to customer satisfaction and more business. Column 4 in Table 11–2 might be representative of a company that registers a participant in a course on best practices in project management. Some companies believe that if a seminar participant walks away from a training program with two good ideas for each day of the program and these ideas can be implemented reasonably fast, then the seminar would be considered a success. In this example, the objectives are to identify best practices in project management that other companies are doing and can be effectively implemented in the participant's company.

There can be differences in training objectives, as seen through the eyes of management. As an example, looking at columns 3 and 4 in Table 11–2, objectives might be:

- Learn skills that can be applied immediately to the job. In this case, ROI can be measured quickly. This might be representative of the PMCP course in column 3.

TABLE 11–2. TYPICAL PROGRAM OBJECTIVES

		Objectives	
Level	Description	Typical PMCP Training	Typical Best Practices Training Course
1	Reaction/satisfaction	Understand principles of PMBOK® Guide	Understand that companies are documenting their best practices
2	Learning	Demonstrate skills or knowledge in domain groups and knowledge areas	Demonstrate how best practices benefit an organization
3	Application	Development of EPM processes based upon PMBOK® Guide	Develop a best practices library or ways to capture best practices
4	Business impact	Measurement of customer and user satisfaction with EPM	Determine the time and/or cost savings from a best practice
5	Return on investment	Amount of business or customer satisfaction generated from EPM	Measure ROI for each best practice implemented

- Learn about techniques and advancements. In this case, additional money must be spent to achieve these benefits. ROI measurement may not be meaningful until after the techniques have been implemented. This might be representative of the best practices course in column 4.
- A combination of the above.

11.5 DATA COLLECTION LIFE-CYCLE PHASE

In order to validate that each level's objectives for the training course were achieved, data must be collected and processed. Levels 1–4 in Figure 11–1 make up the data collection life-cycle phase.

To understand the data collection methods, we revisit the course on best practices in project management, which covers best practices implemented by various companies worldwide. The following assumptions will be made:

- Participants are attending the course to bring back to their company at least two ideas that can be implemented in their company within six months.
- Collecting PDUs is a secondary benefit.
- The course length is two days.[10]

Typical data collection approaches are shown in Table 11–3 and explained below for each level.

TABLE 11–3.   DATA COLLECTION

Level	Measures	Data Collection Methods and Instruments	Data Sources	Timing	Responsible Person
Reaction/ satisfaction	A 1–7 rating on end-of-course critique	Questionnaire	Participant (last day of program)	End of program	Instructor
Learning	Pretest, posttest, CD-ROM, and case studies	In-class tests and skill practice sets	Instructor	Each day of course	Instructor
Application	Classroom discussion	Follow-up session or questionnaire	Participant and/or PMO	Three months after program[a]	PMO
Business impact	Measurement of EPM continuous improvement efforts	Benefit/cost monitoring by the PMO	PMO records	Six months after program	PMO
Return on investment	Benefit/cost ratios	PMO studies	PMO records	Six months after program	PMO

[a] Usually for in-house program only. For public seminars, this may be done by the PMO within a week after completion of training.

---

10. Some companies have one-day, two-day, and even week-long courses on best practices in project management.

Level 1: Reaction and Satisfaction

Level 1 measures the participant's reaction to the program and possibly an action plan for implementation of the ideas. The measurement for level 1 is usually an end-of-course questionnaire where the participant rates the information presented, quality of instruction, instructional material, and other such topics on a scale of 1–7. All too often, the questionnaire is answered based upon the instructor's presentation skills rather than the quality of the information. While this method is most common and often serves as an indication of customer satisfaction hopefully leading to repeat business, it is not a guarantee that new skills or knowledge have been learned.

Level 2: Learning

This level measures specific skills, knowledge, or attitude changes learned during the course. Instructors use a variety of techniques for training, including:

- Lectures
- Lectures/discussions
- Exams
- Case studies (external firms)
- Case studies (internal projects)
- Simulation/role playing
- Combinations

For each training technique, a measurement method must be established. Some trainers provide a pretest at the beginning of the course and a posttest at the end. The difference in scores is usually representative of the amount of learning that has taken place. This is usually accomplished for in-house training programs rather than public seminars. Care must be taken in the use of pretests and posttests. Sometimes, a posttest is made relatively easy for the purpose of making it appear that learning has taken place. Out-of-class testing can also be accomplished using take-home case studies and CD-ROM multiple-choice questions.

Testing is necessary to validate that learning has taken place and knowledge has been absorbed. However, simply because learning has taken place is no guarantee that the information learned on best practices can or will be transferred to the company. The learning might simply confirm that the company is doing well and keeping up with the competitors.

Level 3: Application of Knowledge

This level measures changes in work habits or on-the-job performance as well as implementation of knowledge learned. Measurement at this level is normally done through follow-up sessions or follow-up questionnaires. However, for publicly offered courses with a large number of participants, it is impossible for the instructor to follow up with all participants. In such cases, the responsibility falls on the shoulders of the PMO. Participants may be required to prepare a short one- or two-page report on what they learned in the course and what best practices are applicable to the company. The report is submitted to the PMO that might have the final decision on the implementation of the ideas. Based on the magnitude of the best practices ideas, the portfolio management of projects may be impacted. However, there is no guarantee at this point that there will be a positive impact on the business.

Level 4: Business Impact   This level measures the impact on the business as a result of implementation of the changes. Typical measurement areas are shown in Figure 11–2.

The critical terms in Figure 11–2 are:

- Critical Success Factors (CSFs): This measures changes in the output of the project resulting from implementation of best practices. Hopefully, this will lead to improvements in time, cost, quality, and scope.
- Key Performance Indicator (KPI): This measures changes in the use of the EPM system and support received from functional management and senior management.
- Business Unit Impact: This is measured by customer satisfaction as a result of the implementation of best practices and/or future business opportunities.

The measurement at level 4 is usually accomplished by the PMO. There are several reasons for this. First, the information may be company sensitive and not available to the instructor. Second, since there may be a long time span between training and the

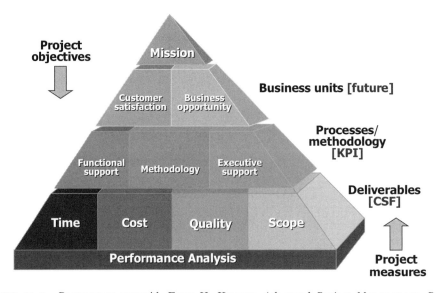

FIGURE 11–2. Postmortem pyramid. From H. Kerzner, *Advanced Project Management: Best Practices in Implementation,* 2nd Ed. New York: Wiley, p. 302.

implementation of best practices, the instructor may not be available for support. And third, the company may not want anyone outside of the company talking to its customers about customer satisfaction. Although the implementation of best practices may have a favorable business impact, care must be taken that the implementation was cost effective.

As shown in Figure 11–1, an important input into level 4 is *isolate the effects of training*. It is often impossible to clearly identify the business impact that results directly from the training program. The problem is that people learn project management from multiple sources, including:

- Formal education
- Knowledge transfer from colleagues
- On-the-job experience
- Internal research on continuous improvements
- Benchmarking

Because of the difficulty in isolating the specific knowledge, this step is often overlooked.

11.6 DATA ANALYSIS LIFE-CYCLE PHASE

In order to calculate the ROI, the business impact data from level 4 must be converted to a monetary value. The information can come from interviews with employees and managers, databases, subject matter experts, and historical data. Very rarely will all of the information needed come from one source.

Another input required for data analysis is the cost of the training program. Typical costs that should be considered include:

- Cost of course design and development
- Cost of materials
- Cost of the facilitator(s)
- Cost of facilities and meals during training
- Costs of travel, meals, and lodgings for each participant
- Fully-burdened salaries of participants
- Administrative or overhead cost related to the training course or approach of participants to attend training
- Possible cost (loss of income) of not having the participants available for other work during the time of training

Not all benefits can be converted to monetary values. This is the reason for the "identify intangible benefits" box in Figure 11–1. Some business impact benefits that are easily converted to monetary values include:

- Shorter product development time
- Faster, higher-quality decisions

- Lower costs
- Higher profit margins
- Fewer resources needed
- Reduction in paperwork
- Improved quality and reliability
- Lower turnover of personnel
- Quicker implementation of best practices

Typical benefits that are intangible and cannot readily be converted to monetary value include:

- Better visibility and focus on results
- Better coordination
- Higher morale
- Accelerated development of managers
- Better project control
- Better customer relations
- Better functional support
- Fewer conflicts requiring some management support

Despite the fact that these benefits may be intangible, every attempt should be made to assign monetary values of these benefits.

Level 5: Return on Investment

Two formulas are required for completion of level 5. The first formula is the BCR, which can be formulated as

$$BCR = \frac{\text{Program benefits}}{\text{program costs}}$$

The second formula is the ROI expressed as a percent. The formula is based upon "net" program benefits, which are the benefits minus the cost. Mathematically, we can describe it as

$$ROI\ (\%) = \frac{\text{net program benefits}}{\text{program costs}} \times 100$$

To illustrate the usefulness of this level, we consider three examples all based upon the same training course. You attend a two-day seminar on best practices in project management. Your company's cost for attending the course is:

- Registration fee $ 475
- Release time (16 hours at $100/hr)   1600
- Travel expenses   800
           $2875

When the seminar is completed, you come away with three best practices to recommend to your company. Your company likes all three ideas and assigns you as the project manager to implement all three best practices. Additional funds must be spent to achieve the benefits desired.

Example 1

During the seminar, you discover that many companies have adopted the concept of paperless project management by implementing a "traffic light" status-reporting system. Your company already has a Web-based EPM system but you have been preparing paper reports for status review meetings. Now, every status review meeting will be conducted without paper and with an LCD projector displaying the Web-based methodology with a traffic light display beside each work package in the work breakdown structure.

The cost of developing the traffic light system is:

Systems programming (240 hours at $100/hr)	$24,000
Project management (150 hours at $100/hr)	15,000
	$39,000

The benefits expressed by monetary terms are:

- Executive time in project review meeting (20 hours per project to 10 hours per project × 15 projects × 5 executives per meeting × $250/hr): $187,500
- Paperwork preparation time reduction (60 hours/project × 15 projects × $100/hr): $90,000
- Total additional benefit is therefore $275,500:

$$\text{BCR} = \frac{\$275,000 - \$39,000}{\$2875} = 82$$

$$\text{ROI} = \frac{\$275,000 - \$39,000 - \$2875}{\$2875} = 8109$$

This means that for every dollar invested in the training program, there was a return of $8109 in net benefits! In this example, it was assumed that workers were fully burdened at $100/hr and executives at $250/hr. The benefits were one-year measurements and the cost of developing the traffic light system was not amortized but expensed against the yearly benefits.

Not all training programs generate benefits of this magnitude. Lear in Dearborn, Michigan, has a project management traffic light reporting system as part of its Web-based EPM system. Lear has shown that in the same amount of time that it would review the status of one project using paper, it now reviewed the status of *all* projects using traffic light reporting.

Example 2

During the training program, you discover that other companies are using templates for project approval and initiation. The templates are provided to you during the training program and it takes a very quick effort to make the templates part of the EPM system and inform everyone about the update. The new templates will eliminate at least one meeting per week at a savings of $550:

$$\text{Benefit} = (\$500/\text{meeting}) \times (1 \text{ meeting/week}) \times 50 \text{ weeks} = \$27,500$$

$$\text{BCR} = \frac{\$27,500}{\$2875} = 9.56$$

$$\text{ROI (\%)} = \frac{\$27,500 - \$2875}{\$2875} = 8.56$$

In this example, for each $1 invested in the best practices program, a net benefit of $8.56 was recognized.

Example 3

During the training program, you learn that companies are extending their EPM systems to become more compatible with systems utilized by their customers. This should foster better customer satisfaction. The cost of updating your EPM system to account for diversified customer report generators will be about $100,000.

After the report generator is installed, one of your customers with whom you have four projects per year informs you they are so pleased with this change that they will now give you sole-source procurement contracts. This will result in a significant savings in procurement costs. Your company typically spends $30,000 preparing proposals:

$$\text{BCR} = \frac{(4 \text{ projects} \times \$30,000) - \$100,000}{\$2875} = 6.96$$

$$\text{ROI (\%)} = \frac{(4 \times \$30,000) - \$100,000 - \$2875}{\$2875} = 5.96$$

In this case, for every dollar invested in the best practices program there was a net benefit of $5.96 received.

Table 11–4 identifies typical ROI cases studies.[11] From Table 11–4, it should be obvious that the application of ROI on project management education could lead to fruitful results. To date, there have been very few attempts to measure ROI specifically on project management education. However, there have been some successes. In an insurance company, a $100 million project was undertaken. All employees were required to undergo project management training prior to working on the project. The project was completed 3 percent below budget.

Unsure whether the $3 million savings was due to better project management education or poor initial estimating, the company performed a study on all projects where the employees were trained on project management prior to working on project teams. The result was an astounding 700 percent return on training dollars.

---

11. Phillips, Patricia Pulliam. *The Bottom Line on ROI*. CEP Press, Atlanta, GA: p. 54, 2002. The Center for Effective Performance, Inc., 1100 Johnson Ferry Road, Suite 150, Atlanta, GA 30342, 800-558-4237, Reprinted with permission. (ISBN: 879618-25-7)

TABLE 11–4. ROI CASE STUDIES

Organization	Industry	Program	ROI (%)	Source
Office of Personnel Management	U.S. government	Supervisory training	150	1
Magnavox Electronic Systems Company	Electronics	Literacy training	741	1
Litton Guidance and Control Systems	Avionics	Self-directed work teams	650	1
Coca-Cola Bottling Company of San Antonio	Soft drinks	Supervisory training	1447	1
Commonwealth Edison	Electrical utility	Machine operator	57	2
Texas Instruments	Electronics	Sales training negotiation	2827	2
Apple Computer	Computer manufacturing	Process improvement	182	3
Hewlett-Packard Company	Computer support services	Sales training	195	3
First National Bank	Financial services	Sales training	555	3
Nassau County Police Department	Police department	Interpersonal skills training	144	3

Sources:
1. J. J. Phillips, Ed., *Measuring the Return on Investment,* Vol. 1. Alexandria, VA: American Society for Training and Development, 1994.
2. J. J. Phillips, Ed., *Measuring the Return on Investment,* Vol. 2. Alexandria, VA: American Society for Training and Development, 1998.
3. P. P. Phillips, Ed., *Measuring the Return on Investment,* Vol. 3. Alexandria, VA: American Society for Training and Development, 2001.

In another organization, the HRD people worked with project management to develop a computer-based project management training program. The initial results indicated a 900 percent ROI. The workers took the course on their own time rather than company time. Perhaps this is an indication of the benefits of e-learning programs. The e-learning programs may produce a much higher ROI than traditional courses because the cost of the course is significantly reduced with the elimination of the cost of release time.

11.7 REPORTING LIFE CYCLE PHASE

The final life-cycle phase in Figure 11–1 is reporting. The acceptance of the results could very well be based upon how the report is prepared. The report must be self-explanatory to all target groups. If assumptions are made concerning costs or benefits, then they must be justified. If the ROI numbers are inflated to make a training program look better than it was, then people may be skeptical and refuse to accept the results of future ROI studies. All results should be factual and supported by realistic data.

11.8 CONCLUSIONS

Because of the quantity and depth of available project management training programs, the concept of measuring ROI on training dollars can be expected to grow. Executives will recognize the benefits of this approach and its application to project management the same way it is applied to other training programs. Project management training organizations will be required to demonstrate expertise in ROI analysis. Eventually, PMI might even establish a special investigation group on ROI measurement.

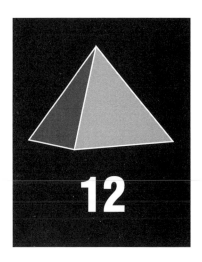

12 The Project Office

12.0 INTRODUCTION

As companies begin to recognize the favorable effect that project management has on profitability, emphasis is placed upon achieving professionalism in project management using the project office (PO) concept. The concept of a PO or project management office (PMO) could very well be the most important project management activity in this decade. With this recognition of importance comes strategic planning for both project management and the project office. Maturity and excellence in project management do *not* occur simply by using project management over a prolonged period of time. Rather, it comes through strategic planning for both project management and the PO.

General strategic planning involves the determination of where you wish to be in the future and then how you plan to get there. For PO strategic planning, it is often easier to decide which activities should be under the control of the PO than determining how or when to do it. For each activity placed under the auspices of the PO, there may appear pockets of resistance that initially view removing this activity from its functional area as a threat to its power and authority. Typical activities assigned to a PO include:

- Standardization in estimating
- Standardization in planning
- Standardization in scheduling
- Standardization in control
- Standardization in reporting
- Clarification of project management roles and responsibilities
- Preparation of job descriptions for project managers
- Preparation of archive data on lessons learned
- Benchmarking continuously

- Developing project management templates
- Developing a project management methodology
- Recommending and implementing changes and improvements to the existing methodology
- Identifying project standards
- Identifying best practices
- Performing strategic planning for project management
- Establishing a project management problem-solving hotline
- Coordinating and/or conducting project management training programs
- Transferring knowledge through coaching and mentorship
- Developing a corporate resource capacity/utilization plan
- Supporting portfolio management activities
- Assessing risks
- Planning for disaster recovery

In the first decade of the twenty-first century, the PO became commonplace in the corporate hierarchy. Although the majority of activities assigned to the PO had not changed, there was now a new mission for the PO:

- The PO now has the responsibility for maintaining all intellectual property related to project management and to actively support corporate strategic planning.

The PO was now servicing the corporation, especially the strategic planning activities for project management, rather than focusing on a specific customer. The PO was transformed into a corporate center for control of project management intellectual property. This was a necessity as the magnitude of project management information grew almost exponentially throughout the organization.

During the past 10 years, the benefits to executive levels of management of using a PO have become apparent. They include:

- Standardization of operations
- Company rather than silo decision making
- Better capacity planning (i.e., resource allocations)
- Quicker access to higher-quality information
- Elimination or reduction of company silos
- More efficient and effective operations
- Less need for restructuring
- Fewer meetings which rob executives of valuable time
- More realistic prioritization of work
- Development of future general managers

All of the above benefits are either directly or indirectly related to project management intellectual property. To maintain the project management intellectual property, the PO must maintain the vehicles for capturing the data and then disseminating the data to the various stakeholders. These vehicles include the company project management Intranet, project websites, project databases, and project management information systems. Since much of this information is necessary for both project management and corporate strategic planning, then there must exist strategic planning for the PO.

12.1 TYPES OF PROJECT OFFICES

There exist three types of POs commonly used in companies.

- *Functional PO:* This type of PO is utilized in one functional area or division of an organization such as information systems. The major responsibility of this type of PO is to manage a critical resource pool, that is, resource management. Many companies maintain an IT PMO, which may or may not have the responsibility for actually managing projects.
- *Customer Group PO:* This type of PO is for better customer management and customer communications. Common customers or projects are clustered together for better management and customer relations. Multiple customer group POs can exist at the same time and may end up functioning as a temporary organization. In effect, this acts like a company within a company and has the responsibility for managing projects.
- *Corporate (or Strategic) PO:* This type of PO services the entire company and focuses on corporate and strategic issues rather than functional issues. If this PMO does manage projects, it is usually projects involving cost reduction efforts.

12.2 UNIVERSAL UNDERWRITERS GROUP

Some organizations rush into the establishment of a PMO and then hope for the best. Others take a more methodical approach. Kathleen Jeffries, PMP®, Manager of Project Support Services (PSS) at Universal Underwriters Group (UUG) in Overland Park, Kansas, describes the evolutionary process in her company:

> Over the course of four long years, UUG has successfully implemented and evolved its PMO into a thriving catalyst for effective project management. The UUG PMO was recognized in 2003 as being in the top four in a seven-state region in two categories. The categories were "training and mentoring project managers through the PMO" and "PMO sponsorship." How we got to where we are today is the result of traveling down a winding and twisting road littered with overthought processes and a few ideas that just did not work as hoped [like the birth and demise of the enterprise project officer (EPO)]. One of the most valuable lessons we learned is how important it is to have a good outline of your process before you try to implement *anything.* Buy-ins and thorough communication are keys to the success of any new PMO. Following are a few trials and tribulations of the UUG PMO:
>
> 1998: Getting started
> - All project plans in common format
> - Project managers trained on project management software
> - Roll out tracking/scheduling software
> - Base processes set up

1999–2000: Process development
- Project review board set up
- Project support services established
- Reports developed
- EPO created

2001: Process improvement:
- Processes streamlined
- EPO moves back to IT
- PMO streamlined
- PSS develops training venues

2002: PMO acknowledgment and rejuvenation
- Project managers involved earlier in initiation phase
- PMO receives award for mentoring/training
- PSS executes lunch/learns, webinars, and PMP study group
- Reports updated to show approved figures/variances

2003: PMO outreach
- PMO marketing
- PSS open forum for project work
- Easier access to historical information
- Reports autogenerated and distributed

2004: PMO process improvement
- Project success factors clearly defined for all
- Communication plan best practices
- Document management, one-stop shopping for project artifacts
- Project plan development best practices

2005: PMO "practice what we preach"
- Project management process—batten down to hatches
- Change control and expectation management focus
- Accountability of other areas that support project management
- Measurement milestones for all key project resources

12.3 CERIDIAN[1]

While everyone seems to agree on the importance of project management, there is always the question of the importance of a PMO and whether it adds value to a company. Ben Stivers, PMP®, Director of the PMO at Ceridian, states his views on this:

The PMO, Tools of the Trade and Thriving in a Chaotic World

While the PMBOK® Guide is a good basis for building project manager competencies, a PMO it does not comprise or broach. Early on, however, it became apparent that our

---

1. Headquartered in Minneapolis, Ceridian (NYSE: CEN) is a multinational company providing the broadest range of solutions to manage all of your human resources and employee effectiveness needs. More than 100,000 clients and their 20 million employees worldwide rely on Ceridian to help them better manage their businesses and achieve work–life balance every day.

PMO was going to need to use additional advanced tools besides standard project management tools in order to build a world-class PMO that could meet the needs of the business. Questions were quickly going to arise (right around the time of the first budget cycle) such as:

- Doesn't project management take longer?
- Is this really the most efficient way to run projects?
- Is the PMO becoming more productive year-over-year? Is it causing the rest of the corporation to become more productive?
- How do we know we are working on the right projects?

Needless to say, there were many more questions that arose, but the purpose here is to discuss the short list of questions above and how we prepared *in advance* for the questions that would inevitably arise.

The PMO and Six Sigma

Processes that are not written down are not worth the paper on which they are not written. Our PMO has a fully documented process life cycle (to allow continuous process improvement), project life cycle, and portfolio management process suite. Once those processes were described, the PMO educated all of its project managers at the Six Sigma Green Belt level (and we have aspirations of Black Belt soon) and put them through our company's Six Sigma certification program.

The purpose was twofold—first, to ingrain the importance of process into every PMO member and, second, to instrument the PMO processes to ensure that we were constantly improving them. For instance, we know our staffing "tolerance" for a specified number of projects. After that, the matrixed members of the project teams become unfocused. Because of that, we look at several data points, and when the numbers start to climb too high, we begin to see other indicators, such as "number of change requests," of how we were getting "too far out over our skis." When this occurs, we know we need to bring some projects to closure and perhaps delay less important active projects. In short—go slower, so we can go faster. Such findings are backed by data from control charts, showing the number of "special management reviews" we must conduct. These reviews (by written policy) must be conducted any time a project slips more than 10 days on the critical path.

Our processes track a variety of trends, including:

- Percentage of projects funded
- Planning as a percentage of the life cycle
- Planning time versus reduction of cycle time in execution
- ROI and net present value (NPV)

Many of our projects prior to the PMO ran on for at least a year, some as long as two years. When we inventoried those projects while setting up the Portfolio Management Center of Excellence, we found that too many of the active projects had inadequate funding, or schedule, or deliverables, but people were working on them. All of that has been corrected.

Today, using portfolio management, we track vital statistics for all portfolios. Projects are ranked by an objective scoring system during the initiation phase and trended over time. Six Sigma is constantly and consistently employed to monitor our processes and enhance our productivity.

The PMO and Other "Best Practices"

But Six Sigma is not our only ally. We have adopted Goldratt's theory of constraints to help in scheduling, buffering contingency, and determining the best mix of projects.

We use earned value management to track project schedules, cost, status, and progress. We used the CMMI to model our base policies that laid the groundwork for creating executive buy-in and the written procedural guidebooks and education program we put in place for our project managers.

The PMO and Education

Getting the message of project management, process management, and portfolio management out to the masses is not good enough to build a sustainable PMO. In order to get such culturalization established in the corporate DNA, the PMO undertook an aggressive in-house education program called "The PMO boot camp." In two years, the PMO grew from having 13 percent of its project managers PMP certified to 87 percent certified. This, however, would not be good enough to establish the dramatic change we needed to make in the corporate thought processes. In this, the PMO was very lucky in the strength of its executive sponsor, Senior Vice President of Information Technologies Sid Hebert.

Sid made it mandatory for his resource managers to also attend the PMO boot camp in the first and second years of the PMO rollout. The boot camp is full of interactive games and gave the resource managers a first-hand view of how projects could and should be run plus how they could contribute to the project success. This indoctrination was particularly important as the PMO rolled out organizational resource management that was built into the Web-based project management tools. Additionally, it gave the PMO an opportunity to understand the challenges the resource managers faced and to assist them by shifting scheduling to accommodate faster throughput.

This blending of cross-functional education then began to filter out into the enterprise, and in our second year, the PMO began teaching project managers from other business units through the project management boot camp and ultimately became a part of the corporate university, with project and program managers teaching other project and program managers the best practices in our guidebook.

The PMO and Process

The PMO, despite the broad spectrum of technologies it has brought to enhancing our service to the business, could not have done so without a firm foundation in process engineering. We are process zealots but see our processes as ever-improving artifacts of our work rather than project management dogma. We have installed a Web-based feedback system for any artifact or process in the PMO process suite that allows anyone to send in a suggestion for improvements, suggest new items, or correct process errors. In the second year of the PMO, we processed 192 of those process improvements, many of them based on Six Sigma metrics and nearly as many based on the lessons learned by working with new units of the business and the project managers who work both inside and outside the PMO. As the business changes, the PMO adapts in agile fashion while maintaining discipline and order. It is this combination of mindset that sets us apart from the many other PMOs that we have seen.

Previously, we discussed the benefits of the PMO, especially the fact that many executives now realize that the PMO allows them to perform their job better. Sidney Hebert,

Senior Vice President for Information technology at Ceridian Corporation, discusses his beliefs about the value of a PMO:

> As the senior vice president of information technology at Ceridian, I could not adequately manage the investments and the workload without the PMO. The PMO helps me to rationalize decisions about strategy, capacity (facilities, capital, human resource, technology, information), and investments. In order to have a PMO that can provide this type of advantage, the PMO must take on the role of service provider rather than a purveyor of tools.
>
> I have seen PMOs that function as the recommender of tools—that is, some templates, some facilitation—a bit of begging and pleading to the executive sponsor to do the right things. Robust PMOs cannot deliver significant value to the organization without taking ownership of the business outcomes and providing a key leadership role in managing all resources and methods necessary to deliver the desired business outcome. Instead of giving the internals a toolbox of processes, templates, and facilitation, the PMO should do what it does best: provide professional program and project management services to the organization on behalf of the shareholders. This can only be done by effectively ingraining core values, disciplined and structured processes, toolset enablement, and dedication to the education and professional development of project managers.
>
> The PMO must be responsible for the development of the processes it uses, continuous process improvement (we use Six Sigma as a framework), and must be given the authority to execute. As partners with the resource managers and corporate executives, the PMO should be the one-stop-shopping service center for programs and projects as the owners of those projects and the results that are produced.
>
> This is often not easy for the executive who chooses to champion the PMO in its infancy. A service-oriented PMO that encompasses process management, project management, program management, and portfolio management will force a company to reexamine many of the paradigms under which it currently operates. Distribution of power will be an issue as the project managers assume more responsibility for the outcomes of their programs. This assumption will change the basic strategies of companies, ranging from risk management to fiscal management of their projects. In most cases that shift of authority will not be popular—but it will provide significant return to the company and the shareholders.
>
> These simple concepts are the premise upon which Ceridian sponsored the PMO and one to which the individuals within strive to achieve. In the twenty-first century, those companies who are the most agile will be so because of the quality produced by their process infrastructures, the ability to anticipate, and their ability to bring innovations to market in the shortest possible time. We intend to be first to the finish line and the PMO will provide the services to ensure that we are.

12.4 STONEBRIDGE GROUP

Project offices can reside anywhere in an organization. However, it is vitally important to recognize that the existence of the PO is to service the entire organization, and therefore whatever type of PO is developed, it must be networked with the business areas and share information. Brad Ruzicka, Senior Consulting Manager at the StoneBridge Group, comments on information systems (IS) POs:

> We have been contracted to establish such an entity (i.e., PMO) for our clients. In general, we recommend the project office have strategic responsibilities for project definition in partnership with business management. The project office can reside on either the IS or business side but should be jointly sponsored by IS and business management. The project office would generally have a core staff of project managers responsible for managing larger, complex, strategic projects as well as providing mentoring services to both IS and business areas.

Lessons-learned reviews have become commonplace. Brad Ruzicka believes:

> StoneBridge Group recommends a postproject assessment be performed on every project. Generally, our approach is to produce a postproject report. Depending on the nature of the project and the preference of the client, we may review the report with the entire team, key team members, the sponsor, and/or senior management. The key in any postproject review is to keep the focus on the project and not personalities. Lessons learned are generally in the categories of sponsorship, management, scope and requirements definition, change control, and resources.

12.5 MOTOROLA

Not all companies assign to their PMO all of the activities identified previously. The needs of the company may not require all of these activities. At Motorola, Charles Rankin, PMO Manager, describes the responsibilities of the PMO:

> At Motorola, the PMO is a standard term to mean program management organization. It refers to our entire staff.
>   Functions include:
>
> - Project scheduling, tracking, and reporting—responsible for on-time delivery
> - Cross-functional coordination
> - Field test planning
> - Prototype build planning
> - Customer communications
> - Status reporting at all levels
> - Product requirements change control board chair
> - Leads core development team, calls team meetings, sets agenda
> - Cross-functional risk and issue identification, mitigation, and management

The success of the PMO is often based upon where it reports in the organizational hierarchy. Generally speaking, the higher up the PMO reports, the more effective it becomes.

At Motorola, according to Charles Rankin, the director of program management reports to the Division GM. Also, according to Rankin, the PMO does have some Six Sigma responsibility for project management to the point of leading process improvement projects.

12.6 DTE ENERGY

Although functional POs can be developed anywhere in an organization, they are most common in an information systems environment. DTE Energy maintains an information systems PMO. According to Tim Menke, PMP®, Senior Project Manager, Software Engineering, Methods, and Staffing:

> At DTE Energy the customer service PMO functions with the customer service program management (CSPM) group reporting to the vice president of customer service. The CSPM group consists of the PMO, the process management team, and the customer contact channel management team.
>
> The PMO provides project management support for the continuous improvement initiatives within the department. These initiatives are designed to achieve the customer service strategy.
>
> Specific functions of the PMO include:
>
> - Developing and maintaining the project management methodology
> - Maintaining the portfolio of customer service continuous improvement projects
> - Collecting and disseminating project data and metrics
> - Providing project management tools and templates
>
> The customer service portfolio contains projects from the six departments within customer service (consumer affairs, customer care, credit and collections, billing, data acquisition, and CSPM). The projects improve customer service, increase operational efficiency, and/or achieve savings from operations.
>
> The PMO enables and facilitates the application of the project management process. The employees in the PMO have extensive background in project management and act as consultants, liaisons, and coaches for their respective projects.

As stated previously, the PMO can also participate in the portfolio management of projects. This is common in companies that wish to make maximum use of the talent in their PMO. Tim Menke explains:

> We select projects at the enterprise level based on various indicators including return on investment (ROI), internal rate of return (IRR), and net present value (NPV). This annual process involves the highest levels of organizational leadership and is integral to the prioritization and budgeting process.

Our PMO engages with the project manager on "approved" projects. Our PMO aggregates projects into portfolios aligned by business unit. This approach allows us to analyze "trade-offs" between projects within a business unit in an effort to elevate performance of the portfolio.

As successes from this approach mount, our interest in performing portfolio management across business units increases. Our future focus includes a greater emphasis on resource allocation in accordance with enterprise strategies as opposed to business unit strategies.

12.7 HALIFAX COMMUNITY HEALTH SYSTEMS

In the previous section, we saw that the PMO at DTE Energy participated in the portfolio management of projects. The same is true for Halifax Community Health Systems. Nancy Jeffreys, Portfolio and Program Manager at Halifax Community Health Systems, discusses their role in portfolio management:

The enterprise project management office (EPMO) at Halifax Community Health Systems prepares the portfolio of projects and presents them to management for their approval. In January, the EPMO manager sends a memo to the department managers asking for their input for their projects for the next fiscal year (starting in October). The managers have until mid-March to submit their proposals.

When all of the requests are completed, the senior project managers and manager of EPMO review the requests with the executives. These are one-on-one meetings with all of the requests that fall under that executive's area of responsibility. The executive determines if a request is worthy to pursue. If so, a project manager is assigned to the project. The project manager meets with the requestor to complete an executive summary. The executive summary is presented to the executive responsible for the area, who prioritizes the projects.

After all of the executives have prioritized their requests, the EPMO team meets to review each request and to rate the request. We have a scoring system that rates each project according to:

1. Workflow impact
2. Strategic focus area alignment
3. Regulatory or absolute need
4. Perceived risk and rate of return.

The manager of the EPMO meets with the Technology Advisory Council (TAC) committee to review the scores. They confirm or change any of the scores. After this meeting, the requests are returned to the project manager for any revisions. They meet with the requestor to make the revision.

The EPMO then prepares a Gantt chart with all of the requests and an expected timeline for the requests. This Gantt chart is taken back to the TAC for final approval. This becomes the portfolio for the next fiscal year. This process is completed before the budgeting process begins for the next fiscal year. These projects are then planned for in the budget.

12.8 KEYBANK

KeyBank also uses project management for support during portfolio management activities. Vicky Bartholomew, IT Communication Specialist, Enterprise Project Management at KeyBank, discusses some of the portfolio management activities at KeyBank:

- Technology cost is capped for the corporation; each line of business (LOB) has allocation.
- LOBs have financial allocations within which their projects must fit; large projects and all projects seeking "top-of-house" funding are reviewed and prioritized by cross LOB governance committee.
- Portfolio metrics are analyzed by project health and type of investment.
- Portfolio health is analyzed by investment and number of projects.
- Portfolio data are used to forecast resource supply and demand.
- Portfolio managers work with lines of business to plan technology project investments appropriate to their portfolio goals and allocations. Portfolio analysts (members of the PMO) assist them in understanding risks and constraints (e.g., resources) while planning and reserving resources.
- Quarterly cross-organizational pipeline review of upcoming projects to identify resource needs and constraints.

12.9 SATYAM[2]

Satyam Computer Services Limited (SCSL) is one of the largest Indian IT service providers. Satyam started Enterprise Business Solutions (EBS) in the mid-1990s ahead of its peer-group companies. EBS grew at 60 percent CAGR over the last six years, expanding its reach to 45 countries. Satyam has established itself in the leadership position in EBS among Indian IT service providers, as rated by leading analysts like Gartner.

Being a leader in EBS, Satyam has constantly innovated to stay ahead of the pack. That was never simple. The challenge of EBS's growth was compounded by the complexity of managing:

- Blend of functional and technical skills and vertical industry knowledge
- Increasing geographical spread and ability to understand local requirements
- More fixed-price projects, compared to other IT services
- Growing demand for business value by customers

An integrating force was needed to oversee project delivery, standardize processes across solutions, products, and regions and induce consultants to adopt best practices in

---

2. Satyam material has been graciously provided by Dr. Subhash C. Rastogi, formerly Head, Project Management Center of Excellence, Satyam Learning Center; Anu Khendry, Principal Consultant, Corporate Quality; and Rajkumar Periaswamy, Principal Applications, Satyam Computer Services Ltd., Hyderabad, India.

managing delivery. Satyam adopted the PMO, a nascent concept in the Indian IT services industry, as a change enabler to derive these benefits.

The objectives of the PMO for the business unit are:

- To build a structured project management approach by consolidating, formalizing, standardizing, and maturing project management practices, processes, and tools
- To enhance client visibility on globally delivered engagements
- To build a strong review-and-recognize culture, which not only helps in early identification of risks and issues but also recognizes practice and contribution to best practices
- To guide project managers in managing projects and extend shared services support to project teams in the area of project analytics

Universally, the sponsors for the PMO look at short-term return cycles due to quarterly pressures from Wall Street! While that is a tempting trap, integrated development working at various levels of the pyramid over a period of time is required to deliver sustainable improvements.

The core challenge since the inception of PMO is to balance the focus between short- and long-term results. The PMO adopted an evolutionary development model to make the changes more persistent. A three-phase approach was followed to lay a strong foundation in the early phases that would support the subsequent broad-based and rapid improvements.

We provide here the journey traversed and the practices adopted in getting the PMO operational and delivering value to the global service delivery model (RightSourcing model).

Stages of PMO Evolution   The evolution of the PMO, spread across three stages (as shown in Figure 12–1), helped ensure its success and measure the performance at regular intervals. The first stage was called formative. In this stage, the group was formed; the vision, mission, goals, and plans were developed. The time frame and success criteria for subsequent stages were defined during this stage. Facilitation of project delivery methodology enhancements was one of the key initiatives carried out during this stage

The second stage was the normative stage. The objective was on expanding the reach to all project teams with focus on incremental improvements. The normative stage was important to ease the shift in culture needed. Project data analytics and the management dashboard are good examples of initiatives introduced at this stage.

The last stage of evolution was termed the definitive stage. In this stage, the objective was on shifting to breakthrough actions with focus on performance, data, productivity, culture, and innovation. To make the PMO effective and deliver results, the balance between define, control, and support activities was maintained.

Successful Implementation   Various initiatives were started as part of the successful evolution of the PMO. A clearly defined process runs through from identifying, delivering, and maturing these initiatives. Various parameters were identified to measure the

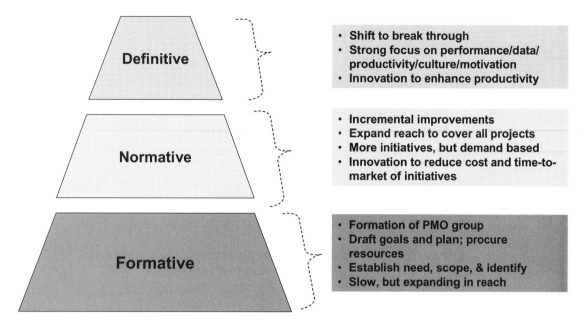

FIGURE 12–1. PMO evolution stages.

maturity of these initiatives at each of the maturity stages. Table 12–1 shows the various maturity stages an initiative passes through.

The maturity of various initiatives is shown in Figure 12–2. The growth of the consulting practice drives these initiatives. Different initiatives can be broadly categorized as:

- Enhancing customer perception
- Enabling leadership team
- Enabling project managers
- Enabling paradigm shift

A snapshot of the most critical initiatives under each category is given in Figure 12–3.

Enhancing Customer Perception Various initiatives have been taken to enhance customer perception. One of them is Nautilus portal (Figure 12–3a). It provides visibility on

TABLE 12–1. MATURITY STAGES OF INITIATIVES

Optimize	Optimize for better ROI
Stabilize	Extend, reach, and stabilize groupwide
Evolve	Launch (pilot) and improve design
Design	Design of initiative and deliverables
Define	Definition of scope, resource, and strategy
Identify	Identification and portfolio analysis of initiative

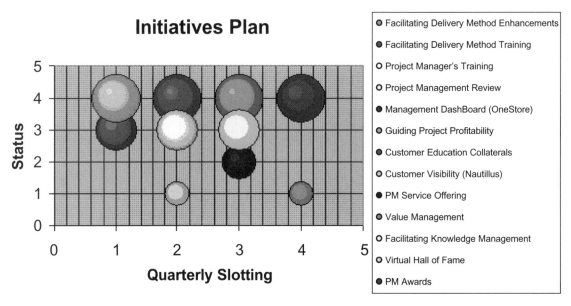

FIGURE 12–2.   Maturity of initiatives.

global engagements to the senior management of customers. It also provides collaborative work space for both teams (customer and Satyam) so that they have common understanding about project issues and status of deliverables.

Enabling Leadership Team   Satyam leadership is enabled with the right kind of information at the right time in the right format. A management dashboard (Figure 12–3b)—One Store—has been developed to fulfill the information needs of the leadership team. This dashboard enhances their decision-making with the help of performance data. Problems are identified at early stages enabling them to take proactive steps to resolve them. It also helps in comparing the performance against the group baselines as well as between projects.

Enabling Project Managers   To help project managers improve project performance, the PMO kicked off several initiatives. Traditionally, in the IT industry, the project managers grew through the technical or consulting function. Project management needs a different kind of learning mechanism, achieved through real-life project cases. Enhancement of project delivery methodologies was one of the initiatives in this category. The collective project management experience was mined to improve on the existing methodologies. Shared services support functions like project analytics were also introduced as part of this category.

Enabling Paradigm Shift   Over the last decade, Satyam's global engagements grew in size and number by several times. The PMO focused on increasing the collaboration between global delivery teams. Therefore, to develop better customer relationship, a com-

FIGURE 12–3(a). Satyam's Nautilus portal.

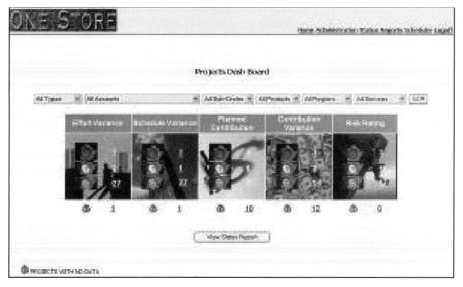

FIGURE 12–3(b). Management dashboard.

prehensive training program (IMPACT) was developed on overcoming cross-culture differences. This program focused on integrity, mannerism, personality, attitude, culture, communication, and tact. Enterprise consulting is about leveraging effectively the combined experience of the entire team. Weblogs are being used to connect global teams and enable tacit knowledge sharing.

Going Forward   The PMO for the business unit has evolved steadily since its inception. Going forward, the PMO would focus on the sustenance and optimization of initiatives. As the globe shrinks and the global IT services delivery model expands, project management practices would continue to evolve. No stationary framework would be suited to handle this evolution. If you are looking at a PMO for your organization, we recommend an evolutionary framework with multiyear focus tailored to suit your organization's cultural context.

12.10 EXEL

For multinational companies, there can exist several POs that must function in a coordinated effort. According to Francena D. Gargaro, PMP®, Director Project and Resource Management, Americas for Exel:

> Exel's enterprise project management (EPM) group serves the global organization as a project management center of excellence supporting project managers from all regions and sectors.
>
> The mission of the EPM is to provide thought leadership and training of Exel's project management tools, techniques, and methodology. It is also responsible for the development of a strategic business plan that will leverage strengths of both project and resource management disciplines. The EPM group provides a single-source solution for Exel's internal customers (sector PMOs and project managers). The Exel EPM is responsible for the following:
>
> - Center of excellence, supporting project management tools and techniques
> - Creation and deployment of an enterprise-wide project management methodology
> - Project management training for all sectors
> - Consulting and mentoring of project managers in the Americas
> - Facilitation and support for the establishment of PMOs in Latin America, Asia, Europe/U.K., and Canada
> - Visibility to Exel's project portfolio and resource capacity across the organization
> - Executive-level strategic reporting for EPM initiatives
>
> Additionally, there are regional PMOs, established in North America, South America, Mexico, U.K./Europe, and Asia Pacific—Exel's primary theaters. Each of these regional PMOs provides dedicated project management in their respective regions and have dotted-line reporting to the EPM, based in the United States.
>
> The EPM group serves a number of roles. Primarily responsibility involves managing the foundation for project management in the organization.
>
> The roles of the EPM group can be categorized into three major elements—visibility, collaboration, and globalization:
>
> - Access to the global project pipeline via internal opportunity/leads database
> - Assists account teams in the establishment and support of projects
> - Executive-level reporting and resource capacity planning via enterprise software

- Collaboration
- Project management strategy and customer relationship management
- Project management support of sectors/departments
- Project management support of internal/functional projects
- Internal/external marketing and communications about project management practices at Exel
- Development, maintenance, and delivery of project management training and certification assistance
- Development, maintenance, and deployment of project management tools
- Career path development
- Benchmarks and metrics
- Globalization
- Establishment and support of regional PMOs
- Global training curriculum
- Globally consistent tools (multilingual)

Regional PMOs (as shown in Figure 12–4) are groupings of project management associates (project managers, team members, etc.) who perform project management duties within specific regional or industry-specific areas.

Primary PMO responsibilities are:

- Promotion of Exel's project management methodology
- Promote use of project management tools
- Project execution and delivery
- Subject matter expertise

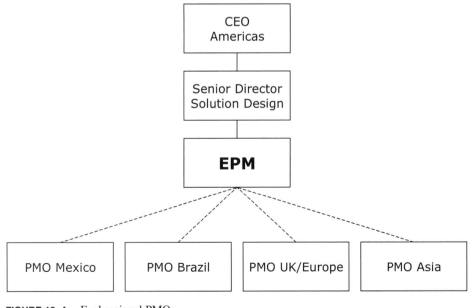

FIGURE 12–4. Exel regional PMOs.

Global PjM Organization Structure
Responsibilities

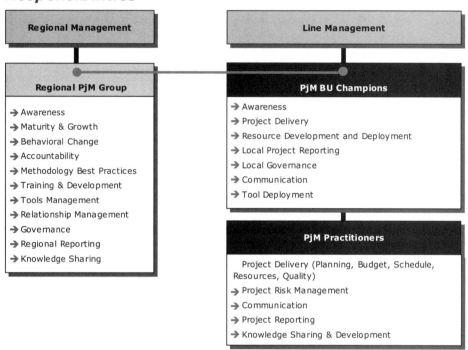

FIGURE 12–5. Global project management organization structure: matrix model.

The EPM group, on occasion, will manage or assist with the project management of internal/functional projects. For example, in the past five years, the EPM group has managed a Canadian payroll improvement project, a corporate office move project, and an EPM application implementation. In these cases, a member of the EPM group will perform the duties of project manager, managing the day-to-day project activities of functional project teams.

Today, a globally consistent project management organization has been created to ensure continuity, collaboration, and global visibility to all project management activity. (See Figures 12–5 and 12–6.[3]) This revitalized organizational structure follows a matrix model and allows for the scalability of the methodology to accommodate cultural differences.

Each project management group has specified roles and responsibilities that allow the project management community to mature while supporting the individualized needs of the internal business community and Exel's growing customer base.

---

3. The following acronyms are used in the Exel figures:
DePICT—acronym for the five phases of Exel's project management methodology: define, plan, implement, control, transition.
EMEA—Acronym for Exel's Europe, Middle East, Africa region.
APAC—Acronym for Exel's Asia-Pacific region.
PjM—Acronym for "project management" used as an identifier within the Exel Way program, as PM could have been confused with performance management.

Global PjM Organization Structure
Responsibilities

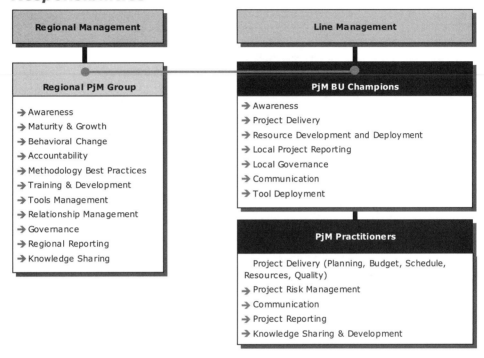

Regional Management

Regional PjM Group

→ Awareness
→ Maturity & Growth
→ Behavioral Change
→ Accountability
→ Methodology Best Practices
→ Training & Development
→ Tools Management
→ Relationship Management
→ Governance
→ Regional Reporting
→ Knowledge Sharing

Line Management

PjM BU Champions

→ Awareness
→ Project Delivery
→ Resource Development and Deployment
→ Local Project Reporting
→ Local Governance
→ Communication
→ Tool Deployment

PjM Practitioners

Project Delivery (Planning, Budget, Schedule, Resources, Quality)
→ Project Risk Management
→ Communication
→ Project Reporting
→ Knowledge Sharing & Development

FIGURE 12–6. Global project management organization structure: responsibilities.

12.11 HEWLETT-PACKARD

Another company that has recognized the importance of a global PMO is Hewlett-Packard. According to Ron Kempf, PMP®, Director PM Competency & Certification, HP Services Engagement PMO at Hewlett-Packard:

> For large, global companies the need for project management (PM) standardization and support is essential. To solve this problem, companies have developed a network of global PMOs all coordinated from a single source. At Hewlett-Packard, this network is referred to as the HP Services Project Management Office.
>
> "In the 80's our organization had spread across the world and inevitably we ran into some problems on project margins, our ability to deliver on time and to the expected budget," says Renee Speitel, Vice President HP Services Program Management Office. "We set a goal to increase project management performance, consistency, and financials." A global PMO was established to provide central management and mentorship.

The characteristics of a global PMO as defined by HP Services are:

- Manages across geographies and multiple projects
- Involves organizational and business responsibility in addition to project disciplines
- Long-term impact on organization and business
- Responsible for the professional development of PM community of practitioners
- Functional responsibility for PM infrastructure deployment

HP Services PMO structure supports more than 2500 project managers in 160 countries with regional offices located in the Americas, Asia-Pacific, Europe, Middle East, Africa, and Japan. Three focus areas are health of the portfolio, PM development, and processes.

Health of the portfolio considers the status and profit of projects. "Portfolio tracking systems enable us to keep status on more than 2400 active customer projects around the world," says Speitel. "A typical PMO scorecard includes customer satisfaction, portfolio financial performance (actual vs. budget), number of problem projects, number of certified project managers, and project manager utilization. The objective is to improve portfolio status year over year. PMO activities within this area include:

- Managing escalations
- Supporting project start-up activity
- Reviewing and auditing projects regularly
- Implementing review and approval process
- Troubleshooting projects in difficulty

Project management development involves formal training and certification as well as informal development. Project management is a core skill and competency for HP Services. The award-winning Project Management Development Program is organized by core PM courses, advanced PM topics, courses specific to HP Services practices, and professional skills training. The 35-course curriculum is taught in multiple languages. Other PMO-sponsored activities that support PM development include:

- Driving PM certification programs
- Updating and managing the formal training curriculum in coordination with workforce development
- Driving and participating in major events like PMI congresses and regional PM training/ networking events
- Encouraging informal communication and mentoring
- Providing mentorship to field project managers

Project management processes include business practices, methods and tools, and rewards and recognition programs. HP Services' Opportunity Roadmap is a project life-cycle architecture that defines the major business activities required to successfully pursue a customer engagement. It provides a process to determine scope and evaluate risk and price in order to win and succeed over a project lifetime.

The Opportunity Roadmap also incorporates the solution opportunity approval and review (SOAR) process, which facilitates appropriate levels of cross-business-unit involvement, review, and approval of global deals. This is shown in Figure 12–7. The global

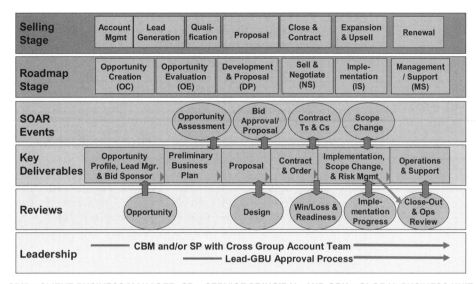

CBM = CLIENT BUSINESS MANAGER, SP = SERVICE PRINCIPAL, AND GBU = GLOBAL BUSINESS UNIT

FIGURE 12–7. Opportunity Roadmap and SOAR.

method for program management provides project managers with methodologies and a standardized approach using industry best practices and incorporating the added value of HP's experience. This is shown in Figure 12–8. The PMO is also responsible for defining and maintaining policies, procedures, and other business practices relating to project management.

Speitel summarizes, "The goals of our program management offices are to deliver a quality solution, provide business value, and meet customer needs. Our project performance has improved nearly 70 percent of our projects within or under budget. This

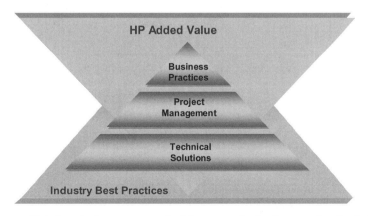

FIGURE 12–8. Global method, program methodology: standardized approach using industry best practices with company added value.

compares with an industry average of 50 percent. The PMO structure and consistent approach enhance our ability to manage global projects and provide the flexibility to acquire and retain qualified project managers where we need them."

12.12 EDS

Doug Bolzman, Consultant Architect, PMP®, ITIL Service Manager at EDS, discusses the PMO approach at EDS:

> Most organizations have a PMO established and this was generated from the view that their individual projects required oversight. This is a significant jump for many organizations that 10 years ago did not see value in project managers and are now funding a PMO. But most of them are paying the price to staff the PMO but still do not see the value; they see it as a necessary evil. In other words, things would probably be worse if we did not staff the PMO.
>
> Major functions include project oversight, status reporting, and project conformance. Since release frameworks were not in place, companies had the situation where their main supplier organizations simply threw the solution over the fence to the next supplier. The PMO was created to facilitate these transactions. (See Figure 12–9.)
>
> The problem with the implementation of this approach is that there never was a single model developed for this type of framework and the PMO would add additional constraints, bureaucracy, or workloads. The PMO was looked at to plan the direction of the company though the implementation of individual projects. Instead, another model was developed to have all of the suppliers contribute to every stage of a release, which shares the accountability of planning and designing, while providing the PMO the proper level of functionality. (See Figure 12–10.)

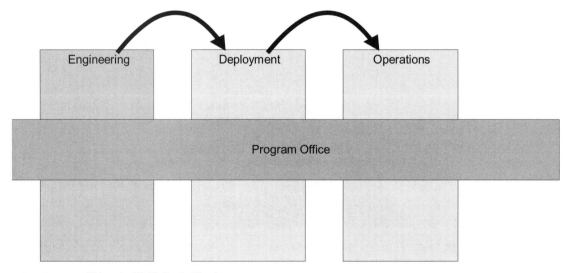

FIGURE 12–9. Using the PMO for facilitation.

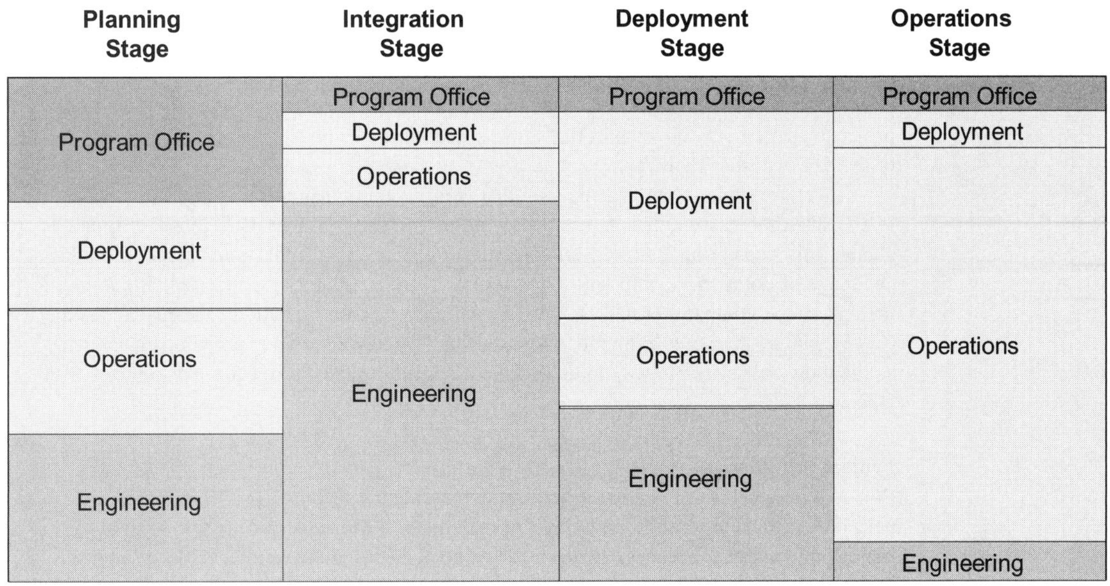

Planning Stage	Integration Stage	Deployment Stage	Operations Stage
Program Office	Program Office	Program Office	Program Office
	Deployment		Deployment
	Operations	Deployment	
Deployment			
	Engineering		Operations
Operations		Operations	
		Engineering	
Engineering			Engineering

FIGURE 12–10. Mapping the PMO to functionality.

12.13 AMEREN

Whenever companies discuss their growth and maturity in project management, the PMO concept always appears in the discussion. Doug Ascoli, PMP®, PE, Supervisor, PMO at Ameren—Information Technology, discusses his views on Ameren's journey to excellence in project management:

> The IT function of Ameren has traditionally utilized project management techniques in the deployment of systems and applications. In recent years, IT leadership has recognized the need for more consistency in the approach to project management and the incorporation of project management best practices into the methodologies. To this end, the organization leadership has taken steps to build on past successes and grow the use of a body of standards and best practices. Project management is considered a core competency, and an employee development program leading to project management certification is now in place.
>
> **Project Management Process at Ameren IT**
> Employing project management principles on its projects is not new to Ameren IT. But, recently project management has become a core competency for Ameren IT. The project management process at Ameren IT has evolved over the years to a more standardized process. Project and program managers have access to a more standards-based project management methodology that includes guidelines, definitions, forms, templates, checklists, and examples.
> Many of the guidelines and templates embody best practices from prior methodologies, lessons learned, and other industry standards. Ameren IT has embraced the Project Management Institute's Project Management Body of Knowledge (PMBOK® Guide) and incorporated many of its recommended techniques into our methodologies.

While the project management process at Ameren IT is standards based, it also recognizes the need for flexibility to address the unique requirements of individual projects. To that end, we have a set of published methodologies from which the manager can choose. These methodologies are scaled to the project as necessary, producing only those project management deliverables that make sense for the level of management appropriate to the risk exposure to the company.

There are some in our organization that feel project management is just an overhead. It will take more testimonials from successful program and project managers over time to change this perception. Further, our organization, like many other companies, face the challenge of doing more with less in the future. More computer systems are being implemented in the company each year yet IT continues to face operations-and-management (O&M) budget pressures to maintain low staffing levels. We see good project management as the most cost-effective way to deliver a successful project and meet the challenges we face.

Project Initiation

Potential projects for IT are identified through an annual planning process with the business lines of the corporation. In today's environment, the business lines drive most of IT's major project work. Business cases are developed for candidate projects, describing the proposed project, project assumptions, alternatives considered, dependencies, impacts, work tasks, and cost and schedule estimates. A financial analysis or EVA (economic value added) is developed to show project payback. Generally we expect a three-year payback for all discretionary IT systems.

If a project business case is approved, a project manager is assigned. The role of project manager is typically assigned to an engineer, specialist, or supervisor in the department where the bulk of the project work will be done.

If the project plan was not developed in conjunction with the business case, the first deliverable for the project team is to develop the project plan. A critical step in the process of constructing the project plan is to incorporate the business line requirements and approval.

Project Execution, Methodologies, and Life Cycle

IT has two distinct types of methodologies: software development and infrastructure. Each methodology identifies the project management deliverables throughout the life cycle of the project. The centerpiece document of both methodologies is the project plan. As the key document, the project plan is approved initially by the project approval committee (PAC). All subsequent changes must be approved by the PAC. The core components of the project plan include definition of the project goal, objectives (success metrics), project description, organization, scope, cost estimate, schedule, issues, and risks. Other components such as training plans, testing plans, and so on are added depending on the project. Guidelines and templates are available to assist the project team in developing the project plan.

Every effort is made to identify issues as soon as possible. As issues are identified, an owner is assigned to manage the issue through resolution. Issues are assigned a priority of high, medium, or low as a way to better focus resources on the major problems. Risks are also identified and managed with a standard process. Probability, impact, mitigation, and contingencies are developed and monitored. Owners of issues must report progress on a regular basis, typically the weekly or biweekly project status meeting.

Software Development

The software development groups utilize two levels of the software development project management methodologies: major projects and small projects. The primary elements of both methodologies include a guidelines document for developing the project plan, an Excel template for project estimating, a schedule template with the life-cycle phases, and a checklist of deliverables by phase. The methodologies also include several forms and templates for issues management, scope management, roles and responsibilities, and communications management.

The small-projects methodology was developed as an alternative to the more robust and comprehensive major-projects methodology. The PMO worked with the managers and representatives of the software development departments in downsizing the project management deliverables as compared to the large-projects methodology. The life-cycle phases of the small-projects methodology are the same as the major-projects methodology: planning, design, build/test, implementation, and close-out. The deliverables checklist for the software development small-projects methodology is shown in Table 12–2.

Infrastructure

The infrastructure project management methodology has its own life cycle based on the more traditional construction process: conceptual, definition, execution, and close-out. The PMO worked with representatives from the telecommunications department of IT to refine, validate, and document its project management process. Figure 12–11 is a graphic of the life cycle and deliverables.

Project Management Office

While the value of solid project management has long been recognized at Ameren IT, the triggering event that institutionalized the PMO in IT was the merger of Union Electric Company and Central Illinois Power to form Ameren and the effort needed to merge the IT systems of the two companies into a single set of systems.

According to Bill Herr, then IT's program manager for the merger, a process was put in place that utilized a methodology with estimating standards and templates. A project management tool was also used for project schedule management. Metrics were collected weekly from the project managers and project status meetings were held to review schedules and discuss issues. With the success of the IT efforts in integrating the systems of the merging companies, the PMO demonstrated in a real way that it would add value to the organization. Today, the PMO serves as both a "center of excellence" and a source for project and program management resources. The PMO is the trustee of the project management methodologies and provides project management tools, coaching, mentoring, and training. The PMO function resides in the planning section of IT's security and planning department. The staff of the PMO has increased to include more senior-level project managers as they now perform project manager and program manager responsibilities as well as providing support to others throughout the IT organization who serve as project managers.

Earned Value

As an organization, Ameren IT has only recently begun to utilize earned value for project performance measurement. On major programs and projects we have historically used curves, which compare actual hours (burned) to the plan hours across time. The most recent initiative of the PMO has been to encourage the use of the earned value analysis tech-

TABLE 12–2. SMALL-PROJECTS METHODOLOGY DELIVERABLES CHECKLIST

Phase	Activity	Comment
Planning	**Create project plan**	Use project plan form
	Contact enterprise architecture	
	High-level estimate	High-level estimate to be ±20% of baseline estimate
	Create project work plan/schedule	Determine activities, estimates, resources, deliverables
	Conduct kickoff meeting	Review project plan with stakeholders
	Determine if project software is to be capitalized	
	Economic evaluation (EVA)	Contact the financial planning group for template
	Capital funding committee (CFC)	Submit EVA to CFC if the project is >$100,000
	Obtain project approval	
	Update IT's milestone schedule	Use project toolbar
	Determine service request (SR)	Contact your supervisor for appropriate SR to charge time
	Fill out work order/ process	As applicable
Design	High-level design	Define interfaces, activity diagram, ERDs, DFD
	EWTA approval, if applicable	
	Data architect approval	
	Revise estimate	High-level design estimate to be ±10% of baseline estimate
	Revise project plan	Based on final design, new economic evaluation, etc.
	Obtain project approval	
	Update IT milestone schedule	
	Detailed design	Finalize interfaces, ERDs, DFDs, physical data model
Build/test	Build programs	
	Unit test	
	Functional test	
	Cross-application test	
	Performance test	
	Develop implementation/conversion plan	
	Develop training plan	Identify operations/help desk personnel that need training
	Update IT milestone schedule	
Implement	Migrate/convert for final training/testing	
	Conduct training	
	Install/implement system	Generate/convert data
	Update IT milestone schedule	
Close out	Complete documentation	
	Final schedule and cost updates	
	Send out project evaluation	Use IT toolbar to access form
	Close project plan/firstcase	
	Update IT milestone schedule	
	Document outstanding issues/support requirements	

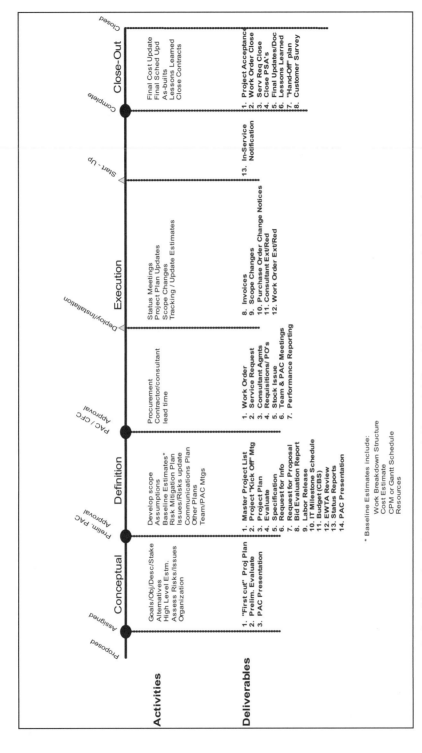

Activities

Conceptual
Goals/Obj/Desc/Stake
Alternatives
High Level Estm.
Assess Risks/Issues
Organization

Definition
Develop scope
Assumptions
Baseline Estimates*
Risk Mitigation Plan
Issues/Risks update
Communications Plan
Other Plans
Team/PAC Mtgs

Execution
Procurement
Contractor/consultant
lead time

Status Meetings
Project Plan Updates
Scope Changes
Tracking / Update Estimates

Close-Out
Final Cost Update
Final Sched Upd
As-builts
Lessons Learned
Close Contracts

Deliverables

Conceptual
1. "First cut" Proj Plan
2. Prelim. Evaluate
3. PAC Presentation

Definition
1. Master Project List
2. Project "Kick Off" Mtg
3. Project Plan
4. Evaluate
5. Specification
6. Request for Info
7. Request for Proposal
8. Bid Evaluation Report
9. Labor Release
10. IT Milestone Schedule
11. Budget (CBS)
12. EWTA Review
13. Status Reports
14. PAC Presentation

Execution
1. Work Order
2. Service Request
3. Consultant Agmts
4. Requisitions/ PO's
5. Stock Issue
6. Team & PAC Meetings
7. Performance Reporting

8. Invoices
9. Scope Changes
10. Purchase Order Change Notices
11. Consultant Ext/Red
12. Work Order Ext/Red

13. In-Service Notification

Close-Out
1. Project Acceptance
2. Work Order Close
3. Serv Req Close
4. Close PSA's
5. Final Updates/Doc
6. Lessons Learned
7. "Hand-Off" plan
8. Customer Survey

* Baseline Estimates include:
Work Breakdown Structure
Cost Estimate
CPM or Gantt Schedule
Resources

Phases: Proposed / Assigned / Conceptual / Prelim. PAC Approval / Definition / PAC / CFC Approval / Deploy/Installation / Execution / Start - Up / Complete / Close-Out / Closed

FIGURE 12–11. Project life cycle: project management activities and deliverables for telecommunications projects.

nique as the standard project performance metric for projects in IT. We will also continue to report the other traditional metrics such as budget variance, percent complete, schedule variance, and so on alongside the earned value metrics.

We see the benefit of earned value analysis in that it integrates project scope, costs, and schedule into one currency-based metric for a quick overall assessment of project performance. Many are not familiar with earned value so we are gradually implementing the technique into the project management process, starting with the monitoring of the two performance indices: the cost performance index (CPI) and the schedule performance index (SPI). With the implementation of the Microsoft Enterprise Project Management tool, which has built in earned value functionality, we are now able to more easily deploy and use the technique.

On a recent major program, the PMO monitored the CPI and SPI for a quick read on schedule and cost performance to date. The PMO decided that if a project's CPI or SPI fell below 0.8, we would further discuss the areas of the project that contributed to the low index. We also discussed cost or schedule implications and the corrective action to bring the project back on track. In this way, earned value's greatest benefit was to point us quickly to areas of poor performance so that our time was spent on areas that needed our attention most.

As with anything new, we also recognized some lessons to be learned in using earned value. Teams must have great discipline to update their schedules regularly. Also, every effort must be made to level resource workloads initially and thus avoid overly optimistic schedules. These are lessons to be learned as we continue to deploy the technique.

Project Close-Out

IT has traditionally defined project success as meeting budget, schedule, and customer satisfaction. After each project is completed, a project evaluation form is sent out to the project owners indicating the contracted cost and completion date along with the actual costs and completion date. Variances are noted on the form. They are asked to rate the project in 10 areas on a five-point scale:

1. Effectively determined your requirements
2. Met project objectives
3. Provided quality deliverables
4. Delivered results on time
5. Kept you informed on the status of the project
6. Effectively managed project activities
7. Effectively managed scope changes
8. Communicated in terms that you could understand
9. Responded to all questions, concerns, issues
10. Professional, thoughtful, and courteous

This evaluation is taken very seriously, with any rating below a 3 (neutral) followed up by IT management. Over time, this survey has contributed to a marked improvement in business line satisfaction with IT.

As part of project close-out, project managers hold postimplementation reviews to present final metrics and compare to those estimated in the project plan. The variance is often instructive in improving future project justifications and project executions. It also enhances corporate accountability in terms of getting the promised business value from technology initiatives.

Project teams also discuss lessons learned in project execution and overall project management and communications. This information is considered a potential improvement opportunity in the PMO and may result in methodology updates.

Conclusion

Chuck Bremer, Vice President of IT, summarizes his thoughts on the future of project management at Ameren IT: "While the implementation of project and program management techniques is a key element of a successful IT function, the PMO must be vigilant in ensuring that the methodologies continue to evolve to meet the needs of both IT and its customers. Every effort must be made to ensure that the methodologies minimize overhead and maximize value. While they should be standards based and encourage best practices, at the same time they must be sufficiently flexible to meet the vagrancies of the individual projects. If all of that can be accomplished, the PMO will continue to deliver value to the organization."

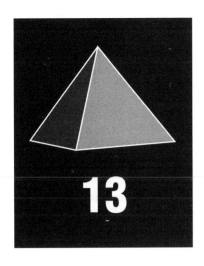

13

Six Sigma and the Project Management Office

13.0 INTRODUCTION

In the previous chapter, we discussed the importance of the PMO for strategic planning and continuous improvements. In some companies, the PMO was established specifically for the supervision and management of Six Sigma projects. Six Sigma teams throughout the organization would gather data and make recommendations to the PMO for Six Sigma projects. The Six Sigma project manager, and possibly the team, would be permanently assigned to the PMO.

Unfortunately, not all companies have the luxury of maintaining a large PMO where the Six Sigma teams and other supporting personnel are permanently assigned to the PMO. It is the author's belief that the majority of the PMOs have no more than four or five people permanently assigned. Six Sigma teams, including the project manager, may end up reporting "dotted" to the PMO and administratively "solid" elsewhere in the organization. The PMO's responsibility within these organizations is primarily for the evaluation, acceptance, and prioritization of projects. The PMO may also be empowered to reject recommended solutions to Six Sigma projects.

For the remainder of this chapter we will focus on organizations that maintain small PMO staffs. The people assigned to the PMO may possess a reasonable knowledge concerning Six Sigma but may be neither Green nor Black Belts in Six Sigma. These PMOs can and do still manage selected Six Sigma projects but perhaps not the traditional type of Six Sigma projects taught in the classroom.

13.1 PROJECT MANAGEMENT–SIX SIGMA RELATIONSHIP

Is there a relationship between project management and Six Sigma? The answer is definitely "yes." The problem is how to exchange the benefits such that the benefits of Six

Sigma can be integrated into project management and, likewise, the benefits of project management can be integrated into Six Sigma. Some companies, such as EDS, have already recognized this important relationship, especially the input of Six Sigma principles to project management. Doug Bolzman, Consultant Architect, PMP®, ITIL Service Manager at EDS, discusses this relationship:

> We have incorporated the Information Technology Information Library (ITIL) into the information technology enterprise management (ITEM) framework to design the operational model required to maintain and support the release. ITIL operations components are evaluated and included within each release that requires an operational focus. Six Sigma models have been generated to assist the organization in understanding the capabilities of each release and how to manage the requirements, standards, and data for each of the established capabilities.

Today, there is a common belief that the majority of traditional, manufacturing-oriented Six Sigma failures are because of the lack of project management; nobody is managing the Six Sigma projects as projects. Project management provides Six Sigma with structured processes as well as faster and better execution of improvements.

From a project management perspective, problems with Six Sigma Black Belts include:

- Inability to apply project management principles to planning Six Sigma projects
- Inability to apply project management principles to the execution of Six Sigma projects
- Heavy reliance on statistics and minimum reliance on business processes
- Inability to recognize that project management is value added

If these problem areas are not resolved, then Six Sigma failures can be expected as a result of:

- Everyone plans but very few execute improvements effectively.
- There are too many projects in the queue and poor prioritization efforts.
- Six Sigma stays in manufacturing and is not aligned with overall business goals.
- Black belts do not realize that executing improvements are projects within a project.

Six Sigma people are project managers and, as such, must understand the principles of project management, including statements of work, scheduling techniques, and so on. The best Six Sigma people know project management and are good project managers; Black Belts are project managers.

A possible solution to some of the Six Sigma failures is to require Six Sigma personnel to use the enterprise project management methodology. Jason Schulist, Manager—Continuous Improvement, Operating Strategy Group at DTE Energy, discusses this:

> In 2002, DTE Energy developed an operating system framework to enable systemic thinking around continuous improvement. We blended a lean tool and Six Sigma implementa-

tion strategy to develop our current "Lean Sigma" systemic approach. This approach utilizes a four-gate/nine-Step project management model.[1]

Members of the various business units submit ideas for projects. A review committee prioritizes the projects within each business unit using a project selection document. Once prioritized, each business unit allocates 1–2 percent of its organizational staff to full-time continuous improvement initiatives. Most of these resources are either Lean Sigma Black Belt certified or in training. These resources use the four-gate/nine-step project management model for all projects.

Four-Gate/Nine-Step Management Model

In steps 1–3, the project lead scopes the project opportunity, forms a team, and analyzes the current reality using rigorous data analysis techniques. By using the $y = f(x)$ tool, teams are able to quantify their metrics and scope their projects to the appropriate level. All Black Belt certified projects must achieve at least $250,000 in savings or have a significant impact in safety or customer service. The team develops a project charter, which the champion signs along with the gate 1 review form.

In steps 4–6, the team defines the ideal-state design that most effectively improves the metrics agreed to in gate 1. The team identifies gaps and develops countermeasures [using the failure mode and effect analysis (FMEA)] to migrate the initiative from the current state to the ideal state. The team develops a master plan for implementing the changes and commits to targets for each of the metrics. The team measures both input and output metrics and measures the success of the project with respect to improving these metrics. The champion signs off gate 2.

In step 7, the team implements its plan and course corrects as necessary in order to achieve the metrics. At gate 3 the team reviews its performance to plan, addresses gaps and plan countermeasures, discusses progress to project targets, and ensures that outcomes will be achieved.

In steps 8 and 9, the team measures project progress, sustains the goals, acknowledges the team, reflects on the project, and communicates the results. The team performs an after-action review (AAR) to inculcate the learning from the project and reduce mistakes in future implementations. The team must achieve the project metrics from gate 2 before the sponsor signs off at gate 4. If the team does not reach its targets, the team most likely returns to gate 2 to redefine the ideal state and confirm that the original targets are still feasible.

The DTE Energy Sarah Sheridan award recognizes many successful completed projects using the four-gate/nine-step project management model. Operating systems improvements using the project methodology have saved DTE Energy over $40 million in 2003 and over $100 million in 2004.

13.2 INVOLVING THE PMO

The traditional PMO exists for business process improvements and supports the entire organization, including Six Sigma Black Belts, through the use of the enterprise project management methodology. Project managers, including Black Belts, focus heavily upon

---

1. The model is shown in Figures 4–3, 4–4, and 4–37.

customer value-added activities, whether is be an internal or external customer. The PMO focuses on corporate value-added activities.

The PMO can also assist with the alignment of Six Sigma projects with strategy. This includes the following:

- Continuous reprioritization may be detrimental. Important tasks may be sacrificed and motivation may suffer.
- Hedging priorities to appease everyone may result in significant work being prolonged or disbanded.
- A cultural change may be required during alignment.
- Projects and strategy may be working toward cross-purposes.
- Strategy starts at the top whereas projects originate at the middle of the organization.
- Employees can recognize projects but may not be able to articulate strategy. Selecting the proper mix of projects during portfolio management of projects cannot be accomplished effectively without knowing the strategy. This may result in misinterpretation.
- "Chunking" breaks a large project into smaller ones to better support strategy. This makes it easier for revitalization or rejection.

The PMO can also assist in solving some of the problems associated with capturing Six Sigma best practices, such as:

- Introducing a best practice can "raise the bar" too soon and pressure existing projects to possibly implement a best practice that may not be appropriate at that time.
- Employees and managers are unaware of the existence of the best practices and do not participate in their identification.
- Knowledge transfer across the organization is nonexistent and weak at best.
- Falling prey to the superstitious belief that most best practices come from failures rather than from successes.

Simply stated, the marriage of project management with Six Sigma allows us to manage better from a higher level.

13.3 TRADITIONAL VERSUS NONTRADITIONAL SIX SIGMA

In the traditional view of Six Sigma, projects fall into two categories: manufacturing and transactional. Each category of Six Sigma is multifaceted and includes a management strategy, metric, and process improvement methodology. This is shown in Figure 13–1. Manufacturing Six Sigma processes utilize machines to produce products whereas transactional Six Sigma processes utilize people and/or computers to produce services. The process improvement methodology facet of Six Sigma addresses both categories. The only differ-

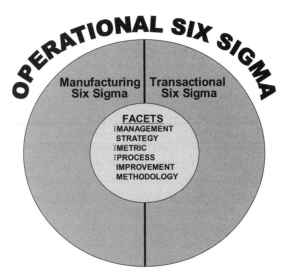

FIGURE 13–1. Six Sigma categories (traditional view).

ence is what tools you will use. In manufacturing, where we utilize repetitive processes that make products, we are more likely to use advanced statistical tools. In transactional Six Sigma, we might focus more on graphical analysis and creative tools/techniques.

The traditional view of a Six Sigma project has a heavy focus on continuous improvement to a repetitive process or activity associated with manufacturing. This traditional view includes metrics, possibly advanced statistics, rigor, and a strong desire to reduce variability. Most of these Six Sigma projects fit better for implementation in manufacturing than in the PMO. Six Sigma teams manage these manufacturing-related projects.

Not all companies perform manufacturing and not all companies support the PMO concept. Companies without manufacturing needs might focus more on the transactional Six Sigma category. Companies without a PMO rely heavily upon the Six Sigma teams for the management of both categories of projects.

Those companies that do support a PMO must ask themselves the following three questions:

- Should the PMO be involved in Six Sigma projects?
- If so, what type of project is appropriate for the PMO to manage even if the organization has manufacturing capability?
- Do we have sufficient resources assigned to the PMO to become actively involved in Six Sigma project management?

PMOs that are actively involved in most of the activities described in Chapter 12 do not have the time or resources required to support all Six Sigma projects. In such a case, the PMO must be selective as to which projects to support. The projects selected are commonly referred to as nontraditional projects that focus more on project management–related activities than manufacturing.

Figure 13–2 shows the nontraditional view of Six Sigma. In this view, operational Six Sigma includes manufacturing activities and all other activities from Figure 13–1, and transactional Six Sigma now contains primarily those activities to support project management.

In the nontraditional view, the PMO can still manage both traditional and nontraditional Six Sigma projects. However, there are some nontraditional Six Sigma projects that are more appropriate for management by the PMO. Some of the projects currently assigned to the PMOs include enhancements to the enterprise project management methodology, enhancements to the PMO tool set, efficiency improvements, and cost avoidance/reduction efforts. Another project assigned to the PMO involves process improvements to reduce the launch of a new product and improving customer management. Experts in Six Sigma might view these as nontraditional types of projects. There is also some concern as to whether these are really Six Sigma projects or just a renaming of a continuous improvement project to be managed by a PMO. Since several companies now refer to these as Six Sigma projects, the author will continue this usage.

Strategic planning for Six Sigma project management is not accomplished merely once. Instead, like any other strategic planning function, it is a cycle of continuous improvements. The improvements can be small or large, measured quantitatively or qualitatively, and designed for either internal or external customers.

There almost always exists a multitude of ideas for continuous improvements. The biggest challenge lies in effective project selection and then assigning the right players. Both of these challenges can be overcome by assigning Six Sigma project management

FIGURE 13–2. Six Sigma categories (nontraditional view).

best practices to the project management office. It may even be beneficial having Six Sigma specialists with Green Belts or Black Belts assigned to the PMO.

13.4 UNDERSTANDING SIX SIGMA

Six Sigma is not about manufacturing widgets. It is about a focus on processes. And since the PMO is the guardian of the project management processes, it is only fitting that the PMO have some involvement in Six Sigma. The PMO may be more actively involved in identifying the "root cause" of a problem than in managing the Six Sigma solution to the problem.

Some people contend that Six Sigma has fallen short of expectations and certainly does not apply to activities assigned to a PMO. These people argue that Six Sigma is simply a mystique that some believe can solve any problem. In truth, Six Sigma can succeed or fail but the intent and understanding must be there. Six Sigma gets you closer to the customer, improves productivity, and determines where you can get the biggest returns. Six Sigma is about process improvement, usually repetitive processes, and reducing the margin for human and/or machine error. Error can only be determined if you understand the critical requirements of either the internal or external customer.

There are a multitude of views and definitions of Six Sigma. Some people view Six Sigma as merely the renaming of total quality management (TQM) programs as Six Sigma. Others view Six Sigma as the implementation of rigorous application of advanced statistical tools throughout the organization. A third view combines the first two views by defining Six Sigma as the application of advanced statistical tools to TQM efforts.

These views are not necessarily incorrect but are incomplete. From a project management perspective, Six Sigma can be viewed as simply obtaining better customer satisfaction through continuous process improvement efforts. The customer could be external to the organization or internal. The word "satisfaction" can have a different meaning whether we are discussing external or internal customers. External customers expect products and services that are a high quality and reasonably priced. Internal customers may define satisfaction in financial terms, such as profit margins. Internal customers may also focus on such items as cycle time reduction, safety requirements, and environmental requirements. If these requirements are met in the most efficient way without any non-value-added costs (e.g., fines, rework, overtime), then profit margins will increase.

Disconnects can occur between the two definitions of satisfaction. Profits can always be increased by lowering quality. This could jeopardize future business with the client. Making improvements to the methodology to satisfy a particular customer may seem feasible but may have a detrimental effect on other customers.

The traditional view of Six Sigma focused heavily on manufacturing operations using quantitative measurements and metrics. Six Sigma tool sets were created specifically for this purpose. Six Sigma activities can be defined as operational Six Sigma and transactional Six Sigma. Operational Six Sigma would encompass the traditional view and focus on manufacturing and measurement. Operational Six Sigma focuses more on processes, such as the enterprise project management methodology, with emphasis on continuous

TABLE 13–1. GOALS OF SIX SIGMA

Goal[a]	Method of Achievement
Understand and meet customer requirements (do so through defect prevention and reduction instead of inspection)	Improvements to forms, guidelines, checklists, and templates for understanding customer requirements
Improve productivity	Improve efficiency in execution of the project management methodology
Generate higher net income by lowering operating costs	Generate higher net income by streamlining the project management methodology without sacrificing quality or performance
Reduce rework	Develop guidelines to better understand requirements and minimize scope changes
Create a predictable, consistent process	Continuous improvement on the processes

[a] From *The Fundamentals of Six Sigma.* New York: International Institute for Learning, pp. 1–24.

improvements in the use of the accompanying forms, guidelines, checklists, and templates. Some people argue that transactional Six Sigma is merely a subset of operational Six Sigma. While this argument has merit, project management and specifically the PMO spend the majority of their time involved in transactional rather than operational Six Sigma.

The ultimate goal of Six Sigma is customer satisfaction, but the process by which the goal is achieved can differ whether we are discussing operational or transactional Six Sigma. Table 13–1 identifies some common goals of Six Sigma. The left-hand column lists the traditional goals that fall more under operational Six Sigma, whereas the right-hand column indicates how the PMO plans on achieving the goals.

The goals for Six Sigma can be established at either the executive levels or the working levels. The goals may or may not be able to be completed with the execution of just one project. This is indicated in Table 13–2.

Six Sigma Initiatives for project management are designed not to replace ongoing initiatives but to focus on those activities that may have a critical-to-quality and critical-to-customer-satisfaction impact in both the long and short terms.

Operational Six Sigma goals emphasize reducing the margin for human error. But transactional Six Sigma activities managed by the PMO may involve human issues such

TABLE 13–2. GOALS VERSUS FOCUS AREAS

Executive Goals	PMO Focus Areas
Provide effective status reporting	• Identification of executive needs • Effective utilization of information • "Traffic light" status reporting
Reduce the time for planning projects	• Sharing information between planning documents • Effective use of software • Use of templates, checklists, and forms
Improve customer interfacing	• Templates for customer status reporting • Customer satisfaction surveys • Extensions of the enterprise project management methodology into the customer's organization

as aligning personal goals to project goals, developing an equitable reward system for project teams, and project career path opportunities. Fixing people problems is part of transactional Six Sigma but not necessarily of operational Six Sigma.

13.5 SIX SIGMA MYTHS[2]

Ten myths of Six Sigma are shown in Table 13–3. These myths have been known for some time but have become quite evident when the PMO takes responsibility for project management transactional Six Sigma initiatives.

Works Only in Manufacturing   Much of the initial success in applying Six Sigma was based on manufacturing applications; however, recent publications have addressed other applications of Six Sigma. Breyfogle[3] includes many transactional/service applications. In GE's 1997 Annual Report, CEO Jack Welch proudly states that Six Sigma "focuses on moving every process that touches our customers—every product and *service* (emphasis added)—toward near-perfect quality."

Ignores Customer in Search of Profits   This statement is not myth but rather a misinterpretation. Projects worthy of Six Sigma investments should (1) be of primary concern to the customer and (2) have the potential for significantly improving the bottom line. Both criteria must be met. The customer is driving this boat. In today's competitive environment, there is no surer way of going out of business than to ignore the customer in a blind search for profits.

TABLE 13–3.   THE TEN MYTHS OF SIX SIGMA

1. Works only in manufacturing
2. Ignores the customer in search of bottom-line benefits
3. Creates a parallel organization
4. Requires massive training
5. Is an add-on effort
6. Requires large teams
7. Creates bureaucracy
8. Is just another quality program
9. Requires complicated, difficult statistics
10. Is not cost effective

2. Adapted from F. W. Breyfogle III, J. M. Cupello, and B. Meadows, *Managing Six Sigma.* New York: Wiley, 2001, pp. 6–8.
3. F. W. Breyfogle, III, *Implementing Six Sigma; Smarter Solutions Using Statistical Methods.* New York: Wiley, 1999.

Creates Parallel Organization   An objective of Six Sigma is to eliminate every ounce of organizational waste that can be found and then reinvest a small percentage of those savings to continue priming the pump for improvements. With the large amount of downsizing that has taken place throughout the world during the past decade, there is no room or inclination to waste money through the duplication of functions. Many functions are understaffed as it is. Six Sigma is about nurturing any function that adds significant value to the customer while adding significant revenue to the bottom line.

Requires Massive Training   Peter B. Vaill states:

> Valuable innovations are the positive result of this age (we live in), but the cost is likely to be continuing system disturbances owing to members' nonstop tinkering. Permanent white water conditions are regularly taking us all out of our comfort zones and asking things of us that we never imagined would be required. It is well for us to pause and think carefully about the idea of being continually catapulted back into the beginner mode, for that is the real meaning of being a continual learner. We do not need competency skills for this life. We need incompetency skills, the skills of being effective beginners.

Is an Add-On Effort   This is simply the myth "creates a parallel organization" in disguise. Same question, same response.

Requires Large Teams   There are many books and articles in the business literature declaring that teams have to be small if they are to be effective. If teams are too large, the thinking goes, a combinational explosion occurs in the number of possible communication channels between team members, and hence no one knows what the other person is doing.

Creates Bureaucracy   A dictionary definition of bureaucracy is "rigid adherence to administrative routine." The only thing rigid about wisely applied Six Sigma methodology is its relentless insistence that the customer needs to be addressed.

Is Just Another Quality Program   Based upon the poor performance of untold quality programs during the past three to five decades,[4] an effective quality program would be welcome. More to the point,[5] Six Sigma is "an entirely new way to manage an organization."

---

4. J. Micklethwait and A. Wooldridge, *The Witch Doctors of the Management Gurus.* New York: Random House, 1997.

5. T. Pyzdek, "Six Sigma is Primarily a Management Program, *Quality Digest,* 1999, p. 26.

Requires Complicated, Difficult Statistics

There is no question that a number of advanced statistical tools are extremely valuable in identifying and solving process problems. We believe that practitioners need to possess an analytical background and understand the wise use of these tools but do not need to understand all the mathematics behind the statistical techniques. The wise application of statistical techniques can be accomplished through the use of statistical analysis software.

Is Not Cost Effective

If Six Sigma is implemented wisely, organizations can obtain a very high rate of return on their investment within the first year.

13.6 USE OF ASSESSMENTS

One of the responsibilities that can be assigned to a PMO is the portfolio management of projects. Ideas for potential projects can originate anywhere in the organization. However, ideas specifically designated as transactional Six Sigma projects may need to be searched out by the PMO.

One way to determine potential projects is through an assessment. An assessment is a set of guidelines or procedures that allows an organization to make decisions about improvements, resource allocations, and even priorities. Assessments are ways to:

- Examine, define, and possibly measure performance opportunities
- Identify knowledge and skills necessary for achieving organizational goals and objectives
- Examine and solve performance gap issues
- Track improvements for validation purposes

A gap is the difference between what currently exists and what it should be. The gaps can be in cost, time, quality, and performance or efficiency. Assessments allow us to pinpoint the gap and determine the knowledge, skills, and abilities necessary to compress the gap. For project management gaps, the assessments can be heavily biased toward transactional rather than operational issues, and this could easily result in behavior modification projects.

There are several factors that must be considered prior to performing an assessment. These factors might include:

- Amount of executive-level support and sponsorship
- Amount of line management support
- Focus on broad-based applications
- Determining who to assess
- Bias of the participants
- Reality of the answers
- Willingness to accept the results
- Impact on internal politics

The purpose of the assessment is to identify ways to improve global business practices first and functional business practices second. Because the target audience is usually global, there must exist unified support and understanding for the assessment process and that it is for the best interest of the entire organization. Politics, power, and authority issues must be put aside for the betterment of the organization.

Assessments can take place at any level of the organization. These can be:

● Global organizational assessments
● Business unit organizational assessments
● Process assessments
● Individual or job assessments
● Customer feedback assessments (satisfaction and improvements)

There are several tools available for assessments. A typical list might include:

● Interviews
● Focus groups
● Observations
● Process maps

Assessments for Six Sigma project management should not be performed unless the organization believes that opportunities exist. The amount of time and effort expended can be significant, as shown in Figure 13–3.

The advantages of assessment can lead to significant improvements in customer satisfaction and profitability. However, there are disadvantages, such as:

● Costly process
● Labor intensive

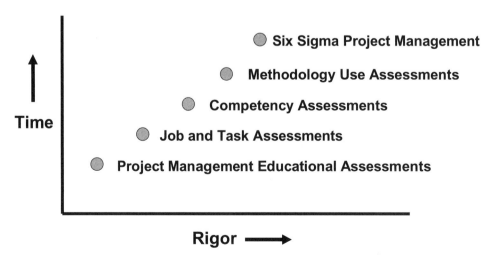

FIGURE 13–3.   Time and effort expended.

- Difficulty in measuring which project management activities can benefit from assessments
- May not provide any meaningful benefits
- Cannot measure a return on investment from assessments

Assessments can have a life of their own. There are typical life-cycle phases for assessments. These life-cycle phases may not be aligned with the life-cycle phases of the enterprise project management methodology and may be accomplished more informally than formally. Typical assessment life-cycle phases include:

- Gap or problem recognition
- Development of the appropriate assessment tool set
- Conducting the assessment/investigation
- Data analyses
- Implementation of the changes necessary
- Review for possible inclusion in the best practices library

Determining the tool set can be difficult. The most common element of a tool set is a focus on questions. Types of questions include:

- Open ended
  - Sequential segments
  - Length
  - Complexity
  - Time needed to respond
- Closed ended
  - Multiple choice
  - Forced choices (yes–no, true–false)
  - Scales

Table 13–4 illustrates how scales can be set up. The left-hand column solicits a qualitative response and may be subjective whereas the right-hand column would be a quantitative response and more subjective.

It is vitally important that the assessment instrument undergo pilot testing. The importance of pilot testing would be:

- Validate understanding of the instructions
- Ease of response

TABLE 13–4. SCALES

Strongly agree	Under 20%
Agree	Between 20 and 40%
Undecided	Between 40 and 60%
Disagree	Between 60 and 80%
Strongly disagree	Over 80%

- Time to respond
- Space to respond
- Analysis of bad questions

13.7 PROJECT SELECTION

Six Sigma project management focuses on continuous improvements to the enterprise project management methodology. Identifying potential projects for the portfolio is significantly easier than getting them accomplished. There are two primary reasons for this:

- Typical PMOs may have no more than three or four employees. Based upon the activities assigned to the PMO, the employees may be limited as to how much time they can allocate to Six Sigma project management activities.
- If functional resources are required, then the resources may be assigned first to those activities that are mandatory for the ongoing business of the firm.

The conflict between ongoing business and continuous improvements occurs frequently. Figure 13–4 illustrates this point. The ideal Six Sigma project management activity would yield high customer satisfaction, high cost reduction opportunities, and significant support for the ongoing business. Unfortunately, what is in the best interest of the PMO may not be in the best, near-term interest of the ongoing business.

All ideas, no matter how good or how bad, are stored in the "idea bank." The ideas can originate from anywhere in the organization, namely:

- Executives
- Corporate Six Sigma champions

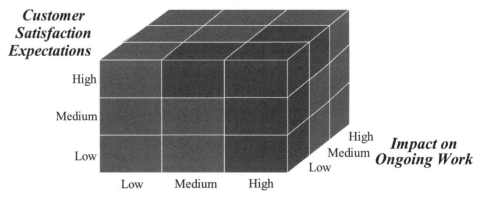

FIGURE 13–4.   Project selection cube.

- Project Six Sigma champions
- Master Black Belts
- Black Belts
- Green Belts
- Team members

If the PMO is actively involved in the portfolio management of projects, then the PMO must perform feasibility studies and cost–benefit analyses on projects together with prioritization recommendations. Typical opportunities can be determined using Figure 13–5. In this figure, ΔX represents the amount of money (or additional money) being spent. This is the input to the evaluation process. The output is the improvement, ΔY, is the benefits received or cost savings. Consider the following example.

Convex Corporation   Convex Corporation identified a possible Six Sigma project involving the streamlining of internal status reporting. The intent was to eliminate as much paper as possible from the bulky status reports and replace it with color-coded "traffic light" reporting using the company Intranet. The PMO used the following data:

- Burdened hour at the executive level = $240
- Typical number of project status review meetings per project = 8
- Duration per meeting = 2 hours
- Number of executives per meeting = 5
- Number of projects requiring executive review = 20

Using the above information, the PMO calculated the total cost of executives as:

(8 meetings) $\times$ (5 executives) $\times$ (2 hr/meeting) $\times$ ($240/hr) $\times$ (20 projects) = $384,000

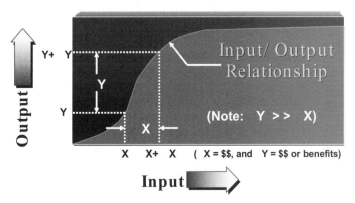

FIGURE 13–5. Six Sigma quantitative evaluation.

Convex assigned one systems programmer (burdened at $100/hr) for four weeks. The cost for adding traffic light reporting to the Intranet methodology was $16,000.

Six months after implementation, the number of meetings had been reduced to five per project for an average of 30 minutes in duration. The executives were now focusing on only those elements of the project that were color coded as a potential problem. On a yearly basis, the cost for the meetings on the 20 projects was now about $60,000. In the first year alone, the company identified a savings of $324,000 for one investment of $16,000.

13.8 TYPICAL PMO SIX SIGMA PROJECTS

Projects assigned to the PMO can be operational or transactional but mainly the latter. Typical projects might include:

- *Enhanced Status Reporting:* This project could utilize traffic light reporting designed to make it easier for customers to analyze performance. This could be Intranet based. The intent is to achieve paperless project management. The colors could be assigned based upon problems, present or future risks, or title, level, and rank of the audience.
- *Use of Forms:* The forms should be user friendly and easy to complete. Minimal input by the user should be required and the data inputted into one form should service multiple forms if necessary. Nonessential data should be eliminated. The forms should be cross-listed to the best practices library.
- *Use of Checklists/Templates:* These documents should be comprehensive yet easy to understand. They should be user friendly and easy to update. The forms should be flexible such that they can be adapted to all situations.
- *Criteria of Success/Failure:* There must exist established criteria for what constitutes success or failure on a project. There must also exist a process that allows for continuous measurement against these criteria as well as a means by which success (or failure) can be redefined.
- *Team Empowerment:* This project looks at the use of integrated project teams, the selection of team members, and the criteria to be used for evaluating team performance. This project is designed to make it easier for senior management to empower teams.
- *Alignment of Goals:* Most people have personal goals that may not be aligned with goals of the business. This includes project versus company goals, project versus functional goals, project versus individual goals, project versus professional goals, and other such alignments. The greater the alignment between goals, the greater the opportunity for increased efficiency and effectiveness.
- *Measuring Team Performance:* This project focuses on ways to uniformly apply critical success factors and key performance indicators to team performance metrics. This also includes the alignment of performance with goals and rewards with

goals. This project may interface with the wage and salary administration program by requiring two-way and three-way performance reviews.

- *Competency Models:* Project management job descriptions are being replaced with competency models. A competency criterion must be established, including goal alignment and measurement.
- *Financial Review Accuracy:* This type of project looks for ways of including the most accurate data into project financial reviews. This could include transferring data from various information systems such as earned value measurement and cost accounting.
- *Test Failure Resolution:* Some PMOs maintain a failure-reporting information system that interfaces with FMEA. Unfortunately, failures are identified but there may be no resolution on the failure. This project attempts to alleviate this problem.
- *Preparing Transitional Checklists:* This type of project is designed to focus on transition or readiness of one functional area to accept responsibility. As an example, it may be possible to develop a checklist on evaluating the risks or readiness of transitioning the project from engineering to manufacturing. The ideal situation would be to develop one checklist for all projects.

This list is by no means comprehensive. However, the list does identify typical projects managed by the PMO. Some conclusions can be reached by analyzing this list. First, the projects can be both transactional and operational. Second, the majority of the projects focus on improvements to the methodology. Third, having people with Six Sigma experience (i.e., Green, Brown, or Black Belts) would be helpful.

When a PMO takes the initiative in Six Sigma project management, the PMO may develop a Six Sigma toolbox exclusively for the PMO. These tools most likely will not include the advanced statistics tools that are used by Black Belts in manufacturing but may be more process-oriented tools or assessment tools.

Index